MADISON'S SORROW

MADISON'S SORROW

SORROW

TODAY'S WAR ON THE FOUNDERS
AND AMERICA'S LIBERAL IDEAL

KEVIN C. O'LEARY

PEGASUS BOOKS
NEW YORK LONDON

MADISON'S SORROW

Pegasus Books Ltd.
148 W. 37th Street, 13th Floor
New York, NY 10018

First Pegasus Books cloth edition May 2020

Library of Congress Cataloging-in-Publication Data is available.

ISBN: 978-1-64313-434-5

10 9 8 7 6 5 4 3 2 1

Printed in the United States of America
Distributed by Simon & Schuster
www.pegasusbooks.us

To

Lita Elen Robinow

I would not wish any companion in the world but you.

—Shakespeare

CONTENTS

Seldom have two ages the same fashion in their pretexts and the same modes of mischief. Wickedness is a little more inventive. Whilst you are discussing fashion, the fashion is gone by. The vice assumes a new body. The spirit transmigrates; and, far from losing its principle of life by its change of appearance, it is renovated in its new organs with the fresh vigour of a juvenile activity. It walks abroad; it continues its ravages.

—Edmund Burke,
Reflections on the Revolution in France, 1790

Your purpose, then, plainly stated, is that you will destroy the Government, unless you be allowed to construe and enforce the Constitution as you please, on all points in dispute between you and us. You will rule or ruin in all events.

—Abraham Lincoln,
Cooper Union Address, 1860

I've struggled to understand how people who've spent a lifetime chest-beating about patriotism can be so willing to burn liberal democracy to the ground to protect a man they wouldn't trust to sell them a used car.

—Michelle Goldberg,
The New York Times, 2019

PREFACE

I think the Enlightenment project is dead. The Left is so tribal, that a few on the right have decided that well, like it or not, those are the terms of engagement." A conservative friend sent me an email that opened with these two sentences. I hope Scott is wrong because modern constitutional democracy is the child of the Enlightenment. In proclaiming all people fundamentally equal—with the capacity to think critically for ourselves and to debate with others—the United States showed the world that it is possible for a people to govern themselves instead of turning power over to kings or authoritarian dictators. In this, America is the Enlightenment's grand experiment.

Theories abound about what has gone wrong. Yes, America is more partisan and polarized; the Blue/Red divide has deepened since the 1990s. Yes, gerrymandering has contributed to fewer swing seats oscillating between the two parties. This causes lawmakers to think more about electoral challenges from zealots on their partisan flank than from the middle. Yes, the digital revolution has created a new economic reality, and global competition, coupled with immigration fears, has produced a populist reaction. Yes, the younger generation is less white and more cosmopolitan than the baby boom generation that now counts grandchildren.

But something deeper—something tectonic—has shaken our political core. Like the Civil War, this crisis is political, not economic. It's about our identity as Americans and our commitment to the ambitious ideal that has set us apart as a nation. Do we continue as "the city upon a hill, the eyes of all people are upon us"—the message of Pilgrim John Winthrop and President Ronald Reagan? Or will a new and powerful combination of sinister social forces—the mixture of which we have never experienced before—set us on a different road?

In 1787, at the conclusion of the Constitutional Convention, Elizabeth Willing Powell, one of the most important women of the founding era, addressed Benjamin Franklin, "Well Doctor, what have we got—a republic or a monarchy?" Franklin replied, "A republic, if you can keep it."[1] In order to invigorate, protect, and keep our democratic republic, it is imperative to know what threatens it.

The Birth of Reactionary America

T he moment when a new and powerful Frankenstein monster first walked onto the American political stage can be marked with precision. In July 1964, at the high-water mark of New Deal liberalism, Arizona Senator Barry Goldwater was preparing to accept the Republican Party's nomination as its presidential standard-bearer. Goldwater had earned a reputation for his severe libertarian, strict-constitutionalist philosophy. Because of his unequivocal opposition to New Deal reform liberalism, and especially because of his "principled" stance against civil rights, Goldwater was approached by an unusual emissary just prior to the GOP's national convention in San Francisco. A Goldwater Republican from Alabama arrived carrying an outrageous—yet prescient and politically potent—request to the Arizona senator.

Darling of the New Right, Goldwater broke with his Republican colleagues in the Party of Lincoln to side with white Southern Democrats in opposing the Civil Rights Act of 1964. Facing a Democratic Party championing civil rights, Goldwater told a group of Atlanta Republican activists that it was time "to go hunting where the ducks are." He understood that white Southerners—the ducks—would only abandon their longstanding commitment to the Democratic Party if Republicans suddenly became "conservative" on race. In his 1960 best seller, *The Conscience of a Conservative*, Goldwater wrote that race issues were best decided by the states and during the Senate's debate on the Civil Rights Act he declared that while he personally opposed racial discrimination, national legislation would result in a "federal police force of mammoth proportions" and lead to neighbors spying on neighbors.[1]

The Republican delegate coming to meet Goldwater was Jim Martin, a former United States Senate candidate. Martin was mowing his lawn the day before he was scheduled to fly to San Francisco when his wife, Margaret, called him to receive a call from the governor. George Wallace told Martin that he was sending a state plane to the local airport and wanted him to fly to Montgomery—immediately—and secretly meet in the governor's suite at the Jefferson Davis Hotel. As Martin took his car keys, Margaret objected that he still had his yardwork clothes on. Jim told her not to worry, as he would be back soon. Security men hid Martin from view when he arrived for his meeting with Governor Wallace, the leading political voice defending Southern white supremacy and a wily foe of Presidents Kennedy and Johnson and the civil rights movement led by Martin Luther King Jr.

Eager to cement his status as the idol of the white racist South, Wallace was a shrewd politician. He understood that the only way the South could fight off a second Reconstruction was by making an alliance with Northern business interests and the anti–New Deal wing of the Republican Party. Wallace met with Martin for three hours, whereupon Martin was informed that the governor would be the perfect choice as Goldwater's vice presidential running mate. As Martin's jaw dropped (Wallace was a Democrat, not a Republican), the governor continued: "Now you've got to pretend that this is your original idea . . . It didn't come from me, but you think you can persuade me." One participant recalls Wallace saying in the racist speech that was typical of the pre–civil rights South, "it must be apparent to a one-eyed nigguh who can't see good outa his other eye, that me and Goldwater would be a winning ticket. We'd have the South locked up, then him and me could concentrate on the industrial states of the North and win."[2]

Martin replied that a Goldwater-Wallace ticket would be very strong in the South but that its success in the rest of country would remain uncertain and "unknown." Not wanting to antagonize the governor, who was known to be contemplating a third-party run, Martin told Wallace that he would be sure to mention the idea to Goldwater when he arrived in San Francisco the next day.

"No," Wallace said. "I want you to go tonight." Martin looked down at his dirty clothes and said, "Well obviously, I'm not prepared to go, you know . . . I don't have any money with me."

"That's no problem," said Wallace, who turned to an aide and told him to give Martin a thousand dollars in cash so he could buy suitable clothes when he got to California.

On Sunday afternoon, July 12, 1964, with the official opening of the Republican National Convention just twenty-four hours away, a member of Goldwater's presidential staff ushered Martin to a secret meeting with the Arizona senator on the rooftop of the Mark Hopkins Hotel.

While they stood looking out at San Francisco Bay, Goldwater and his aide Vern Stephens listened as Martin spoke. "Mr. Wallace has suggested that he would like to be a candidate with you as your vice presidential nominee on the Republican ticket."

On a nearby rooftop, a freelance photographer for *Life* magazine focused his telephoto lens and began recording the scene. Stephens, looking down with his hands in his pockets, wore a worried expression; Goldwater, in shirtsleeves and tie flying, looked as if "someone had just reported a death in the family." Goldwater considered Wallace a racist thug, and thought the request was absurd. He told Martin it just wasn't possible. Moreover, George Wallace was a lifelong Democrat and "this *was* a Republican convention."[3]

In that clandestine rooftop meeting, the Old South and the antigovernment New Right made contact; two powerfully charged wires crossed and the ensuing electric shock jolted the world's oldest continuous democracy in ways we are only now recognizing. Previously isolated and marginalized in terms of their impact on national politics, the yin and yang of America's illiberal future found each other and were soon inseparable.

The "Goldwater-Wallace ticket" is the secret inner logic of the modern conservative movement, the Reagan presidency, and today's ferociously illiberal right. It is well known that the 1964 Goldwater campaign was a galvanizing moment in the rise of the right as a national political force.[4] It is less well understood that in and of themselves, the libertarian ideals of F. A. Hayek, Ayn Rand, and William F. Buckley were insufficient to create an illiberal onslaught powerful enough to overwhelm classic conservatism and the Republican Party. The additional necessary ingredient was Southern racial rage, which George Wallace skillfully sublimated and repackaged as wrath against liberals, government, and Washington. Luminaries of the right such as Rush Limbaugh, Ann Coulter, Newt Gingrich, and Donald Trump have followed Wallace's playbook.

The two most reactionary elements in American politics confronted each other in 1860 and occupied different universes in the century that followed. Across American history, the right-wing business class and Southern whites had always been minority voices in *different* political parties. Their interests had to be considered when political calculations were made, but they did not dominate their parties or the national conversation. Traditionally, American political parties were large heterogeneous grab bags in which diverse groups coalesced around common goals. White Southerners with less than modern views on race in Roosevelt's Democratic Party and hard-right CEOs applauding the brutality of unregulated capitalism in Eisenhower's GOP were considered outliers in their respective parties. They were an embarrassment, akin to a disagreeable uncle who is sure to say something offensive during holiday dinners or a friend who has had a few too many at the company party. This changed as the two previously marginalized groups discovered that *together* they could reinvent and radically transform the party of Abraham Lincoln, Teddy Roosevelt, Dwight Eisenhower, and Richard Nixon.

In recent years, the few remaining congressional Republican Party conservatives have been defeated in primaries (Mike Castle of Delaware), scurried furiously to reposition themselves to the right to win reelection (the late Senator John McCain of Arizona), or voluntarily retired (Senators Olympia Snowe of Maine and Jeff Flake of Arizona and Congressman Charlie Dent of Pennsylvania). Wrongly labeled "moderates" or RINOs (Republican in Name Only) by their illiberal foes, classic conservatives have largely vanished from the halls of Congress and the state legislatures. Those who survive take care to balance their conservative views with illiberal stances. And lacking a charismatic champion at the national level, the millions of traditional conservatives in the electorate remain adrift listening to an onslaught of illiberal messages. Scholars tell us that since the 1980s, the base of the Republican Party has shifted sharply to the right.[5] For more than thirty years, the Karl Roves of the GOP happily taught the right to hate Washington; it should come as no surprise then that the Tea Party/Trump generation of Republicans have no respect for Madisonian democracy and the delicate checks and balances of the American constitutional system.[6]

AUTHORITARIAN POLITICS IN THREE ACTS

For two centuries, the United States has been the modern Athens for those seeking a society that values democracy, equality, and freedom. President Trump and his most ardent supporters vehemently reject that legacy, preferring instead the ancient authoritarian principles of privilege, hierarchy, inequality, and exclusion that divide societies into winners and losers based on ethnic identity, gender, social status, and economic power. The president's disdain for the democratic norms that have guided the nation for decades, his targeted cruelty aimed at the weak and those he considers his enemies, his utter disrespect for the duties of the presidency and possible disloyalty to the nation he leads, and the Republicans' shameful devotion to power politics no matter the cost to the public believing in the legitimacy and rule of law were all on display during a few short weeks in 2018.

It was then that the administration announced its "zero-tolerance policy" on immigration on the southern border, the president embraced and praised Russia's Vladimir Putin while insulting Western leaders as he flirted with the idea of withdrawing from NATO—America's most important security alliance—and Justice Anthony Kennedy announced his retirement from the U.S. Supreme Court. The president's actions and the strong Republican support he received spoke volumes about the nature of America's reactionary right and the crisis the nation faces. Echoing the "Muslim ban" established in the administration's first months and the president's inability to criticize the white nationalists and neo-Nazis who rallied violently in Charlottesville, Trump signaled to the world that he is leading the United States down a reactionary road.

Act I: President Donald J. Trump is in a league of his own when it comes to disregarding the truth. A pathological liar of massive proportions, the president lies so often on matters large and small that the public can't keep up. Instead of knowing that the president told a whopper, the public ends up dazed, not realizing that something is seriously amiss. In a profession that requires elected officials to persuade constituents with different beliefs and priorities that they are on their side, politicians often shade the truth; it's part of the formula of success. Partisans from both sides of the aisle choose facts and spin narratives that favor their preferred course of action; this we know and expect. But a democracy depends on truth being the primary currency of political debate.

In an act of bravado, Trump amped his game in the summer of 2018. In a barefaced lie, he repeatedly blamed Democrats for his incredibly cruel policy of separating children from their parents at the border. The president told reporters that he hated "to see the separation of parents and children," but that "Democrats forced the law upon our nation." South Carolina Republican Senator Lindsey Graham spoke the truth when he told CNN that the president could direct the Department of Homeland Security to change the policy. "President Trump could stop this policy with a phone call," Graham said. "I'll go tell him: 'If you don't like families being separated, you can tell DHS, Stop doing it.'"

Technically, the Trump administration did not have a policy stating that illegal border crossers must be separated from their children. But the decision to enforce a zero-tolerance policy resulted in unlawful immigrants, including those seeking asylum because of violence in their home countries, being taken into federal criminal custody; when this happened, their children were taken away. Immigration rights lawyers reported that even those not being criminally prosecuted were being separated from their children.

"They are being arrested, prosecuted like common criminals for a misdemeanor offense, not knowing when or if they will ever see their kids again," said then–Texas representative Beto O'Rourke, who led a Father's Day march from El Paso to a tent city set up in Tornillo to house children under detention for immigration violations.

Compounding the trauma, shelter workers were not allowed to touch the children. "She doesn't have her mother, and none of us can fix that," Dr. Colleen Kraft told the *Washington Post* about a little girl crying in a

Texas shelter. The shelter workers, who wanted to comfort the child, were instructed that they could not touch, hold, or pick her up. That was the rule, Dr. Kraft was told.[7]

It appeared the Trump administration's goal was to inflict as much harm as possible on the innocent. For decades, the Office of Refugee Resettlement was in charge of caring for children whose parents were deemed worthy of criminal prosecution by immigration services. In most cases, these children were given to relatives living in the United States while their parents went through the legal process. Under the Trump administration, U.S. Immigration and Customs Enforcement (ICE) took over the refugee resettlement role. As a result, if an undocumented relative came to interview for a child, ICE arrested and deported them, leaving the child alone to experience a nightmare worthy of Kafka.

In the age of slavery, the United States sanctioned the separation of children and parents. The Trump administration decided to do it again.

As public fury mounted, Trump again falsely blamed the Democrats for a child separation policy that placed children in wire cages. He then sought to dehumanize the victims of his cruelty by saying the policy was necessary to stop the south-of-the-border flood of violence from spilling northward. Reporters quickly cited numerous government studies showing that little of this violence washes into the United States. When one lie doesn't work, Trump moves to another. This president's relationship to truth and lies is the same: he will say whatever he thinks will help him at the moment. How can a democracy function when the nation's top elected official is incapable of telling the truth?

National outrage appeared to cause the president to reverse a barbarous policy, but kidnapped children and their parents remained separated for months and the Justice Department argued that it had the authority to hold migrant families in detention indefinitely. In the summer of 2019, attention again focused on overcrowded detention centers along the southern border. Children, teenagers, and adults were living in filth and sleeping on concrete floors (if they could find space) amid reports that the policy of forced separation of young children, including even infants, from their parents had continued.[8]

Act II: For decades, Republicans treated foreign affairs with the utmost seriousness. The party's presidential nominees had the résumés of Dwight Eisenhower (a five-star general in charge of D-Day and victory over Nazi Germany), Richard Nixon (twice vice-president and a chessmaster at global politics), or George H. W. Bush (envoy to China and U.N. ambassador). But then the Soviet Empire collapsed and suddenly foreign policy was no longer important.

At the summer G7 meeting in Canada, President Trump played the disrupter. He quarreled with the Europeans, Japanese, and Canadians and pushed for the reinstatement of Russia four years after it was cast out for its aggression against Ukraine. The other leaders criticized Trump's embrace of protectionism. Trump responded with name calling, labeling Canadian Prime Minister Justin Trudeau "weak." Then the president was off to his Singapore summit, where he cozied up with North Korean dictator Kim Jong-un. Trump heaped praise on a homicidal dictator with nuclear weapons and Kim got what he wanted—sharing the stage with an American president in a way that instantly elevated his international status. The president seemed to think that treating Kim as if they were stars in a Hollywood buddy movie was the way to solve the North Korean dilemma. Only weeks later did the U.S. government report that North Korea had restarted its nuclear weapons program.

At his joint Helsinki press conference in July with Vladimir Putin, Trump again, in a stunning rebuke, rejected the unanimous consensus among U.S. intelligence agencies that Russia interfered in the 2016 presidential election. Trump said: "Dan Coates [Director of National Intelligence] came to me and some of the others and said they think it's Russia. I have President Putin; he just said it's not Russia. I will say this: I do not see any reason why it would be . . . President Putin was extremely strong and powerful in his denial today."[9] Before the world, Putin conceded that he wanted Mr. Trump to win because of his promises of warmer relations with Moscow. Granular details of how Putin's GRU intelligence hackers had penetrated Democratic campaign computer networks and stole sensitive information—including valuable data analytics on the key Clinton support groups of idealistic liberals, young women, and African Americans—were revealed in the indictments of twelve Russian military officers by Special Counsel Robert Mueller just days before the Helsinki summit.

The president's overseas meetings with heads of state fit a pattern: Trump is far more comfortable with authoritarians than he is with democrats. This singular fact raised sinister questions: Was Trump out to destroy the West? Was he going to dismantle NATO, which has defended Western Europe for nearly seventy years? Was Trump a Vladimir Putin stooge doing Russia's dirty work?

On trade, the border, and North Korea, Republicans could make the case that Trump was elected to shake things up and see if an unorthodox approach could bring about progress toward long-sought U.S. goals, among which would be a fairer trade relationship with China, a reduction in illegal immigration across the southern border (already accomplished by the Obama administration), and a decrease in the threat posed by a nuclear North Korea. But Trump's continuous praise of Putin, his genetic inability to utter a critical word about one of the world's most dangerous men, and his continual denigration and sharp criticism of the West make no sense in terms of advancing America's interests. Quite the opposite. Appalled by Trump's behavior, then gravely ill Republican senator John McCain wrote from his home in Arizona, "No prior president has ever abased himself more abjectly before a tyrant."

There were three rival explanations for Trump's extraordinary performance in Helsinki variously described as disgraceful, pathetic, or traitorous. Either the president is crazy and thus continually utters nonsense when it comes to Russia, or he is Putin's devoted puppet (because of the assistance Russia gave his campaign and/or because the Russians have compromising material on the president). Perhaps Trump just feels at home with reactionary white nationalist authoritarians such as Putin, who claim to be defending Christian values when they attack the cosmopolitan diversity of modern democracy. Trump, Putin, Marine Le Pen, Steve Bannon, and Stephen Miller scorn the liberal world order epitomized by women and people of color having an equal seat at the table. All three explanations may have been at play. Alternative rationales for a U.S. president kissing the ring of the leader of the former Soviet Union while at the same time doing everything in his power to further Russia's No. 1 foreign policy goal: weakening the Western alliance in general and NATO and the EU in particular—lost believability.

◆

Act III: When Justice Anthony Kennedy announced his retirement from the U.S. Supreme Court the news was greeted with joy among Republicans and panic among Democrats. On the surface, the nomination of Judge Brett M. Kavanaugh by President Trump for the U.S. Supreme Court appeared normal. Kavanaugh had the credentials: A graduate of Yale Law School, a former clerk to the retiring Kennedy, a White House aide for President George W. Bush, and a judge on the U.S. Court of Appeals for the D.C. Circuit since 2006.

But liberals were justifiably alarmed that Kavanaugh would fulfill President Trump's promise that he will only nominate individuals for the nation's highest court who are committed to overturning *Roe v. Wade*. Liberals knew that Kavanaugh's confirmation would shift the court sharply right not only on women's rights and reproductive freedom, but also on the Affordable Care Act and protections for preexisting conditions as well as voting rights, religious liberty, environmental protection, protections for workers and consumers, and gun laws. Beyond the trepidation that a second Trump appointment would lock in a hard-right court majority for decades lurked a deeper issue, arguably just as grave. It was a problem of legitimacy that should give pause to conservatives who believe in tradition and who understand that democracies depend on standards of fair play to survive.

It is one thing for a president to sweep into office with a landslide majority and in his first term have the good fortune to make not just one but two Supreme Court appointments. This is the reward for being an FDR, a Lyndon Johnson, or a Ronald Reagan. The ideological balance of the nation's highest court is an echo of presidential elections, and elections have consequences. But the Trump nomination of Kavanaugh was entirely and egregiously different. After winning the electoral college with a few thousand votes from three states while having lost the popular vote by nearly three million, President Trump then inherited a Supreme Court pick in his first months in office, hijacked from the prior president of the *other* party.

Senate Majority Leader Mitch McConnell and his Republican colleagues violated both the letter and spirit of the Constitution in the last year of the Obama presidency when they denied even a hearing for Merrick

Garland, President Obama's nominee in the wake of Justice Antonin Scalia's death. It was Machiavellian power politics pure and simple. The Constitution says nothing about waiting for the results of the next election. Trump's pick of a hard-right ideologue such as Kavanaugh only tilted the balance of the court because the GOP stole the seat Neil Gorsuch now holds. In playing to win with loaded dice, no matter the cost, no matter what values and norms are smashed in the process, the GOP revealed an authoritarian streak that violates the country's most sacred principles.

We want the courts, especially the Supreme Court, to represent our better angels. From kindergarten onward, American children are taught to believe that judges have a deep respect for and belief in justice, equality before the law, and the rule of law no matter who appointed them to the court. Granting the courts the power of judicial review—to be the final arbiter of what is constitutional and right in our system of separated powers—has helped citizens not to lose faith in the country when the other party wins an electoral battle. But a power-hungry GOP, led by McConnell and Trump, crumpled the sacred legitimacy of the courts. The opportunity for President Trump to fundamentally alter the balance on the court for a generation with the appointment of Kavanaugh was the gift of McConnell's foul deed—the illegitimate seating of Neil Gorsuch on the high court.

As with American society and politics in general, the legal world has split into three camps—liberal, conservative, and reactionary. The divide on the right is between classic American conservatives—such as Chief Justice John Roberts and former Justice Anthony Kennedy—and the radical right. Few would deny that Justices Samuel Alito, Clarence Thomas, Neil Gorsuch, and Brett Kavanaugh are closely allied with the illiberal right that steers the Republican Party. In the age of Reagan, opposition to Soviet Communism was the glue that held the Republican coalition together; in the age of Trump, the holy grail for the business class, NRA zealots, and right-to-life evangelicals is control of the Supreme Court.

POLITICS WITHOUT CONSERVATIVES

As a journalist who has reported for *Time* and a political scientist with a doctorate from Yale, I have been a close observer of the political scene for more than thirty years. I have written about political events on deadline; by temperament and training, I am respectful of others' political opinions and the reasons they give for their views. However, if we are to make sense of this current political crisis, a different type of reporting is necessary—one that combines history, institutional analysis, knowledge of political thought, and a willingness to follow the truth of the matter to conclusions that step beyond the polite journalistic norm of accepting the labels that people and groups give themselves.[10] This book speaks to the present through a historical lens. It addresses a simple yet essential question: How did we get *here*?

Linguistic confusion adds to our political vertigo. The traditional labels—conservative versus liberal, Republican versus Democrat—are a façade; they obscure the reality of 21st-century American politics. For example, we often speak of the Republican Party as having a strong evangelical contingent as well as a freewheeling libertarian wing that wants as few social controls as possible. As a surface understanding of the GOP, this has utility. Yet the evangelical Republican Party is predominately white and Southern and holds views strongly connected to an authoritarian racist past.[11] Professing adherence to Christian principles, these churchgoers support a president who struggled to denounce the Ku Klux Klan and neo-Nazi marchers in Charlottesville and strongly endorsed an Alabama Senate candidate credibly accused of sexual misconduct with minors. Similarly, an examination of libertarian thought—which inspires a great many Republican leaders—reveals an ugly, reactionary reality.

No longer conservative, the powerful post-Reagan right is, indeed, a new political phenomenon and thus, as with a newly discovered planet or species, deserves its own distinctive name. In the past, the words "reactionary" and "illiberal" typically were reserved to describe authoritarian politics abroad; regrettably, the American homeland is not as isolated from the political extreme as we once believed. Jonathan Swift counseled "proper words in proper places."[12] It is time to change the terms of debate. *Illiberal, reactionary,* and *the right* are interchangeable words for the same phenomenon. Once a marginal, if constantly visible, outer planet in our political solar system, the right has exploded into a supernova that dominates the Republican Party.

Today's GOP long ago abandoned classic conservative principles such as caution, belief in government, respect for experience and tradition, abhorrence of crackpots and political amateurs, and hatred of revolution-aries who propose destroying the present social order. The Republican right is not conservative. Instead of urging slow, cautious reform (à la Edmund Burke), these illiberal revolutionaries have little respect for the institutions and norms of contemporary society. Romanticizing the past, they yearn for a time when America was whiter, the power of men unquestioned, and the national government barely existed.

Antiquated and balky, the American political system—bequeathed to us by Madison and the founders, and then modified/reformed/improved (take your pick) by Andrew Jackson, the Progressives, Franklin Roosevelt, and the participatory upheavals of the 1960s—has worked fairly well for nearly 250 years.[13] Once upon a time, liberals and conservatives argued, fought, and worked together in Washington, D.C. and the state capitols and the result was a string of public policy successes that included the Interstate Highway System of the Eisenhower administration, Lyndon Johnson's pas-sage of Medicare, and Ronald Reagan's tax reform of 1986. Major public policy success happens when the two parties talk to each other and work together. No more. In the Trump era, traditional elected conservatives are either dead, retired, or excommunicated. They are lobbyists doing the bidding of their client (Bob Dole's new gig), conversos—the name given to Jews who became Catholic to survive the Spanish Inquisition—such as former Tennessee Senator Bob Corker and Ohio Senator Rob Portman (publicly with the rightward shift of the GOP but not altogether happy about it), mild critics such as Utah Senator Mitt Romney (who turned his back on his principled criticism of Donald Trump to prostrate himself as he chased appointment as secretary of state only to show true courage voting for conviction in the impeachment trial), or full-blown sycophants like Senator Lindsey Graham (once a voice of reason but now Donald Trump's best friend in the Senate). Conservatives, such as Romney and Maine Senator Susan Collins, struggle to persevere in the tradition of the late Senator McCain.

How would conservatives feel if liberals suddenly became marginalized or extinct and the Democratic Party were taken over by Marxist-Leninists bent on subverting democracy and destroying capitalism? Forced into a zero-sum game that encourages intransigent behavior, liberals confront a political foe who demonizes them, who accuses them of hating America, and who seeks total victory. In the post-Gingrich era, Republicans refuse to participate in good-faith compromise; liberals have come to understand that the new Republican Party has no interest in the old dance. Viewed as ideal types, conservatives and illiberals differ in the following ways:

- Conservatives follow Edmund Burke, Alexander Hamilton, and George F. Will in viewing government as a good and essential thing. Illiberals do not.
- Conservatives value civility, the give-and-take of politics, and believe in compromise. Illiberals do not.
- Illiberals seek a society governed nearly exclusively by white male authority and the market. Conservatives do not.
- Illiberals have a Manichaean fundamentalist (good or evil) mentality. Conservatives do not.
- Illiberals have qualms about democracy and express misgivings about majority rule if they lose at the ballot box and are in the minority. Conservatives do not.

On each of these measures, conservatives and illiberals hear a different drumbeat and march in opposite directions. Traveling a different road than either liberals or conservatives, reactionaries smash longstanding norms in the pursuit of power. Identified by their lack of empathy and belief that winning is everything, many see their task as either to convert or to destroy.

Neither traditional conservatives nor European fascists, the Republican right can best be understood as a radical movement to remake America in the image of ungenerous and unlovely ideals. Unlike traditional liberals and conservatives (both adherents to Locke's liberalism), reactionaries either explicitly or implicitly accept and encourage public policies that enshrine and institutionalize the core illiberal values—privilege, hierarchy, inequality, and exclusion—particularly for white males and their families. These are the foundational values of the feudalism that the founders fled. Many Republicans will deny this as an accurate portrayal of their personal politics. Indeed, a considerable number of Americans vote Republican out of habit, accept uncritically the harsh caricature of liberals they absorb from Fox News, and do not realize just how far the Republican Party has shifted rightward over the past thirty years. For them, the political contest still appears to be between conservatives and liberals, as it was during the Reagan years.[14] That may be true to an extent, for them, but it is naive.

It is understandable that auto workers in Ohio and Michigan voted for Trump after voting for Obama out of a sense of desperation to avert—to no avail—yet another shuttered factory.[15] The creative destruction of capitalism that results in lost jobs and damaged dreams, especially when combined with rapid changes in demographics and social norms, prompts those on a downbound train to seek a reversal of fortune.[16] Seymour Martin Lipset termed the periodic appearance of backlash politics the "continuing revolt against modernity."[17] In thinking about the sharp cultural and political divisions in the U.S. and Europe, Russ Dalton, one of my colleagues at the University of California, Irvine, offers these wise words: "Some people are too extreme, and go beyond the boundaries of democratic tolerance and respect for human rights—these excesses should be identified and criticized. But many on the 'other side' are friends or relatives, who have different value orientations but good intentions."[18] This is true. That said, it is vitally important that voters of all political stripes understand the forces that have transformed—almost beyond recognition—what was once the Party of Lincoln. There are millions of conservatives in the population who are uncomfortable with the illiberal turn of the base and the elected. In part, this book is written for them.

The adamant opposition by the right to nearly all policy proposals made by liberals and moderates makes perfect sense once we understand the illiberal values that animate today's Republican Party. A witches' brew of antigovernment libertarianism, misogyny, and Southern racism, illiberalism galvanizes grievances, harnesses hatreds, and celebrates cold hearts. Rejecting dialogue and compromise and standing well outside the mainstream American political tradition, the political engine that is the right views the press, Democrats, Republican political opponents, persistent women, minorities, and immigrants of color as "enemies of the people" and "others" to be marginalized and/or subdued.[19]

As the contemporary Republican Party has escalated its attack against the New Deal state and the norms of Madisonian democracy, it has deserted the conservative tradition of Edmund Burke. Railing against the French Revolution, the father of modern conservatism argued that change must be gradual, not abrupt, and certainly not chaotic. Instead of valuing individual liberty as an abstract value to be held above all others, as many on the right today demand, Burke said commitments to liberty must be balanced with other worthy goals if a society is to function successfully.[20] In his governing philosophy, Burke fundamentally rejects the illiberal anthem—"extremism in the defense of liberty is no vice"—articulated by Barry Goldwater in his 1964 presidential campaign.

With traditional conservatives marginalized, the threat from the right is dramatic. If the illiberal camp triumphs over the next decades—electing strongly reactionary presidents, holding the majority in the House and Senate, and packing the Supreme Court with ideological copies of Justice Scalia—it is highly probable that *Roe v. Wade* will be overturned, Social Security, Medicare, and the New Deal safety net shredded, and the Affordable Care Act abandoned. Other key investments in society, education, public infrastructure, and scientific research also will be considerably weakened. Distressing trends will worsen—stagnating wages for 80 percent of the workforce, escalating economic and political inequality, the shrinkage of the middle class, and the exclusion of minorities and women from positions of authority and power. If reactionaries hold sway, and the tipping point may arrive sooner than we expect, the United States could cease being the constitutional republic famously celebrated by Alexis de Tocqueville in *Democracy in America* and instead join the authoritarian oligarchies of Latin America.

Then there is the right's steadfast and insane denial of the climate emergency, a stance that threatens the very survival of civilization as we know it.[21] The rejection of science and fact-based argument has now reached a point where the Grand Old Party now embraces the moniker "Flat Earth Cult." Chasing ideological nirvana, reactionaries are hell-bent on annihilating liberalism even if this means not only the destruction of Madisonian democracy but the planet on which the children and grandchildren of millennials may well struggle to survive.[22] Again rejecting Burke's conservative counsel, reactionaries fail to recognize that government is a good and necessary thing and that human society is a partnership across generations "between those who are living, those who are dead, and those who are to be born."[23]

Marriages reach the breaking point when couples have a shared disdain for each other. When there is contempt for the other person, the relationship is beyond saving, says marriage therapist John Gottman. Similarly, past experience shows democracy reaching a breaking point when partisanship becomes radically polarized and each side sees the other as an enemy that must be defeated.[24] When a win-at-all-cost mentality takes hold among the political elite, then possibilities for pragmatic compromise cease to exist. In an America where politics is a contest between liberals and conservatives, political argument translates into bipartisan dialogue; policy accomplishment—often incrementally and rarely a 'whole loaf'— is the norm. However, when one party becomes ideologically extreme and uncompromising in its goals, the complex system of American government—carefully constructed by James Madison and the framers in 1787—begins to freeze up and break down.

The ancient Greeks understood that without harmony, there is no democracy. Social harmony allows for people to rule themselves in their own interests, but absent common interest, there is no harmony.[25] What does "government of the people, by the people, and for the people" mean if the people become so divided that there is little they want, together? Without unifying principles, government rules in the interest of one group at the expense of another. Recognizing a lack of harmony and common purpose, many people think the political game is rigged and see no point in taking part in elections; others cynically conclude that they must achieve their goals through fearmongering; still others attack democratic politics by flooding the Internet with fake news and disinformation.[26]

Instead of a president, we have a mad king, an elected authoritarian who hurls insults, embraces cruelty, feeds on chaos, stokes the nation's racial divides, and consistently challenges both the Constitution and the ideals upon which this nation was founded. But Donald Trump is an outcome, not a cause; the GOP set the stage, then embraced him. We face a political crisis because our ideological consensus—perhaps the key factor in our political success—has been shattered in a way not seen since the Civil War. Our dilemma is not a single election; it is a malignant turn by one of the two major parties.[27] The hard-right zealots who control the Republican Party are driven by a hatred of modern liberals—such as Franklin Roosevelt, Barack Obama, and Hillary Clinton—and a hostility toward the core liberal beliefs that have governed American politics since 1776. Largely absent conservatives among elected Republicans, the United States is increasingly a nation of liberals and illiberal reactionaries.

Over the course of the nation's history, the liberal and reactionary sides of America's civic identity have engaged in three pitched battles. The forces of liberalism first defeated the Southern plantation barons on the blood-drenched battlefields of Shiloh, Antietam, Gettysburg, and Vicksburg. Later, Presidents Theodore Roosevelt, Woodrow Wilson, and Franklin Roosevelt checkmated the Gilded Age business tycoons in the Progressive and New Deal eras. Seen in hindsight, fighting first one side of illiberal reaction and then the other gave an advantage to liberal America. In this third momentous clash, the two worst parts of the American political psyche lock in a tight embrace that, in other major nations, has been a recipe for the death of democracy and the birth of deeply authoritarian politics. Today's sinister marriage of unreconstructed whites with moneyed libertarians is no run-of-the-mill political partnership. Instead, it is extraordinarily dangerous.

Until recently, the U.S. was fortunate in never having the plutocracy link arms with the landed elite—or their ideological descendants. Now our history has caught up with us. Our racist past and our capitalist present have combined to threaten American democracy. It is no longer possible to ignore or sugarcoat the illiberal reality of American politics. No longer the party of Lincoln, Theodore Roosevelt, Dwight Eisenhower, Gerald Ford, Howard Baker, George H. W. Bush, Robert Dole, and John McCain, the contemporary Republican Party has pitched its tent at the intersection of racism and greed. The two sides of illiberalism—united into a single powerful reactionary army—are waging a counterrevolutionary struggle against the ideals upon which the United States was founded. The reactionaries will not stop unless and until America's better angels clearly and loudly say, 'Enough and no more.' Like our forefathers confronting dark times in 1860 and 1932, the children of light must step forward to cage the demons of darkness.

The beating heart of the Trump presidency is the illiberal assumption that the United States is a white Anglo-Saxon nation. His rallies are near lily-white and his strong support in the deep South and the white ethnic neighborhoods of the north maps the appeal of Alabama Governor George Wallace's renegade presidential runs in 1968 and 1972. During the summer of 2019, President Trump told four congresswomen to "go back" to the countries they came from.[28] Just in case there was any confusion as to whether Trump's attacks on women of color in the House of Representatives had a racist edge, Kellyanne Conway, the president's counselor, told a Fox News audience, "They represent a dark underbelly of people in this country."[29] While many Republicans, from regular voters to lawmakers to White House aides, say the president's blatant misogyny and verbal attacks on minorities and immigrants are "indefensible," the *Wall Street Journal* reports that many in the president's party are "willing to publicly give Mr. Trump a pass" because they believe the president is the "best bet to keep the economy—one of the few issues that most Americans are willing to give him credit for—on an upward trajectory."[30] The post-Gingrich GOP—led in Congress by Senate Majority Leader Mitch McConnell, the sphinx of reaction and modern master of obstruction—has waved goodbye to conservatives with character. It is supported by a substantial portion of the business class that remains staunchly Republican joined by significant elements of the white middle and working classes; together they have rallied around a president who has made explicit racist and nativist appeals the calling card of his administration.

Similar to the 1930s, democracy is under attack globally and it is a tragedy of immense proportions that one of America's two major political parties is at the forefront of this illiberal wave. Yet many Republicans are content with an elected authoritarian incapable of telling the truth as commander in chief if that is what it takes to capture the White House and control at least one chamber of Congress.

Republicans are seemingly blasé about a chief executive who adores murderous dictators, who bullies foreign governments to smear his political opponents, and who muses about being president for life.[31] When lawmakers remain silent in the face of a lawless president, they are complicit in allowing autocratic design to corrupt the public mind. If looking the other way while the Constitution is under attack on multiple fronts, if kowtowing to the NRA's every wish on gun rights even as innocents are slaughtered in mass attacks by terrorists firing weapons of war, if supporting a president who leads rallies where the joy of hatred is celebrated and cheered is what is required for political success, then the end certainly justifies the means, as illiberal Republicans and their moderate allies continually tell themselves. But does it? If trampling human rights, violating the Constitution, and defacing democracy constitute part of the cost, then it's worth recalling that white Southerners during the lynching era and Romans living at the end of their Republic also enjoyed public spectacle and populist demagogues.[32]

The United States is experiencing more than a culture war. We are in the midst of an illiberal mutiny—driven by a Republican Party that has veered to the extreme in what, in part, is a nativist revolt and patriarchal reassertion by white men, just as the nation is becoming more diverse, tolerant, and equal in opportunity for all its citizens.[33] In the past two decades, this mutiny has escalated into a full-fledged reactionary revolution, one in which radicals on the right continually get outflanked by radicals even more extreme. And President Trump is the counterrevolutionary par excellence—at war with the Republican establishment, the Democrats, the Constitution, norms of decency and, critically, the fundamental principles of liberalism that have been central to American identity since before the founding.

This book tracks the two illiberal impulses—racism and the insatiable desire for power by the ultrarich—across American history and chronicles the consequences of their capture of the Republican Party. Madisonian democracy works when the two major parties share similar values while disagreeing about public policy. In the past quarter century, however, our traditional approach to politics and government has disappeared over the cliff. Marching steadily rightward, the GOP now displays its worst aspects while deserting an honorable tradition. Leaving behind the values and virtues endorsed by the founders, Lincoln, Eisenhower, and Bush 41, Republicans have stubbornly supported a man manifestly unfit for the nation's highest office. Whether the impeached president is someday removed from office, decisively defeated at the polls, or reelected, Donald J. Trump is certain to go down in history as one of the nation's worst presidents. But this book is not about Trump. Instead, it is about the toxic ingredients in our political culture that created a Republican electorate which accepts, tolerates, and thrills to hateful rhetoric while insisting that government protect the privilege, power, and wealth of white upper-class America. With national politics trapped in a period of prolonged and bitter gridlock and insurrection from the right, the roots of our political crisis (a calamity that goes well beyond the presidential debacle, which is but a chapter in a larger story) are to be found in the realm of history and ideas. A single question lies at the heart of our epic struggle: Is the United States, in fact, a *liberal* nation?

MADISON'S
SORROW

I

John Locke Invents America

Viewed from Europe, the United States once appeared as a culturally and politically conservative country.[1] But philosophically, America has been a deeply liberal nation, founded by people who rejected the old ways of Europe and sought a new path forward. In authoring the Declaration, Thomas Jefferson famously cribbed from John Locke.[2] We not only borrowed the right to revolution and property from Locke, but just as important, we adopted his wholesale refutation of the ancien régime—the political and social system of hereditary monarchy and feudalism—and his radical philosophy that spurned the Old World based on caste and class; Americans wanted the New World to be different. Locke's articulation of rational liberty, defense of the sanctity of the individual, embrace of the reality of human equality, and belief that people have a right to choose the government under which they live have been deeply ingrained in American culture and modern liberalism.

America's political consciousness has been largely restricted to Locke's intellectual universe and the language of Thomas Paine, Thomas Jefferson, and Abraham Lincoln. For generations, Americans have been fortunate in this regard. It was Locke, more than any other thinker, who supplied the American founders with their conceptions of liberty, equality, property, natural rights (a powerful mental and moral fiction, not an historic fact, for Locke), and government by consent. Lockean liberalism, at once radically egalitarian and protective of individual rights and initiative, provides the philosophic canopy under which Americans of a progressive and conservative mindset have worked together for more than two centuries. While liberals and conservatives have often disagreed on public policy, they both operate in the world created by Locke and celebrated in the American Revolution. The illiberal right does not.

A century before 1776, Locke, an Oxford University philosopher by trade and a political activist by inclination, found himself needing to invent an argument that would give the people of England the right to rebel against a bad king. Locke and his political friends faced a challenge: King Charles II's brother James had converted to Catholicism and he was heir to the throne in a nation that since the reign of Henry VIII was strongly Protestant. A Puritan fearful that a Catholic king would reverse the Reformation in England, Locke wrote his celebrated *Two Treatises of Government*. In so doing, he provided the American colonists with arguments and rhetoric they would later use against King George III.

To understand Locke and his American disciples such as Jefferson, Madison, and Alexander Hamilton, it is critical to see what they opposed; they "explicitly challenged the fixed hierarchical arrangements taken for granted almost everywhere seventeenth-century Europeans lived."[3] The people who first colonized America, and those who followed, did so to find religious liberty and to escape a stifling caste system in which people were born into a certain class and remained there; their freedom of action and ambition were sharply limited by their social station. Americans en masse rejected the ancien régime and sought to construct a New World based on Locke's principles that we as a people—rich or poor, black, brown, or white, women or men—are equal as human beings and each of us, as individuals (with the exception of the mentally impaired and children), are blessed with the ability to think and judge for ourselves what we want our lives to be and what we want our government to do. Of course, the reality of America often has conflicted with our ideals; but it has been our liberal values that have driven us forward as a nation.

The birth of the United States opened a new chapter in world history; this theme reverberated among the founding generation. In dedicating to

George Washington his book defending the French Revolution, Thomas Paine wrote: "That the Rights of Man may be as universal as your Benevolence can wish, that you may enjoy the Happiness of seeing the New World regenerate the Old."[4] Both liberty and equality are central to the American creed. The aim of American liberalism is to allow *all* members of society the equality and liberty to pursue their dreams—not only white men, not only the business class and their families, not only those born to privilege and status—giving everyone a "fair shot," in President Obama's words, at leading a life of dignity and respect in which they can utilize their abilities and talents. Thus, the reform liberalism of Abraham Lincoln, Woodrow Wilson, and Franklin Roosevelt was not a violation of the founders' vision, as many on the right insist, but a fulfillment and ennobling of it. Moderate Republicans—such as Presidents Dwight Eisenhower, Gerald Ford, and George H. W. Bush, and former Senate Majority Leader Bob Dole—are traditional American conservatives and thus *liberals* in this deeper meaning.[5]

Modern liberals and traditional conservatives share an allegiance to the principles of "life, liberty and the pursuit of happiness." In addition, today's liberals, moderates, and many conservatives are distinctly modern in two senses. First, they insist that all American citizens be granted social and political equality no matter their race, creed, or religion. This is the great project of inclusion that began with Lincoln and the Emancipation Proclamation and continues today with gay and transgender rights. For much of our history, many Americans remained "servants in the shadows." Women and minorities, denied the opportunity to participate in the full sweep of American life, spent their lives serving, supporting, and watching heterosexual white men. The struggle to gain access to the promised land of equality has been one of the central themes of liberalism ever since Thomas Paine and Mary Wollstonecraft wrote in support of the American and French revolutions in the late 18th century.[6] From the suffrage movement before World War I, to the civil rights movement (which brought formal rights to African Americans and opened the door to a much fuller participation in American society by all people of color) and the modern women's movement led most prominently by Betty Friedan and Gloria Steinem, to the current push for LGBTQ rights, Americans who were formerly less than full-fledged citizens have fought to be included.

Second, modern liberals and their conservative sparring partners understand that corporate capitalism, with all its dynamism and productive powers, requires strong regulation of food safety, air traffic control, clean water, and carbon emissions into the atmosphere; and a safety net to protect the most vulnerable and disadvantaged members of society. In addition, they recognize that to preserve and maintain a vibrant democracy "we must keep on rescuing capitalism from the capitalists," in Arthur M. Schlesinger Jr.'s apt phrase.[7] The tragedy of the Great Depression, which devastated working families around the world and gave rise to fascism and World War II, taught the Western democracies that free markets left to their own devices will inevitably run off the cliff. As a result, Wall Street trading is now regulated, and when economic inequality becomes extreme the task for democratic governments is to devise ways to rebalance the economic game so that the rules do not overwhelmingly favor the rich and well connected.

I am not arguing that Locke was a 21st century liberal. No, he was a man of his historical period. But even if he accepted a degree of inequality and hierarchy that a modern liberal might question, his ideas contain a dynamic and a direction that have been developed by his followers.[8] His writing as a whole—especially his major philosophical work, *An Essay Concerning Human Understanding* (1689), and not the second *Treatise* taken alone—is the seed from which the tree of modern liberalism sprang forth.

WHY JOHN LOCKE STILL MATTERS

Locke remains important in the 21st century because he—more than any other intellectual—invented both America and the modern world. Hugely influential for more than three centuries because of his ideas and accessible style, Locke is the philosopher of liberalism par excellence and his liberalism is about both liberty and equality.[9] First and foremost, liberalism is about the individual. But, as Locke, the founders, and Alexis de Tocqueville knew, a spirit of radical egalitarianism powers the liberal creed.[10] Liberalism puts a "stress on equal concern and respect for the rights of every human being," writes University of Pennsylvania scholar Rogers M. Smith. Critically, liberalism, both in its classic and reform modes in the

United States, rejects as artificial social norms and institutions that allow some people to lord over others.[11] Following from Locke's egalitarian premises, inequalities are not accepted as given in the new world that is America; instead, the onus is on those who seek to protect or reinstate social, economic, and institutional inequalities to offer reasons why these inequities are valid and legitimate in a liberal democratic order. It is this antifeudal sensibility that makes America special.

Radical for his time, Locke saw human beings as fundamentally equal in that all adults have the capacity to reason and to think about the world with intelligence. Prior to 1650, when the Enlightenment burst onto the scene, European intellectuals and the Church taught that the human mind knows things because people are born with certain ideas imprinted on the brain, a tradition extending back to Aristotle.[12] By contrast, Locke argued that people are born tabula rasa and held that knowledge of the world may be derived from two sources—personal experience and the ideas that we construct in our minds. For Locke, rational or inner liberty is the capacity to pause and think through the consequences of alternative forms of action before acting. In the *Essay*, Locke issued a powerful critique of ancient and medieval forms of knowledge and called for a revolution in thinking that amounted to a "democratization of the mind."[13]

Living in the modern world that Locke helped create, it is difficult for us to grasp the magnitude of his accomplishment. In 1632, when Locke was born (in Bristol, 100 miles west of London), the modern idea of the autonomous individual did not yet exist. People were only understood in reference to their proper station and role within the organic structure of society that mirrored the cosmic order.[14] In this premodern world, life was thought to be ruled by a Great Chain of Being, which decreed that all humanity was linked together in a descending hierarchy, beginning with God and kings, followed by nobility and church figures, knights, squires, soldiers, merchants, vassals, and finally, powerless peasants toiling in the fields. For centuries, European society was a rigid caste system characterized by radical inequality, and it occurred to very few that it could be otherwise. Locke fundamentally challenged the ancien régime by arguing that human beings were equal in their ability to reason, and that differences of intelligence were largely the result of upbringing and education. His pathbreaking philosophy attacked a world based on radical inequality, hereditary hierarchy, and and entrenched privilege, which viewed those at the top of the hierarchy as innately superior.

BETWEEN PEASANT AND KING: THINKING AND FREEDOM

The key to understanding Locke is to recognize that his political theory, *Two Treatises of Government*, fits together with and flows from the *Essay*. Critically, many of the arguments presented in the second *Treatise* are a means to an end and are not foundational; for example, the famous arguments in the second *Treatise* regarding individualism, natural rights, limited government, and property are polemic and situational. By contrast, Locke's argument regarding liberty in the *Essay* is foundational to his overall philosophy and liberalism. If we wish to understand liberalism in America, we must start with the great *Essay*.

The American and the French revolutions first required a revolution of consciousness. Locke supplied this in his *Essay*, which promoted a deeply subversive theory of knowledge that placed one in control of one's own life and demanded that authoritative institutions and rules be examined "under the searing light of reason." For Locke, between the peasant and the king there was no intrinsic distinction; the capacity to think and operate in the world was the same. In a feudal culture where privilege, hierarchy, class, inequality, and exclusion were deeply woven into the fabric of society, this was a radical doctrine indeed. In his philosophy, Locke conceptualized the individual as being autonomous and freed of the weight of tradition, custom, and the inequality of rank, privilege, and status that defined premodern society. In this way, he turned the received mental world of the 17th century upside down. Giving the average person agency and power, his theory of knowledge exploded a static, settled social order. After Locke's stunningly successful attack, authority, privilege, hierarchy, inequality, class, and exclusion were no longer safe from examination and critique. His egalitarian philosophy followed from Protestant theology's insistence that people have a direct relationship with God unmediated by priests and high clergy; Locke's genius translated Calvinist theology into a social and civic philosophy.

For Locke, the essence of human freedom lay in the individual's ability to construct complex ideas out of simple ones based on personal experience and reflection. He understood that thinking was hard work, but also rewarding and something that all human beings can do: "For all Reasoning is search, and casting about, and requires Pains and Application."[15] Locke believed that our knowledge of the world was based on two things: empirical sensory observation and internal reflection.[16] Reflection is the mental ability to first construct simple ideas and then more complex with which to think, analyze, and make reflective judgments about the best course of action. Together, sensation and reflection produce three types of knowledge:

- Simple ideas;
- Complex ideas made up of multiple simple ideas that the mind combines; and
- Mixed modes, the high-level abstract thinking that is unique to human beings.

Of these, mixed modes are the most abstract form of complex ideas because they are not related to what is found in nature.[17] For example, mathematics and moral and political ideas (such as "ethics" and "justice") do not depend on anything in nature; instead, they are constructions and inventions of the human mind.[18]

Instead of passively receiving messages from authorities about how to think and act, Locke recommended that people use their God-given capacity to think for themselves. In his *Essay*, he demonstrated how this was indeed possible and natural. At the core of Locke's philosophy is the inner freedom of thought—the ability to perceive, think, make judgments, and invent sophisticated concepts in the mind—which allows us to deal with the external environment in an astute and moral way.[19] Rational liberty, for Locke, is the ability to "examine, view, and judge, of the good and evil of what we are *going to do*."[20] This ability to pause and think before acting is not, he insists, a "restraint or diminution of *Freedom*"; instead, it is "the end and benefit of our *Liberty*." If our actions are "determined by anything but the last result of our own Minds, judging the good or evil of any action, we are not free."[21] Lest modern readers think that Locke's philosophy is hopelessly outdated, modern science agrees with him. A *New York Times* article featured this headline: "Scientists are beginning to recognize that foresight is what distinguishes human beings from other animals."[22]

The essence of liberty is this *internal* freedom of judgment, which all human beings possess.[23] The advocacy of rational liberty lies at the heart of Locke's political and moral vision; the rest of his philosophy unfolds from this foundation.[24] For Locke, human freedom, equality, dignity, and happiness are based on our ability to "comprehend our world and ourselves, to deliberate on the possibilities and aspirations we find therein, and to choose and execute our preferred courses to the greatest degree practicable."[25] According to Locke, God had joined together virtue and happiness. Though we may be less sure of this today, an optimistic, progressive hopefulness remains central to the ethos of liberalism.

In an important sense, Locke's religious faith is the key to his philosophy.[26] Because we are God's creatures, we have the capacity to reason; as equal children of God we have the capacity to think and our challenge is to develop the powers of abstraction and then to test our ideas in experience.[27] Locke views mankind as being governed not by pure self-interest but by an ethic of mutuality that bears a striking affinity to what Alexis de Tocqueville would later call "self-interest properly understood." In a crucial passage in the second chapter of the second *Treatise*, Locke writes: "The *State of Nature* has a Law of Nature to govern it, which obliges every one; And Reason, which is that Law, teaches all Mankind, who will but consult it, that being all equal and independent, no one ought to harm another in his Life, Health, Liberty, or Possessions."[28] Locke believed that man's ability to think in a sophisticated, moral way enables every adult, who will but consult his mind and the world around him, to live by the principles of autonomy, equality, and mutual benefit. This sense of self-possession and equality means that—in a Lockean world—people neither live in subordination to others nor do they treat others as merely instruments or tools for their purposes.[29] To reject these two pillars of aristocratic and feudal life is to imagine a world in which unquestioned privilege, hierarchy, inequality, and exclusion no longer define the human condition.

In a number of ways, Locke remains a distinctly modern thinker. First, he rejected the classical insistence on the cognitive connection between human beings and an "extrinsic intellectual, moral or spiritual end, or *telos*."[30] Such a belief was essential for premodern societies that believed in a cosmic world order. In this way, Locke, a devout Puritan, began the disenchantment of the modern world that would later occupy Max Weber. Second, he rejected the speculative philosophy that attempted to discover a "single set of metaphysical principles governing" natural and moral philosophy. He strenuously resisted system building (a characteristic of philosophers as divergent as Hobbes, Spinoza, Hegel, Marx, Spencer, and Hayek), which seeks to construct a "comprehensive account of being."[31] Locke argued instead that the ultimate truth of the universe was beyond human capacity to know and thus his philosophical project was more modest.[32] In the Introduction to the *Essay,* he wrote: "'Tis of great use to the Sailor to know the length of his Line, though he cannot with it fathom all the depths of the Ocean . . . Our Business here is not to know all things, but those which concern our Conduct."[33] For Locke, the task was to use reason to live a good and proper life. Given a limited ability to know the universe with certainty, Locke (and his American followers) counseled that what we needed to do was use our reason to reflect on the best mode of conduct in any circumstance given the information and scientific knowledge that we possess at the time.[34] Unlike animals, we can use our *inner liberty*—our rational minds that direct our actions—to overcome unconscious drives, bad habits, and public opinion based on dogma or misinformation. Third, the egalitarian premises of Locke's empiricist epistemology rejected the ancient idea that there were innate moral principles. If these principles were innate and stamped on our minds, we would not transgress moral rules with such confidence and serenity; if they were innate, why, asked Locke, would some cultures practice infanticide or cannibalism?[35]

Armed with a new philosophy, Locke and his followers had a powerful tool with which to loosen the bonds of an oppressive society.[36] In 1789, 100 years after Locke's books appeared in print, France's Third Estate rose in revolt against King Louis XVI and the ancien régime was swept away. Little more than a decade earlier, in *Common Sense* (1776), Thomas Paine drew on Locke's ideas to ridicule the belief that there are innate differences between people—critically between a king and his subjects—and eviscerated the very idea of monarchy. Leading the way, Locke, Paine, and the Americans had opened the door to a new world.[37] Without the belief that there were radical biological differences between people, the feudal system of aristocrat and serf—and its accompanying norms of hierarchy, strict caste, massive inequality in life prospects, and the exclusion of the many from the privileges of the few—suddenly gave way, fell to earth, and vanished in a billow of smoke.[38]

Reading Locke in this way runs counter to views on the left and right of Locke as a proponent of modern capitalism—a political philosopher who was first and foremost a champion of capitalist accumulation and possessive individualism. This conception of Locke—based on a narrow ahistorical reading of the second *Treatise*—is in error and does a disservice to his philosophy of liberalism.[39] Seeing Locke as propounding a doctrine of absolute property rights and free market expansion comes from reading the second *Treatise* in isolation from his overarching philosophy in the *Essay* and his attack on absolute monarchy in the first *Treatise,* as well as failing to understand that the second *Treatise* is a polemic work written at a specific time for a very specific purpose.[40] Locke's concern is the liberty of the king's subjects, not the free market of modern capitalism.

WHAT LOCKE'S RHETORIC REVEALS

When the *Essay* and both *Treatises* are read together, the change in tone and style between the three works is startling; it is apparent that Locke was writing with different tasks in mind, being at ease with some subjects and uncomfortable with others. In the *Essay*, the writing is confident, almost casual, as Locke systematically explains to his audience how their minds and the world work. In the first *Treatise*, he adopts a slashing style of attack and ridicule as he systematically destroys Robert Filmer's claim that kingly authority descends from Adam and that, as a result, we are all slaves in a world made by God. Locke writes with zest and joy, using his knowledge of the Bible to repudiate Filmer's argument for absolute monarchy and the divine right of kings.[41]

By contrast, the famed second *Treatise*, whose authorship Locke strove to keep secret (thus delaying publication of both *Treatises* for years) is filled with compact, incisive, nearly somber prose. There is no levity in this *Treatise*; Locke knows he is making a radical argument that could well send him to the scaffold. Famous and beloved across Europe for his *Essay*, the mild-mannered philosopher was forced, by exceptional circumstance, into a role he disliked; the change in tone clearly signals that Locke would rather someone else be available to play the role of revolutionary intellectual. Yet, because of his loyalty to his mentor and sponsor, Lord Shaftesbury, and his fear of the consequence of a Catholic king of England, Locke felt compelled to be bold and forceful and drafted the *Two Treatises* in an unstable and dangerous political environment.[42] Knowing that England might soon have a Catholic king, Locke had to mount a convincing attack against the divine right of kings and frame an original argument as to why the subjects of a king could, in some instances, be justified in rebelling against authority.

◆

In the first *Treatise,* Locke takes on Filmer, one of the leading advocates of absolute monarchy, and reduces to ash his argument that no man is born free and all government is monarchy. He unleashes a polemic blowtorch beginning with his opening salvo: "Slavery is so vile and miserable an Estate of Man, and so directly opposite to the generous Temper and Courage of our Nation; that it is hardly to be conceived, that an *Englishman,* much less a *Gentleman,* should plead for it."[43] The essence of Filmer's view of absolute monarchy was that all authority among human beings was of the same type—the authority of a domineering father over his family. Rulers received their right to rule from God as descended from Adam, and they ruled over their subjects as they wished. Conversely, the political responsibility of the subjects was simply to do what they were told—honor and obey authority.[44] Armed with a stiletto, Locke destroys Filmer. He writes that in Filmer's treatise, "which was to provide Chains for all Mankind, I should find nothing but a Rope of Sand." In the introduction to the first *Treatise,* Locke says that Filmer's "System lies in a little compass, it is no more than this: *That all Government is absolute Monarchy,*" and the ground upon which Filmer builds his argument "is this, *That no Man is Born free.*"[45] Filmer argues that God gave all power and authority to Adam, but Locke responds by saying that if men had nothing left to them but their slavery they might at least "have such undeniable Proofs of its Necessity."[46] Locke argues that Filmer supplies nothing of the kind. Across the pages of the first *Treatise,* the rhetorical technique is refute, refute, refute. When Filmer claims that

Adam's power as monarch has since passed down to all the monarchs in the world, Locke attacks. Three passages in Chapter XI ("Who Heir?") give a flavor of Locke's argument. First, "all this ado about Adam's Fatherhood, the greatness of its Power, and the necessity of its supposal, helps nothing to Establish the Power of those that Govern, or to determine the Obedience of Subjects."[47] A few pages later Locke writes, that to make good on the title of his book, *Patriarchy*, the author "begins the History of the descent of Adam's Regal Power in these words: 'This Lordship which Adam by command had over the whole World, and by Right descending from him, the Patriarchs did enjoy.'" Locke asks: How does he prove that the Patriarchs by descent "did enjoy" this power?[48] Finally, he pulls the Bible out from under Filmer's argument, writing: "The Scripture says not a word of their Rulers or Forms of Government, but only gives an account, how Mankind came to be divided into distinct Languages and Nations; and therefore it is not to argue from the Authority of Scripture, to tell us positively, *Fathers* were their *Rulers*, when the Scripture says no such thing."[49]

◆

In the second *Treatise*, Locke utilizes the radically democratic philosophy he had developed in the *Essay* and invents—out of whole cloth—a mental universe that would stand as an alternative to an absolute monarchy. This theory, writes Cambridge University political scientist John Dunn, was "a very radical theory, a theory of political equality and responsibility, resting on the judgment of each individual adult" that, in turn, is based on the philosophy of knowledge set forth in the *Essay*.[50] The second *Treatise* is justly famous because it contains lucid and original reasoning about the state of nature, natural rights, limited government, the consent of the governed, property, and a conception of people existing prior to society. These are the rhetorical arguments of a lawyer making his case. Locke used all of this to advance and defend *his primary goal*—justifying the right to revolution and resistance to a bad king; everything else in the second *Treatise* is secondary and supportive of this core argument.[51]

Under an absolute monarchy, the king's subjects had no rights (even to their lives) and no liberty of their own outside the monarch's purview. Whether *any subject* lived or died, from lowly wench to powerful baron, was at the king's discretion and his alone. Locke's goal was to create a space outside the king's reach in which his subjects could stand as independent, autonomous beings. His additional goal was to create an alternative political narrative to absolute monarchy that would allow the people an opportunity to voice their disapproval of a bad king, and if necessary to depose him. Against the idea of absolute monarchy, Locke countered with the abstractions of the state of nature and natural rights—which together supply the idea that people are born equal and have the fundamental rights to life, liberty, and property, an idea that has priority ahead of any government under which a society happens to live.[52]

Both of Locke's ideas—the "state of nature" and "natural rights"—are artificial and fictional in the sense that neither exists in nature. Today, we see these ideas as sophisticated mental abstractions employed by people to make sense of the society in which they live; these creations of the mind exert power across society and strongly influence how people act. Many of Locke's readers did not catch this subtlety and viewed his argument for natural rights not as a mental invention but as a discovery of actual fact. In doing this, many readers of the second *Treatise* understood natural rights in the same way that the defenders of monarchy saw the divine right of kings—as an innate reality of the world. Locke, of course, would laugh at this. But as a rhetorical device, an argument of Logos (as when a lawyer stresses certain facts and ignores others to make the best case) as against strict logic, Locke was able to utilize natural rights to destabilize and eventually destroy the ancien régime across Europe.

If we want a straightforward, easy to grasp definition of liberalism—one from which people living and working in the 21st century can benefit—we can do far worse than to think of Locke and his rejection of authoritarian feudalism.[53] Defining Locke in the negative—as opposing privilege, hierarchy, inequality, and exclusion—allows us see what the founding generation sought to achieve and how the ideals of liberty, equality, and democracy, once unleashed, transformed—and continue to transform—the world. Explaining the meaning of American liberalism in this way makes it easily understood by corporate executives, service workers, and schoolchildren. It helps us grasp exactly why America has been a deeply liberal nation and why modern liberals and conservatives typically can talk and argue with one another and arrive at solutions to the nation's problems.

STUART KINGS, LOCKE, AND SLAVERY IN AMERICA

Like Jefferson, Locke is a liberal hero who has long endured the reputation of a hypocrite. His critics point to Locke's authorship of *The Fundamental Constitutions of Carolina* (1669), which explicitly endorsed both slavery and hereditary nobility.[54] The traditional view of Locke is expressed thus:

> To introduce slavery in the Carolinas, then, was to establish, as fundamental to the political order, an institution at variance with everything about how Locke understood civil society. "Every Freeman of Carolina shall have absolute power and Authority over his Negro slaves," Locke's constitution read. That is to say, notwithstanding the vehement assertion of a natural right to liberty and the claim that absolute power is a form of tyranny, the right of one man to own another—impossible to conceive in a state of nature or under civil government, impossible to imagine under any arrangement except a state of war—was not only possible, but lawful, in America.[55]

In addition, detractors point to Locke's ownership of stock in the Royal African Company, responsible for Britain's African slave trade. Criticism of Jefferson's hypocrisy is justified, but such criticism of Locke is unfair; groundbreaking scholarship overturns our understanding of Locke's role in promoting slavery.[56] It liberates the author of the *Two Treatises of Government* from being entangled in the promotion of slavery and colonialism—accusations that "cast a shadow over Western liberalism."[57]

Western slavery emerged from ideas about the divine and absolute rights of kings and people being born into distinct and separate castes.[58] In Plato's *Republic*, for example, society is divided into gold, silver, and bronze orders. Similarly, under feudalism, a prince was born to be a king, an aristocrat was born to be a nobleman, a subject was born to obey his master and the king, and a slave was born to be a drone; each with the obligation to obey those above their station. At the time of colonies, the English kings were deeply involved in the slave trade. Following the English Civil War, Charles II (1660–1685) pursued slavery vigorously and the tax revenue from the crops produced by slaves helped finance the monarchy. In the American colonies,

Charles offered generous rewards of land to settlers who purchased slaves or indentured servants and put his brother James in charge of the new Royal African Company to encourage the slave trade. In the early 18th century, one of Charles II's successors—Queen Anne—obtained a grant to supply the Spanish empire with all of its slaves for thirty years. That contract made Britain the main importer of slaves to the New World by 1750. This is the world in which Locke lived and worked, and the world he struggled to reform.

Living in 17th century England, Locke knew fully well the life-crimping reality of inherited status. As part of his work as a mid-level bureaucrat, Locke did indeed draft the Carolina constitutions. But he did so as a secretary—much like a lawyer composing a legal document today—and he wrote the document for the eight men who owned the Carolinas (gifted to them by Charles II). The constitutions championed hereditary nobility and slavery but these ideas reflected the views of their owners, not Locke. About the Carolina constitutions, historian Holly Brewer writes:

> The principles it espoused—including hereditary nobility and slavery—both predated Locke's involvement, and reflected the ideals of the owners. It is a deep error, therefore, to contend that Locke's role in the Carolina constitutions should guide interpretation of his later work, much less liberalism.[59]

Similarly, while working as Lord Shaftesbury's personal secretary, Locke became the scribe for the Council of Foreign Plantations, and in 1672–73, Charles II paid Locke in Royal African Company stock. Shaftsbury oversaw England's overseas colonies and, as the Council's clerk, Locke wrote considerably about African slaves.

As he grew older, Locke came to see slavery as the most extreme example of the evils issuing from inherited status. Turning against Charles II, Shaftesbury and Locke began to argue "that absolutism possessed a common essence, and took different forms—of kings in imperial policymaking, and masters over slaves—but that all forms were wrong."[60] In 1675, Shaftesbury and Lock cowrote and published debates in the House of Lords questioning whether Charles II sought too much "absolute" power. When Charles ordered the book burned as seditious, Locke fled to France and Shaftesbury was imprisoned without trial in the Tower of London. After spending the first part of his career promoting the feudal ideals and practices of the Stuarts and British royalty, Locke turned sharply against them. In the end, Locke supported slavery only as a punishment for a terrible crime for which the death penalty could apply. He opposed slavery on the same grounds as hereditary monarchy; people should not inherit their status.

After the Glorious Revolution of 1688 placed William and Mary on the throne, the party of reform, Shaftesbury's Whigs, gained control of Parliament. William III appointed Locke to the Board of Trade, a new and powerful council overseeing the colonies. Concerned with abuse of power in Virginia, Locke wrote a forty-page plan for legal reform. For centuries, his Virginia plan gathered dust in the Bodleian Library at Oxford, where it was recently discovered rolled into a cubby hole in Locke's desk. It turns out the reforms in this plan substantially overturned many of the earlier colonial policies that had promoted hierarchy, inherited status, and slavery. In particular, Locke's plan challenged Charles II's policy of granting masters fifty acres of land for each slave purchased, a policy that fostered the large estates and bound labor of Virginia's gentry. As part of the reform effort, Locke arranged for the appointment of a new Virginia governor—Francis Nicholson. By a 1699 court decision, Nicholson eliminated the land bounty for purchasing a slave, and sent a copy of the ruling to England. In the margin of the court ruling that masters would no longer be rewarded with large estates for the "Importation of Negroes," Locke wrote, "Well Done."[61] When Locke began the first *Treatise*: "Slavery is so vile and miserable an Estate of Man . . . that it is hardly to be conceived" that anyone would support it, he meant what he said.[62] Those words—"Well done"—are proof of his effort to overturn one of the royal policies that promoted African slavery in the new world, says Brewer. The policy of land for slaves and indentured servants had a major political impact; the king appointed the men with the most land to powerful colonial political positions. Connecting "property in people to property in land to political power" had a profound effect on the legal, cultural, and political development of America.[63]

> The extent of Locke's objection to property in people is evident in his objections even to indentured servitude: he supported bound labor *only* for criminals sentenced to hang . . . Instead

of servants indenting themselves to servitude to pay their passage, Locke urged the king to pay. Skilled tradesmen, the poor, "Native Irish," and "French Protestants," should arrive without debt and receive land. He encouraged the king to diversify production on smaller farms.[64]

Unfortunately for Locke and the future of America, when Queen Anne, allied with the high Tories, took the throne in the early 18th century, she aggressively supported slavery across the empire. In 1706, her Board of Trade reversed Locke's reform measures and approved a Virginia law that again granted two hundred acres per servant or slave to masters who purchased more than five (and ten new slaves earned their owner two thousand additional acres). They also approved a new Virginia law which compensated masters for the value of executed slaves, ushering in a severe system of punishment, and another that allowed "plantation owners to create permanent estates over generations, with slaves and their descendants attached to these estates . . . to the lord and his heir *ad infinitum*."[65] Locke was the original reform liberal; he fought against illiberalism in his age just as we do in ours.

When we unpack the philosophy of Locke, whose influence on Jefferson and the Declaration was profound, we see how the liberalism of Abraham Lincoln, Franklin Roosevelt, and Barack Obama is, in fact, a continuation and flowering of Locke's ideas.

His rejection of privilege, hierarchy, inequality, and exclusion lies at the heart of the American liberal ideal.

2

Our Imperfect Founders

American political consciousness operates at a different level than party politics. Its three primary ideological components—liberal, civic republican, and illiberal—should not be confused with being a Democrat or a Republican. The liberal hemisphere, dominant and broadly familiar, celebrates life, liberty, the pursuit of happiness, and government by consent. Our civic republican lobe—which traces back to Aristotle, Rome, and the Italian Renaissance—champions patriotism, civic virtue, and citizen participation, and excites a fear that elite corruption will spoil our grand democratic experiment. Civic republican idealism triggers great passion and was critical to both the American Revolution and the outburst of participatory democracy in the 1960s. It was also a factor in the Tea Party revolt. The promise of American life flows from our liberal and civic republican heritage. These are the ideals that make us proud to be Americans. By contrast, illiberalism lurks like a tumor—sometimes latent, sometimes growing rapidly, but always malignant. This ancient part of our political brain defends the feudal values that define monarchy, the ancien régime, and modern authoritarians. Pre-democratic, it is comfortable with high degrees of inequality and white male privilege, has no problem with hierarchy (especially when white males are in charge), and is happiest when certain groups—women, racial minorities, recent immigrants, and the LGBT community—are excluded from full membership in American society. Illiberalism found its purist expression in the feudalism of the Old South—first the slave South and then the segregated racist South that functioned as a one-party white nationalist oligarchy from 1865 to 1965.

If our Lockean consciousness flows like the mighty Mississippi, the civic republican and illiberal streams are tributaries akin to the Missouri and Ohio rivers.[1] There are periods when liberal and republican ideals have been stronger than the illiberal strain. At other times (the 1920s and the post-Gingrich era, for example), the illiberal tradition—and its arguments for the preservation of the norms, prerogatives, and privileges of the white Protestant nation—has been ascendant. The mix of the three ideological streams is not simple. Sometimes, the three ideologies are encapsulated in a single person's political career. Thomas Jefferson and the Georgian Tom Watson, for example, painfully personified the liberal/illiberal contradiction at the heart of the American experience.[2] As every schoolchild knows, the principal author of the Declaration also owned slaves.[3] Watson led the agrarian populist movement in the South that formed an alliance between poor whites and blacks against the Southern upper class in the 1890s. In civic republican fashion, the populists rallied against a corrupt economic system that favored the banks and railroads over the nation's farmers, and Watson stood squarely in liberal tradition when he declared, "The accident of color can make no difference in the interests of farmers, croppers, and laborers." But after the defeat of the populist crusade, a disheartened, bitter Watson turned against the liberal-republican ethos and became a vehement racist.[4]

Across the nation's history—up to and including the present—there has been strong resistance to the liberal principles of equality and inclusion by those who benefit from the illiberal norms of hierarchy, exclusion, and exploitation.[5] For many young people growing up in an increasingly cosmopolitan and diverse United States, a commitment to inclusion is both natural and right. For example, most Americans younger than age thirty-five support gay marriage. At the same time, hostility to equal rights and full opportunity continues even among millennials.[6] The reactionary attitudes of the white slaveholding South—evolved and often "reconstructed" so as not to be as blatantly racist as in the past—remain a central part of the American political mind.

LIBERTY AND PATRIOTISM

Locke's ideas are supplemented by civic republican norms. For much of the 20th century, scholars saw only the dominant liberal stream, almost to the point of claiming Americans were all about Locke and only Locke and, especially, those parts of the second *Treatise* focused on individual rights, minimal government, and, most of all, property rights.[7] Then Hannah Arendt, Bernard Bailyn, and J. G. A. Pocock discovered that civic republican ideas both sparked the American Revolution and were integral to the patriots' thinking. The colonies only risked rebellion against the world's reigning superpower because Americans became convinced that the British government had become irrevocably corrupt and despotic. If liberty was to be saved, the colonies had to unite in a patriotic cause, dropping their plows and becoming citizen soldiers not unlike the citizens of the early Roman republic. "Give me liberty or give me death" is not from Locke. It flows instead from the three choices men faced in the ancient world: freedom, slavery, or death. Addressing the Second Virginia Convention in March 1775, Patrick Henry famously said:

> The question before the house is one of awful moment to this country. For my own part I consider it as nothing less than a question of freedom or slavery . . . Has Great Britain any enemy, in this quarter of the world, to call for all this accumulation of navies and armies? No sir, she has none. They are meant for us: they can be for no other. They are sent over to bind and rivet upon us the chains which the British ministry have been so long forging . . . Is life so dear or peace so sweet, as to be purchased at the price of chains and slavery? Forbid it, Almighty God! I know not what course others may take: but as for me, give me liberty, or give me death![8]

It would appear that liberalism and republicanism are fundamentally at odds. They sprang from separate wells and had distinctive attributes that seemed to compete and conflict. But in the American case, liberalism both emerged from and merged with republicanism.[9] Thomas Jefferson and other American leaders modernized republicanism by making it less about an

upper-crust gentry and more about the common man by insisting that all
yeoman farmers were entitled to full citizenship.[10] Abandoning the elitist
classical belief that the gentry are uniquely situated for disinterested citizenship, Americans shifted to a liberal worldview while retaining a celebration
and concern for public happiness and political participation. Critically, the
generation of Jefferson, Alexander Hamilton, and James Madison did not
think self-interest alone was a sufficient basis for citizenship. In the new
republic, citizens did not regard government as existing solely to protect
the private pursuit of happiness, nor were they totally comfortable with the
greed and wealth generated by the emerging capitalist economy. As liberals,
the founding generation broke with a social and political order anchored
in hereditary privilege and sought to establish and institutionalize a New
World social system based on individual equality and talent. As republicans,
the founders fixated on public duties as well as private rights, on politics
as well as commerce.

America's ideas about freedom have a republican tinge. While Americans
think of freedom primarily in terms of individual liberty, we also understand that an active, engaged public exercising political liberty together is
what guarantees that our government protects the liberty of all and not just
the freedom of a few. The belief that it is, indeed, possible for a "people to
shape its own political destiny" inspires republican thought.[11] This, in turn,
is connected to a unique form of human pleasure. Engaging in discussion
and argument with their political equals, something unimaginable for
their European cousins, Americans living during the time of the American
Revolution and the decades after experienced a type of public happiness
that differs from private enjoyments. In *On Revolution*, Arendt writes:

> What was a passion and a 'taste' in France was clearly an
> experience in America and the American usage which, espe-
> cially in the eighteenth century, spoke of 'public happiness',
> where the French spoke of 'public freedom' . . . the Ameri-
> cans knew that public freedom consisted in having a share in
> public business, and that the activities connected with this
> business by no means constituted a burden but gave those
> who discharged them in public a feeling of happiness they
> could acquire nowhere else.[12]

Instead of abandoning the civic republicanism, Americans modernized it. Led by Jefferson, Thomas Paine, and Madison, the revolutionaries retooled republican concepts, and, in so doing, they invented the American form of liberalism that has endured.[13] The governmental apparatus and democratic creed that Tocqueville observed in the 1830s reflected this blend of liberal and republican values. Thus, the liberalism invented by Locke and developed by the Americans is not the austere, solitary liberalism associated with Immanuel Kant or John Rawls nor the liberalism of personal liberation associated with John Stuart Mill. Instead, the republican liberalism of early America championed public involvement as essential and encouraged a sense of community at the same time that it defended individual rights. The search for what is good and necessary in life was not discarded as an empty exercise as Americans chased commercial success; instead, people in the New World built a society they saw as good and worthwhile based on their rejection of the entrenched caste and class of the Old World.

JEFFERSON AND THE DECLARATION

In writing the Declaration, Jefferson catapulted politics into a new era. Making use of the intellectual capital of the *Essay*, the second *Treatise*, and the "common sense" philosophy of the Scottish Enlightenment, Jefferson looked to the future and saw a world in which people would be free of feudal authoritarianism. Drawing on the English revolutionary tradition, and particularly its foremost proponent Locke, Jefferson and his colleagues in the Continental Congress put forth a bold liberal argument:[14]

> When in the Course of human Events, it becomes necessary for one People to dissolve the Political Bonds which have connected them with another, and to assume among the Powers of the Earth, the separate and equal Station to which the Laws of Nature and of Nature's God entitle them, a decent Respect to the Opinions of Mankind requires that they should declare the causes which impel them to the Separation.
>
> We hold these Truths to be self-evident, that all Men are created equal, that they are endowed by their Creator with

certain unalienable Rights, that among these are Life, Liberty, and the Pursuit of Happiness—That to secure these Rights, Governments are instituted among Men, deriving their just Powers from the Consent of the Governed, that whenever any Form of Government become destructive of these Ends, it is the Right of the People to alter or to abolish it, and to institute new Government, laying its Foundations on such Principles, and organizing its Powers in such Form, as to them shall seem most likely to effect their Safety and Happiness.[15]

The Lockean doctrine of a right to revolution was in the air; Jefferson used it as he crafted the first draft of the Declaration.[16] In addition, the influence of Locke's *Essay* is both tangible and pungent in the sense of the revolutionaries using their minds to make judgments about the government under which they live. Writing about the Declaration's famous preamble, Harvard political theorist Danielle Allen references the *Essay* when she says, "Human equality is grounded, fundamentally, in the capacity for judgment."[17]

Famously, Jefferson was the third choice to draft the Declaration. On the small committee of five tasked with writing a ringing announcement of independence, Benjamin Franklin had taken ill with gout and John Adams saw the political value of having the primary author hail from Virginia instead of Massachusetts. In addition, Adams did not want his work edited by a committee. That left the aloof, erudite, and shy Jefferson as the natural choice. Jefferson retired to the second-floor study of the house that he rented on the then-outskirts of downtown Philadelphia. Having studied and copied many of the leading works of political thought, both contemporary and ancient, Jefferson had access to a "formidable . . . internal lexicon" as he set to work.[18]

Jefferson was at his most radical when he was assigned the lead role in drafting the Declaration of Independence. Evidence of this can be seen in the three passages that Congress deleted from the final document as well as in Jefferson's use of the famous triad of "Life, Liberty and the Pursuit of Happiness" instead of the traditional Lockean triplet of life, liberty, and property.[19] The first passage that did not survive the editing process was an evocative section condemning the king for his role in the slave trade:

He has waged cruel war against human nature itself, violating
its most sacred rights of life and liberty in the persons of a distant people who never offended him, captivating and carrying
them into slavery in another hemisphere, or to incur miserable
death in their transportation hither. This piratical warfare, the
opprobrium of *infidel* powers, the warfare of the *Christian* king of
Great Britain. Determined to keep open a market where MEN
should be bought and sold, he has prostituted his negative for
suppressing every legislative attempt to prohibit or to restrain
this execrable commerce. And that his assemblage of horrors
might want no fact of distinguished die, he is now exciting those
very people to rise in arms against us and to purchase that liberty
of which he has deprived them by murdering the very people
on whom he has obtruded them, thus paying off former crimes
against the *liberties* of one people, with crimes which he urges
them to commit against the *lives* of another.[20]

Of course, it was a fiction that George III was responsible for forcing
slavery on blameless Americans; earlier Stuart kings pursued colonial
slavery as a policy and many settlers eagerly participated. But this piece of
propaganda made revolutionary sense; in a bill of particulars against the
King and Great Britain, Jefferson was including a statement endorsing
emancipation. If this passage had remained, Americans would have avoided
the hypocrisy of declaring "all men are created equal" while ignoring
slavery. However, the signers of the Declaration of Independence as a group
desperately wanted to keep slavery unmentioned and out of sight. To talk
about slavery in this fashion would put them on record as opposing slavery
in principle. What the delegates from the deep South, especially South
Carolina, would not allow appears to have been the young Jefferson's hope.
It was not his first attack on slavery. In the House of Burgesses in 1769,
he helped propose a bill permitting slave owners in Virginia to free their
slaves without first gaining permission from the governor or council, as
colonial law then required.

In another passage, Jefferson inserted his belief that American colonialists were descendants of the Saxon race that had lived for generations in
equality and freedom until the Norman invasion introduced feudalism to

England; this romantic fiction fit with the antifeudal narrative he was constructing. The American Revolution was much more than simply the colonies severing ties with Great Britain. For Jefferson and Paine, it was the vanguard of a global movement away from monarchy and feudalism and toward democracy and equality. When the subjects suddenly became equal beings who could think for themselves, the once solid ground beneath monarchy liquefied. Rejecting the idea of divine right, Paine and Jefferson knocked the king down to size. In *Common Sense* (and later in *Rights of Man*), Paine demolished the idea of hereditary monarchy, calling it biologically absurd; because of royal inbreeding, European nations were sure to experience an imbecile as king. In *A Summary View of the Rights of British America* (1774), Jefferson argued that the king was "no more than the chief officer of the people, appointed by laws, and circumscribed by definite powers, to assist in working the great machine of government."[21] In the decades prior to the Revolution, the American colonies had been schooling themselves in the norms and practices necessary for self-government. The Declaration was not only a break with Great Britain, it was a repudiation of more than "a thousand years of entrenched feudal traditions."[22] However, for the other delegates to the Continental Congress, it stretched credulity too far to claim that the original English settlers in America had come "at the expense of our own blood and treasure; unassisted by the strength of Great Britain."[23] When the Continental Congress placed themselves into a committee of the whole on July 2, 1776, they decided that the Virginian's doctrine of expatriation was too Jeffersonian for their taste.

The committee of the whole also eliminated Jefferson's final charge against King George and the British—the emotional climax of his argument for independence. Here, Jefferson spoke of the pain of parting ways with what once was family:

> These facts have given the last stab to agonizing affection, and manly spirit bids us to renounce for ever these unfeeling brethren. We must endeavor to forget our former love for them, and to hold them as we hold the rest of mankind enemies in war, in peace friends. We might have been a free and a great people together; but a communication of grandeur & of freedom

it seems is below their dignity. Be it so, since they will have it.
The road to happiness & to glory is open to us too. We will
tread it apart from them.

Jefferson's word choice of grandeur, glory, and happiness shows the
influence of republican ideas. In renouncing their ties to a people who had
chosen not to hold their rulers to account, the Americans decided they
would not accept the status of abused and silent second-class subjects;
instead, they would seek glory as heroic, virtuous citizens. Here we also see
the influence on Jefferson of the Scottish thinker Francis Hutcheson, who
extolled affection and emotional connection as the essential glue of society,
much like Edmund Burke would do later in *Reflections on the Revolution
in France* (1790). Jefferson, Paine, and Patrick Henry all spoke of Americans struggling to maintain a relationship with the mother country but at
last reaching a breaking point. In *Common Sense*, Paine wrote in a fashion
similar to Jefferson:

> To talk of friendship with those in whom our reason forbids
> us to have faith, and our affections wounded through a thou-
> sand pores instruct us to detest, is madness and folly. Every
> day wears out the little remains of kindred between us and
> them . . . Ye that tell us of harmony and reconciliation, can
> ye restore us the time that is past? Can ye give to prostitution
> its former innocence? . . . There are injuries which nature
> cannot forgive; she would cease to be nature if she did . . . The
> Almighty hath implanted in us these unextinguishable feelings
> for good and wise purpose . . . They distinguish us from the
> herd of common animals.[24]

While Jefferson was not happy with the edits his draft endured, on
balance, the text that emerged was stronger and more concise; more than
80 percent of Jefferson's original draft survived to become the official
Declaration. But if Jefferson lost three of his cherished paragraphs, his
language in the preamble survived. And here the words that became
the American creed were radical, in part, because Jefferson substituted the
phrase "pursuit of happiness" for "property." The prose Jefferson had

before him as he wrote was George Mason's May 1776 draft of Virginia's *Declaration of Rights*:

> That all men are born equally free and independent, and have certain inherent natural rights, of which they cannot, by any compact, deprive or divest their posterity; among which are the enjoyment of life and liberty, with the means of acquiring and possessing property, and pursuing and obtaining happiness and safety.[25]

By writing "pursuit of happiness," a more expansive phrase than simply "property," Jefferson's famed felicity of expression may have taken over. This rendering allowed him to express more concisely and movingly what Mason stated without grace and at greater length.[26]

Jefferson's foremost goal was to express sentiments that were well understood in as compact and eloquent a fashion as possible.[27] But in making the decision not to write "life, liberty, and property," Jefferson broke with the argument of Locke's second *Treatise* which put great emphasis on property.[28] And in substituting "pursuit of happiness" for "property," Jefferson may have intentionally smuggled a covert antislavery argument into the Declaration. This is the position of Joseph Ellis, a leading scholar on Jefferson and the Revolutionary generation. "By dropping 'property' altogether, Jefferson deftly deprived slaveholders of being able to claim that owning slaves was a natural right protected by law," Ellis writes. "On this score there can be little doubt that he knew what he was doing."[29] If so, in drafting the Declaration Jefferson acted in a way similar to Madison later in regard to the Constitution. At the Constitutional Convention in 1787, Madison used his considerable political skill to make sure that neither "slavery" nor the phrase "property in man" found its way into the Constitution. Critically, both Jefferson and Madison strove to keep illiberal ideals out of America's founding documents.

In monarchies of the past and many authoritarian regimes of the present, those in power largely leave alone the private lives and private freedoms of individuals.[30] By contrast, public freedom exists only when the people have control of government and make decisions for themselves. Arendt put forth another reason why Jefferson's use of "pursuit of happiness" expresses what is exceptional about American democracy, arguing that the immigrants to America who left England were motivated, in part, by a "dissatisfaction with the rights and liberties of Englishman" in the home country and inspired by the desire to enjoy a novel type of freedom available in the New World. This freedom "consisted in the citizen's right of access to the public realm, in his share in public power—to be 'a participator in the government of affairs'" in Jefferson's revealing phrase.[31] When this is the case, the possibility exists for the "public happiness" that the Virginian spoke of at the beginning of *A Summary View of the Rights of British America.*[32]

In an early draft of the Declaration, Jefferson wrote that "all men are created equal and independent."[33] The word independent fits well with both the vaunted individualism of the second *Treatise* and the autonomous, freestanding republican who speaks his (or her) own mind and is under the thumb of no other when participating in the public sphere. Jefferson's great accomplishment was weaving together strands of liberal and republican thinking into one coherent ideology for a nation at the forefront of a global democratic revolution. Across his political career, he inspired Americans to think and act in a bold new fashion—as equal citizens and equal men in the world's first liberal democratic nation.

CREATING A NATION

It is useful to think of the American Revolution as a two-stage affair, stage one being the revolt against the British monarch, a Declaration announcing a new nation dedicated to both liberty and equality, and the creation of a citizen-led republic. Stage two being the realization that a confederation of states was a recipe for failure and that to survive, America had to unite as one nation with a strong central government. This the Constitution did—debated in the same room of the Pennsylvania State House in which the Declaration was signed—with a preamble that began "We the People of the United States." With these words, Gouverneur Morris made sure that the nationalist agenda animating James Madison and George Washington triumphed over the defenders of the Articles of Confederation.[34] It was nothing less than an extralegal coup against the Articles, but one that was sorely needed. Once the Revolutionary War ended, all the political forces and incentives built into the Articles—a loose alliance of sovereign states with conflicting interests—were centrifugal.[35] Fortunately, Madison, Washington, Hamilton, and the other nationalist radicals recognized this and engineered the intellectual and political refounding of the nation that was the Constitutional Convention. The debate in Philadelphia, the successful campaign for ratification, and the accompanying explanation provided by Madison, Hamilton, and Jay in *The Federalist Papers* placed the American republic on sturdy ground at a time when the Confederation was in danger of dissolution.

While hardly perfect, the new government could rightly call itself representative in a way that the Articles never could. Under the Articles, each state had one vote while the people had none. Under the Constitution, the people elected both the members of the House of Representatives and, in a fashion, the president (with the electoral college added because the framers were cautious democrats), while the Senate was selected by state legislatures until the Seventeenth Amendment in 1913 during the Progressive reform era. The Articles of Confederation was a treaty between separate sovereign powers. Under the Constitution, sovereignty was based in the American people as a whole and reflected in the federal government.

With the Constitution in place, the United States became the "dominant model for the liberal state in the modern world."[36] Why is the U.S. Constitution profoundly liberal? Four reasons stand out:

- it self-consciously separates and divides power at the national level so as to avoid monarchy in a new form;
- it makes the courts and the Congress coequal branches of government with the executive;
- it formally added Madison's Bill of Rights to enumerate the legally protected rights of individuals and the press;
- and it put into practice Madison's concept of democracy in which a wide variety of groups can both be heard and compete for political power.[37]

The heart of Madison's constitutional vision has two chambers: the extended sphere of representation across geographic space and Congress as a forum for deliberative democracy.[38] The separation of power and federalism, institutional mechanisms there for everyone to see, act as insurance plans in case the first two methods fail to achieve a just and well-reasoned polity.[39] The formal, written Constitution instituted a government of laws, not men; one in which citizens and the media can freely criticize any and all government officials without fear of retribution. Critics of the government are protected by the First Amendment, which built on the English constitutional tradition and John Milton's *Areopagitica* (1644). Milton's classic defense of free speech and expression anticipated Locke's later arguments about "the duty of every intelligent man as a rational being, to know the grounds and take responsibility for his beliefs and actions. Its corollary was a society and a state in which decisions are reached by open discussion . . . in which political unity is secured not by force but by consensus that respects variety of opinion."[40]

Modern life has taught us that democratic norms and a government of laws are essential to the maintenance of freedom. Marx's two massive mistakes were his dismissal of constitutional government and his belief that there was no need to maintain a separation between the government and the economy and thus establishing a sector of power outside of the government. By contrast, the framers and the liberals who followed them understood that tyranny is a continuing danger and constitutional government is essential. They established a society where both government and the private market exist and thrive. Modern liberals such as former President Obama and the historian Arthur M. Schlesinger Jr. champion a more powerful, more activist government than do conservatives, but they believe in a vibrant private sector. American liberals understand that while the government can regulate and set the rules for a market economy, freedom depends on citizens having economic wealth and resources independent of the government.[41]

But if the Constitution was liberal in some aspects it was profoundly illiberal in others. Two of the most important were its violation of political equality in establishing the U.S. Senate as a legislative chamber consisting of two representatives from each state, regardless of population, and allowing slavery to exist in the states where it was established, a gigantic contradiction to the very ideals of freedom and equality enunciated in the Declaration.

THE SENATE'S VIOLATION OF POLITICAL EQUALITY

While Americans have divergent views about economic equality, on political equality there is wide agreement that people's votes should count equally. James Madison concurred. Entering the Constitutional Convention, he thought it essential to establish proportional representation by population in *both* branches of the legislature. Only proportional representation by population would permit the Congress to speak for the American people and thus justify the framers' coup.[42] Yet, much to Madison and George Washington's dismay, the infamous Connecticut Compromise gave small states the same representation in the U.S. Senate as large population states. Madison understood that the real issue at the time was not large state versus small state, but rather Southern slaveholding states versus Northern free states, and that giving small states extra clout in Congress did not protect minority rights.

Ironically, while the United States was far ahead of other nations in its democratic revolution, the Constitution of 1787 is embedded with provisions that violate the norms of equality, majority rule, and one-man, one-vote.[43] Its purposeful aristocratic design has provided structural protection to the reality of exclusion, inequality, hierarchy, and privilege in a liberal capitalist society. For example, two centuries of experience since the founding era has confirmed Madison's judgment about the U.S. Senate. Yale University political scientist Robert Dahl wrote, "Unequal representation in the Senate has unquestionably failed to protect the fundamental interests of the *least* privileged minorities" and often has "served to protect the interests of the *most* privileged minorities." The small state bias arguably protected slavery before 1860, allowed the Southern states to defeat Reconstruction after the Civil War, made it possible for powerful illiberal Southern politicians to craft New Deal reforms as being for whites only, and helped defeat efforts to end segregation until the Civil Rights movement combined with Lyndon Johnson's landslide win in the 1964 presidential election enabled LBJ to muscle the Civil Rights acts through Congress.[44]

The seminal 1964 one-man, one-vote rule is rarely criticized today. In *Reynolds v. Sims*, the Supreme Court ruled that one person's voting power ought to be roughly equivalent to another person's *in the same state*. To which we should ask, why only in the same state? The Senate's violation of political equality is a major flaw in the Constitution that badly distorts contemporary politics. In 2020, with a population of roughly 39.8 million, California has two senators. So does Arkansas with only 3 million residents (the same population as Orange County, California), Nebraska with only 1.9 million residents, and Montana with only 1 million residents. The vote of a Nebraska resident is, in effect, worth about twenty-one times the vote of a California resident. The same pattern holds true if we compare Texas (with 28.7 million residents) to Oregon (with 4.2 million) and Vermont (with 623,960 residents—less than the average House district of approximately 750,000 voters).[45] The small state bias in American politics is both profound and consequential:

- In a nation of nearly 330 million people, the 40 senators from the 20 smallest states (33.3 million) represent a population base of just 10 percent.
- The 50 senators from the 25 smallest states (52.7 million Americans) represent a minuscule population base of only 16.1 percent.

Today, senators from small population rural states—such as North and South Dakota, Vermont, West Virginia, New Mexico, Mississippi, Oregon, Oklahoma, and Kentucky—represent not even one-fifth of the nation's total population. Of the 50 senators from small population rural or partially rural states, 29 are Republicans (58 percent) and 19 are Democrats plus two Independents who caucus with the Democrats (42 percent). Of the 53-seat majority held by Senate Republicans in the 116th Congress *more than half* (54.7 percent) come from the 25 smallest states by population and represent less than 1 in 6 Americans (just over 50 million people).[46]

In a prophetic *New Republic* article, Thomas Geoghegan foresaw in 1994 that the political inequality of the Senate could lead to nativist politics as the nation became more cosmopolitan and diverse. As the non-Hispanic white population has dropped in percentage, the new Latino, Asian, and Middle-Eastern minorities live overwhelmingly in big states such as California, Texas, and Florida. In the new multiracial America, these big state minorities individually have even less voting power than they did a generation ago.

The vote of each such person (e.g., not New York's but each New Yorker's) will count for substantially less. As the U.S. becomes more multi-racial and stranger to the people-of-the-interior, the non-Hispanic whites in most of the small states will get more and more heavily weighted votes. Talk radio will get louder. The "new ideas" will get smaller. We may be way past gridlock, and heading into something worse.[47]

A serious effort at making the Constitution truly liberal would attack the problem of a U.S. Senate that represents states instead of people. One such solution would be to give the largest population states—such as California and Texas—ten senators and the smallest states with populations of less than a million—such as Alaska, Vermont, and Wyoming—a single Senate seat. States in between would have between two and nine senators. Such a proposal sounds strange to our ears and is probably impossible to enact but only a constitutional reform such as this would cure the massive political inequality at the heart of our political system.

SLAVERY AND THE CONSTITUTION

Twenty-five of the fifty-five delegates who attended the Constitutional Convention owned slaves, but by the time of the Constitutional Convention, a "conditional antislavery mentality" had become prevalent across much of the country. As a result, slavery was abolished in the North, prohibited in the West, and put on the defensive in the South.[48] Even so, the proponents of slavery were able to craft a Constitution that largely accepted slavery as it existed, causing the great 19th century abolitionist William Lloyd Garrison to label the Constitution a "covenant with death" and "an agreement with Hell."[49] The word slavery was never mentioned in the Constitution, but its presence lurks.[50] Five provisions of the U.S. Constitution—including the infamous three-fifths clause—dealt directly with slavery and gave special treatment to the South's "peculiar institution."[51]

The full proslavery position was first explicitly articulated in Congress in 1790 after two Quaker delegates presented petitions to Congress, one from the Pennsylvania Abolition Society signed by Benjamin Franklin, demanding that the federal government immediately end the African slave trade. Reminding the House that the recently ratified Constitution explicitly stated that the slave trade could not be disturbed until 1808, Representative James Jackson from Georgia and William Loughton Smith from South Carolina set forth the Southern position on slavery, along with its racial component. At the core of Smith's speech: The Constitution recognized slavery's existence and any attempt to renegotiate what had been agreed to would mean the dissolution of the Union. To Smith, a racially mixed United States was an abomination:

> If the blacks did not intermarry with the whites, they would remain black until the end of time; for it was not contended that liberating them would whitewash them; if they did intermarry with the whites, then the white race would be extinct, and the American people would all be of the mulatto breed.

If blatant racism voiced in the halls of Congress was new, the attitudes were familiar and drew on the assumption that the United States was and would be a white Anglo-Saxon nation.[52] Abolitionist sentiment was growing in the white North, but it was based on empathy, not direct self-interest. By contrast, maintaining slavery was everything for South Carolinian planters. Without black slaves working in the tropical heat, their economic El Dorado would be worthless. And freeing slaves, who outnumbered whites eight to one in the lush coastal regions, appeared to be a recipe for suicide.[53] Thus the intensity of the delegates from the deep South to protect their privileged minority status at home and among the other states.[54]

But if the framers were complicit in allowing slavery to continue, the majority were adroit in their commitment to the nation's liberal ideals. In three crucial respects, the antislavery proponents were successful. They kept the words "slave," "slavery," and "property in man" out of the final document and drafted the clauses in the Constitution that pertained to slavery to apply only to the states and not the national government.[55] This provided Abraham Lincoln, the Republicans, and the abolitionists the ammunition they needed to win the war of ideas with the South. In the decade before the

Civil War, Southerners, including Supreme Court Chief Justice Roger B. Taney in the 1854 Dred Scott decision, argued that "the right of property in a slave is distinctly and expressly affirmed in the Constitution." Lincoln, in his 1860 Cooper Union address, argued emphatically, that "no such right is specifically written in the Constitution. That instrument is literally silent about any such right . . . neither the word 'slave' nor 'slavery' is to be found in the Constitution, nor the word 'property,' even, in any connection with language alluding to things slave, or slavery."[56]

Second, while Southerners argued that they had a Constitutional right to take slaves into the federal territories and to hold them there as property, the founders forbade slavery in the Northwest territories and gave the federal government the authority to close the door on the expansion of slavery if so desired. By Lincoln's count, twenty-one of the thirty-nine who signed the Constitution later voted for legislation that gave the federal government the power to control or ban slavery in the territories. The prohibition of slavery in the territory that became the states of Ohio, Indiana, Illinois, Michigan, and Wisconsin proved critical. During the 19th century, slavery would have been economically viable in southern Illinois and Indiana; had the two become slave states the nation's political balance would have shifted in favor of the South.[57]

Third, the slave trade's end in 1808 accelerated the difference in population and industrialization between the North and the South. Without access to freshly arrived slaves from Africa, plantation owners in the newly created cotton belt of Alabama, Louisiana, and Mississippi purchased hundreds of thousands of slaves from slaveholders in Maryland and Virginia and marched the slave labor South. Less dependent on slavery, the Upper South developed an economy based on free labor.[58] As a result, at the start of the Civil War, the border slave states of Kentucky, Maryland, Delaware, and Missouri chose the Union. Additionally, the population and economy of the North boomed as white immigrants forsook the South; advantages in demographics and industrialization made all the difference once shots were fired at Fort Sumter in April 1861.[59]

Madison played a crucial role in setting in motion slavery's demise. During the debate over the slave trade clause, Madison said it would be wrong to "admit in the Constitution the idea that there could be property in men." He did this because he recognized that slavery violated the fundamental principles of republican government and, like most of the Convention, he thought that slavery had no place in national law.[60] As with Jefferson's substitution of "pursuit of happiness" for "property" in the Declaration, Madison's subterfuge in combating slavery in the Constitution has not been fully appreciated. Speaking for many Southerners during the fight over ratification, Virginia's Patrick Henry warned that should Northerners win dominant control over the federal government, there would be every reason to believe that they would someday move to abolish slavery. Henry argued that the Constitution needed an explicit provision that would "secure us that property in slaves, which we now hold."[61] Instead, the exclusion of such a clause was accomplished by design by Madison, a slaveholder, and his allies. The main architect of the Constitutional Convention could not be candid on this point while debating Henry because Madison recognized:

> revealing to Virginia's slaveholders, even indirectly, that he and the convention majority had deliberately excluded property in man might have risked losing ratification in Virginia, which would have severely endangered the Constitution itself. (It might also have ruined Madison's political career.)[62]

In "Politics as a Vocation," Max Weber reminds us that politics is not for purists. Madison, Washington, Hamilton, and their nationalist allies understood that framing a new Constitution that would replace the Articles of Confederation was audacious, necessary, and carried no guarantee of success. Because preserving the union was the top priority of delegates, Northerners were forced to make important concessions to the Southern states. Most historians agree with Harvard Law professor Michael Klarman: "To have expected the Constitution to be less protective of slavery than it was probably would have been unrealistic."[63]

MADISON'S VISION

The Constitutional Convention succeeded in drafting a Constitution that the states then ratified not because of popular demand but because the nation's political elite feared that the young confederation of states would soon break apart.[64] Madison did not succeed in all of his aims in Philadelphia.[65] But Madison and his like-minded colleagues achieved much of their nationalist and anti-populist agenda: they repudiated the Articles, vastly expanded the power of the federal government by granting it the authority to tax, regulate commerce, and have primacy over state laws, and made it resistant to democratic populist cries for "fairness" and redistribution.[66] Among the founding generation statesmen few, such as Thomas Jefferson (who did not attend the Constitutional Convention), Benjamin Franklin, and Pennsylvania's James Wilson, were committed democrats.[67] In sharp contrast, a large majority of the fifty-five delegates who attended at least a portion of the Constitutional Convention were horrified by Shays's Rebellion and skeptical of popular participation. A decade later, the Jeffersonians quarreled with the Federalists, in no small part because a majority of the Federalists were elitists who wished to banish ordinary people from active participation in politics.

A republic the scale and size imagined for the United States was unprecedented and Madison recognized that America's first national government lacked an overarching source of sovereignty larger than the narrow interests of the states.[68] Challenged, Madison constructed a novel theory of government. His boldness showed when he rejected received political wisdom from Aristotle to Montesquieu claiming that republics were restricted to city-states. Recognizing that politics outside of a monarchy or a dictatorship must involve a contest between various interests, Madison theorized that he could avoid the bitter feuds of small republics by expanding the scale of democracy to nation-state status and employing representation instead of direct democracy. This is how Madison posed the problem:

> How to render government 'sufficiently neutral between the different interests and factions, to control one part of the society from invading the rights of another, and at the same time sufficiently controlled itself, from setting up an interest adverse to the whole of society.' While a king might be 'sufficiently neutral toward his subject,' he would also 'frequently sacrifice their happiness to his ambition or his avarice.' By contrast, in a republican form of government, where the majority 'ultimately gives the

law,' nothing restrained that majority 'from unjust violations of the rights and interests of the minority, or of individuals.'[69]

Madison argued at the Convention and later in *Federalist* No. 10 that a larger geographic political community would feature a greater variety and diversity of interests than a small polity and lessen the danger of a single majority faction imposing its will on minorities. He also held that large congressional districts would favor the election of distinguished men who could rise above petty grievances, display a calmness of temper, and be capable of the sort of intelligent, deliberative debate that he saw at the Convention. Madison was adamant that the people were the ultimate sovereigns. Yet, he sought to insulate the national government from majority will and together with the other delegates to the Constitutional Convention he designed a constitutional system with numerous hurdles standing in the way of majority rule. As a result, American government is a form of democracy where a supermajority is often necessary to enact major legislation and the minority whose rights are most often protected is the financial elite.

Afraid of the working-class rabble—poor farmers and the mechanics who rallied around Jefferson and Thomas Paine's vision of the future—the authors of the Constitution were timid democrats. Influenced by Greek writers such as Plato who were critics of popular rule, neither Alexander Hamilton nor James Madison in *The Federalist* issued praise for the pure direct democracy that existed in ancient Athens where every male citizen, no matter how poor or rich, had the right to attend the Assembly (*ekklesia*), which met at least 40 times a year, and exercise the paramount principle of democracy *isegoria*—the universal right to speak and address his peers.[70] Educated, successful members of America's upper class, Hamilton and Madison had watched with dismay when the unicameral state assemblies had bowed to popular pressures to issue paper money and enact tax and debt relief legislation in the 1780s. Most of the Philadelphia delegates agreed with South Carolina planter Pierce Butler that "the great object of government" was to protect and secure private property.[71] Agreeing that one branch of the federal government, the House of Representatives, should be directly elected by the people, the delegates found solace in Madison's design: "A small House with vast constituents would loosen connections between representatives and the people."[72] Breaking from monarchy and establishing a republican form of government, the early Americans were at the forefront of the global democratic revolutions to come. If the Constitution had been written two decades later it would have been radically more egalitarian and liberal; this, in turn, would have made it less likely for contemporary illiberal jurists to make a fetish out of "original intent." As it was, the Constitution of 1787 crystalized a fleeting moment when the nation had rejected monarchy and aristocracy but was not yet fully committed to democracy.

FROM THE VIRTUOUS GENTRY
TO JACKSONIAN DEMOCRACY

In the years after the Constitution, the democratic ethos transformed and revolutionized not just politics, but American society as a whole. While colonial America did not possess the rigid caste structure of the Old World, the upper-class gentry steered society, and everyone deferred to them. The 18th-century monarchical order with its "emphasis on kinship, patronage, hierarchy, and dependency" was quite visible in America.[73] Elites were granted political authority in accord with their established economic and social superiority and family rank. Such was the case across colonial America from the great Tidewater planters of Virginia to the wealthy landowners of the Connecticut River valley.[74] Historian Gordon Wood argues persuasively that "Americans were not born free and democratic in any modern sense." Rather they became so, in large part, because the American revolution was both a political and social revolution that destroyed the mental universe of aristocracy that had ruled the world for two millennia.[75] Colonial America was divided into gentlemen and commoners. Regular people were the herd—George Washington labeled small farmers "the grazing multitude"—and ordinary people accepted their second-class status. In this unequal universe of the leisured few and the laboring many, the American gentry shared qualities with the European aristocrats. Freedom was defined as the freedom from the necessity of work.[76] But the American system of class was permeable while Europe's was not; as soon as Benjamin Franklin became wealthy from his entrepreneurial exploits, he retired from business at the age of forty-two and became a man of leisure.[77]

In this Old World mindset, hierarchy, inequality, and the privilege of a few was the norm and people were expected to contribute to society according to their social rank. Independent gentlemen of leisure and education supplied government leadership; office holding was a duty. According to classic republican teaching, only the upper class had the capacity for "disinterested" service for the community as a whole. At the time of the Revolution, it was expected that these elite gentlemen would always think about the common good and that it would be apparent to all exactly who were the men of exceptional vision and virtue. But when the public, state governments, and Congress failed to act in this idealized fashion, the framers quickly rejected classical republican wisdom as wrong-headed and inadequate. Dismayed that the "self-sacrifice and patriotism of 1774–75 soon seemed to give way to greed and profiteering at the expense of the public good," and confronted with the reality of self-interest, Madison, Hamilton, and the framers revised their thinking. Classical ideas of civic republican virtue dominant at the time of the Declaration gave way to liberal ideas of separation of power, the clash of interests, and ambition checking ambition in the design of the Constitution.[78]

The American Revolution was a radical revolution of psychology first put into motion by Locke and then into practice when ordinary Americans discarded ancient habits of inferiority, humility, and deference before "better men." In *The Rise of American Democracy: Jefferson to Lincoln*, Princeton historian Sean Wilentz writes:

> Democracy appears when some large number of previously excluded, ordinary persons—what the 18th century called "the many"—secure the power not simply to select their governors but to oversee the institutions of government, as officeholders and as citizens free to assemble and criticize those in office. Democracy is never a gift bestowed . . . it must always be fought for.[79]

The possibility of radical democracy became real in the Pennsylvania constitution of 1776, drafted by Benjamin Franklin and the followers of Thomas Paine. Instead of fearing the people, this constitution featured a unicameral representative assembly that functioned as an upper house, while the people as a whole "out of doors" retained their power to legislate. This was done by virtue of the extraordinary Article 15, which required every bill passed by the Pennsylvania legislature to be circulated for consideration by the people at large before becoming law in the next legislative session. In contrast to the Federalist elite who framed the Constitution, Pennsylvania radicals brought the affairs of government intimately into the hands of the people.[80]

Politics began to change prior to the American Revolution when opposition groups critical of the royal governors began to mobilize the electorate. Competing factions of the gentry elite vied with each other to be seen as a friend of the people and thus secure electoral advantage. After the Declaration proclaimed that all men are created equal and Tom Paine's *Common Sense* eviscerated the idea of monarchy, the genie was out of the bottle; the republican age dumped feudal tradition into the dustbin.[81] By the 1780s, ordinary men began to think they should be represented by people like themselves.[82] Suddenly, as William Thompson, a little-known Charleston tavern keeper, did when he quarreled with the aristocrat John Rutledge in South Carolina, social and political upstarts bragged about their hard work, low status, and refusal to comprehend their supposed inferiority. In his 1784 feud, Thompson wrote that "opulence and influence" when combined with "intermarriage" or patronage were "calculated to subvert Republicanism."[83]

Across America, inspired by the popular and egalitarian ideas of the Revolution, average people sought office and displaced the older hierarchy. Hustling egalitarian politicians brought out new voters and, as a result, turnout skyrocketed from 20 percent in the 1790s to 80 percent or more in the first decade following Jefferson's election as president in 1800. With Jefferson and Madison leading the Republicans and Hamilton, Adams, and Burr heading the Federalists, the United States was the first country to develop modern political parties to organize and mobilize a mass electorate. And this mass drive for democratic equality made black slavery a stark anomaly. To a certain extent, colonial America was a continuation of European feudalism where the "brutality and inequality of life" was taken for granted and there were multiple ranks of freedom and unfreedom. Suddenly, after 1800, slavery was no longer just the "most base and degraded status" in a society with multiple castes.[84] Instead, slavery in 19th century

America was glaringly conspicuous and could only be justified by virulent racism. Unfortunately, in a repeat of the Virginia colonial experience and a foreshadowing of Jim Crow, as the white man gained the vote in the early 19th century, the free black man lost it.[85]

Thomas Jefferson's razor-thin victory in the 1800 presidential election drove the democratic tide and announced the political equality of the American public. It was a victory of the "poor-ragged democrats" over the "well-fed, well-dressed, chariot-lolling, levee-reveling federalists," wrote one Jefferson supporter.[86] The world in which uppity gentlemen could expect grateful deference from humble inferiors disappeared. Instead, the new Lockean world that elected Thomas Jefferson and Andrew Jackson president was one of Tocquevillian equality and mass democracy, and President Jefferson had a keen grasp of the psychology of democracy. He astutely "steered the country toward a fresh, indeterminate, emotional space where citizens, not subjects, might experiment with new ways of being free."[87] A famous example of Jefferson's drive to instill self-respect in the American public and to obliterate deference was when he greeted a British ambassador wearing slippers and casual dress. When Ambassador Anthony Merry complained that Jefferson's slovenliness and indifference to appearance was an insult, James Madison told him that he could no more expect and demand social distinctions in the United States than an American diplomat could ask for equality at the Court of St. James's.[88]

True, America's democratic revolution in the age of Jefferson and Jackson focused on white men, but the ideals of Locke and the Revolution set in motion the antislavery and women's rights movements of the 19th century and all the movements for equality and inclusion since. The drastic difference between democracy in America and class-bound Europe could be seen in property qualifications and suffrage at the time of the Revolution. Because property-owning was so widespread, the American colonies enjoyed the broadest suffrage of any people in the world—between 60 to 80 percent of adult white males could legally vote. In England, by contrast, the working class had to wait until 1867 to get the vote.[89] Taken together, the social and political revolution triggered by 1776 created the most cosmopolitan, the most democratic, the most liberal, the most business minded, and the most thoroughly modern nation in the world.[90]

THE IMPORTANCE OF THOMAS PAINE
AND ALEXIS DE TOCQUEVILLE

To the future United States, Locke bequeathed the ideals of liberalism that proved to be extraordinarily powerful in shaping our political culture. Two other writers—one an Englishman who adopted America as his home and the other a visiting Frenchman who sought to explain America to the world—demonstrated exceptional eloquence and insight to capture the essence of American democracy. One might say Thomas Paine, author of *Common Sense* (1776) and *Rights of Man* (1791–92), and Alexis de Tocqueville, author of *Democracy in America* (1835–1840), played a role equal to that of Jefferson, Hamilton, and Madison in defining and explaining just how the United States would be different and exceptional compared to Europe. When he wrote, "What Athens was in miniature, America will be in magnitude," Paine succinctly stated the lofty ambition of the American experiment.[91]

Paine's audacity ignited the American Revolution. His clear, impassioned prose and the boldness with which he attacked the very idea of monarchy made *Common Sense* a sensation. While others argued for moderation and negotiation with Great Britain, Paine made the case for an independent, democratic America. Simplifying Locke for the average reader, he spoke of natural rights allowing men to come together to make a social compact. In this slim volume, government was the enemy because, prior to the revolution, the tyranny of monarchy was the only government people knew. Thus, among the first lines of *Common Sense*: "Society in every state is a blessing, but government even in its best state is but a necessary evil."[92] Paine's target was the special evil that is monarchy, particularly hereditary monarchy:

> To the evil of monarchy we have added that of hereditary succession; and as the first is a degradation and lessening of ourselves, so the second, claimed as a matter of right, is an insult and imposition on posterity . . . One of the strongest natural proofs of the folly of hereditary right in kings is that nature disapproves of it, otherwise she would not so frequently turn it into ridicule by giving mankind an *ass for a lion*.[93]

Among the most radical democrats of the founding generation, Jefferson and Paine believed in the "equal moral worth of every individual." Strikingly different in life experience and temperament, they shared a belief in the moral goodness of ordinary people.[94] Because Jefferson pursued a political career that depended on popularity, he was cautious about giving full expression to his political views. But he and Paine agreed on most everything political except slavery: Paine was a staunch abolitionist. Wood argues that if Jefferson had written a treatise on politics it would have resembled Paine's second masterpiece, *Rights of Man*.[95]

Defending the fledgling French Revolution and declaration of the Rights of Man by the French National Assembly against the intellectual and rhetorical onslaught by Edmund Burke in *Reflections on the Revolution in France*, Paine made his most mature and sustained argument for liberalism. He begins *Rights of Man* by ridiculing Burke for defending the authority of the dead over the living, whereby every successive generation is bound by decisions made by people centuries before:

> The vanity and presumption of governing beyond the grave, is the most ridiculous and insolent of all tyrannies . . . The circumstances of the world are continually changing, and the opinions of men change also; and as government is for the living, and not for the dead, it is the living only that has any right in it.[96]

Later, in defining a legitimate government, Paine made a crucial distinction that remains valid today. What matters is whether government arises "*out* of the people, or *over* the people."[97] In healthy democracies, people are making decisions via their representatives based on informed consent. And if a government is a democracy, the people can decide, as they wish, what government should and should not do. Outside of fundamental rights, nothing is ruled out. Nothing in Paine says government must be small and weak. In a prophetic chapter titled "Ways and Means of Improving the Condition of Europe," Paine put forth the contrary, a plan that foreshadowed Franklin Roosevelt's New Deal two centuries later. He said a government should have as its objective "*general* happiness," and when it operates instead to increase wretchedness, something is wrong. After protesting that in Old World Europe "a vast mass of mankind are degradedly thrown into the background of the human picture, to bring forward with greater glare, the puppet-show of state and aristocracy," he proposed a humane alternative. In societies that have escaped authoritarian rule and where democracy reigns, citizens can choose to educate the young and help provide for the two groups of people who cannot provide for themselves—poor children and "old people past their labour" via a system of progressive taxation.[98]

Visiting America in 1831, Tocqueville wrote, "I admit I saw in America more than America, it was the shape of democracy itself which I sought, its inclinations, character, prejudices, and passions."[99] Impressed by the social and political equality that existed in the North and West and by a political culture in which the norms of participation and engagement in the New England townships seemed to permeate the political culture of the nation as a whole, Tocqueville discovered that norms count more than the laws or constitutions in determining whether a nation is and remains democratic. The power of equality overwhelmed him; *Democracy in America* begins: "No novelty in the United States struck me more vividly during my stay there than the equality of conditions . . . all my observations constantly returned to this nodal point."[100]

Tocqueville saw in America a nation where the individualism natural to a liberal democratic society was balanced by the tendency of Americans to join groups and associations to get things done and by a spirit of "self-interest properly understood."[101] He saw this spirit of engagement by political equals as the genius of American politics and that our visceral dislike of elites and top-down authority induced the skills and outlook necessary for cooperation, compromise, and self-government. The Frenchman wrote, "one sees that by serving his fellows man serves himself and that doing good is to his private advantage . . . the doctrine of self-interest properly understood does not inspire great sacrifices, but every day it prompts some small ones; by itself it cannot make a man virtuous, but its discipline shapes a lot of orderly, temperate, moderate, careful, and self-controlled citizens."[102] In a longer passage, Tocqueville elaborated:

> Though private interest, in the United States as elsewhere, is the driving force behind most of men's actions, it does not regulate them all. I have often seen Americans make really great

sacrifices for the common good, and I have noticed a hundred cases in which, when help was needed, they hardly ever failed to give each other trusty support. The free institutions of the United States and the political rights enjoyed there provide a thousand continual reminders to every citizen that he lives in society. At every moment they bring his mind back to this idea, that it is the duty as well as the interest of men to be useful to their fellows.[103]

Thus, in Tocqueville's mind, the American rejection of aristocratic society led people in the United States to develop a new and wondrous political culture in which middle class virtues and objectives were the goal of society, not the feudal excesses of a rarified upper class that lived off the work of others.

Of course, not all of the United States rejected the aristocratic model. Sailing down the Ohio River that separated free Ohio on the northern bank from slave Kentucky on the southern bank, Tocqueville made this observation:

On the left bank of the Ohio work is connected with the idea of slavery, but on the right with well-being and progress; on the one side it is degrading, but on the other honorable; on the left bank no white laborers are to be found; for work people must rely on Negroes; but one will never see a man of leisure on the right bank: the white man's intelligent activity is used for work of every sort. Hence those whose task it is in Kentucky to exploit the natural wealth of the soil are neither eager nor instructed, for anyone who might possess those qualities either does nothing or crosses over into Ohio so that he can profit by his industry, and do so without shame.[104]

Democracy in America remains the single most brilliant examination of the American character ever written, even though its author was biased in his celebration of the United States because he focused overwhelmingly on the mores of America's North and West, not its feudal South.

3

Illiberal Challenge from
the Plantation Elite

Illiberalism has its origin in a simple fact. The great divergence in opportunity between 19th century Europe and America—which amazed Tocqueville and others familiar with both continents—largely advantaged males of Anglo-Saxon ancestry. What Tocqueville observed was true: President Andrew Jackson's 1830 America was a dream paradise in terms of liberty, economic opportunity, and the freedom to achieve one's ambitions. Limited only by their ingenuity, talent, and drive, nearly all white males could be independent farmers, tradesmen, or merchants. But the wide-open liberal universe of the mid-19th century, when Abe Lincoln and Samuel Clemens came of age, excluded women, people of color, black slaves in the South, and newcomers from China, Ireland, and Italy. All were second-class citizens, or worse.

Illiberalism is the ugly side of America's political consciousness. It encapsulates the heritage of racism and white male patriarchy as well as the mean-spirited, antigovernment libertarian streak that accepts the privilege, hierarchy, and radical inequality generated by unregulated corporate capitalism as a "natural" condition. Among the upper- and upper-middle classes, illiberalism articulates the values of a would-be aristocratic elite on American soil; the plantation homes of slaveholders and the modern estates of the financial elite mimic Old World chateaus. Among the GOP's upper-middle class and Trump's working-class supporters, illiberalism comes dressed in the attitude of white male privilege and a resentment of programs—such as affirmative action for college admission and employment, Pell Grants for college, and equal pay for equal work—designed to improve the life chances of minorities and women. Compared to liberals and conservatives, illiberals seem to have no problem with Old World values as long as they are the ones benefiting from them.

Paradoxically, illiberals often speak in the liberal dialect and, in doing so, sound similar to liberals and conservatives. But if we listen carefully, we recognize that illiberals use liberal rhetoric to preserve the liberty of action and equality of opportunity *for themselves* at the expense of others. During the civil rights struggle in the South, for example, white resisters used the rhetoric of rights, saying that freedom of association gave them the rights to choose with whom to associate and how to educate their children. Said a white Atlanta father in 1956, "Is it not every father's and mother's inalienable right and duty to choose, for their children, associates and companions for life?"[1] Thus, to understand the American right, it is necessary to see how it operates both inside *and* outside the bounds of classic liberalism. It boasts that it believes in the basic Lockean rights of life, liberty, property, and the pursuit of happiness, yet violates the spirit of liberalism by jealously trying to preserve liberal principles for a subset of the population—white men, particularly of the middle and upper classes. Across American history there have been two completely different and opposing ideals of liberty arguing with each other: one being the liberty of powerful individuals to do whatever they please (even if it means trampling on the liberties of others) and the other being a society in which freedom and liberty are widely shared and constitute a common good. For hard-core reactionaries—the Donald Trumps and Roy Moores, the Tea Party faithful, and their billionaire enablers—the world of the 19th century, which celebrated only the freedom and equality of white men, is as far as they want to go.

For illiberals, the feudal values that liberals reject have stubbornly persisted and their expression has been refashioned as circumstances have allowed. In *Civic Ideals: Conflicting Visions of Citizenship in U.S. History*, University of Pennsylvania political scientist Rogers M. Smith finds a persistent pattern of discrimination and exclusion against women, minorities, and non-Anglos based on the "ascriptive" or hierarchical values of white Protestant nationalism—specifically, the belief that a bloodline stretching back to northwest Europe is what fully qualifies someone for American citizenship.[2] Smith's Pulitzer-nominated work makes it clear that the 20th century consensus school of American history (to which Louis Hartz, Daniel Boorstin, and Richard Hofstadter belonged) glossed over Southern slavery, post-slavery Jim Crow segregation, xenophobia, and the persistence of caste in the United States.[3] In the Jacksonian period, white males enjoyed exceptional liberty and equality. Yet, "intertwined with their liberal democratic arrangements," Smith writes that Americans had "extensive institutions and ideological traditions supporting white supremacy and slavery, Protestant hegemony, patriarchy, and Anglo-Saxon predominance."[4] For generations, white Anglo-Saxon Protestant Americans believed they had been in some way "chosen" by God, history, or nature to possess superior moral and intellectual traits that were conveniently linked to race (Anglo-Saxon) and gender (male).[5] Until the middle of the 20th century, northern Europeans ruled America's political economy based on the myth that they were biologically and culturally superior beings compared to people with black, brown, or yellow skin whose homelands had been colonized by imperial powers. For a large portion of our history, the American Anglo majority excluded certain racial and ethnic groups from the mainstream and treated them as lower caste.[6] Men naturally ran the family and society; African Americans and Latinos were consistently portrayed in white culture as "lower-caste people, born to serve." African Americans, in particular, were viewed by white supremacist ideologues as an "inherently unprogressive race, incapable of joining the modern world."[7]

Being colorblind has been part of our civic mythology since 1965; however, a clear-eyed view of American political and social history—including the post–civil rights era—says otherwise. Smith makes a strong case that illiberalism and racism are part of America's "constitutive, fundamental ideological" makeup—just as important in our history as the ringing liberal call for equal rights for all in the Declaration of Independence.[8] Unlike Gunnar Myrdal, the Swedish sociologist who argued that racism was not central to American political identity, Smith does not see bias and prejudice fading away; instead, he sees it taking new forms and shapes.[9] The surge of illiberal racial expression that began during Obama's presidency and has spiked with Donald Trump's confirms Smith's sober and pessimistic view about the persistence of anti-Lockean attitudes in the American psyche.[10]

HOW SLAVERY AND RACISM CAME TO AMERICA

In early colonial times, blacks and whites mixed easily and the poor of both groups were indentured servants to the more well-to-do. Small farmers tilled the soil for themselves, but the gentry with large estates in Virginia and other Southern colonies could sell for the market, especially if they had a dependable labor supply. Yet large estates had trouble finding enough manpower in a world that was land-rich but labor-poor. Slave labor provided a solution. After all, in ancient republics the equality of male citizens was premised on foreign-born slaves—often captured in war—doing the hardest and dirtiest jobs. But what group should draw the unluckiest of straws in America? Enslaving Native Americans left planters open to raids by other indigenous tribes. Putting additional numbers of white Europeans into servitude—and making it permanent—brought with it the danger of a political rebellion by the yeoman farming class against the planter aristocracy. Accelerating the importation of human cargo from Africa was the safest option. In a cavalier, cruel way, it was nothing personal, it was just business. In *The New Jim Crow*, Michelle Alexander reminds us that the concept of race, fathered by European imperialism, is only a few centuries old.[11] In the New World, racial identity allowed for a sorting among Africans destined for a life of bondage; Native Americans marked for war, removal, and genocide; and whites entitled to the Lockean ideals of liberty and equality. Making slavery race-specific had the additional bonus of showing poor whites that they held a privileged position in society.

In America, land was abundant and labor scarce; in England, the reverse was true. Hungry, masterless men crammed the roads looking for work and bread when the population surge of the 16th and 17th centuries set off an explosion of landless laborers. Seeking a better life, many of the poor sailed to colonial Virginia to become indentured servants where they faced an appalling death rate while serving as "a machine to make tobacco for someone else."[12] To make the most out of the high price of tobacco, landowners pushed the laboring class hard. In 1620s Virginia, a servant's choice was either work for the master or escape into the wilderness populated by Native Americans. Still, ordinary poor Englishmen came to Virginia because land was everyone's hope for security. As the mortality rate began to fall in the second half of the 17th century those who graduated from servant status could find land and grow crops. But Virginia's increase in population did not solve the problem of the larger planters. When servants became free and turned to farming, they added to the volume of the tobacco crop and helped depress the price. In the competition between the larger planters and the small farmers, it was the small planters who lost.

As more poor immigrants poured into Virginia, the class of freedmen grew. Discontent surged as servants freed after 1660 found it increasingly difficult to find land that was not already claimed. To avoid life on the edge of the frontier, they had to rent land from the "big men." When years of hard work first as a servant and then as a small farmer left men still grasping for security, they became angry. The men who came to Virginia as laborers knew they would be exploited but saw land and independence as an achievable goal. When this dream was exposed as dubious, some became vagabonds living off the land like the masterless men back in England; others grew rebellious. The wealthy planters and officials regarded these "terrible young men" as both labor lost and a danger to society. Unlike in England, in America nearly every man had a gun. This was useful for a wartime march against Native Americans, but men with guns could be dangerous. Fearing poor farmers, frontiersmen, and the rabble who dodged taxes, in 1670 their former masters deprived homeless freedmen of the vote. But unrest continued and in 1676 a messy civil war broke out in the form of Bacon's rebellion—the largest revolt in any American colony before the revolution. Nathaniel Bacon led the freedmen against Virginia's Governor William Berkeley, who expected from his subjects the same loyalty that he himself gave his king. A confusing rebellion, it began as a crusade against American Indians (whom Bacon hated) and ended as a series of plundering raids against the upper class who stuck with Berkeley.[13] According to Yale historian Edmund Morgan:

Considering the grievances of Virginia's impoverished freemen, it is surprising that [Bacon] was able to direct their anger for so long against the Indians . . . for those with eyes to see, there was an obvious lesson in the rebellion. Resentment of an alien race might be more powerful than resentment of an upper class.[14]

Having quelled the insurrection but facing a swelling number of disgruntled poor farmers and landless men, the Virginia elite sought a new way to compel maximum output without posing a threat of rebellion. The solution: retire indentured servitude of the restless English poor in favor of the slavery of Africans.[15] In the Virginia tobacco fields, servitude already came closer to slavery than anything known at the time in England. "Men served longer, were subject to more rigorous punishments, were traded about as commodities already in the 1620s."[16] Although slavery did not exist in England, all of Europe knew that the Spanish treasure chest was dug by slave labor and that the sugar plantations of the West Indies were profitable because of African slaves.

The Virginia elite could have transformed indentured servitude into actual slavery, but not only did this risk rebellion, it required a public decision. However, the market option was available. Virginian planters could simply choose to purchase slaves instead of servants. This option became economically attractive when life expectancy in Virginia improved in the second half of the 17th century. Previously, when a man's probability of dying during his first five years in Virginia were better than fifty-fifty, English servants with a five-year term were a "better buy" than slaves.[17] The tipping point came in the 1660s. Setting mortality aside, the economic benefit for the master was obvious: there was no limit to the work or the time that a master could command from his slaves, other than allowing them to eat and sleep so they could work again. The shift to slavery solved the Virginia elite's most pressing political problem: in a slave society, the flood of newly freed servants slowed to a seep.

Americans had developed a plantation system without slavery or racism; both suddenly came to the fore as the tradeoff for social and political stability. Racism came into the picture because to induce slaves to work as hard as the plantation system required, masters had to be willing to beat, torture, injure, and kill.[18] In the West Indies, the sugar planters literally worked their slaves to death to make a profit. Death was not necessary in the tobacco fields of Virginia, but savagery was endemic to slavery. If slaves were of a dark-skinned race they could be viewed as alien beings who were not really human. Slavery was illegal in England, but in Barbados, masters were authorized to inflict severe punishment on their bound labor that went well beyond English law because the African slaves were "a brutish sort of People."[19]

Paradoxically, African slaves came to Virginia (and America) without it being a decision of public policy. The same was not true of racism. In England, the poor were portrayed as "vicious, idle, dissolute."[20] In the early decades of the 17th century, Virginia planters voiced similar complaints about their indentured servants and restless freedmen. With freedmen no longer a threat, these attitudes were transferred to African slaves and Native Americans. In the new economy, the wealthy elite faced a choice: they could squeeze out the small planters, as they were trampled in Barbados the prior century, or they could work to make the poor farmers part of the white ruling class. They choose the second option, in part, because the wealthy planters wanted poor whites to come to their assistance in the case of a slave insurrection.

To aid in this effort, the Virginia assembly passed a series of laws designed to foster racism against blacks and Native Americans. In 1680, the assembly legalized thirty lashes on the bare back "if any negroe or other slave shall presume to lift up his hand in opposition against any Christian."[21] Allowing former servants to whip black slaves *without fear of legal penalty* made lower-class whites psychologically equal with their former masters, as now they too could partake in such shameless sadistic behavior. In proclaiming all white men superior to dark-skinned people, Virginia's ruling class also offered socially inferior whites economic support. To help former servants get a start on an independent life, the Virginia assembly in 1705 required their masters to give them corn, money, and a gun. In addition, at the insistence of the English government, servants on becoming free were entitled to fifty acres of land. Finally, the colony's ruling elite drastically reduced the poll tax and thus invited the freedmen to participate in politics. As the small farmer's economic and social standing improved, so did his political position.

By the middle of the 18th century, slavery was well established in the mid-Atlantic and Southern colonies. Between 1660 and 1710, nearly every

English colony in the Americas put in place laws defining slaves as "convey-
able property" that could be moved or sold at the owner's will.[22] The danger
of unruly poor white farmers presenting a political challenge to the wealthy
elite or rising up in arms à la Bacon's rebellion was long past. The fear and
contempt that the English upper class felt for the masterless men and the poor
had mutated into racism in the Southern slave colonies. In 18th century
America, Native Americans, mulattoes, and African slaves were lumped
into a single pariah class. Above them stood a master class in which the
planter elite were privileged in the extreme and small farmers enjoyed
the benefits of a socially constructed identity—"whiteness."

> But race is the child of racism, not the father . . . the belief in
> the preeminence of hue and hair, the notion that these factors
> can correctly organize a society and that they signify deeper
> attributes, which are indelible—this is the new idea at the heart
> of these new people who have been brought up hopelessly, tragi-
> cally, deceitfully, to believe that they are white.[23]

There is a critical difference between a *society with slaves* and a *slave
society*. Early America, especially New England and the mid-Atlantic states,
was an example of a *society with slaves*. Here the line between slave and
free was fluid, slavery was just one form of labor among many, and slaves
were marginal to core economic productivity. While slaves could be treated
with cruelty in societies with slaves, this was the way the upper class
treated all subordinates, whether indentured servants, debtors, slaves, or
the poor. By contrast, in the *slave societies* that developed in the American
South, bondage "stood at the center of economic production, and the
master-slave relationship provided the model for all social relations," and
slaveholders held power. Other forms of labor—whether family labor,
indentured servants, or wage labor—declined, as the new powerful slave
economy drove small farmers to the margins. By the middle of the 17th
century, Virginia and the Southern colonies were fully established slave
societies. A salable commodity—such as tobacco or sugar or cotton—was
a necessary condition for the development of a slave society, but it was not
sufficient. What distinguished the post-1670 Chesapeake region was
neither the cultivation of tobacco nor slave power, but a planter class that

commanded the region's resources and mobilized the power of the state. A slave society emerges when the slaveholding class becomes the preeminent leadership element and marginalizes its political and economic rivals.[24]

The American North and South splintered when Southern colonies became full-fledged slave societies centered on plantations: "a radically different form of social organization and commercial production controlled by a new class of men whose appetite for labor was nearly insatiable." As part of this transformation, imported Africans were designated slaves for life based on their pigmentation. "These two words, Negro and Slave," became "by custom grown Homogeneous and convertible," when the plantation masters in the Caribbean and North America redefined people of African ancestry in the eyes of Europeans.[25] Until slavery became "color-coded," *African* slavery was just one of many forms of subordination—a common circumstance in a feudal world ruled by hierarchies. But in the American South, *African* slavery became the foundation of the social order. And what would become the world's most powerful slave society justified its cruelty and unbridled power by inventing and perfecting the ideology of white supremacy.[26]

KING COTTON HELL AND THE PLANTATION ELITE

The tobacco slavery of 1750 Virginia, Delaware, and Maryland was not nearly as violent and destructive as when slavery moved south to Georgia and then west to the great Black Belt (so named for the rich soil) cotton fields of Alabama and Mississippi. In the mid-Atlantic states, slave families often were allowed to stay together and by the 1780s many white Americans, including slaveholders such as Virginia's George Mason, believed slavery should be abolished. At the Constitutional Convention, Mason boasted that Virginia and Maryland had already banned the Atlantic slave trade, the "infernal traffic," but he worried that the planters in South Carolina and Georgia would push for the expansion and growth of slavery.[27] His fears were realized.

At the same time as the Revolution, the United States embarked on Caribbean-style plantation slavery; the plantation elite did not invent mass slavery—they just copied the great sugar plantations of the West

Indies. The estates in Barbados, Jamaica, and Saint-Domingue were the 18th century equivalent of the Silicon Valley and made their British and French owners fabulously wealthy.[28] After Eli Whitney invented the cotton gin in 1793—increasing productivity by a factor of fifty—ambitious, wealthy Southern whites made a pact with the devil and conveniently compartmentalized the Lockean part of their brain from the feudal-slave capitalist side.[29] In an open letter to British abolitionist Thomas Clarkson, one South Carolina planter wrote that *only* slaves could be made to work so hard while costing the owner so little.[30] After 1780, more than a million slaves were marched south crossing the barrier between the old slavery in the mid-Atlantic states and the new torture chamber that was the deep South. This massive deportation, named the Second Middle Passage by historians, traumatized black people after the American Revolution and expanded slavery westward. "Hurrying in lock step, the thirty-odd men came down the dirt road like a giant machine. Each hauled twenty pounds of iron, chains that draped from neck and wrist to wrist, binding them all together." For eighty years, these coffles of bound men and women walked for weeks, many covering 700 miles or a million and a half steps, to reach the cotton frontier in Alabama, Mississippi, and Texas. There they cleared the forest, plowed the fields, and picked the white gold that made their masters rich, spurred on by the brutal cuts of rawhide whips.[31] The planter's hegemony required that slaves stand in awe of their masters, an awe based on the ever-present threat of violence.[32]

For nearly its entire history, a powerful landed elite led the South's business and commercial class. In antebellum and post–Civil War America, the masters of the great plantations exercised a power that knew no limit. Practiced in the art of domination, they communicated their purported natural right to rule via stately houses, fine clothes, swift carriages, and grand gestures.[33] Everyone knew where they stood in the social hierarchy that began with the family patriarch and flowed down a long chain until the bottom link: the Negro field hand, whether slave or tenant farmer. In such a situation, the broad social equality that Tocqueville celebrated, and Northern men of varied economic levels experienced, was unknown. The Southern aristocracy—wealthy because of the harsh exploitation of others' labor—was the one piece of the puzzle that fit the feudal traditions of Europe much better than the great democratic bourgeois experiment that was America.

Unlike the rest of the nation, the South did not reject the notion of status based on birth, the cornerstone of European aristocracy. Instead, Southern planters defended a caste society just as it was falling out of favor in Europe, where the bourgeoisie and liberals were rushing to catch up with the American Revolution. As the North moved ahead, the South turned and walked back. The idea that all men were created equal contradicted the facts of daily life in the South. Slavery offered no inconvenience to capitalism *per se*, but "bourgeois conceptions of freedom" and the ideals of the American and French revolutions were severely subversive doctrines to the South; they struck at the foundation of the Southern economy, property in slaves.[34] Emphasizing aristocratic and preindustrial traits—courtesy, grace, leisure, politeness, and a preference for the country estate—the plantation elite created a reactionary oasis for themselves inside a nation that was otherwise a Lockean dream world in which free men had finally escaped the Old World restrictions of inequality, caste, and class.[35]

Slavery was not simply an economic system. As the foundation of Southern culture, forced labor was the basis for an authoritarian state of mind. Situated by power and station atop the social pyramid, the planters were, in every regard, feudal lords. They considered everyone else—their slaves, their poor white employees, their less powerful neighbors, and finally their wives and children—as grossly "inferior to themselves in social status and personal rights."[36] Jefferson wrote in his *Notes on the State of Virginia*:

> The whole commerce between master and slave is a perpetual exercise of the most boisterous passions, the most unremitting despotism on the one part, and degrading submissions on the other. Our children see this, and learn to imitate it . . . The man must be a prodigy who can retain his manners and morals undepraved by such circumstances.[37]

These slave kings literally owned the life, liberty, and property of their chattel. Slaves were lumped in with cattle and horses—all existed to do the work that the master needed done. The planter and his overseers had total control over a worker's life. Owning other human beings molded the very core of the planter's personality. How else could it be when on their estates, America's landed elite were at once masters, wardens, employers, lawmakers, prosecutors, judges, jailers, and executioners?[38] In the habit of exercising power, the slave owners grew accustomed to the obsequious deference of others. Like authoritarians before and since, they justified injustice and inhumanity on the grounds that it was necessary because every great society is built on a division of labor between a superior elite and a group of drones "naturally" suited for those jobs that are the most menial, exhausting, and unrewarding. Southern slave owner James Henry Hammond wrote:

> In all social systems, there must be a class to do the menial duties, to perform the drudgery of life. That is, a class requiring but a low order of intellect and but little skill. Its requisites are vigor, docility, fidelity. Such a class you must have, or you would not have that other class which leads progress, civilization, and refinement.[39]

Masters of their world, the plantation elite chafed at the idea that society or government might have claims that ran counter to their desires. Government was to be kept as weak and minimal as possible, at least in terms of interfering with master power and prerogative.[40] Like reactionaries today, slaveholders wanted to minimize government, except when it would strengthen their power and grow their bank account.

Plantation and slave owners represented a very small minority of society in the antebellum South. By 1850, there were fewer than 350,000 slave owners in a total white population of approximately 6 million in the slaveholding regions. Counting their families, they numbered, at most, a quarter of the white population; and within this group, a smaller minority owned most of the slaves. By 1860, an estimated 7 percent of Southern whites owned more than 70 percent of the slaves. There was a hierarchy and power structure to the planter class. Black slaves were the most valuable piece of property white people owned in the antebellum South; owning just a few slaves elevated a farmer from the crowd. The average master owned four to six slaves. Men who owned at least twenty human beings were given the title of "planter" by the federal census bureau. One in eight Southern masters were included in the nearly 50,000 planters who owned more than half of the South's slaves. Owning fifty or more slaves, the planter aristocracy stood above everyone else; these 10,000 families ran the South. In 1860, 3,000 of these families owned at least 100 slaves, a mere 300 planters each owned at least 250, and at the very pinnacle of Southern society stood the 50 masters whose slave ownership topped 500.[41]

At the bottom of the social pyramid stood a large number of yeoman farmers working on small properties without slaves and, finally, poor whites outside the cash crop system struggling as subsistence farmers. Critically, the small farmers in the South accepted the political leadership of the big planters.[42] Recognizing the danger of poor whites and poor blacks uniting against their illiberal power, the planter aristocracy encouraged poor white farmers to understand the value of their skin. The self-made Joseph E. Brown, Georgia's governor just prior to the Civil War, told his constituents, "with us, every white man . . . feels and knows that he belongs to the ruling class."[43]

SLAVERY AS WAR CAPITALISM

As every schoolchild learns, the Civil War pitted the industrial North against the agrarian slave South. The abolitionists argued that slavery was static and inefficient compared to the free labor North. Yet recent scholarship reveals that antebellum slavery was ruthlessly efficient and that before the factory, capitalism grew in the fields.[44] Harvard historian Sven Beckert says "war capitalism" was the foundation from which the more familiar industrial capitalism evolved.[45] Capitalism's early phase—the United States being the exemplary case—required the removal and extermination of indigenous inhabitants and domination of masters over slaves.[46] In the American South, a region as large as Great Britain, France, Spain, Austria, and Prussia combined, violence drove an economic engine that powered the new global economy. In 1860, slaves in the American South picked two-thirds of all the commercially grown cotton in the world and nearly 80 percent of the cotton consumed by Great Britain's massive textile industry. The United States enjoyed access to the lowest-cost, most-available labor in the world.[47] Slavery not only provided plantation owners cheap labor, but it was also used as collateral to secure mortgages. The flow of credit between

British banks and the United States depended to a significant degree on human property.[48]

New World slavery yoked the ancient tradition of bondage to a "decidedly modern purpose—the large-scale, profit-oriented production of commodities for a capitalist world market," writes Edward Baptist.[49] Similar to Detroit's automobile industry in the 20th century, the 19th century cotton empire in the American South mobilized huge numbers of workers and relied on tight managerial control, all in the pursuit of great profit. Slavery, we now understand, was essential to early industrialization. For nearly a century, from 1770 to 1860, with British cotton manufacturers as well as the North's embryonic industry demanding huge amounts of the commodity, industrial capitalism lived off and invigorated war capitalism.[50] Instead of the "free market," radical un-freedom is what fueled explosive American economic growth.[51]

> Slave traders, slave pens, slave auctions, and the attendant physical and psychological violence of holding millions in bondage were of central importance to the expansion of cotton production in the United States and of the Industrial Revolution in Great Britain.[52]

The introduction of the gang labor system and daily picking quota, along with the adoption of new hybrid seed varieties, increased cotton production dramatically.[53] The brutal metaphor "whipping machine" spoke to the central technology of the antebellum cotton empire: calibrated pain. Inflicted day after day and week upon week, the threat of the whip and the pain of the beatings spurred enslaved workers to pick faster still. In this way, productivity—the metric of capitalism's efficiency—continued to climb. Planters called this new method of labor control the "pushing system": Each slave was assigned a daily picking quota, which increased steadily over time.[54] Picking cotton was a skill that required good eyes, quick hands, and stamina. If a new "hand" couldn't meet the set quota, he or she would have to quickly improve or the whip would settle the account. Slave societies require violence that is systematic and relentless.[55] Between 1790 and 1860, there was no mechanical innovation of any kind to speed up the harvesting of cotton and certainly "human bodies, the only 'machine' that worked the cotton fields," did not change.[56] Yet cotton yields increased almost every year from 1800, when African American slaves picked 1.4 million pounds of white gold, to 1860, when the enslaved harvest reached nearly 2 billion pounds.[57]

CALHOUN AND SLAVERY AS A "POSITIVE GOOD"

In the decades preceding the Civil War, John C. Calhoun of South Carolina was the most important proslavery politician in the nation. A congressman, senator, cabinet member, and vice president, Calhoun addressed the Senate in his most famous speech in February 1837. Instead of excusing slavery as a "necessary evil," as had been the practice of many illiberal Southerners, Calhoun declared it a "positive good":

> the existing relationship between the two races . . . is indispens-
> able to the peace and happiness of both . . . Never before has
> the black race of Central Africa, from the dawn of history to the
> present day, attained a condition so civilized and so improved,
> not only physically, but morally and intellectually . . . the rapid
> increase of numbers, is conclusive proof of the general happiness
> of the race, in spite of all the exaggerated tales to the contrary.[58]

Furthermore, Southern slavery held an important advantage over industrial capitalism based on wage labor, said Calhoun. In advanced societies, he observed, there is an inevitable "conflict between labor and capital" but the special situation of the South—its regime of slave labor—"exempts us from the disorders and dangers resulting from this conflict." Here he proudly enunciated the enduring illiberal position: "There never has yet existed a wealthy and civilized society in which one portion of the community did not, in point of fact, live on the labor of the other." For Calhoun and the plantation class for which he spoke, Locke, Paine, Jefferson, and Tocqueville were chasing a mirage. The creation of a liberal democratic society based on equality and inclusion in opposition to and as an alternative to the rigid class structure of Old World Europe was an impossible dream. Ripping the liberal ideological cover off industrial capitalism, in a fashion similar to Marx's critique of the French and American revolutions, Calhoun asserted that exploitation exists in every society.[59] "It would not," the South Carolinian said, "be difficult to trace the various devices by which the wealth of all civilized communities has been so unequally divided, and to show by what means so small a share has been allotted to those whose labor it was produced, and so large a share given to the non-producing classes." If some means involve "brute force," others, Calhoun noted, are achieved by modern "subtle and artful fiscal contrivances."

The exploitation of labor in the South was, at once, more honest than above the Mason-Dixon Line and resulted in a political condition "much more stable and quiet than that of the North," Calhoun proclaimed.[60] Militant racism was not an incidental part of the slaveholder's philosophy, it formed its core; the class structure was stable in the South because an inferior race played the part of the laborer. In his *Memoir On Slavery* (1838), South Carolina College chancellor William Harper wrote, "If there are sordid, servile, and laborious offices to be performed, is it not better that there should be sordid, servile, and laborious beings to perform them?"[61] Born as the child of slavery, racism only grew stronger and more autonomous after slavery's end. Historian George Fredrickson says, "the treatment of blacks, if originally inspired by exploitative interests and rational calculations, engendered a cultural and psycho-social racism that after a certain point took on *a life of its own* and created a powerful irrational basis for white supremacist attitudes and actions."[62]

NORTHERN VICTORY AND THADDEUS STEVENS

After the North's victory in the Civil War, the Radical Republicans held power in the victorious North and mounted an attack on the plantation system itself. Between 1865 and 1868, they demanded sweeping land reform, the seizure of plantation properties, and the division of great estates into smaller farms for both blacks and whites—the famed "40 acres and a mule."

> Freedpeople believed, for good reasons, that only access to land would secure their newfound freedom, and they argued that

their support for the Union war effort and their unpaid labor under slavery had given them the right to such lands. . . . Slavery amounted to the theft of the just rewards of their labor—a theft now compensated by the redistribution of land.[63]

The Radical Republicans understood, as others did not, that only the seizure of land would "break the power of the planters" and end their dominance over Southern society.[64] Congressman Thaddeus Stevens of Pennsylvania insisted that the South had to be treated not as a group of wayward states, but as a defeated enemy; if not, the power structure and social norms that had produced the evil of slavery would remain in place, even though slavery had been abolished. In impassioned speeches, Stevens told audiences in Congress and across the North: "But reformation must be effected; the foundation of their institutions both political, municipal and social *must* be broken up and *relaid*, or all our blood and treasure have been spent in vain. This can only be done by treating and holding them as a conquered people."[65]

While President Lincoln struggled to prevent the Civil War from degenerating into "a violent and remorseless revolutionary struggle," Stevens understood that this was precisely what was required. He saw the peace that followed the war as an opportunity to create a "perfect Republic" purged of the legacy of slavery and racism. For Reconstruction to succeed, the plantation estates—source of the planters' economic and political power—had to be destroyed and the slaves given not only political freedom but economic standing as well. Stevens believed in the civic republican faith associated with the founding generation "which identified freedom with economic independence."[66] Historian Staughton Lynd wrote:

Reconstruction failed after the Civil War, not because the North tried to compel social change at a bayonet point, not because the North should have kept troops in the South longer, but because political change was not reinforced by economic change. The freedman was given the vote but he was not given the land. Had the plantations of the leading Confederates been divided among the former slaves, the Southern Negro would have had at least the beginnings of economic independence to support his new political power. In fact Negro suffrage was supported *only* by bayonets, and Negroes ceased to vote independently when troops were withdrawn. The mistake of Congress, in this view, was to set up a stool with two legs—Negro suffrage and a Federal presence—which needed the third leg of economic revolution in order to stand by itself.[67]

In *Black Reconstruction in America 1860–1880* (1935), W. E. B. DuBois made the same point: "The truth of the insistence of Stevens was manifest: without land and vocation, the Negro voter could not gain that economic independence which would have protected his vote."[68]

Stevens, more than anyone else of the Civil War generation, saw the future and anticipated the awfulness that would result if nothing were done to curb the massive power of the planter class. Understanding that an incomplete revolution would leave the Confederate despots who had ruled the South in charge, he put forward a plan to seize the property of the largest plantation owners and redistribute the land to poor blacks *and* whites. Believing that human character is shaped by circumstances, Stevens rejected racist arguments that the freed slaves would be unable to work independently. He told audiences, "Nothing is so likely to make a man a good citizen as to make him a freeholder. Nothing will so multiply the productions of the South as to divide it into small farms. Nothing will make men so industrious and moral as to let them feel they are above want." As historian Eric Foner notes, this was classic Jeffersonianism.[69]

Stevens's plan focused only on the largest Southern plantations; those estates valued at more than $10,000 or who owned more than 200 acres of land. These holdings, he estimated, amounted to 400 million acres. Each adult former slave, male and female, would receive 40 acres, which would total an estimated 40 million. The remaining 360 million acres would be sold in small units to help pay off the national debt; compensate Unionists, North and South, for losses they suffered during the war; and finance pensions for Union veterans. The congressman said:

> This plan, would, no doubt, work a radical reorganization in southern institutions, habits, and manners. It is intended to revolutionize their principles and feelings . . . The whole fabric

of southern society must be changed, and never can it be done if this opportunity is lost . . . The Southern States have been despotisms, not governments of the people. It is impossible that any practical equality of rights can exist where a few thousand men monopolize the whole landed property . . . How can republican institutions, free schools, free churches, free social intercourse exist in a mingled community of nabobs and serfs; of the owners of twenty thousand acre manors with lordly palaces, and the occupants of narrow huts inhabited by 'low white trash'? If the South is ever to be made a safe republic, let her lands be cultivated by the toil of the owners or the free labor of intelligent citizens. This must be done even though it drive the nobility into exile . . . If we do not make [Southern] institutions fit to last through generations of free men, a heavy curse will be on us.[70]

The Union victory gave the North the chance to radically transform the South and change American history.[71] Stevens understood that "a landed aristocracy and a landless class are alike dangerous in a republic, and by a single act of justice he would abolish both," remarked William D. Kelley, a congressional colleague. Only confiscation would break the power of the plantation ruling elite, reinvent Southern social structure, inject liberal norms into Southern society, and create the basis for a Southern Republican Party made up of black and white small farmers.[72]

It was not to be. The war-weary northern public did not have the patience, focus, or energy to ensure the destruction of the planter class and its illiberal, racist ideology.[73] Critically, when Lincoln was assassinated by John Wilkes Booth, Southern sympathizer Andrew Johnson became president and the plantation elite reclaimed their "firm hold on power." By the end of 1865, Johnson had allowed Southern whites to reclaim confiscated land. Moving expeditiously, the former Confederate states constructed a new caste system based on so-called Black Codes that forced freed slaves to work as indentured servants and sharecroppers.

In South Carolina, blacks were confined by law to their plantations, forced to work from sunup to sundown. In Florida, blacks who showed "disrespect" to their bosses or rode public conveyances reserved for whites could be whipped and pilloried. In Mississippi, it became a criminal offense for blacks to hunt or fish, heightening their dependence upon white employers. Thus, within six months of the end of the Civil War, there arose a broadly based retreat from many of the ideals that had motivated the northern war effort.[74]

Supporting the Reconstruction Acts passed by Congress, General Ulysses S. Grant sided with the Radical Republicans in pressing for political rights for the former slaves and led the effort to crush the Ku Klux Klan as president. However, he opposed land redistribution when his support could have made a difference.[75]

In the aftermath of the war, Reconstruction failed and the South preserved its radically unequal, illiberal, and antidemocratic mode of life. The rigid class hierarchy and the racist ideology that defined the world's strongest slave society were left untouched. Without land, the freed blacks were easily converted into agricultural proletarians; by 1900, three-quarters of black farmers in Alabama, Arkansas, Georgia, Louisiana, Mississippi, and South Carolina were impoverished sharecroppers.[76] Looking back in 1890, Frederick Douglass observed that if Stevens's twin strategy of plantation confiscation and land redistribution had been followed, "the negro would not today be on his knees, as he is, supplicating the old master class to give him leave to toil."[77]

A decade after 1865, there were no more slaves and the South was producing more cotton than ever. The empire of cotton survived the war because war capitalism was indifferent to the method of exploitation: indentured servants, slaves, or sharecroppers all supplied cheap labor.[78] Stevens correctly saw that the problem of the South was about more than just slavery; what mattered just as much was the authoritarian mindset of the planter elite and the virulent racism used to divide the working class into black and white serfs. He understood that the illiberal political culture of the South was deeply antithetical to the democratic free labor ethic of the North. Instead of slaves, the plantation elite now commanded, dominated, and exploited a work force of impoverished sharecropping peasants. Slave owners fought the Civil War to save bondage; they lost their property in slaves, but retained their way of life.

◆

After surrendering at Appomattox, the South proceeded as a strange anomaly in American politics—an illiberal one-party nation unto itself—until the civil rights revolution and federal action put an end to a brutal racial regime. Actual slavery transmigrated into oppressive legal and cultural chains. Following their successful defeat of Reconstruction, the planters put down the populist revolt of the 1890s and systematically disenfranchised blacks and working-class whites from the voting rolls while imposing Jim Crow apartheid. In the 100 years between the Civil War and 1965, a small oligarchy ruled each Southern state with an iron hand.[79] Premised on elite rule, Southern politics insisted that blacks bow to white authority in a racial caste system based on savage suppression, public lynching, and radical inequality in education, jobs, and living conditions. Not surprisingly, it promoted race baiting to keep restless hill country whites on the side of the bourbon elite. Today, even with Jim Crow put to rest, many of the habits and attitudes of the Old South stubbornly persist.

In December 2017, Roy Moore would have won the Alabama Senate special election against Democrat Doug Jones even though he pronounced America great in the age of slavery, made multiple outbursts against Muslims, Latinos, and gays, and refused to abide by federal judicial orders that resulted in his twice being removed as the state's chief justice. What sank Moore's campaign were allegations that, decades before, he pursued and molested several white teenage girls. This was too much for some die-hard white Republicans. "My grandmother was a pro-segregationist and she says this will be the first time she votes for a Democrat since George Wallace," said one Democrat active in state politics. "She says she can't vote for a pedophile. There are other Republicans like her."[80]

4

Social Darwinism with a Vengeance

The twin pillars of the antebellum economy collided in the Civil War. Afterward, Northern industrialists and Southern plantation owners remained powerful in different ways. In the South, the feudal planter class was defeated; its quest to dominate national politics and the economy finished when the ashes turned cold in Atlanta. Yet leading the fight against Reconstruction with tenacity and terror, the plantation barons continued to rule Southern society. After the war, the big planters maintained their power by quickly altering their economic model from slavery to tenant sharecropping. During the Populist rebellion, the white elite in the cotton Black Belt allied with conservative city dwellers to defeat the hardscrabble white radicals who farmed the hill country where few blacks lived.[1] In the North, the war unleashed a single great economic burst, which then accelerated in a series of boom-and-bust cycles over the next three decades. Exhausted by war and politics, the nation turned its attention to economic expansion and it seemed as though every man was an entrepreneur expecting to get rich. Post–Civil War America was a time of Horatio Alger dreams; some, such as John D. Rockefeller and Andrew Carnegie, succeeded to an amazing degree. Americans prided themselves on being able to compete and thrive in an economy in which

men were measured on individual initiative, hard work, and guile. But in a
laissez-faire/anything-goes economy, more than a few businessmen played
a rigged game.

The Civil War redeemed democracy in America. The Gilded Age
betrayed it and gave birth to the hard-right libertarian doctrine that government is the enemy of progress and the most powerful capitalists should
be able to do as they wish with little or no pushback from the rest of society.[2] In the often-inhumane factory system in the North, the owners of
the means of production re-created the feudal norms that Americans had
sought to escape. In Massachusetts' textile mills one could see "children
nine years of age . . . on their feet for more than twelve hours . . . carrying
sixteen-pound boxes up four stories."[3]

In the United States, a political system premised on equal citizens is paired
with an economic system that accepts and, in fact, encourages inequality.
Writing about the Gilded Age, H. W. Brands observes that inequality is not
"simply a side effect of capitalism. A capitalist economy can't operate without
it . . . participants in a capitalist economy arrive at the marketplace with
unequal talents and resources and leave the marketplace with unequal
rewards . . . which reinforce the original differences."[4] The Industrial Revolution and the glorification of riches in the Gilded Age established sharp class
divisions among Americans. Inequality, hierarchy, and privilege soared to
new heights in the age of Carnegie, J. P. Morgan, Rockefeller, and Cornelius
Vanderbilt, thus undermining the widespread equality and liberal ethos of
the Jeffersonian and Jacksonian periods. While some degree of inequality
is inevitable and, in fact, desirable in a capitalist economy, the citizens of
liberal democracies have to decide just how much inequality is acceptable
and to what degree a social safety net should assist those unable to compete
economically (e.g., the elderly, disabled, and children) as well as workers left
in the lurch when the capitalist engine goes speeding in new directions. In
the 19th century, American government actively assisted business while
inhibiting the efforts of workers.

Thomas Jefferson and Benjamin Franklin famously worried about the
negative impact that mass manufacturing might have on the new nation.
Both had witnessed the squalor of Europe's major cities and saw the independent yeoman farmer as the secret to the young republic's success.[5] One
can read President Jefferson's land grab from the French in the Louisiana

Purchase as his attempt to ensure that an agrarian, small town America would endure. Emphatically, he did not want Alexander Hamilton's famed *Report on Manufactures* (1791) to foretell the future. But, of course, it did. Tocqueville, too, saw the threat. In *Democracy in America*, he warned:

> The manufacturing aristocracy which we see rising before our eyes is one of the hardest that have ever appeared on earth . . . the friends of democracy should keep their eyes anxiously fixed in that direction. For if ever again permanent inequality of conditions and aristocracy make their way into the world, it will have been by that door that they entered.[6]

AN ACTIVIST SUPREME COURT UNLEASHES CORPORATE CAPITALISM

In the first half of the 19th century, business leaders vigorously lobbied the state and national governments to assist with infrastructure projects (such as roads, canals, and ports) and duties (such as tariffs against foreign goods) so that domestic industry would take root and grow. In sharp contrast to the myth that *laissez faire* was the norm until the Progressive Era, American government played an active role in the development of the economy—on the farm, on the railroad, and in the factory.[7] Emerging manufacturing interests relied on significant support from state governments in the decades prior to 1860.[8] Yet, before Gettysburg and Appomattox, the United States was rural and most organizations were local and small. How did the nation suddenly become an economic behemoth featuring some of the world's largest privately held corporations with minimal regulation by the government? Three reasons stand out. First, the Articles of Confederation created a federal government that was divided, small, and weak. The Federalists, led by Hamilton and Madison, championed a more powerful national government, but the new Constitution with its separation of powers and federalism remained far less powerful than the centralized European states. Second, our continental space opened up the possibility of a massive national—versus regional—market. Once the transcontinental railroad was completed, the largest and best capitalized companies enjoyed a distinct competitive advantage. Third, U.S. courts rendered business entities largely free of government interference. Key Supreme Court decisions early in the 19th century paved the way for the bigger-is-best mentality of the Gilded Age.[9]

Visiting Great Britain in 1810, Massachusetts businessman Francis Cabot Lowell encountered the corporation, an economic entity which allowed many people to invest small amounts of money while imposing few restrictions on the actions of executives.[10] The beauty of this unique legal fiction was the ability to raise the vast amounts of capital required to build very large companies. Lowell immediately recognized the value of such an organizational structure and brought the idea back to the United States. However, for the corporation to have currency, America's laws had to change.[11] The wait was not long. In *Dartmouth College v. Woodward* (1819), the U.S. Supreme Court issued a monumental ruling that fundamentally shaped the country's nascent economy. The case concerned a tax-exempt private college that benefited from state assistance; to ensure accountability, New Hampshire officials wanted to place politically appointed trustees on Dartmouth's corporate board. The college sued and claimed that it needed independence from state interference. Chief Justice John Marshall carefully orchestrated the case to legalize a powerful new form of business organization.[12] The decision conferred private rights on corporations, thus treating them like flesh and blood people; eliminated the requirement that corporate boards have public representation; and placed chartered corporations above individual state law. The Court's decision that private corporations should have the same rights as natural persons to contract and enforce those contracts enabled companies to operate with limited liability. This allowed owners to maintain their personal wealth separate from their business and protected corporate officers from being personally responsible for business debts. Spurring America's economic growth, entrepreneurs could fail and start again with the costs of failure being borne by society. Suddenly, debts were ruled harmless if the amounts were large and attached to corporations or partnerships; small debts attached to workers, however, could still lead to prison.[13]

The *Dartmouth* decision effectively eliminated local control—that is, state, county, and city control—over corporations. It didn't matter whether these corporations were colleges, dry goods companies, or textile mills. As a result, because the federal government barely existed in early 19th century America, the national economy became essentially unregulated—and the consequences of this uncontrolled economy would be enormous.[14] In *Gibbons v. Ogden* (1824), the Supreme Court ruled that the power to regulate interstate commerce, granted to Congress by the commerce clause, gave the national legislature the power to regulate commerce on waterways.[15] Reinforcing *Dartmouth*, *Gibbons* freed business entities from most attempts by state and local governments to set rules on market competition.[16] Furthermore, *Dartmouth College* involved a flight from English common law that held that a company chartered as a corporation by the state was required to serve the public interest and have a public representative on its board. The *Dartmouth* ruling eliminated this requirement in American law and inspired the privatization of what, in other nations, were public goods under public control.[17] In England and France, railroads and other major pieces of infrastructure essential to commerce were deemed too important to simply parcel out to wealthy individuals.

GOVERNMENT AND THE RAILROADS

If the textile mills of New England were America's first big business, railroads came next. A seminal example of the dynamism and creative destruction of American capitalism, the rise of the lightly regulated yet massively subsidized railroads was Lowell on steroids.[18] Major railroad companies set the pattern for big business going forward, as they were the first to separate ownership from management, the first (along with the Southern cotton plantations) to acquire capital beyond the local region, and the first to spark large-scale construction and modern investment banking.[19] Railroad development in the United States was different from Europe's, distinguished by the strength and intrusiveness of government. The national government was strong and centralized in France, divided in Britain, and relatively weak in the United States; only the United States permitted the privatization of an immense public good.[20]

The British rail system combined private capital, ownership, and management with regulation by state agencies set up by Parliament. Great Britain, in contrast to France, did not have a strong unitary state. Instead, power was dispersed among members of Parliament and the royal family. Fearing large independent organizations that might threaten its power, the crown made it difficult to amass large amounts of capital, and was cautious in granting partnership agreements. Owned and managed by the gentry and the new manufacturing class, the railroads were privately held, but did not operate in an unregulated market. Realizing that unrestricted competition could lead to oligopoly, the British Parliament allowed the formation of cartels that controlled competition. Nonintervention in the market was a key economic principle in both Britain and the United States during the 19th century.[21] But the British believed independent small railroads kept the industry competitive and efficient and established cartels to protect small rail lines from predatory capture by large firms.[22] Their policy allowed a multitude of small entrepreneurs to compete without interference from government or from larger, more powerful firms.[23] The British did not see this as a violation of free-market norms.

In contrast, the United States had a weak central government that was largely limited to the "courts and parties"—the federal bench, the Post Office, and the patronage system of the two major political parties.[24] Some state governments sought to regulate the railroads, but it was quickly apparent that they were no match for the power of the big railroad companies. By the Civil War, the railroad industry was privatized, largely unregulated, and prone to corruption. The corruption was a means to an end: the railroads wanted public funds (approximately half the rails' construction costs were covered by government money), and they used legal and extra-legal means to secure legislation and judicial rulings that consolidated their power.

Compared to those in Europe, 19th century American railroads were dangerous, inefficient, overbuilt, ill constructed, and leisurely to adopt innovations. Railroads were not built ahead of demand; nevertheless, rail lines were decisive in America's industrialization.[25] When the basic network of rails east of the Mississippi was completed by 1860, cutting the time of a trip from Chicago to New York from three weeks to less than three days, the mechanized transportation grid set off an explosion of factory production.[26] The railroad represented the first corporation in the American experience to employ thousands of workers, first across regions and then the nation. Earlier businesses—textile mills, plantations, trading houses, and the clipper ships flying around Cape Horn—had supervisors directing workers. But railroad corporations built a multilayered bureaucracy of "supervisors over supervisors (over supervisors)," allowing them to gauge market performance, increase efficiency, and pay close attention to a multitude of tasks.[27] This pyramid of administration became the model for other businesses. Executives at the top wielded great power over thousands of workers below and the railroad's organizational structure was celebrated in management theory as the model for both public and private organizations in America.[28] Hierarchy and inequality had entered American life in a new and dramatic way.

FEUDAL LABOR LAWS FOR AMERICA'S WORKERS

The capitalist transformation of the North began in the countryside in the 1790s when New England farmers faced competitive demands of a rapidly commercializing agricultural sector that forced them to steadily increase their productivity. Over the ensuing decades, agriculture productivity in the North and West exploded even as many people left the farm to join newly arrived immigrants in the cities. Indentured servitude and apprenticeship contracts were replaced by wage contracts and by the 1820s "a day's pay for a day's work" became the norm as a new, highly mobile form of free labor developed in the North.[29] Yet while owners of businesses could look to the government for tariffs and the law for protection, workers were second-class citizens.

For most of the nation's history, American labor law violated the heart of the Lockean project of producing a New World that was neither feudal nor coercive. In the South, slavery was a gross violation of our liberal goals. In the North, coercion was inflicted by the universal application a master-servant concept of labor relations that overwhelmingly favored the employer and denied workers their rights. While U.S. courts abandoned English common law in relation to the corporation, American judges continued to rely on common law precedent in the field of labor relations. In fact, the ancient law of master and servant—which traced back to the English Statutes of Labourers first enacted in 1349 under Edward III and was the law of the land in Tudor England—formed the basis for American labor law until the New Deal. Only in 1937, in the landmark *N.L.R.B. v. Jones & Laughlin Steel Corp.*, did the Supreme Court finally move authority for labor relations to statutes made by Congress and the state legislatures.[30] In the Gilded Age, the robber barons J. P. Morgan, Andrew Carnegie, John D. Rockefeller, Cornelius Vanderbilt, and Leland Stanford fought a bloody class war against labor, which they won.[31] The capitalists won on the street with the help of police forces and private security details; they were victorious in court because the law required "virtual absolute obedience to the master" in the workplace.[32]

Holding fast to English common law—passed down in Sir William Blackstone's *Commentaries* of the 18th century—the American judiciary prescribed enforceable obligations upon employees as a legal status, thus defying the principle of the sovereign individual. This status was conferred upon a person separate from any specific action or contract. To understand "status," take, for example, vagrancy. Vagrancy was deemed a crime not because of an action or inaction taken in itself but because of personal characteristics and membership in a predetermined legal category.[33] Across the United States, not to work or to be seeking work, if one was an able-bodied person without other visible means of support, was judged a crime, punishable by a monetary fine or imprisonment. How did the master-servant relationship work in practice? In the all-important railroad industry, the flexible, expansive dynamic of the market was superimposed upon the "rigid, highly constrained regime of the workplace," all to the advantage of those in charge. With impunity, railroad management cut wages, stretched hours, delayed payrolls, and placed extra burdens on employees. All of this was sanctioned by the courts because the employee was at the complete disposal of the master. For example, the law of master-and-servant established a workday from twilight to twilight, or approximately fourteen hours in the summer, unless otherwise specified by contract, but railroad companies could change the contracts of at-will employees at any time. The courts viewed union organizing as "hostile remedies" that destroyed "confidence" and broke up the "friendly intercourse" of the workplace.[34] Across the board, pre–New Deal labor law was highly biased in favor of employers.

HERBERT SPENCER: THE ORIGINAL LIBERTARIAN
AND THE MYTH OF *LAISSEZ FAIRE*

In 1890, the United States had liberal ideals but was far from achieving them: Industrial workers occupied a feudal status in American law, women were classified as second-class citizens denied the right to vote, and African Americans freed from slavery would soon be stripped of all rights in the approaching Jim Crow–era South. At the same time, America's new business elite had found their manifesto and voice in British social scientist and philosopher Herbert Spencer, who pioneered the libertarian doctrine that continues to pulsate in illiberal hearts today. Glorifying liberty while accepting radical inequality, Spencer preached a gospel that legitimized the massive wealth and extreme power of the Gilded Age business elite.

In *Social Darwinism in American Thought, 1860–1915*, Richard Hofstadter explains the libertarian's influence on post–Civil War America: "Spencer's philosophy was admirably suited to the American scene. It was scientific in derivation and comprehensive in scope. It had a reassuring theory of progress based upon biology and physics." The vogue of Spencer filled a vacuum between the decline of the transcendentalism of Emerson and the turn-of-the-century pragmatism of Charles Peirce, William James, and John Dewey. A systems thinker trying to produce an all-encompassing intellectual system that explained the world in an age in which religion was under attack, Spencer defended a savage capitalism. His thinking was a product of the English Industrial Revolution, the large factories that made Great Britain the superpower of the late 19th century, and a fear of an advancing Marxism. Those who had lost faith in traditional Christian theology found in Spencer a new certainty to latch onto, while the still religious were heartened that Spencer claimed that some things were "unknowable." Steel mogul Carnegie, one of Spencer's leading cheerleaders in Gilded Age America, wrote that after he read Darwin and Spencer: "I remember that light came as in a flood and all was clear. Not only had I got rid of theology and the supernatural, but I had found the truth of evolution. 'All is well since all grows better,' became my motto, my true source of comfort."[35]

In his influential *Social Statics: or the Conditions Essential to Human Happiness Specified* (1851), Spencer infused *laissez faire* with the imperatives of biology.[36] The result was a philosophy of capitalism with the moral heart of Genghis Khan. The book combined rigorous logic about government being the only coercive force in society with a view of human progress that required the lower classes to be sacrificed, *literally*, for the good of the species.[37] In Spencer's utopian libertarian heaven, the state—an evil force in society that is only lingering proof of our once-degenerate nature—will disappear and the underclass of parasites and paupers will become extinct, leaving a new generation of active producers to stand tall as moral citizens.[38] Spencer believed in the inheritance of acquired characteristics, Jean-Baptiste Lamarck's theory that modifications that occur during an organism's lifespan are passed on to its descendants.[39] In Spencer's view, those who were successful in the new capitalist order were the most adept adopters. Conversely, the gene pool of the weak, the poor, the inept, the downtrodden, the untalented had to be eliminated before breeding again. According to Spencer, if the government interfered with the process of natural selection, by seeking to correct social problems, then "growth ceases; and in its place commences retrogression."[40] His illiberal philosophy, with its sharp division between the producers and the slackers, the advancing business class and a biologically deficient underclass, and its willingness to sacrifice the poor and the powerless to lives of degradation—or worse—remains central to the right's mindset.

When contemporary conservatives and illiberals speak of "classical liberalism" they are referring to Spencer and the 19th century *laissez-faire* school, not Locke. A self-taught engineer and social thinker, Spencer was a leading architect of "Manchester liberalism" used by the owners of the means of production in England and America to beat back the socialist critique unleashed by Karl Marx and Friedrich Engels in *The Communist Manifesto* (1848). In *Wealth of Nations* (1776), Adam Smith argued that European governments—all monarchies, it should be noted—interfered needlessly with the economy with their mercantilist policies. Spencer went far beyond Smith to argue that individual rights and property were sacrosanct, that the government did nothing but harm, and that anything the government did was by its very nature coercive; his radical argument steers away from complete anarchism only because he allows government an umpire role in economic affairs. In announcing the libertarian creed, Spencer's writings broke with the liberalism of Locke, Jefferson, and Paine, whose singular goal was not to eliminate government, but to make sure that citizens had control of the government, not the other way around.

Spencer enjoyed enormous influence with the American business class during the Gilded Age. His rallying cry of market freedom at the cost of all else, found in *Social Statics* and *The Man Versus the State* (1884), were wildly popular with the new industrial elite. Carnegie hosted Spencer when he traveled to the United States to lecture, and his ideas penetrated deep into the culture. Yale sociology professor William Graham Sumner, author of *What Social Classes Owe to Each Other* (1883), became a passionate disciple and proselytizer. Spencer's impact on the American business and legal community can be seen in the landmark case *Lochner v. New York* (1905), in which the U.S. Supreme Court held that state legislation forbidding bakers from working more than 10 hours a day or 60 hours a week violated the Due Process Clause of the Fourteenth Amendment by infringing on an individual's liberty to make a contract. In his dissent, Justice Oliver Wendell Holmes famously felt it necessary to write: "The Fourteenth Amendment does not enact Mr. Herbert Spencer's *Social Statics*."

In a long passage in *Social Statics* about the Poor Laws, Spencer offers a clear exposition of his harsh views:

> Meanwhile the well-being of existing humanity, and the unfolding of it into this ultimate perfection, are both secured by that same beneficent, though severe discipline, to which the animated creation at large is subject: a *discipline which is pitiless in the working out of good*: a felicity-pursuing law which never swerves for the avoidance of partial and temporary suffering. *The poverty of the incapable, the distresses that come upon the imprudent, the starvation of the idle, and those shoulderings aside of the weak by the strong, which leave so many 'in shallows and miseries,' are the decrees of a large, far-seeing benevolence.* It seems hard that an unskillfulness which with all his efforts he cannot overcome, should entail hunger upon the artizan. It seems hard that a labourer incapacitated by sickness from competing with his stronger fellows, should have to bear the privations. It seems

hard that widows and orphans should be left to struggle for life or death. Nevertheless, when regarded not separately, but in connection with the interests of universal humanity, these harsh fatalities are seen to be full of the highest beneficence—the same which brings to early graves the children of diseased parents, and singles out the low-spirited, the intemperate, and the debilitated as the victims of an epidemic.[41]

As with Marx, his ideological rival, Spencer was a 19th century historic determinist who believed that the ultimate development of the ideal man was logically certain. Spencer begins *Social Statics* by positing that as civilization advances, progress means that there is less need for government and, in the not too distant future (perhaps in our age of smartphones and search engines?) the state will wither away. As evolution proceeds, the human species improves and, correspondingly, the percentage of "good, talented people" in society increases. As this happens, there will be less and less need for government.[42] He predicts that as civilization advances, "the tendency to repudiate governments will increase," as people decide that government is both useless and needless. It was Spencer's opposition to Marx and socialism that animated his resolve to define the proper purpose of government as narrowly as possible.[43]

John Stuart Mill wrote of Spencer, "He is a considerable thinker though anything but a safe one."[44] Recognizing Spencer's intellectual deficiencies, Hofstadter wrote, "[His] influence far outstripped [his] merits . . . in the three decades after the Civil War it was impossible to be active in any field of intellectual work without mastering Spencer."[45] In addition to basing his philosophy on Lamarck's flawed biological theory, Spencer's political thinking has two serious weak points that put his philosophic edifice at risk. In *Social Statics*, Spencer argues that the first condition of social life must be the rule that "Every man has freedom to do all that he wills, provided he infringes not the equal freedom of any other man." The problem is that he never defines and defends what he means by *infringes*.[46] Second, in a chapter titled "The Right to Use the Earth," Spencer, like Locke, first defines property as the right of each person to freely "use the earth for the satisfaction of his wants."[47] But in the following chapter, "The Right to Property," he narrows the definition of property and reveals his bias toward the most productive members of society.[48] Spencer speaks about freedom to pursue, but says nothing about unequal starting points or resources.[49] He makes the unwarranted assumption that those who have property and wealth secured their place at the top of society because of brains, talent, and drive, when inherited position and luck often play a strong role as well.

Spencer wondered when (if ever) regulation and state coercion would stop.[50] He feared an incremental increase of state authority and power that would result in what he called "The Coming Slavery."[51] There is cruel irony here. Spencer's illiberal philosophy, with its binary division between the worthy and the lazy, grafted easily with the slave capitalism of the Old South and has a strong affinity with the racism against people of color that remains embedded in modern American society.

WHY SPENCER REMAINS IMPORTANT

Spencer, similar to modern-day followers such as Ayn Rand, Paul Ryan, Mitt Romney, and anti-tax advocate Grover Norquist, obsessed that there were two components of the community—one "industrious and prudent," and the other "idle and improvident"—and that the less fortunate demanded relief and support from the prosperous producers.[52] For Spencer, legislation or regulation to protect public health and safety was unnecessary and harmful.[53] In *The Man Versus the State*, he bemoaned efforts by liberal reformers to increase workplace safety by making single-shaft coal mines illegal, extending compulsory vaccinations to Scotland and Ireland, and restricting the employment of women and children in open-air bleaching, as well as various other acts of Parliament that placed regulations on private employers. Spencer's libertarian creed counseled that inequality and injustice were facts of life outside our control. When land reform advocate Henry George, author of *Progress and Poverty* (1879), asked Spencer devotee Edward Livingston Youmans what could be done about social problems, the editor of *Popular Science Monthly* exclaimed:

> Nothing! You and I can do nothing at all. It's all a matter of evolution. We can only wait for evolution. Perhaps in four or

five thousand years evolution may have carried men beyond this state of things. But we can do nothing.[54]

In the triumph of the industrial capitalism that followed the Civil War, the focus was on private gain, not government or the public good. Critically, the embrace of Spencerian thought by civic leaders and the new industrial elite encouraged a "paralysis of the will to reform."[55] We no longer recall Spencer's massive influence because his particular theory of evolution has been debunked. But his impact continues because his libertarian approach to public policy is now deeply ingrained in the thinking of many in business and on the right. Examples from the past century and today illustrate the power of Spencer's social Darwinist viewpoint. "You can't make the world all planned and soft," a Midwestern businessman told Robert and Helen Lynd in their famous study of an average American city, *Middletown in Transition* (1937). "The strongest and the best survive—that's the law of nature after all—always has been and always will be."[56] More recently, in *Strangers in Their Own Land* (2016), a study of working-class whites in the refinery region of Louisiana, Arlie Hochschild discovered that "What seemed like a problem to liberals—the fact that conservatives identify 'up,' with the 1 percent, the planter class—was actually a source of pride for the Tea Party people I came to know. It showed you were optimistic, hopeful, a trier . . . Why would you want to blame a guy if he got all the way to the top? they wondered."[57]

Contrary to Spencer, the idea that a market economy can exist outside and apart from government is simply wrong. It is clear from the historical record that capitalism could not exist apart from governments that are strong and efficient.[58] When you look at the success of European powers to industrialize, as against nations such as Egypt and India that were stymied, what stands out is the importance of "state capacity" to industrialization. Without a powerful state, it was all but impossible to launch industrialization. Creating markets, safeguarding domestic industry, inventing tools to raise revenues, guarding borders, and fostering changes that allowed for the mobilization and concentration of wage workers are government actions that are crucial.[59]

But as capitalism and government matured, government responded to demands from multiple constituents, and industry sectors competed against each other for attention. As the political economist Charles Lindblom famously wrote, business enjoys a "privilege position" of being the government's most important constituent because jobs and tax revenue disappear without investment.[60] Still, from the perspective of the capitalist class, the government appeared Janus-faced, because while it enabled the emergence and growth of industrial capitalism, it later responded to workers calling for better working conditions and better wages.[61] Like the eldest child jealous of the attention paid to a younger sibling, the business class wants government to focus all its attention and resources to assist the private sector in making money. When governments in Europe and the United States listen to and respond to other groups, such as those organizing for labor rights and environmental protection, business elites often turn to the libertarian creed of Spencer and the mantra of minimal government.

5

Why Liberals Love Government: The Progressive Era

odern liberalism sprang to life as a response to the abuses, corruption, and great inequality of the Gilded Age. By the end of the 19th century, the social and political equality of the Jacksonian era had vanished. The sense of loss upset Americans in a way that is hard to understand in a 21st century world dominated by large complex organizations, private and public bureaucracy, and a powerful economic elite—the wealthiest of the wealthy, particularly the billionaires of the 1%—having immense power across the economic, social, and political spheres. This is in sharp contrast to earlier periods of American history. In the Jacksonian era, observed Yale political scientist Robert Dahl, "adult white male citizens lived with fewer social, economic, and political inequalities than any large number of persons in history had existed up to that time, and very likely since."[1] The middle decades of the 19th century were a time of incredible equality for white males, economically, socially, and politically, and thus somewhat similar to the widespread middle-class equality of the 20th century postwar era. Yet, the economic equality of the 1830s, '40s, and '50s receded rapidly during the brisk industrialization following the Civil

War. Between 1870 and 1900, dynamic, chaotic growth changed the face of America. Millions left farms and small towns for the booming cities to work in factories, and giant corporations began to dominate the economy. The dizzying shift to an urban, industrial America with national markets at the end of the 19th century confused and terrified ordinary citizens. Watching industrial capitalism bestow fabulous fortunes, many Americans grew angry at an economic system that rewarded greed and market power but seemed stacked against honest hard work. As industrial capitalism ramped into full gear, Americans began to experience what Karl Marx and Friedrich Engels foresaw: a "constant revolution of production, uninterrupted disturbance of all social conditions, everlasting uncertainty and agitation . . . All fixed, fast-frozen relations . . . swept away, all new-formed ones become antiquated before they can ossify."[2] Reacting to the excesses of the Gilded Age, America's liberal democratic ethos applied the brakes to the private accumulation of wealth and power, clawed back popular power from the plutocracy, and implemented a series of reforms—such as the eight-hour workday and an end to child labor—that made industrial America more humane.[3]

The reform era began when the railroads and eastern bankers, seeking to maximize their profit margins in the 1880s, squeezed America's farmers to the brink of financial ruin. No matter how hard farmers in the Midwest and South worked their fields, they could not escape debt and foreclosure. Hundreds of thousands of farmers began to believe that "hard work availed nothing."[4] Those who fed the nation began talking among themselves about their troubles and read books such as Henry George's *Progress and Poverty* (1879), a treatise on poverty among plenty and what to do about it. Banding together, farmers created the Populist movement in the 1890s with a distinct culture and cooperative economic ideology. At once liberal and democratic, "the Populists believed they could work together to be free individually."[5] The farmers sought to establish a system of economic self-help based on the world's first large-scale working-class cooperative. Mass democratic movements are notoriously difficult to form and sustain, but the Populists succeeded by making a fetish out of education and mobilization. A network of 40,000 lecturers spread the Populist gospel across the rural Midwest and the South; it was social media on foot and horseback.

Ultimately, the Populist movement joined the Democratic Party, with William Jennings Bryan carrying its flag in 1896, one of the nation's historic elections. Turnout was extremely high, passing an astounding 90 percent of eligible voters in many places, with Republican William McKinley edging Bryan 51.0 to 46.7 percent in the popular vote while triumphing in the Electoral College 271 to 176.[6] Campaigning against the business class, Democrats lost because they were unable to enlist the ethnic working class of the urban east to vote with the Western and Southern farmers. By the time the labor movement came into its own in the 1930s, a sizeable portion of America's farmers had left the fields or had descended into the helplessness of tenant farming and sharecropping. As historian Lawrence Goodwyn observed, "When the labor movement was ready . . . the mass of farmers no longer were."[7]

The free-market ideas of Adam Smith, limited government, and the economically independent yeoman citizenry of Thomas Jefferson constituted the ideals of the 19th century liberalism that Americans knew and loved; the Populists were no exception. The United States of the early and mid-19th century matched Smith's portrait of England in the 1770s in *The Wealth of Nations* with its apprentices, journeymen, and rising capitalists. In Smith's England and pre–Civil War America, business was competitive, the average factory was small, prices rose and fell as demand grew and ebbed, and prices, undistorted by corporate power, invoked changes in output and occupation. "It was a world in which each agent was forced to scurry after his self-interest in a vast social free-for-all."[8]

This 19th century world disintegrated as Adam Smith capitalism gave way to the "trusts" and corporate capitalism. Until the 1890s, the number of large corporations in the United States remained small. Over a ten-year span, however, mega-corporations sprang to life. Many of the 200 largest corporations that still dominate their industries today were formed during this period. As the old economic world vanished, Americans became outraged that the great conglomerates were overwhelming smaller competitors and rigging the game in their favor.[9] This realization set off first the Populist movement and then the great spurt of liberal reform of the Progressive Era.

IDA TARBELL VERSUS
JOHN D. ROCKEFELLER

When Ida Tarbell wrote *The History of the Standard Oil Company* in 1904, her deeply researched book captivated the nation as few have.[10] One of the nation's first investigative journalists, Tarbell unearthed damning evidence demonstrating beyond question that John D. Rockefeller had used unethical and illegal means to eliminate competitors as he built the nation's most powerful monopoly. When the yearlong magazine exposé became a book, it spanned more than 1,000 pages. Tarbell revealed that Rockefeller had operated in a ruthless, underhanded fashion—using predatory pricing to crush rivals, market power to secure illegal rebates from railroads, kickbacks to corrupt state legislatures, and even a national espionage system to track his competitors' every delivery. Gradually, systematically, and mercilessly, Rockefeller put his rivals out of business—first the independent oil producers in Pennsylvania, then his fellow Cleveland refineries, and afterward whoever stood in his way nationally. One modern biographer says Rockefeller relished predatory pricing; the tycoon "figured out every conceivable way to restrain trade, rig markets and suppress competition."[11] Driven by the goal of monopoly and domination, Rockefeller and his fellow plutocrats displayed a burning desire to destroy any and all competitors—respect for rules and laws be damned. When Tarbell and her fellow muckrakers lifted the veil, the resulting firestorm of moral outrage transformed American politics.[12]

Tarbell's central complaint against Standard Oil was that before Rockefeller arrived on the scene, small entrepreneurs had been "meeting their own needs" and living happily in the world of Adam Smith and John Locke. Before the appearance of Standard Oil, all sorts of individuals had made a successful living as independent businessmen in the oil business; the same was true across scores of industries. Then,

> Suddenly, at the heyday of this confidence, a big hand reached out from nobody knew where, to steal their conquest and throttle their future. The suddenness and the blackness of the assault on their business stirred to the bottom of their manhood and their sense of fairplay.[13]

In her outrage, Tarbell was speaking for millions of Americans, including her own father, an independent oil producer in Pennsylvania. Frank Tarbell's business collapsed and his partner committed suicide because of Standard Oil. These men had seen their life's work ruined by the great corporations that took what they wanted and broke the rules of decency and fair play at every chance. Playing the role of Dorothy in *The Wizard of Oz*, Tarbell drew back the curtain on Rockefeller and dealt a blow to the billionaire's reputation from which he never recovered. Once one of America's most admired men, Rockefeller died a hated villain.

In telling the truth about Rockefeller, Tarbell eviscerated the romantic image that the robber barons had fostered of themselves and their businesses. Rockefeller, Carnegie, Vanderbilt, Stanford, and Morgan preached initiative and the virtues of hard work. But their unchecked power dwarfed that of the state governments and their dishonest methods made a mockery of free-market "competition." After Tarbell's sensational bestseller, it was clear that the idyllic world of 19th century American capitalism was dead and gone. The nouveau corporations, based on market power and monopoly, had no interest in following Locke's dictum of leaving enough for others to succeed.[14] In this new 20th-century economy, small companies had to grow large or be swallowed, and men who previously flourished as independent business owners were forced to become employees, mere cogs in the corporate bureaucracy.

Tarbell, Upton Sinclair, and Lincoln Steffens—the original "muckrakers" who laid bare the brutal reality of industrial, urban America—touched the heartstrings of the public with their revelations, and recognition grew that something had to be done.[15] Progressivism was an effort to restore the economic individualism and political democracy that had been destroyed by the rise of the giant corporations and corrupt urban political machines.[16] In the United States, resistance to mighty trusts came as much from smaller capitalists as it did from blue-collar workers. Small businessmen and entrepreneurs, as well as labor groups, powered the liberal reform movement at the turn of the 20th century. Those aligned against the trusts included small landowners (who wanted their family farms to turn a profit), merchants and entrepreneurs (who wanted to run their own businesses), and owners of mid-sized and regional companies (who desired a chance to compete in the marketplace). These groups believed that a market controlled and dominated by massive corporations operating on a national or international scale was both profane and wrong.

Reformers fought for a return to Smith's vision of competitive capitalism without monopolies and corporate giantism. But how could this happen? Who had the capacity and power to fix the economic marketplace so it would work as the Scottish Smith said it would, and require everyone to play by the rules of fair competition—thus allowing thousands of small entrepreneurs the chance to succeed in the marketplace? What entity could take on the power of the mighty captains of industry and return America to the liberal heaven preached by John Locke and Adam Smith in which every man who worked hard had a chance at success? President Theodore Roosevelt stepped into the breach: "Great corporations exist only because they are created and safeguarded by our institutions; and it is therefore our right and our duty to see that they work in harmony with these institutions."[17]

Roosevelt sent a shot across the bow of the corporate elite when he directed the Justice Department to file an antitrust suit against Northern Securities, the J. P. Morgan railroad combine, and won the Supreme Court case in a 5-4 decision. Liberal Justice John Marshall Harlan, who famously dissented when the Court sanctioned racial discrimination in *Plessy v. Ferguson* in 1895, wrote the opinion. Roosevelt was among those impressed by Tarbell's investigative work and lucid pen, and soon the newly created federal Bureau of Corporations was conducting its own probe of Standard Oil.[18] In 1906, President Roosevelt directed the Department of Justice to use the Sherman Antitrust Act to break up the mighty Standard Oil Co., and in 1911 the Supreme Court issued a decision validating the dismantling of America's most powerful corporation into 33 smaller companies.[19] If the state governments were powerless to control the new corporations, a dynamic, forceful president demonstrated that the national government had the clout to take on the industrial titans.

Louis Brandeis addressed the Economic Club of New York on the issue of competition and monopoly in 1912. The future Supreme Court Justice claimed that the huge profits of the corporations were not due to efficiency, but instead were "due to control of the market," and that unless there existed "regulation of competition, its excesses will lead to the destruction of competition, and monopoly will take its place."[20] Teddy Roosevelt and Herbert Croly, author of *The Promise of American Life* (1909), took the position that certain monopolies could not be prevented and thus their regulation became the proper aim of the government. But Brandeis, a key adviser to President Woodrow Wilson (who appointed Brandeis to the Supreme Court), held that Roosevelt's stance would "legalize monopoly" and concede too much to the great industrialists. These tycoons had shown that they saw nothing wrong with destroying competition by a wide variety of unfair methods. Brandeis believed the largest corporations were too big and thus a distinct danger to democracy. Outlining the liberal reform position succinctly, he told his audience: "Private monopoly in industry is never permissible; it is never desirable, and is not inevitable; competition can be reserved, and where it is suppressed, can be restored."[21]

As part of his presidential campaign, Wilson declared that the nation's money supply must be controlled by the public sector. "The control of the system of banking" and of the money supply "must be vested in the Government itself, so that the banks may be the instruments, not the masters, of business and of individual enterprise and initiative." In a monumental move that shifted power from New York to Washington, D.C., President Wilson and Congress passed the Federal Reserve Act of 1913 to put the nation's money supply under the control of the Federal Reserve Board, whose members are nominated by the president and approved by the Senate. This single action dramatically and decisively changed the balance of power between American capitalism and democracy.[22]

THE TRIANGLE FIRE AND MODERN LIBERALISM

In 1911, the Triangle Shirtwaist Company in lower Manhattan burst into flames, killing 146 workers. Workplace fatalities were common at the time. By some estimates, 100 or more Americans "died on the job *every day*" in the roaring industrial economy at the start of the 20th century.[23] Mines collapsed, tunnels flooded, ships sank, hot liquid steel spilled, trains collided, machinery tore and mutilated. In David Von Drehle's vivid retelling of the March 25, 1911 inferno, the Triangle fire moved swiftly, consuming the eighth and ninth floors of a building in lower Manhattan: "Burning vigorously along the wooden machine tables, devouring the wooden chairs, marching in ragged formation across the room, the flames drove the last forty victims toward the Greene Street windows. A reporter on the scene wrote, 'Girls were burning to death before our eyes. There were jams on the windows. No one was lucky enough to jump, it seemed. But one by one the jams broke. Down came bodies in a shower, burning, smoking, lighted bodies, with the disheveled hair of girls trailing upward . . . There were thirty-three in that shower.'"[24]

In the aftermath of the Triangle tragedy, New York political and business elites felt intense public pressure to do something more than simply mourn the dead. In the prior year, workers had struck the Triangle factory over both pay and unsafe conditions. After the fire, union activists united with wealthy and powerful women in New York City urging politicians to act. In part, the impetus came from young urban progressives such as Frances Perkins, who later helped create Social Security as President Roosevelt's Secretary of Labor. A witness to the fire, Perkins was college educated and passionately devoted to the idea that "an active, humane government" could make a large difference in the lives of average Americans. She believed in women's suffrage and in unions. Perkins had been working in Albany for the Consumer League of New York, lobbying for a bill that "would limit the workweek for women and minors to fifty-four hours—nine hours a day, six days a week." The bill went nowhere. The New York City Tammany Hall machine controlled the state government, and Charles F. Murphy, Tammany's "Boss," decided what legislation lived and died. Tammany was about power, not reform, and served two constituencies—the wealthy and its traditional Irish Catholic ethnic base.[25]

In 1910, however, Boss Murphy surprised observers by placing legislative leadership in the hands of two young men—Robert F. Wagner and Alfred E. Smith. Though more intelligent and talented than the regular machine hacks, these future political stars still carried out Murphy's orders. A savvy political leader, Murphy saw the great surge of immigrants coming to New York, the growing power of the union movement, and calls by reformers such as Perkins to improve workplace conditions; he also knew how to count votes. When Perkins previously lobbied Tammany on legislation that would limit the number of hours that industrial workers could work, Murphy put his political donors above the needs of workers, and said no. Then came the Triangle factory inferno, and Murphy recognized it was time to act. The New York City of his younger days was gone. The city had multiplied sixfold in population, factories jammed the boroughs, new immigrants poured into the city with "little sense of debt toward Tammany and even less affection." The Triangle fire hit the working poor whose votes he and his political machine needed most.[26]

In Albany, a nine-member Factory Investigating Commission formed with Robert Wagner named chairman and Alfred Smith vice chairman. The commission had broad powers to subpoena witnesses, utilize experts, and change its own rules. The legislature created the Commission, but Murphy, Wagner, and Smith controlled it completely. The three Tammany leaders swiftly recast New York's Democratic Party as a party of liberal reform. Riding on the cresting wave of progressive change, they anticipated Woodrow Wilson's winning presidential campaign in 1912.[27] Tammany's timing was impeccable: the urban machine that strongly opposed the strike of female garment workers in 1910 drove change two years later. Smith and Wagner became the liberal heroes of New York politics and the Empire State the leading edge of the Democratic spear that would result in Franklin Roosevelt's New Deal. The Factory Investigating Commission rocketed Smith to the governor's office and a run for the presidency in 1928, with Wagner rising to the U.S. Senate. After two terms as New York governor, Roosevelt was elected president in 1932. In his stellar congressional career, Wagner—"the legislative ramrod of the New Deal"—championed the federal legislation that established Social Security, guaranteed unemployment insurance and workers' compensation, authorized public housing, and authored the Wagner Act, which established the right of unions to organize.[28] The National Labor Relations Act (NLRA) of 1935 remains the single most important piece of labor legislation ever enacted in the United States. Two years later, the Supreme Court's decision in *N.L.R.B. v. Jones & Laughlin Steel*, upholding the NLRA, signaled the official end of master-servant common-law governance of labor relations.

NEW DEAL LEGACY: SETTING LIMITS ON POWER AND THE REACH OF WEALTH

Americans idealize the small town America of Tocqueville and Lincoln for good reason. Across the 19th century, people who were white and male were unusually free and able to follow their dreams—owning their own farms, creating businesses, heading west to find their fortunes, serving on town councils, and worshiping the God of their choice. The goal of liberals in the twentieth and twenty-first centuries is for everyone to have these same opportunities. Liberals and progressives are not socialists; they admire and cheer the economic power of capitalism and have no desire—as true socialists do—to seize control of the means of production or to nationalize large swaths of the economy.[29] In the United States, people have the freedom and opportunity to achieve economic success and acquire great wealth. But doing so, liberals insist, does not empower economic superstars to use their wealth and power to lord over others and create norms of privilege, hierarchy, exclusion, and entrenched inequality. Liberals cheer capitalism, but against the right, liberals argue that economic success should not automatically spill over and dominate other spheres of life, such as politics or culture.[30]

Today, Senators Bernie Sanders and Elizabeth Warren deserve credit for articulating with gusto the age-old conflict between a financial elite who possess more than they earn and average workers who earn more than they possess.[31] Behind attacks by liberal Democrats on the excessive power of Wall Street lies this central principle. The generous freedom of American society sanctions neither radical economic inequality nor a self-perpetuating oligarchy; as a consequence, liberals believe society has the right to set limits on the power and the reach of wealth. Writing more than 300 years ago, Locke defended the idea of private property, but he was not an apologist for unlimited capitalist accumulation.[32] In fact, Locke defended regulating property on behalf of the public good as one of the central purposes of law and government.[33] Neither liberals, moderates, nor classic conservatives want to return the United States to the period of the late 19th century, when the federal government was virtually nonexistent and consisted primarily of the courts, the Post Office, and the Department of War. That, however, is the goal of the antigovernment reactionary right led by House Freedom Caucus leader Mark Meadows, Senate Majority Leader Mitch McConnell, and Trump White House Chief of Staff Mick Mulvaney, who doubles as director of the Office of Management and Budget. They insist that modern liberalism is somehow illegitimate, must be destroyed, and that the nation must revert to the unregulated capitalism of the first Gilded Age. Liberals argue this would be a terrible mistake and point to the wonders of the New Deal state as evidence of how government has improved the lives of average Americans.

WONDERS OF THE NEW DEAL STATE

"History abundantly shows that the intervention of the national government has enlarged liberty, justice, income and opportunity for the average American." So wrote Arthur M. Schlesinger Jr., gazing back on the 20th century just before the millennium. The Pulitzer Prize–winning historian and adviser to President Kennedy regarded capitalism as a necessary condition for democracy because a free market economy ensures that the "people command resources independent of the state." At the same time, Schlesinger argued that the "necessity of capitalism does not argue for the subservience to the capitalists."[34] Progressives and liberals did more than rescue America from the Great Depression and save the world from Hitler and Stalin; Roosevelt and his followers also built the New Deal state. The public sector programs of the New Deal and the Great Society laid the foundation for the largest and most prosperous middle-class society in history. American citizens—illiberals, conservatives, moderates, and liberals alike—have benefited immensely from big government and the New Deal programs launched by Franklin Roosevelt and his brain trust. Americans own the homes they live in due to the thirty-year fixed-rate mortgages, enjoy retirement cushioned by Social Security and Medicare, travel metropolitan freeways and interstate highways built with federal dollars, and flourish in careers made possible because of excellent public universities and/or government-subsidized loans. Activist tax-and-spend government has made life far more productive, bountiful, satisfying, and humane than it would be if these programs did not exist. The seven following examples stand as proof:

THE THIRTY-YEAR FIXED MORTGAGE
AND HOME OWNERSHIP

The thirty-year fixed mortgage is a prime example of government action that has permitted millions of Americans to enjoy a higher standard of living at the same time as it has stimulated private sector growth. Before the Great Depression, few Americans could afford to own their homes. Mortgages had short maturities with homeowners usually renegotiating their loans every year; the typical mortgage had a variable interest rate and a high down payment, and usually included a balloon feature.[35] As the upfront costs of buying a home were far too high for most families, home ownership typically was reserved for the wealthy elite. When the Depression hit, the average price of homes fell 30 to 40 percent, and mortgage foreclosure rates shot skyward. In response, the Roosevelt administration stepped in with HOLC and FHA, alphabet soup for the Home Owners Loan Corporation and the Federal Housing Administration. The HOLC was set up to assist homeowners behind on their payments largely through no fault of their own. The FHA saw the need and the market for a lending product that allowed borrowers in their working years to make affordable payments. Thirty years was viewed as a reasonable amount of time to assume that the borrower would be in the workforce before retiring. The FHA program was an unqualified success and the thirty-year fixed became the conventional mortgage, enabling tens of millions of people to afford a home of their own.[36] When government nudges the economy in a certain direction, the result often is a boon to private sector entrepreneurs and investors. The homebuilders who made fortunes during the rush to build the new suburbs that followed the end of World War II owed their success, in large measure, to the creation of the thirty-year fixed mortgage.

THE GI BILL

Few government programs have been as widely celebrated as the Servicemen's Readjustment Act of 1944, better known as the GI Bill. Following World War II, an estimated 15.7 million veterans returned to the safety and normalcy of civilian life. From this huge veteran cohort, nearly 80 percent, or an estimated 12.4 million, benefited from the GI Bill for college education and training as well as other provisions that allowed them to buy homes, start businesses, or run the farm. When surveys asked what difference it made to these veterans, three-quarters answered, "The GI Bill changed my life." The bill was Roosevelt's New Deal for veterans and

united a liberal president with a conservative Congress.[37] Management guru
Peter Drucker viewed the GI Bill as "the most important event of the 20th
century" because government-subsidized higher education sparked the shift
to a postindustrial, information economy.[38]

SOCIAL SECURITY

Social Security has long been America's most popular government program.
The nation's distinctive form of social insurance is "a collective possession
of all American workers, who earned their old-age, disability, and survivors
benefits by paying for those of the preceding generation."[39] More than 95
percent of Americans participate either as beneficiaries or through payroll
tax contributions. Social Security does not extend lavish benefits; instead, it
provides retirees as well as those who are disabled or survivors of a deceased
breadwinner an income floor. The average monthly Social Security payment to retired workers was $1,461 in 2019 or $17,532 a year.[40] With more
than one in four American seniors with little or no income outside their
Social Security checks, this federal social insurance program keeps millions
of seniors out of the most dire poverty at a time when the private economy
provides less income support for retirees through pensions or other benefits.[41] Only an estimated 30 percent of Americans receive support from
private pensions, while more than 90 percent of retirees receive Social
Security.[42] Approximately two-thirds of seniors relied on Social Security
for half or more of their income; this proportion is even higher for people
of color as well as women, singles, and those who held low-income jobs.[43]

Social Security is strikingly efficient. In terms of the ratio of benefits
delivered to administrative overhead, the social insurance program outper-
forms private insurance plans by a large margin; its benefits are provided at
an administrative cost of less than one penny for every tax dollar collected.[44]
In recent decades, however, critics of Social Security have worked hard to
sow the seeds of doubt about its future solvency. In actuality, the program
is projected to experience no long-term funding problem. Social Security is
not going broke and, as experts Nancy Altman and Eric Kingson write in
Social Security Works!, expanding it would help us all.[45] The much-bandied
2037 end-date for the trust fund surplus is an actuarial projection based on

more stringent accounting practices, not prophecy.[46] If the trust fund does, in fact, need more money, simple fixes are available. First, it is possible to raise the payroll tax gradually and at a rate slower than inflation; this is how Congress kept the program solvent in its first four decades. Second, Congress could raise the cap on the percentage of annual income subject to the payroll tax so that more than 90 percent of all earned income in the country would be taxed to pay for Social Security instead of approximately 86 percent. Third, an increase in the minimum wage and a boost in wages across the economy that helps workers recover some of their decline in earning power over the past three decades would also boost tax receipts. Finally, government action to slow the rapid rise in healthcare costs could help fund the trust. In combination, these steps could keep Social Security solvent far into the future.[47]

MEDICARE

Medicare—the Great Society program that provides medical care to the elderly—is the other cornerstone of income security in modern-day America. Largely because of the advent of Medicare (and its cousin Medicaid) during the Johnson administration, the percentage of seniors living in poverty plunged from 35.2 percent in 1959 to 14.6 percent in 1982.[48] In 2018, only 1 percent of the nation's seniors lacked health insurance, down from nearly half in 1963.[49] Tackling a critical piece of the healthcare challenge, liberals in the 1960s focused on assisting the elderly. The landmark Medicare bill became a reality when Wilbur Mills, the Democratic chairman of the House Ways and Means Committee, combined the Kennedy-Johnson proposal for hospital care (Part A of Medicare) with the Republican support for physician services/outpatient coverage (Part B of Medicare), and then added a third program providing additional assistance to the states for health care for the poor (Medicaid).[50] President Johnson signed the historic act into law on July 30, 1965. With the stroke of his pen, a sizable portion of the nation's population suddenly had healthcare coverage with uniform national standards for eligibility and benefits. The improvement in the lives of the nation's seniors was immediate and profound:

"When Medicare became law, it proved to be a game changer," says Peter Lee Sr. (now 92). Before Medicare, he recalls L.A. County-USC Medical Center overflowing with elderly patients on gurneys who'd been discharged but needed interim care before going home. "So we always had patients in the hall," Lee Sr. says, adding that after Medicare was implemented, "the halls were all empty."

"They were empty because seniors all of a sudden had someone who would pay for long-term care that wasn't there before," says Peter Lee Jr. (now executive director of Cover California). Medicare began paying for transitional nursing home care, hospital care, and other treatments for those 65 and older, no matter their income. "It was a dramatic, overnight change that affected millions of Americans," says Lee Jr.[51]

After battling Medicare as the leading edge of socialism, the American Medical Association and the general medical community accepted the program.

INTERSTATE HIGHWAY SYSTEM

It is nearly impossible to imagine the United States without its massive system of interstate highways and metropolitan freeways "that carry the life of the nation."[52] These ribbons of asphalt and concrete now extend nearly 50,000 miles and carry approximately 25 percent of the nation's vehicular traffic.[53] The federal government paid 90 percent of the construction tab for these arteries of commerce that connect major cities with suburbs. As a young army officer, President Dwight Eisenhower had driven with an army convoy across the United States in 1919 and was singularly disturbed by the poor quality of the roads. The 3,251-mile trip from Washington, D.C., to San Francisco took sixty-two days.[54] Later, as the Supreme Commander of the Allied forces in Europe, Ike saw the German autobahn and envisioned a similar system of superhighways for the United States, and as president he championed passage of the Federal Highway Act of 1956. Few actions by a Congress and a president have had such a monumental effect on American society than this legislation that gave the country a unified freeway/expressway system.[55]

FOOD STAMPS

The Supplemental Nutrition Assistance Program (SNAP) is yet another example of big government working efficiently and humanely. During the Great Recession, SNAP or "food stamps" became the nation's safety net of last resort. In 2007, approximately 26.3 million Americans received food stamps. By the fall of 2011, this number had jumped to nearly 46 million—one in seven people, with a shocking one in four children. When the *New York Times* examined the data in 2009, it discovered there were 2 million families across the country, equaling 6 million people, whose *only* income and daily meals were made possible by food stamps.[56] This figure climbed closer to 3 million families as the pain of the Great Recession persisted and many people found their only shelter in a car.[57]

PAT BROWN AND CALIFORNIA DREAMING

Big government liberalism was not limited to the federal government. California, in particular, was a microcosm of the liberal can-do spirit of the New Deal that built modern America. Under the gubernatorial administration of Edmund G. "Pat" Brown (1959 to 1967), the state put in place an extensive freeway system, a massive water project, and one of the world's greatest university systems. Today, we think of California in terms of Apple, Facebook, Google, Hollywood, and the rich agricultural soil of the San Joaquin Valley. But the private sector entrepreneurship that makes California one of the top 5 or 6 economies on the planet rests on the infrastructure largely constructed during Pat Brown's tenure: freeways and water and a massive system of higher education (10 University of California campuses with 238,000 students, 23 California State University campuses with 484,297 students, and 114 community colleges with 21 million students).

6

The New Deal and Reaction:
The Libertarian Fallacy

FRANKLIN ROOSEVELT AND THE NEW DEAL

In his 1926 essay "The End of Laissez-Faire," John Maynard Keynes wrote that laissez-faire has a powerful grip on the popular imagination for three reasons: it is simple, it conforms to the "needs and wishes" of business, and it graphs easily with Darwin's survival of the fittest. Additionally, the doctrine of noninterference in the economy came into vogue following an 18th century in which everything the state did "seemed, injurious or unsuccessful." If laissez-faire were true, then economists and political philosophers "could retire in favour of the businessman" who can attain the goal of society just by pursuing his own private profit. The trouble, Keynes said, is that laissez-faire often does not work in practice because "the conclusion that individuals acting independently for their own advantage will produce the greatest aggregate of wealth, depends on a variety of unreal assumptions." Keynes explained that instead of being part of the economic theory of Adam Smith, Ricardo, or Malthus, laissez-faire emerged as part of the marketing campaign for free trade waged by the "so-called Manchester School." It further penetrated the public consciousness in grade school books such as *Easy Lessons for the Use of Young People* (1850), which concludes: "More harm than good is likely to be done by almost any interference of Government with men's money transactions, whether letting and leasing, or buying and selling of any kind." Mainstream economists maintained that "the maxim of *laissez faire* has no scientific basis whatever, but is at best a mere handy rule of practice."[1] But while economists of the first rank cast doubt on the truth and efficacy of laissez-faire as sound economic policy, the principle of noninterference in the economy was sacrosanct among conservatives and held sway with a majority of the U.S. Supreme Court from the 1890s to 1937. President Herbert Hoover pursued a largely laissez-faire economic policy in the first years of the Great Depression, with disastrous results.[2]

When President Franklin Roosevelt took office in January 1933, the United States faced a state of emergency, with unemployment climbing toward 30 percent and men fighting for food scraps in garbage cans.[3] Hunger spread across the industrialized West and both capitalism and democracy seemed to be in danger of dying as fascists on the right and communists on the left rose to power; people were desperate for direct, vigorous action and the new president responded. Telling the nation "the only thing we have to fear is fear itself," Roosevelt in his inaugural address said the greatest task was "to put people to work." And he did, as he quickly launched the Civil Works Administration (CWA), the Civilian Conservation Corps (CCC), the Federal Emergency Relief Administration (FERA), the Works Progress Administration (WPA), and the Tennessee Valley Authority (TVA). Administrator extraordinaire Harry Hopkins told Roosevelt he could create four million jobs if he had the money to do it. Hopkins and Roosevelt were aware of the stigma of relief and the importance of protecting people's dignity; CWA job applicants did not have to prove how poor they were. Applications poured in, with 70,000 people signing up in Chicago in one day and 150,000 in North Carolina in a single week. More than 800,000 workers received checks on CWA's first payday in November and in January 1934 Hopkins achieved his goal with 4.2 million Americans earning paychecks, with an average salary of $13 a week. Workers built or renovated 40,000 schools, constructed and repaired 250,000 miles of road, erected 469 airports, laid 12 million feet of sewer pipe, built 250,000 outdoor restrooms, and renovated thousands of public buildings, including state capitols, city halls, county courthouses, libraries, police stations, hospitals, and jails. In the CWA's short life to deal with emergency need, Hopkins was particularly proud "that not a single county in America was omitted from this enterprise." Yet with all these jobs, still some 9 million remained unemployed.[4] The WPA, which succeeded the CWA, employed 8.5 million people in its seven-year history, working on 1.4 million projects ranging from parks and playgrounds to roads, bridges, public buildings, and sports stadiums.[5]

Speaking to Secretary of Labor Frances Perkins, one of the lead architects of the Social Security Act of 1935, Roosevelt summed up the liberal philosophy of the New Deal in a single sentence: "We are going to make a country in which no one is left out."[6] Roosevelt sought to permanently improve the lives of the millions of Americans who were ill-nourished, ill-clad, and ill-housed because of the Great Depression. His fundamental goal was to provide for working Americans some measure of the "economic security and predictability of life's material circumstances that his own patrician class took for granted."[7] The president stressed our interconnectedness in the modern economy:

> Our civilization cannot endure unless we, as individuals, realize our responsibility to and dependence on the rest of the world. For it is literally true that the "self-supporting" man or woman has become as extinct as the man of the stone age. Without the help of thousands of others, any one of us would die, naked and starved. Consider the bread upon our table, the clothes on our backs, the luxuries that make life pleasant; how many men worked in sunlit fields, in dark mines, in the fierce heat of molten metal, and among looms and wheels of countless factories, in order to create them for our use and enjoyment . . . in the final analysis, the progress of civilization will be retarded if any large body of citizens falls behind.[8]

In the blizzard of new laws, agencies, and programs, the early New Deal of 1933–1935 often is distinguished from the second New Deal of 1935–1937. In his first term, FDR and his administration focused on stabilizing the banking system, creating emergency job programs, and promoting cooperative action within industry to increase employment and prevent a spiral of falling prices. After a conservative Supreme Court ruled the National Recovery Act (NRA) and the Agricultural Adjustment Act (AAA) unconstitutional, the second New Deal abandoned industrial cooperation efforts to emphasize antitrust policy as well as larger institutional reforms to provide long-term protection to the vulnerable.[9]

The principle of security linked all the efforts together. "Achieving security was the leitmotif of virtually everything the New Deal attempted," says Stanford historian David M. Kennedy.[10] In 1933, the Glass-Steagall Act improved everyone's financial security by separating commercial banking from riskier investment banks dealing in securities, and the Federal Deposit Insurance Corporation was created to insure deposits. In 1935 the Wagner Act improved job security by establishing the National Labor Relations Board (NLRB), granting labor legal status and unions the right to organize, and the epic Social Security Act provided old-age financial security.

Roosevelt may have been an enemy of his class, but he was a friend of capitalism. His goal was to rescue and strengthen capitalism and make it work for the country at large and not just for a small financial elite. The president and his liberal colleagues in Congress built a larger, stronger national government, but they did not nationalize industries nor did they impose their wishes on society with the heavy hand of an imperial state. In fact, their work often was achieved with a "remarkably delicate hand." Before the New Deal, Wall Street investors lacked information and transparency, which in large part contributed to the 1929 crash. The establishment of the Securities and Exchange Commission (SEC) cured this by mandating the disclosure of detailed information—"such as balance sheets, profit and loss statements, and the names and compensation of corporate officers"—about firms whose securities were being publicly traded. This information required verification by independent auditors. While SEC regulations imposed a reporting burden on public companies, transparency supplied buyers and sellers in the financial markets much improved information on which to base their decisions. The New Deal reforms dramatically improved the financial heart of American capitalism by making Wall Street work the way free markets should work.[11]

In a second example, New Deal housing policies stabilized a major sector of the economy in a skillful public-private partnership that again introduced reliable information into a market system. Similar to those of the financial sector, the housing reforms did not check or hinder capital flows, but instead liberated investment. The New Deal established the Home Owners Loan Corporation (HOLC) and the Federal Housing Administration (FHA) along with the creation of the Federal National Mortgage Association (Fannie Mae). The HOLC introduced uniform national appraisal methods across the real estate industry, the FHA insured long-term mortgages and defined national standards of home construction, and Fannie Mae furnished lending institutions with a mechanism for reselling their mortgages which increased lender liquidity for more construction. Together, these innovations removed unnecessary risk from home buying and selling.

Neither making loans nor building houses, the FHA and Fannie Mae changed the institutional landscape and, as a result, an unprecedented amount of private capital flowed into the homebuilding industry in the post–World War II decades. As lenders became more confident, the thirty-year mortgage with fixed monthly payments became the norm and millions of Americans became homeowners. It was a win-win-win for lenders, builders, and consumers. And it happened because the policy wonks of the New Deal intervened, in a positive, creative way, to structure a "free market" in housing that worked for everyone. Forty years after the New Deal, nearly two-thirds of Americans lived in their own homes; only 1 percent of the population lived in public housing. This stood in sharp contrast to postwar England, where half the population lived in public housing, and France, where more than 30 percent of the public called government-owned housing projects home.[12]

Only two years after he had won the 1936 presidential election in a rout, a conservative backlash handed FDR a stinging defeat. Before the 1938 congressional elections, the president campaigned heavily in the South on the platform of raising factory wages; he wanted to end Dixie's historic low-wage tradition and bring the South into the modern era by accelerating efficiency and mechanization. If he could transform the South, FDR thought he could make the Democratic Party more steadfastly liberal. Instead, the illiberal Southerners he opposed won. South Carolina's "Cotton" Ed Smith declared Roosevelt's Fair Labor Standards Act of 1937 unnecessary because a man could support a family on 50 cents a day in his home state. Reflecting on the recalcitrant nature of the South, Roosevelt mused dejectedly: "It takes a long, long time to bring the past up to the present."[13] The anti–New Deal sentiment was not just in the South. An anti-urban wave stood in opposition to Roosevelt's liberal agenda, not only in the overwhelmingly rural South, but also across New England, the Midwest, and the West. The template for modern Red State America and President Trump's 2016 Electoral College victory from the South to the upper Midwest to the West can be seen in the 1938 midterm results.[14] At the same time, a reactionary ideology crystalized in reaction to the New Deal.[15] A critical piece of this mindset was strongly anti-statist and libertarian and was championed most effectively by two refugees fleeing Europe—the novelist Ayn Rand and the economist F. A. Hayek. Their writings became the holy texts of the reactionary counterrevolution.

AYN RAND SMUGGLES A VICIOUS ELITISM INTO AMERICAN CULTURE

Ayn Rand (1905–1982), a refugee from Lenin's Soviet Union, reinvented herself in early Hollywood as a novelist with a mission. Celebrating a winner-take-all philosophy, her books—especially *The Fountainhead* (1943) and *Atlas Shrugged* (1957)—continue to exert a powerful influence on popular culture. One recent biographer reports that Rand's four novels—all published before 1960—sold more than 800,000 copies in 2008 alone. The reading public named *Atlas Shrugged* and *The Fountainhead* as the greatest English language novels of the 20th century in a Modern Library poll ahead of *Ulysses*, *The Sound and the Fury*, *Catch–22*, and *Invisible Man*.[16] Readers originally snapped up Rand's novels because they were page-turners. With complex plots, mystery, and drama—but absent nuance—the books are romance novels; read another way, they are soap operas with a political argument.[17] Good yarns, the books lack the subtlety of high literature. Instead, they are pulp fiction—similar in writing and plot to run-of-the-mill noir crime fiction, but in Rand's case it is not jealous wives with fingerprints on a bloody knife. Instead, it is the government, the liberals, and moochers playing the villain. For Rand, the noir is the big dark government, the liberal nanny state. Donald Trump's dystopian portrait of America in horrible decline—"rusted-out factories scattered like tombstones ... students deprived of all knowledge ... the crime and the gangs and the drugs ... this American carnage"—is right out of Rand.[18]

Rand's fiction—*We the Living*, about Soviet Russia; *Anthem*, science fiction about equality destroying the world; *The Fountainhead*, about the gifted and arrogant architect Howard Roark contending with "second-handers"; and *Atlas Shrugged*, about the suffering industrial elite finally saying "enough" and going on strike in a futuristic America ruined by socialist ideals—is infused with and unified by two themes: a hatred of Soviet Communism and heroes guided by a harshly illiberal, anti-democratic philosophy of life. The Randian philosophy was inspired, in good measure, by her simplistic, social Darwinist reading of Friedrich Nietzsche (1844–1900). A great philosopher who has influenced hundreds of major writers, Nietzsche is a gifted stylist but notoriously difficult to understand. As with the Bible, readers find a great diversity of ideas in his dozen-plus books. Often writing in a series of aphorisms that may be considered thought experiments, he is not a systemic thinker.[19] In his pathbreaking *Nietzsche: Philosopher, Psychologist, Antichrist*, first published in 1950—which sought to rescue Nietzsche from the crude reading of the fascists—Walter Kaufmann noted, "It was the surprising merit of Karl Jaspers' *Nietzsche* (1936) that he counseled Nietzsche's readers never to rest until they had found passages contradicting those found first."[20] Nietzsche's aphorisms transform the reader's consciousness with "his subversions, teasings, and insults" aiming to shake us out of our compla-cency in our thinking and challenge us to become something more than mediocre. Aphoristic writing at Nietzsche's level challenges the reader to turn a sentence into a paragraph.[21] As a result, he can be read in quite divergent ways; if nothing else, he is a radical philosopher, at odds with modern society.

What he seems to dislike is every aspect of contemporary civilization . . . His underlying view that if we don't make a drastically new start we are doomed, since we are living in the wreckage of two thousand and more years of fundamentally mistaken ideas about almost everything that matters.[22]

Rand's understanding of Nietzsche was shaped by the first generation of scholarship by authors such as Oswald Spengler and H. L. Mencken that shaded in an authoritarian, social Darwinist direction; Rand biographer Jennifer Burns writes that Rand viewed Nietzschean ethics as a call for the strong to dominate the weak. In the first book written in English about the philosopher, Mencken mistakenly equated Nietzsche's "Will to Power" with Arthur Schopenhauer's "will to live," which later scholars view as a gross error.[23] It is true that in beautiful prose, the late 19th century German philosopher presented dark ideas about a noble aristocracy acting out its own moral code; Nietzsche famously wrote that Western morality and Christianity "amounts to a vindictive effort to poison the happiness of the fortunate."[24] But modern scholarship argues that the twisted interpretation of Nietzsche favored by Rand and the European fascists is a gross distortion of the philosopher's intentions. Misconceptions of Nietzsche are famous. For example, misreadings of Nietzsche's famous phrase, "will to power," including its use by the Nazis, arise, in part, because of confusion between *Kraft* (force) and *Macht* (power). Nietzsche makes a distinction between the two, viewing *Kraft* as primordial strength while *Macht* is closely connected to sublimation and "self-overcoming," the conscious directing of *Kraft* for creative purposes.[25] Some of his readers miss the distinction.

Nietzsche's interest was "in greatness rather than goodness" and he argued that traditional morality was refuge of the weak.[26] But his passionate critique of Christian morality and his own morality is easily misunderstood. Kaufmann argues that Nietzsche denounces "not sincere Christianity, but insincere Christianity."[27] In *Beyond Good and Evil*, Nietzsche writes:

The strength of a person's spirit would then be measured by how much 'truth' he could tolerate, or more precisely, to what extent he *needs* to have it diluted, disguised, sweetened, muted, falsified.[28]

Nietzsche charged that the Christian faith too often is the refuge of people who have not pushed themselves to be the superior beings that some people can become. Focusing on the gifted among mankind, such as Socrates, he was contemptuous of ideologies which put people to sleep. He thought greatness was possible, but only a few would pursue it because, as one modern interpreter writes, "there is no greatness without a readiness and capacity to withstand, absorb, and use to the best purpose an immense quantity of pain."[29] Nietzsche was an Abraham Maslow of higher flourishing—exploring the highest reaches of human accomplishment and consciousness. But Kaufmann and other scholars argue that this goal of *self*-perfection—something that philosophers from Plato to Kant saw as the goal of their morality—was not a celebration of the heroic loner, but was something that would be done in community with others. For example, like the Greeks, Nietzsche saw friendship as "a means toward the self-perfection of two human beings." Genuine friends can help one another gain self-mastery.[30]

But a sophisticated reading of Nietzsche is possible while also understanding that his words, on their face, can be read in a savagely illiberal way.[31] In *Beyond Good and Evil*, for example, the philosopher championed "a return to an aristocratic social order in which the happiness of the vast majority would be sacrificed for an elite caste."[32]

> The crucial thing about a good and healthy aristocracy, however, is that it does not feel that it is a function (whether of monarchy or community) but rather its *essence* and highest justification—and that therefore it has no misgivings in condoning the sacrifice of a vast number of people who must *for its sake* be oppressed and diminished into incomplete people, slaves, tools. Its fundamental belief must simply be that society can *not* exist for its own sake, but rather only as a foundation and scaffolding to enable a select kind of creature to ascend to its higher task and in general to its higher *existence*—much like those sun-loving climbing plants on Java (called *Sipo Matador*) whose tendrils encircle an oak tree so

long and so repeatedly that finally, high above it but still supported by it, they are able to unfold their coronas in the free air
and make a show of their happiness."[33]

In Nietzsche, Rand saw a philosopher who argued in favor of the
strong individual. She was obsessed that there were two types of people
in the world: those who think for themselves and those who have a hollow
core—formulating their goals based on what appears important in other
people's eyes. She labeled the second type, "second-handers," those who
follow the ideas and values of others. Based on her reading of Nietzsche's
critique of Judeo-Christian morality, Rand sought to dramatize in nov-
elistic form the advantages of egoism as morality. Howard Roark, the
hero of *The Fountainhead*, was an ideal of what men should be. Presented
initially as "'monstrously selfish,' by the end of the book her readers would
understand that a traditional vice—selfishness—was actually a virtue."
She read Nietzsche's genealogy of morals, his devastating assault on the
development and meaning of traditional Western morality, as having
cleared the field of Christianity and she saw herself as one of the philosophers of the future. Christianity taught the importance of placing
others before the self; this she thought was an ethical mandate for the
collective to dominate the individual. In order to fight the scourge of
communism, it was necessary to preach a new individualistic ethic based
on selfishness.[34]

An authoritarian conception of Nietzsche lurks behind Rand's characters
and plots. Standing aloof and lacking empathy for ordinary people, her
heroes are cold in the special way that she understood Nietzsche believed
befit society's natural nobility. Nietzsche viewed the American and French
revolutions as tragic events because the destruction of aristocratic society
eliminated the possibility of creativity, distinction, and human greatness. He makes this ringing rejection of the Declaration of Independence
and Lincoln: "In the past, every elevation of the type 'human being' was
achieved by an aristocratic society—this will always be the case: by a
society that believes in a great ladder of hierarchy and value differentia-
tion between people and that *requires slavery in one sense or another*."[35] In
Rand's fictional world, superior beings are supremely self-contained and
focus only on themselves; her heroes understand that the "slave morality"

of the Judeo-Christian ethic leads to socialism and that the social welfare policies of modern liberal states are profound mistakes.

In both *The Fountainhead* and *Atlas Shrugged*, Rand celebrates individualism and American capitalism, and much more. She offers moral fables that justify a new aristocracy—that of wealth and money—ruling the land. (It is doubtful that Nietzsche would have seen America's capitalist class as superior human beings.) Speaking to a fellow scion of great wealth, Dagny Taggart, in *Atlas Shrugged*, Francisco d'Anconia says, "We are the only aristocracy left in the world—the aristocracy of money."[36] Celebrating the genius, ingenuity, and energy of the industrial elite would be one thing, but Rand has a Manichaean worldview that sharply divides human beings into two castes—the deserving and the undeserving, the producers and the looters. In the staggering 1,000-plus pages of *Atlas Shrugged*, Rand worships her unfeeling heroes while damning the majority of mankind for being unproductive leeches. Her heroes have a singular focus on their calling, but cannot help noticing the overabundance of "the weakling, the fool, the rotter, the liar, the failure, the coward, the fraud."[37] In a review in *National Review*, Whittaker Chambers wrote, "from almost any page of *Atlas Shrugged*, a voice can be heard, from painful necessity, commanding: "To a gas chamber—go!"[38]

In *Atlas Shrugged*, Rand achieves a clever rhetorical reversal of Marx by creating a sense of suffering and pathos for the "1 percent." A modern bible for an anguished elite and her readers who identify with the capitalist "doers," the narrative is about the mysterious disappearance of all those with talent and drive. Here we have the *true workers* of the world united in a strike that shuts down not just a steel plant or railroad, but the country's *entire* economy; the only labor force that really matters has quit. Rand is relentless, unforgiving, and unsparing in announcing her manifesto of the elite.[39] Readers looking for an explanation for society's collapse find it in John Galt's epic speech at the end of the novel—reminiscent of one of Fidel Castro's tirades against the United States.

Corey Robin makes an excellent point about Rand when he writes, "However much she liked to pit the genius against the mass, her fiction always betrays a secret communion between the two." At the climax of both *The Fountainhead* and *Atlas Shrugged*, her heroes address the unlettered in a lengthy speech that results in the masses recognizing their greatness. The conflict in Rand's novels, says Robin, is not between the super-gifted individual and the masses but "between the demigod-creator and all those unproductive elements of society—the intellectuals, bureaucrats, and middlemen"—who are jealous of his genius and seek to block his freedom of action. This is the great man theory of society and easily becomes part of a Caesar-authoritarian plot line—"it bends toward fascism."[40]

At its core, Rand's political argument is a radically simple gloss on her vulgar reading of Nietzsche. As with her ideological colleagues Spencer and Hayek, she came to the United States from Europe. In the Russian Revolution, her father's business was seized and her family—Jewish members of the bourgeois elite of St. Petersburg—lost its wealth and stature. The grown-up Alisa Rosenbaum never forgot that Bolshevik soldiers, carrying guns and carrying out directives for Comrade Lenin on that winter day in 1918, spoke of fairness and equality and a better society for all. The lesson she absorbed: speaking about helping others was a thin disguise for coercion and power.[41] Armed with her new America identity—the Nordic-sounding Ayn Rand—she used her novels to warn Americans of the collectivist nightmare.

While an undergraduate at the University of Leningrad, Rand discovered Nietzsche and, like other adoring fans of the German philosopher, Rand never doubted for a minute that she was one of the gifted, the potential Supermen of whom her hero spoke.[42] Her love affair was such that a cousin taunted her with a biting critique—Nietzsche "beat you to all your ideas."[43] Rand poured scathing criticism on "second-handers," people who borrow their ideas from others. Yet, just as Peter Keating in *The Fountainhead* feverishly borrowed ideas and inspiration from Howard Roark, so Rand took large elements of her elitist philosophy from her reductionist reading of Nietzsche. During her early days in Hollywood, her journals were filled with the phrases "Nietzsche and I think" and "as Nietzsche said."[44]

A central focus of Nietzsche's philosophy, which finds ultimate expression in *Thus Spoke Zarathustra*, is the creation of the Overman (*Übermensch*) or Superman, a supremely powerful person capable of "affirming all life and all existence."[45] The Overman is "what is extraordinary rather than average, exceptional rather than everyday, rare rather than commonplace and common."[46]

For Rand, her Superman protagonists live "above all other things," and conquer life as they choose.[47] Even laughter has a connotation of superiority for Rand. For Nietzsche, there are two types of laughter, the laughter of the herd and the laughter of the height. The laughter of the crowd making fun of someone often is a scornful, mocking laughter that reveals ignorance. The laughter of the height is a special laughter of the superior being, the *Übermensch*, who realizes the true value of life. Happy with himself, his work, and his place in the universe, he has the transcendent laugh that befits a superior being.[48] *The Fountainhead's* famous first line, "Howard Roark laughed," can best be understood in connection to how Rand understood Nietzsche's thoughts about laughter.[49] This is also how Rand presents Galt and her female protagonists Dominique Francon and Dagny Taggart. In *The Gay Science*, Nietzsche wrote, "Laughter.—Laughter means: to be schadenfroh, *but with clear conscience.*"[50] *Schadenfroh* ("maliciously gleeful"), or literally "harm-joy," is the sadistic feeling of joy or satisfaction when one sees another fail or suffer misfortune.[51] Keating hears Francon "laughing; it was a sound so gay and so cold."[52]

Under cover of John Wayne–type heroes, Rand injected a virulent form of elitism into America's political culture; her message is clear: Hierarchy is natural, exceptional individuals must be allowed to do as they wish, and to believe that the liberals, moochers, and zeros among us can make society work defies logic and world history. There is, of course, something strange and off-putting about Rand's leading men. She conceives of Howard Roark as being "born without the ability to consider others . . . he does not suffer, because he does not believe in suffering," and describes "the cold, pure brilliance of the eyes that had no trace of pity."[53] And we should have known something was amiss while reading the infamous rape scene in *The Fountainhead*: "She felt the hatred and his hands . . . the hands that broke granite . . . He did it as an act of scorn. Not of love, but as defilement. And this made her lie still and submit."[54]

Rand's lasting importance is as a messenger. She retooled and repackaged the illiberal message of Spencer with her bastardized interpretation of Nietzsche and then presented her ideas to a new, innocent audience, largely unaware of their ugly import. Similar to George Wallace, Rand hid behind a "politically correct" cover story. On the surface, Governor Wallace was speaking against the government and liberal elites telling us what to do.

In Rand's fiction, the productive freedom of gifted entrepreneurs is being put at risk by collectivists. But the animating, underlying force behind their rhetoric is Southern racism and a simplistic interpretation of Nietzsche's overlords, respectively.

An émigré who arrived in the United States in her mid-twenties, Rand was tone-deaf to the democratic genius of American politics.[55] She never appreciated that the special quality of our politics is the ability to hold equality and liberty equally dear. Illiberals such as Rand, Spencer, and Hayek missed this point completely. In Rand's black-and-white political universe, the liberty of the elite is precious and must be protected at all cost. Any talk of equality—in any form, for her—is a sin. Rand spread the illiberal gospel by expanding the definition of aristocracy to include the business elite; her mission was to define and defend America's business class as the new nobility.

Rand's powerful influence was exemplified in the 2012 presidential campaign. Speaking to a private meeting of wealthy donors in Florida, unaware that his words would eventually be broadcast to the nation as a whole, Mitt Romney said:

> There are 47 percent of the people who will vote for the president no matter what . . . who are dependent upon government, who believe that they are victims. . . . These are people who pay no income tax. . . . and so my job is not to worry about those people. I'll never convince them that they should take personal responsibility and care for their lives.

Proclaiming that he would be president for a responsible and productive 53 percent of Americans, the Republican nominee's words were taken straight out of Rand's playbook. Promoting a vision of heroic loners rising above the refuse of life's losers begging for a handout, *Fountainhead* and *Atlas Shrugged* took dead aim at the New Deal edifice built by Roosevelt. Yet, while Rand's prose reached a mass audience and her message stirred souls on the right, her novels lacked the weight of social science fact. If Rand could be ignored by liberal elites, F. A. Hayek could not be so easily dismissed. One of his generation's leading social scientists and a founder of the Chicago school of economics, Hayek had credentials.

F. A. HAYEK AND THE FEAR
OF TOTALITARIANISM

At the height of World War II, Hayek penned *The Road to Serfdom* (1944), his polemic against modern liberalism and activist government, arguing that any expansion of the liberal state inevitably leads to totalitarianism.[56] This slender volume remains the King James Bible of the reactionary right and colors most contemporary GOP arguments about the proper role of government and the market. For example, Hayek's thesis is central to the right's opposition to vigorous government action on climate change. In black-and-white logic, Hayek argues that government involvement in the economy is like being a little bit pregnant, with the resulting birth being a hideous monster in the form of a Hitler or a Stalin. The only safe road ahead, Hayek insisted, is the wide-open, unregulated market system and as minimal a government as possible.[57] Discovering in Hayek rhetoric pitch perfect for the Cold War, the American business class launched a crusade against the New Deal state that continues.[58] In the postwar era, William F. Buckley Jr., Milton Friedman, and Barry Goldwater—the leading American reactionary pundit, economist, and politician, respectively—powered the shift from conservative to illiberal. Hayek was the intellectual pillar on which they built their case. Against older Midwestern Burkean conservatism that extolled tradition and experience, hated abstract principle, and embraced prudent good government, Hayek, Buckley, Friedman, and Goldwater redefined "liberty" and "freedom."[59] At its core, the free-market libertarian doctrine states that Americans must accept life as unfettered laissez-faire capitalism allows.[60]

On the surface, Hayek appeared to be making a straightforward, analytical argument about the dangers of totalitarianism. But on another level, he issues a fierce polemic defending the holiness of property and sanctity of elite privilege.[61] Similar to Burke 150 years earlier, Hayek is defending the status quo, which for him represented not the ancien régime of monarchy and feudal orders of the 18th century, but instead the 19th century "Manchester liberal" capitalism that Spencer defended. Hayek asserts again and again that he is a "liberal." But self-identification is not always accurate. Hayek's only works if we accept his narrow definition of "negative freedom" as being the essence of liberalism and collapse the libertarian argument of Spencer into Locke, Madison, Jefferson, Tocqueville, and other defenders of freedom.[62] We need not do this.

TWO ARGUMENTS

In *The Road to Serfdom*, Hayek makes two main points: one valid against central planning and one invalid and pernicious that paints liberals as a "collectivists" and thus totalitarians in bed with Hitler and Stalin. We should accept Hayek's first point and reject the second. He understands that a centrally planned economy is both unworkable and highly toxic to individual liberty and democracy. The very complexity of modern economies means that the only viable method for economic coordination is a price system.[63] There simply is too much information for planners to possess "in order effectively to adjust his decisions to those of others." In contrast to the market, central direction is "clumsy, primitive and limited in scope." Beyond an economic quagmire, central planning threatens freedom; in a centrally planned economy the "will of a few persons decides who is to get what." By contrast, having the means of production divided among many people acting independently prevents the centralization of power that can lead to dictatorship.[64] Numerous liberal intellectuals of the postwar era made the same pluralist point.[65]

Hayek's second argument is central to the illiberal cause; it also is simplistic and false. Having argued that a central planned economy is radically inefficient and a tool of choice in dictatorship and totalitarian states, he then makes an unwarranted leap to assert that all arguments to the left of his "minimal government" position are totalitarian in spirit and practice. Throughout his book, he does this repeatedly. The supposed connection between Nazism and socialism is central to his argument; after all, the Nazis called themselves a socialist workers party. Hayek desperately wants his readers to believe that socialist planning led to the takeover of the German government by the Nazis. Thus, by extension, all liberals, progressives, New Dealers, and democratic socialists are guilty of promoting tyranny. Unfortunately for Hayek, his expertise in the economy did not extend to his skill as a social and historical analyst.

There are at least three more plausible and powerful alternative explanations of why Hitler and the Nazis rose to power in the 1930s.[66] The most obvious explanation—and the one Hayek does not wish to discuss—is that Hitler came to power as a direct result of the meltdown of capital markets that triggered the Great Depression and led to a 25 percent unemployment rate and the destruction of the middle class in Germany. In May 1928, the Nazi Party won only 2.6 percent of the vote in the Reichstag parliamentary elections; in September 1932, the Nazi Party won 37.0 percent.[67] It was the inevitable boom and bust of unregulated capitalism—not socialist planning—that gave Hitler and the Nazi Party their chance to seize power and establish the Third Reich. In this explanation, it is Hayek and his free-market cohorts who are collaborators with the enemy. A second interpretation, one endorsed by Keynes, is that the punitive and severe peace imposed on Germany following World War I spawned bitterness and militarism among the German people.[68] Finally, Alexander Gerschenkron and Barrington Moore Jr. make a compelling case that the Nazis seized power after Germany's reactionary landed elite—the powerful Prussian Junker class—rejected liberal democracy. The Junker aristocracy, despising liberalism and democracy, abandoned the Weimar Republic and threw their clout behind Hitler and his National Socialist German Workers' Party. In England, the upper strata had ceased to be agrarian by the start of the 20th century; their economic base had shifted to industry and trade. By contrast, in Germany agriculture remained dominant and the Junker elite used the state to preserve their position; a coalition of Junker, peasant, and industrial interests united around a program of imperialism and reaction.[69] This philosophy, combined with the machinery of Junker protectionism in agriculture, retarded the development of democratic institutions and norms in Germany. At the end of World War I, the German Revolution of 1918 replaced the Imperial government with a fledgling parliamentary republic. In the turmoil, the Prussian landed elite escaped with their power intact and became strong vocal opponents of the new democracy. The Junker's strength and displeasure over losing the monarchy contributed significantly to the "constitutional weakness and subsequent disintegration of the Weimar Republic . . . The German farmers bear their full share of responsibility for the advent to fascism in that country."[70] As is well known, the Imperial government, the Prussian elite, and the German Army shunned responsibility for defeat in 1918 and sought to place the blame for it on the new democratic government. These three explanations—the Great Depression, the harsh peace, and the power of the illiberal Junker landed elite—taken singularly or together, offer a more historically accurate picture of the dynamics that brought tragedy to Europe, the Jews, and the world. Once we deny Hayek the rhetorical move of painting all his ideological opponents as Nazis, his argument weakens considerably.

◆

At the heart of Hayek's Logos is the assertion that the so-called "middle path," the modern welfare state, is unstable and unsustainable. Oxford political philosopher John Gray writes, "The belief that there is a stable middle way between the socialist command economy and the free-market process [is] the principle target of Hayek's attack in *The Road to Serfdom*."[71] The experience of Western Europe and North America since World War II demonstrates that the "middle path" of New Deal–style reform is viable indeed. The more advanced welfare states in France, Sweden, Denmark, Great Britain, and Germany have not slunk toward totalitarian rule, nor has Canada (with a single-payer health care system, no less) or the United States. In fact, as Gray admits, "none of the advanced industrial democracies has seen the transformation from hampered liberalism to full totalitarian control that Hayek predicted."[72] Still, illiberals today act like Chicken Little insisting that the sky is about to fall.[73]

There is a good deal of arrogance and conceit in Hayek's argument. On the one hand, he argues that human knowledge, for each individual, is severely limited. On the other hand, as a member of the economic priesthood, he claims that he can see the future. Hayek starts by saying his market philosophy is based on people's limited knowledge and rationality, and therefore instead of trying to impose a "rationalist plan" on reality, we are much better off accepting the "natural" order that emerges in a free-market economy. After this assertion, however, Hayek as an "all-knowing economist" then argues that our only choice is between laissez-faire freedom (and the massive privilege, hierarchy, inequality, and exclusion based on the classic split between the upper class and the plebs) and totalitarian rule. How can Hayek plausibly say that the mid-19th century is the absolute high point of human civilization in terms of how we design government and political and economic systems? How is his limited knowledge great enough to make such a claim, especially when he makes the epistemological point that we are all limited in what we can know? There might, in fact, be a noncapitalist market system in the future; this is a possibility that Hayek and illiberals both ignore and fear.

In Hayek's ode to the market, we hear echoes of Rousseau's infamous argument about being "forced to be free." He insists that there can be no direction or interference with the market beyond the basic laws and rules that set it in motion.[74] Once the system is instituted, "the impersonal and anonymous mechanism of the market" must then be left to its own devices.[75] Hayek argues that if there is radical economic inequality, so be it. The people who have property, wealth, and power had to compete in the market and this is far more just than a government bureaucrat deciding who gets what.[76] He says we must *submit* to the market, and doing so will foster a free society because it operates without the personal coercion inherent in previous economic systems, such as feudalism. But why should the word "freedom" be associated with a socioeconomic order in which we submit to forces that we do not fully comprehend and follow paths that we would not choose without compulsion?[77]

For Hayek and illiberals, the supreme value is liberty and in the peculiar way illiberals define freedom, the value must always be chosen at the cost of democracy and equality. For illiberals, it is axiomatic that, as Spencer's American ally William Graham Sumner wrote, "every effort to realize equality necessitates a sacrifice of liberty."[78] By contrast, in the broader conception of freedom favored by Machiavelli, Tocqueville, Jefferson, Lincoln, and modern democrats, a commitment to freedom entails a related commitment to equality, democracy, fairness, and justice.[79] In this civic republican tradition, freedom is based on economic independence and a social status that allows citizens to be seen as equals by their peers. From the liberal/republican point of view, "the freedom to sell one's labor to the highest bidder is not properly speaking freedom at all."[80] In Hayek's market society, this republican understanding of freedom is utterly lost.

A PLATONIC THEORY OF POLITICS
AS AN ALTERNATIVE TO DEMOCRACY

If Hayek's historical analysis is flawed and his denial of a "middle way" economy and republican freedom suspect, his argument for unrestrained capitalism is frightening. In devising an argument that both protects property and provides capitalists with as much latitude as possible to pursue their business goals, Hayek places the market outside of democratic control, endorses a Platonic theory of politics and, in effect, sanctions a modern form of monarchy in which we must submit to the dictates of the market.

Hayek—like many illiberals—had reservations about democratic politics, especially the will of the majority. At the height of World War II, as the freedom-loving democracies sacrificed a generation of youth to defeat the Third Reich and imperial Japan, Hayek wrote, "We have no intention, however, of making a fetish of democracy. It may well be true that our generation talks and thinks too much of democracy."[81] Allowing for democracy, yet fearing majority rule, Hayek sought to restrict the reach of government to areas of policy "where true agreement exists." Common action between individuals should be restricted to "the instances where individual views coincide."[82] Without being explicit, Hayek is making an argument against majority rule and urging that only decisions arrived at by near unanimity be considered legitimate. Such a precept makes reaching decisions on public policy exceedingly difficult. But, of course, Hayek and illiberals do not want government to function; instead, they want the market to govern. According to Robert Dahl, the leading democratic theorist of his generation, majority rule is the fairest decision rule. Asking for super majorities, in effect, sanctions rule by the minority. Dahl writes:

> Majority rule maximizes the number of persons who can exercise self-determination in collective decisions . . . [it] ensures that the greatest number of citizens will live under laws they have chosen for themselves . . . if more than a majority were required in order for a law to be adopted—let's say 60 percent—then a minority of 40 percent (plus one vote) could prevent the majority of 60 percent (less one vote) from adopting its preferred

alternative. As a result, the alternative preferred by a minority would be *imposed* on the majority.[83]

Hayek's perfect market system denies the right of the people to come together to discuss their common fate and make collective decisions about the shape of their lives. This is radically illiberal. Indeed, he does provide for democratic governance. But he wants democracy to defer to the market and leave it autonomous. For Hayek, "the fundamental principle in the ordering of our affairs is that we should make as much use as possible of the *spontaneous forces* of society, and resort as little as possible to coercion," which he defines as arbitrary personal power or the power of government.[84] In making this argument, Hayek, in effect, rules economic issues off the table for political discussion. Yet, when the economy plays such a vast and vital role in modern life, excluding economic issues from political discussion violates *our liberty* to have a voice in deciding our collective fate.

In Hayek's political economy, a soulless market system becomes a dis-embodied, inanimate iteration of the philosopher king.[85] Simply stated, participants in market economies operate with limited knowledge and must willingly submit to a spontaneous and all-knowing superstructure—the price mechanism and "market forces"—in order for the market to operate successfully. Claiming to be a liberal, Hayek articulates a Platonic theory of politics; against utopian planning, his market ideal is itself utopian.[86] In Hayek's perfect society, specially trained philosopher kings are replaced by a powerful and autonomous market system (aided by the Federal Reserve Board), and the people submit. To draw on Albert O. Hirschman's *Exit, Voice, and Loyalty*, in Hayek's utopia there is no voice, only the choices of exit and loyalty. Within the system, people can exercise Hirschman's exit option—they can buy and sell and enter and exit contracts. But they cannot voice their objections to the market system as a whole; they are not allowed to question its logic and are forbidden from pursuing a "middle path" mixed economy with an activist government. Loyalty is demanded, voice is severely constrained, and the exit option exists only for market transactions *within* the closed system. There is no escape from the all-encompassing monarchy of the market.[87]

The parallels between *The Road to Serfdom* and Plato's *Republic* go deep once we recognize the "noble lies" of the market system.[88] Karl Polanyi identifies three "commodity fictions" that are necessary in the organization of a market society. In *The Great Transformation*, Polanyi explains: "labor, land, and money are essential elements of industry; they also must be organized in markets; in fact, these markets form an absolutely vital part of the economic system. But labor, land, and money are obviously *not* commodities; the postulate that anything that is bought and sold must have been produced for sale is emphatically untrue in regards to them."[89] Only by transforming modern man into labor, transforming the space by which he lives into land, and by creating a system by which these are commodified into money, is man forced to submit to the market. One may read these commodity fictions as Hayek's version of Plato: necessary tales we tell ourselves for our society to function.[90] Here, activist government and the possibility of planning and public ownership of certain sectors, such as railroads and utilities, threaten the utopian scheme. Both principles—Plato's noble lie and Hayek's commodity fictions—are motivated to allow the respective utopian societies to function at their full potential. As Plato explained in *The Republic*, the lies quickly become assumptions inherent in the organization of society. In a telling comment, Hayek writes, "The people are made to transfer their allegiance from *the old gods* to the new under the pretense that *the new gods* really are what their sound instinct had always told them but what before they had only dimly seen."[91]

THE MONARCHY OF THE MARKET

After Thomas Paine shredded the case for traditional monarchy in *Common Sense* and *Rights of Man*, the upper class needed a new argument to protect them from questioning from below. The doctrine of laissez-faire capitalism supplied this need in the 19th century, with Spencer leading the way. When the Great Depression sank laissez-faire, Hayek leaped into action inventing a new argument to protect power, privilege, property, and wealth. The message to working people of today: the market must be off-limits to "government interference" and whatever the market generates is by definition "fair and just," because no person arbitrarily decides the outcome. It is an audacious argument: In the service of the new noble lie, the democratic public is to be severely limited from regulating business and should, in a good society, limit the government to minimal protective functions—the police, the army, and the courts—because nearly all other actions violate the dictates of the market. That a hefty portion of the American public has bought into the market myth places us in a similar position to our feudal forefathers who—not yet thinking for themselves, as Locke counseled—passively believed in the divine right of kings.

In 1790, Edmund Burke asserted that generations long dead had decided the English constitutional system once and for all—"and forever"—and that those then living in England in 1790 had no right to change or reform the constitution. In *Rights of Man*, Thomas Paine rightly skewered Burke on this point: "Every age and generation must be as free to act for itself, in all cases, as the ages and generations which preceded it. The vanity and presumption of governing beyond the grave, is the most ridiculous and insolent of all tyrannies."[92] In a perverse way, Hayek's argument about the sanctity of the market echoes Burke proclaiming the necessity and paramount importance of the British monarchy. According to Hayek and Burke, some spheres of life are untouchable and off-limits to any reform impulse or change or democratic voice by the living. Realizing full well that unregulated corporate capitalism is a politicoeconomic system biased in favor of the rich and influential, Hayek and his fellow illiberals implore average people to bow to the *new* king, the monarchy of the market. In Burke's age, the British monarchy was ruled untouchable; in our time, the market is wrapped in a sacred bubble guarded by Nobel laureates. Hayek is frank about the necessity of the modern subjects bowing and submitting to the edicts of King Market:

> It was men's *submission* to the impersonal forces of the market that in the past had made possible the growth of a civilization . . . it is by thus *submitting* that we are every day helping to build something that is greater than any one of us can fully comprehend . . . the only alternative to *submission* to the impersonal and seemingly irrational forces of the market is *submission* to an equally uncontrollable and therefore arbitrary power of other men."[93]

According to Hayek, Friedman, and their acolytes, any direction or regulation by democratically elected officials working in the public interest is deemed unnatural; government must be limited to the protection of—yes—property.[94] As with Burke earlier, Hayek argued that he was defending liberty. However, both Hayek and his predecessor were, as Mary Wollstonecraft understood, "really defending that demon of property." The pioneering feminist and liberal wrote: "Security of property! Behold, in a few words, the definition of English liberty. And to this selfish principle every nobler one is sacrificed."[95]

The United States was the first modern nation to insist that government arise *out* of the people, instead of being imposed *over* them.[96] As a force *over* us to which we must shelf our democratic selves and submit, the divine right of the market is both paradoxical and troubling. If nothing else, Hayek's argument is illiberal because of its absolutist stance. If any growth of the state sets off the inevitable march toward totalitarianism, then any expansion of the state, any growth of the public sector, *must* be stopped. How convenient for those who want to limit the size and power of government to better preserve their wealth, property, and privilege from challenge. Believing Hayek, in effect, sanctions a radical counterrevolution against modern liberalism and American government. As Paine and his cohorts rejected the divine right of kings, so liberals today should challenge the right's blanket reactionary claim about the divine right of the market.

A market system is a supremely powerful tool for economic advancement and social coordination.[97] Used wisely and with good design, markets can do wonderful things. Operated without caution, prudence, or supervision, however, markets can cause great harm; they can fail and cause anguish to tens of millions. To offer a critique of Hayek is neither a rejection of the market nor an endorsement of central planning. What liberals endorse is the freedom to use politics *and* markets, independently and together.[98] We need both tools to deal with the challenges facing American society.

7

Rage Against Government: George Wallace

We all know that the American South celebrated slavery and virulent racism. But why do those collective experiences, *that* history, matter to us now? Because more than a citadel of slavery and segregation, the Old South was staunchly authoritarian, illiberal, and reactionary. Governed by a power structure based on racial separation, radical inequality, and oligarchy, the South was never liberal in the sense of Locke, Jefferson, and Tocqueville.[1] Of course, we have the New South of the past fifty years, but to believe the Old South vanished without a trace is terribly naive and woefully un-Southern. Such a reading of contemporary history would have more resonance if it were not for incidents such as the Ole Miss election rally for Mitt Romney just after President Obama won reelection on November 6, 2012. The Romney rally turned racial when white students torched Obama campaign signs while shouting "the South will rise again" and blasting "Dixie" on their car stereos. Deeply ingrained cultural habits and patterns of thought persist across time. The white Ole Miss students, born more than a quarter century after Selma and Memphis, were taught to feel and act as they did. A black student told

National Public Radio, "It's very interesting kind of experiencing racism in the 21st century. Nobody's going to openly, you know, ostracize you. But there are whispers and there are looks."[2] In 2015, national attention turned to Selma, fifty years after "Bloody Sunday." It says something about the strength of racism in the South that the Edmund Pettus Bridge—the site where armed state troopers attacked Martin Luther King Jr. and nearly killed future congressman John Lewis as they led peaceful civil rights demonstrators in 1965—is still named after a Confederate general who led the Alabama Ku Klux Klan following the Civil War.

Take an example from pop culture. "Sweet Home Alabama," a Lynyrd Skynyrd song recorded in the 1970s and still heard on many rock radio stations, is a defense and celebration of Southern illiberal attitudes. Often while performing, the band would display a huge Confederate flag in the background. Responding to Neil Young's "Southern Man" and "Alabama" and Young's criticism of the racism and savagery of the Old South, the song spoke about the popularity of Governor Wallace, Southerners not needing to hear criticism from Yankees, and asked whether the Watergate scandal was worth the fuss.[3] Skynyrd's popular ballad became so mainstream and accepted that Bank of America used it as the soundtrack for one of its commercials. Many leaders and spokespeople for the Republican Party today claim that they favor racial and ethnic inclusion just as much as Democrats, yet President Trump and others on the right are emphatic in their assertion that white men deserve to stand first in line ahead of everyone else. Hostility, discrimination, and racism are on the rise in Trump's America. And the source of these ugly attitudes is the Old South; the deeper beliefs of an ideology often remain even as time marches forward and modes of expression change.

For 100 years, the South was a defeated colony of the North—overwhelmingly rural, socially isolated, and economically backward. Trapped in a system of sharecropping and tenant farming created by the plantation elite following the Civil War, the South suffered terrible poverty. Dixie's politics were defined by race; its economy desperately underdeveloped. At a funeral in Georgia late in the 19th century, a newspaper editor wrote that, "The South didn't furnish a thing on earth for that funeral but the corpse and the hole in the ground." The tombstone came from Vermont, the pine coffin arrived from Cincinnati, and the shovel used to dig the grave imported from Pittsburgh.[4] It is no wonder that the stories of William Faulkner and Flannery O'Connor picture a world far different than the North. Then, at warp speed, the South changed. Urban blacks led by the Southern Christian Leadership Conference and Martin Luther King Jr. confronted bigotry with a growing wave of nonviolent protests, which led to federal intervention and a dramatic end to American apartheid and the one-party South. An inflow of middle-class professionals and corporate investment prompted an economic boom. The unleashing of a dynamic economy pressed two comparative advantages versus the North: cheaper labor and sunshine. Today, no longer predominately rural and poor, the South boasts shiny urban centers, sprawling upscale suburbs, and an economy that is a mix of industry (auto plants) and postindustrial development (university research parks, banks, and corporate headquarters). The region has transnational connections to the global economy and is increasingly cosmopolitan with Cubans in Florida, Indians and Vietnamese in Louisiana, and Latinos across the region. Among its minority officeholders are two current Republican U.S. senators (Ted Cruz of Texas and Marco Rubio of Florida) and two former Republican governors (Nikki Haley of South Carolina, President Trump's first United Nations Ambassador, and Bobby Jindal of Louisiana).

In the 21st century, the overt verbal racism of the past is largely gone. But a stark separation by race and class persists in the spatial patterns of suburbs and urban centers as well as access to better schools for the affluent. Segregationist resistance failed to stop the civil rights movement, but it nevertheless managed to preserve the world of segregation.[5] The difficulties that minorities and the working poor have in reaching their jobs, particularly in the Southeastern cities such as Atlanta, Charlotte, Memphis, and Raleigh, were highlighted on the front-page of the *New York Times*:

> "Stacey Calvin spends almost as much time commuting to her job—on a bus, two trains and another bus—as she does working part-time at a day care center . . . Her nearly four-hour round-trip stems largely from the economic geography of Atlanta, which is one of America's most affluent metropolitan areas yet also one of the most physically divided by

income . . . This geography appears to play a major role in making Atlanta one of the metropolitan areas where it is most difficult for lower-income households to rise into the middle class and beyond."[6]

It's not only racism, both personal and institutional, but the passive acceptance of power above that characterized Southern society and politics. The authoritarian, illiberal legacy of the Old South endures—and infects national politics. There is a quiescence among working- and middle-class whites who rarely question or challenge the power of those above. This can be colored by racism, as when Lyndon Johnson, a poor son of Texas, upon seeing a group of working-class white women holding up racist signs in Tennessee, said: "I'll tell you what's at the bottom of it. If you can convince the lowest white man he's better than the best colored man, he won't notice you're picking his pocket. Hell, give him somebody to look down on, and he'll empty his pockets for you."[7] Or it can be totally separate from race as when the workers in an Appalachia coal valley are defeated again and again by the Company and resign themselves to the fact that the power of the multinational is too immense and too distant to confront.

> The secrecy, complexity and tightly-held nature of the empire's ownership also helped ensure that the power was not challenged. The consequent powerlessness of the would-be protestors is like that of the farmer in Steinbeck's *Grapes of Wrath*, who, as the absentee-owned bulldozer mows down his crops, pleads but "*who can* we shoot?"[8]

The hill country poor, having been defeated in the Populist rebellion, saw the Bourbon elite above them and poor blacks below and imagined, by hard work and luck, they could escape their marginal life and move up. If you dream that you or someone in your extended family might join the elite, then "Why would you want to blame a guy if he got all the way to the top?"[9] But as Nancy Isenberg, author of *White Trash*, notes, "If the American dream were real, upward mobility would be far more in evidence."[10]

Arizona senator Barry Goldwater and Alabama Republican James Martin shaking hands on the rooftop of the Mark Hopkins Hotel in San Francisco just before the 1964 Republican National Convention is the moment when the reactionary right was born. The two sides of American illiberalism—right-wing libertarianism and Southern racism—connected and set in motion today's reactionary revolution. Martin (shown at center) told Goldwater that Alabama governor George Wallace—a Southern Democrat who led the resistance to the civil rights revolution—wanted to be his running mate. Previously, the two most reactionary elements in American politics, the right-wing business class and Southern whites, had always been minority voices in *different* political parties. Goldwater told Martin "no," but two powerfully charged wires sparked; the "Goldwater-Wallace ticket" is the secret inner logic of the modern Republican Party. The clandestine rooftop meeting was recorded by a freelance photographer for *Life* magazine, standing on another rooftop, and the photo was part of *Life*'s July 24, 1964, cover story. *Photo © Bob Gomel, used by permission of the artist.*

The ideas of a 17th century philosopher, **John Locke**, form the core of America's liberal ideal. Locke supplied the American founders with their conceptions of liberty, equality, property, natural rights (a powerful mental and moral fiction, not an historic fact, for Locke), and government by consent, and his ideas provide the philosophic canopy under which progressives and conservatives have worked together for more than two centuries. In a Lockean world, people neither live in subordination to others nor do they treat others as merely instruments or tools for their purposes. To reject these two pillars of aristocratic and feudal life is to imagine a world in which unquestioned privilege, hierarchy, inequality, and exclusion no longer define the human condition. *Portrait by Godfrey Kneller via Wikimedia.*

British statesman **Edmund Bur**ke is the father of conservatism. He wrote *Reflections on the Revolution in France* (1790) as a statement defending monarchy, but his wise words about the qualities that make a society both stable and virtuous remain seminal. Conservatives follow Burke and Alexander Hamilton in viewing government as a good and essential thing. Illiberals do not. Burkean conservatism extols tradition and experience, hates abstract principle, and embraces prudent government. *From the New York Public Library digital library via Wikimedia.*

Assigned the lead role in drafting the Declaration of Independence, the young **Thomas Jefferson** catapulted global politics into a new era. Jefferson's great accomplishment was weaving together strands of liberal and civic republican thinking into one coherent ideology for a nation at the forefront of a global democratic revolution. Across his political career, he inspired Americans to think and act in a bold new fashion—as equal citizens and equal men in the world's first liberal democratic nation. At the same time, his egalitarianism did not extend to African Americans and his legacy is stained by his ownership of slaves. *Portrait by Rembrandt Peale from the White House Collection via Wikimedia.*

The primary author of the Constitution, **James Madison**, a slaveholder from Virginia, was successful in keeping the words "slave," "slavery," and "property in man" out of the final document. Neither he nor George Washington approved of the infamous Connecticut Compromise that gave small states the same representation in the U.S. Senate as large population states. Madison saw this as a severe violation of political equality. *Portrait by John Vanderlyn from the White House Collection via Wikimedia.*

Thomas Paine's audacity ignited the American Revolution. In *Common Sense* (1776), his clear, impassioned prose made the case for an independent, democratic America. Among the most radical democrats of the founding era, Paine shared a belief with Jefferson in the moral goodness of ordinary people. His *Rights of Man* (1791–92) included proposals for the care of the elderly and the education of the young that anticipated FDR's New Deal. *Portrait by Auguste Millière from the National Portrait Gallery via Wikimedia.*

In 1837, addressing the U.S. Senate in his most famous speech, **John Calhoun** of South Carolina declared slavery a "positive good." To Calhoun and the plantation class, the idea of a liberal democratic society based on equality and inclusion in opposition to the rigid class structure of Old World Europe was an impossible dream. *Portrait by George Peter Alexander Healy from the National Portrait Gallery via Wikimedia.*

At the end of the Civil War, Pennsylvania congressman **Thaddeus Stevens** understood that for Reconstruction to succeed, the plantation estates—source of the planters' economic and political power—had to be destroyed and the land redistributed to poor blacks and whites. That the North did not follow Stevens's advice is arguably the greatest mistake in American history. Born into slavery, **Harriet Tubman** escaped to become the most famous "conductor" of the Underground Railroad and risked her life to lead hundreds to freedom. During the Civil War, she helped direct a Union Army raid that liberated more than seven hundred slaves in South Carolina. *Thaddeus Stevens photo from the Library of Congress Prints and Photographs Division, via Wikimedia. Harriet Tubman photo by H. B. Lindsley, circa1870s, courtesy of the Library of Congress.*

As a dedicated foe of Karl Marx, **Herbert Spencer** glorified liberty while accepting radical inequality. The original libertarian, he preached a gospel for the Gilded Age business elite that infused laissez-faire with the imperatives of biology. His influential *Social Statics* combined rigorous logic about the government being the only coercive force in society with a view of human progress that required the lower classes to be sacrificed, *literally*, for the good of the species. *From the Smithsonian Institution Libraries via Wikimedia.*

When the Populist rebellion flared in the Midwest and South at the end of the 19th century, Georgian **Tom Watson** argued for a political union between white and black sharecroppers. When the Populists were defeated, a bitter Watson became a virulent racist. Like Jefferson, Watson personified the liberal/illiberal contradiction at the heart of the American experience. *Portrait of Thomas E. Watson, in the Thomas E. Watson Papers #755, Southern Historical Collection, The Wilson Library, University of North Carolina at Chapel Hill.*

Friedrich Nietzsche, the great German philosopher who has influenced hundreds of major writers, was interested in greatness rather than goodness, and he argued that traditional morality is the refuge of the weak. Modern scholarship argues that the crude interpretation of Nietzsche put forth by the novelist Ayn Rand and the European fascists in the early 20th century is a distortion of the philosopher's intentions. *Photograph circa 1869, taken at studio Gebrüder Siebe, Leipzig via Wikimedia.*

Operating in a ruthless, underhanded fashion—using predatory pricing to crush rivals, market power to secure illegal rebates from railroads, kickbacks to corrupt state legislatures—**John D. Rockefeller** (shown at left in photo above) systematically and mercilessly drove his rivals to ruin. His company dominated petroleum and kerosene refining, controlling ninety percent of the business nationally, and Rockefeller became the richest person in America. Investigative journalist **Ida Tarbell** unearthed damning evidence demonstrating that Rockefeller had used unethical and illegal means to eliminate competitors as he built the nation's most powerful monopoly. Her book, *The History of the Standard Oil Company* (1904), enraged the nation and helped spark the Progressive Era of reform. In 1906, President Theodore Roosevelt initiated antitrust action that dismantled the nation's most powerful corporation into thirty-three smaller companies. *Photograph of John D. Rockefeller from the Library of Congress Prints and Photographs Division, via Wikimedia. Portrait of Ida Tarbell by James E. Purdy from the Library of Congress Prints and Photographs Division, via Wikimedia.*

A young union organizer when she witnessed the 1911 Triangle Fire, **Frances Perkins** believed in women's suffrage and devoted her life to the idea that an active, humane government could make a large difference in the lives of average Americans. As Franklin Roosevelt's secretary of labor, Perkins drove U.S. adoption of unemployment insurance, federal laws regulating child labor, the minimum wage, and Social Security, America's most popular government program. *From the Library of Congress Harris & Ewing Collection, 1905.*

President Franklin D. Roosevelt summed up the liberal philosophy of the New Deal in a single sentence: "We are going to make a country in which no one is left out." The president and his liberal colleagues in Congress saved capitalism and built a larger, stronger national government. Their work often was achieved with a "remarkably delicate hand." *Portrait of Franklin D. Roosevelt, August 21, 1944, by Leon A. Perskie, Hyde Park, New York. From the FDR Presidential Library & Museum via Wikimedia.*

Ayn Rand, a refugee from Lenin's Soviet Union, reinvented herself in early Hollywood as a novelist with a mission. Smuggling a vicious elitism into American culture, her novels—especially *The Fountainhead* and *Atlas Shrugged*—celebrate a winner-take-all philosophy based on Rand's social Darwinist reading of Friedrich Nietzsche. *From the Everett Collection Inc./Alamy Stock Photo.*

In the early 20th century, Georgia governor **Eugene Talmadge** (above left) and Mississippi senator **Theodore Bilbo** (above right) were classic Southern demagogues who were much more blatant and direct in demeaning blacks than was George Wallace in the 1960s. Like President Trump, they insulted and belittled their targets explicitly and concentrated on providing a venomous, racist form of entertainment for the white working and middle classes. **W. E. B. Du Bois** (left) was the first African American to earn a PhD at Harvard University and was one of the great intellectuals of the 20th century. He wrote, "It must be remembered that the white group of laborers while they received a low wage, were compensated in part by *a sort of public and psychological wage.*" *Photograph of Eugene Talmadge from the Altoona Tribune via Wikimedia. Photograph of Theodore Bilbo from the Library of Congress Prints and Photographs Division, via Wikimedia. Photograph of W. E. B. Du Bois from the Library of Congress Prints and Photographs Division, via Wikimedia.*

In *The Road to Serfdom* (1944), his polemic against modern liberalism and activist government, **F. A. Hayek** (above left) argued that any expansion of the liberal state inevitably leads to totalitarianism. The King James Bible of the reactionary right, it colors most contemporary GOP arguments about the proper role of government and the market. Hayek's thesis is central to the right's opposition to vigorous government action on climate change. Hayek's protégé, Chicago School economist **Milton Friedman** (above right) argued that the public sector should be limited to public safety, defense, and the courts. *Portrait of Milton Friedman from the Friedman Foundation for Educational Choice via Wikimedia. Photograph of F. A. Hayek by Levan Ramishvilli via flickr.*

President Ronald Reagan was one of the founders of the modern right. Yet in his political career he straddled the liberal/reactionary divide. The irony of Reagan's presidency is that while he did more than anyone else to link the Old South to the New Right (and thus create today's reactionary right), he himself remained something of a Lockean liberal. The goal of *National Review* editor **William F. Buckley** was to explode the stereotype that conservatives were dull. Seeking to identify New Deal liberalism as a stalking horse for communism, Buckley was a dedicated reactionary who understood that it was best if the right's most embarrassing characters—such as the John Birch Society and the KKK—were hidden from view. *President Reagan meeting with William F. Buckley in the Oval Office, January 21, 1988. From the White House photo office.*

Big government liberalism was not limited to the federal government. California, in particular, was a microcosm of the liberal can-do spirit of the New Deal that built modern America. Under the gubernatorial administration of **Edmund G. "Pat" Brown** (1959–1967), the state put in place an extensive freeway system, a massive water project, and one of the world's greatest university systems. The private sector entrepreneurship that makes California one of the top five or six economies on the planet rests on that infrastructure. (In photo above, Governor Pat Brown meets with President John F. Kennedy.) *Photograph by Abbie Rowe, White House Photographs, John F. Kennedy Presidential Library and Museum, Boston.*

In the 1960s and early 1970s, Alabama governor **George Wallace** demonstrated to the nation just how Southern illiberalism could survive and thrive in a world that had bid Jim Crow segregation goodbye. In his presidential campaigns of 1968 and 1972, Wallace took the "defeated" planter ideology of the Southern oligarchy to a national audience—with devastating effect. *Photograph from February 8, 1968,* U.S. News & World Report , *Library of Congress, via Wikimedia.*

Martin Luther King Jr. (top left, pictured at the 1963 March on Washington) borrowed Gandhi's concept of nonviolent resistance (satyagraha) to lead African Americans in their struggle to end segregation and to be embraced as full American citizens. The liberal vision and political muscle of **President Lyndon Johnson** (pictured seated at left) made possible his signing into law the Civil Rights Act of 1964, the Voting Rights Act of 1965, and Medicare. Along with fellow Smith College graduate **Betty Friedan** (pictured bottom left), activist and writer **Gloria Steinem** (pictured in 2019 photo below) helped spearhead the modern women's movement. *Martin Luther King Jr. photograph from the National Archives at College Park, National Archives and Records Administration. Lyndon Johnson photograph by Cecil Stoughton, White House Press Office. Betty Friedan photograph courtesy of the Library of Congress. Gloria Steinem photograph by Jay Godwin, November 6, 2019, via Wikimedia.*

House Speaker Newt Gingrich's distinctive combination of ideological commitment and partisan animosity, gift for saying outrageous falsehoods as if they were as true as the sun rising in the East, and zeal in driving home a malevolent message to the Republican base had a transformational impact on the Republican Party. The reactionary revolution only became full-blown after the Gingrich speakership in the 1990s. *Photograph by Gage Skidmore, via Wikimedia.*

In his presidential campaigns and at the 1992 Republican National Convention, former Nixon speechwriter **Pat Buchanan** declared there was a "culture war" taking place for the soul of the nation, and flashed the right-wing Catholic and neo-Confederate flags of the New Right. Buchanan and writer Samuel Francis argued that a coastal "liberal elite" cares little about "flyover country." While Nixon's politics of resentment were more about class than race; with Buchanan and Francis the reverse was true. Sons of the South, they thought of "Middle America" largely in terms of the white Protestant nation of yesteryear. *Portrait of Patrick Buchanan, presidential aide, July 12, 1969. From the Richard Nixon Presidential Library and Museum, National Archives and Records Administration.*

President Barack Obama, who entered the White House believing in the value of dialogue and collaboration, faced blanket opposition from Senate Majority Leader Mitch McConnell and the Republicans. In terms of policy, President Obama achieved "half a New Deal" according to Harvard political scientist Theda Skocpol, but he was unable to make the Democrats the majority party. Both Obama and President Trump have governed during a political interregnum, in which neither party is the majority party. *Official White House portrait by Pete Souza, December 6, 2012, via Wikimedia.*

Owner of the second-largest privately held company in America, Koch Industries, billionaire **Charles Koch**, who sponsors a plethora of reactionary groups ranging from the Cato Institute to Americans for Prosperity, is a hard-core libertarian who has become the face of the 1%. The Koch family is the second-richest family in the world. *Photograph by Gavin Peters, via Wikimedia.*

Former House Speaker **Paul Ryan** of Wisconsin and Texas senator **Ted Cruz** are devotees of Ayn Rand and F. A. Hayek. Ryan achieved his massive tax cut before leaving Congress, while Cruz, who bitterly fought Trump during the 2016 campaign, is a key congressional defender of the president. Blocking any and all legislation proposed by Democrats, **Majority Leader Mitch McConnell** crafted a policy of heavy obstruction and rejection. In sabotaging President Obama's Supreme Court nomination of Merrick Garland, he spurned the Constitution, undermined the nation's founding ideal in the pursuit of power, and revealed himself a dedicated illiberal reactionary. When McConnell violated his impeachment oath saying he would work closely with the White House and ensure that President Trump was not convicted, and then blocked both witnesses and evidence in the 2020 Senate trial, he moved the United States perilously close to "banana republic" status. Before being elected to the U.S. Senate from Pennsylvania, **Patrick Toomey** headed the Club for Growth, a well-funded libertarian group that calls for deep cuts in government programs. (Shown from left: Ryan, Cruz, McConnell, and Toomey.) *Photo by Alex Wong / Getty Images.*

Far from being a serious populist, **President Donald Trump** doubled down on the long-standing Republican commitment to radically inegalitarian policies extremely friendly to the wealthy and major corporations. Says reactionary radio show host Michael Savage of his listeners, "I don't think they care very much about issues. They'll vote for him no matter what because he's not 'them.'" With traditional conservatives marginalized, radicals on the right pursue their twin passions reshaping the power and reach of the federal government to benefit the elite—in President Trump's case, himself—and protecting the power and privilege of white male America. The ambition of conservatives for responsible government focused on solving pressing public problems has been largely abandoned. Following the January 2020 vote by Senate Republican against allowing witnesses and evidence in Trump's impeachment trial, historian Jon Meacham called President Trump "functionally a monarch . . . he's functionally the most politically powerful president in American history." *Staff photograph from the Executive Office of the President of the United States, via Wikimedia*

THE JIM CROW SOUTH: COUNTERING THE
POPULIST REBELLION AND NEOSLAVERY

When the Populist rebellion flared in the Midwest and South at the end
of the 19th century, Georgian Tom Watson argued for a political union
between the white and black sharecroppers who endured poverty at the
bottom of the Southern economic pyramid.

> You are kept apart that you may be separately fleeced of your
> earnings. You are made to hate each other because upon that
> hatred is rested the keystone of the arch of financial despotism
> that enslaves you both. You are deceived and blinded that you
> may not see how this race antagonism perpetuates a monetary
> system that beggars both.[11]

Unlike the right-wing populism of the 1920s and today, the Populist movement of the 1890s was based on racial comity and a sense that
working-class whites and poor blacks had a common interest in opposing
the tyrannical power of the planter elite. Both the social movement toward
integration and the political push for real democracy in the South profoundly threatened the landed elite and their business allies. With Reconstruction dead and black Southerners put back "in their place," the only real
challenge to the Southern planter elite came from poor white farmers. The
Populist revolt in the 1880s and '90s attacked the planter elite by making
economic inequality an issue more important than keeping the black
population submissive. In response, in one Southern state after another,
beginning in the late 1890s and accelerating at the turn of the century, the
planter class rammed through a web of laws that disenfranchised blacks
and poor whites alike.

The public campaign was against restive blacks; but rebellious whites,
destitute and terribly poor, constituted the real target. At the turn of the
20th century, each state in the former confederacy produced electoral movements aimed at "removing large numbers of its eligible voters." Instead of
voter fraud, this was "voter elimination."[12] The driving forces behind the
disenfranchisement movement were the conservative or so-called Bourbon
elements of the Democratic Party, the socioeconomically privileged Black

Belt aristocracy.[13] Sure of its superiority and birthright status, this aristocracy of privileged men "expressed contempt and hostility toward the lower-class and uneducated whites" whose votes they did not control, writes historian Michael Perman. "They disenfranchised these whites as willingly as they deprived blacks of the vote."[14] Lowndes County, Alabama exemplified the toll on blacks. An impoverished Black Belt rural area on the road from Selma to Montgomery, the county was home to 3,000 whites and 12,000 blacks. Not a single person of the county's 5,122 potential black voters was registered. No one had ever *tried* to register in the 20th century; they knew that to do so was a death sentence.[15] Disenfranchisement and the institution of Jim Crow segregation codes ensured the dominance of the white upper class across the South; impoverished whites were encouraged to take out their frustration by kicking the poor blacks below instead of attacking the rich whites above. The contemporary push by the Republican Party to purge voting rolls of those they suspect of being loyal Democratic voters is nothing new; voter elimination was pioneered in the Old South.

With the Southern authoritarians again in full control, the practice of enslavement—this time of black men fraudulently charged of minor crimes such as vagrancy—again reared its ugly head. For years, such terrorism of blacks in the post–Civil War South was viewed as regrettable but incidental. But stunning reporting by the *Wall Street Journal* revealed that neoslavery had been widespread, with hundreds of thousands of poor black men picked up on phony charges by police or other whites in authority, quickly sentenced, and then leased to slave farms and industrial mines where many were quite literally worked to their deaths. Neoslavery was worse than the original enslavement because the new slave masters had no investment in keeping their "prisoners" alive.

Douglas Blackmon's *Slavery by Another Name* (2008) recounts the horrible crimes that blacks suffered in the prison that was the pre–World War II South. Lynching, at least, brought a quick death. Blackmon writes, "The horror of the mortality rates and living conditions was underscored by the triviality of the alleged offenses," for which men were imprisoned in work camps, plantations, and mines across the deep South.[16] In the Soviet Union, the Gulag administered and controlled the Soviet forced labor camps under Joseph Stalin. In the United States, a decentralized gulag of hundreds of forced labor camps of a different kind—operated by state and county governments, corporations such as U.S. Steel, and sadistic provincial farmers—sprawled across the mid-century South.

THE POWER OF THE BLACK BELT WHITES

Writing about the post–Civil War South before the civil rights struggle, Yale historian C. Vann Woodward and Harvard political scientist V. O. Key recognized that behind the public front of "White Supremacy" solidarity there raged the longstanding rivalry between the Black Belt and the hill country. This was a struggle of white men for supremacy over other white men and the lines of cleavage separated counties predominantly African American from those primarily white. *Black Belt* was the name for the most fertile plantation areas in the South where a majority of the black population lived, working either directly or indirectly for the planter elite. Though it made up only a small portion of the South and a sliver of the total white population this fertile area was where power resided. The fight went back to slavery, when the white yeoman counties sought to tax slaves as property and prevent masters from counting slaves as a basis for Black Belt representation in state legislatures. In opposition, the slave owners fought for property qualifications for office holding and to prevent the upland counties from increasing their number of elected officials.[17]

The rich planters and their families—minorities in a sea of black faces—needed allies and a stern political order to maintain a "peaceful" and lucrative dominance. The deep and unflinching racism of Black Belt whites was prompted by fear—during the antebellum period, this was the nightmare of a savage slave revolt similar to Haiti's (1791–1804), and in the post–Civil War era, the dread of black vigilantism and score settling. In Black Belt counties, the "real problem of politics" was how a *white minority* could maintain control of a very large, majority "colored population." In sharp contrast to the poor white farmers who labored on small farms in the hill country where the black population was minimal, the whites of the Black Belt had the "deepest and most immediate concern about the maintenance of white supremacy."[18]

In a way that no other study had done, V. O. Key's *Southern Politics in State and Nation*, based on 538 confidential interviews with Southern elites, revealed the inner logic of the region's politics. As one of Key's research associates later wrote, "He correctly felt that informal talk might breed trust, and trust might breed candor, and candor might lead to subjects seldom discussed—and never discussed for attributions."[19] The secret to white power in the South, according to Key, lay in the ability of the planter elite in black-majority counties to win support of the white-majority counties so that whites would continue to support the denial of the vote to blacks. To maintain its feudal-like rule and encourage political passivity, the Southern oligarchy opposed any political program that tended to "elevate or excite the masses, black or white"—that is, any political program outside of race baiting.[20] To this end, the ruling elite in every Southern state consciously and creatively played the "race card" in elections—blaming blacks for the region's poverty and problems—to keep poor whites from the hill country on the side of the planter elite.[21]

In *Let Us Now Praise Famous Men* (1941), James Agee's poetic prose and Walker Evans's stark photos laid bare the abject poverty of poor white sharecroppers during the Depression. Capitalism had transformed the yeoman farmers of the 19th century into sharecroppers locked in poverty similar to their black neighbors. Without land or economic skills, poor Southern whites had little to no chance of climbing up the socioeconomic ladder. However, even the poorest whites knew that their social status rose far above every black person they met; in the semifeudal South, this privileged position meant a great deal. Poor whites "were given public deference and titles of courtesy because they were white," wrote W. E. B. Du Bois.

> It must be remembered that the white group of laborers while they received a low wage, were compensated in part by *a sort of public and psychological wage* . . . They were admitted freely with all classes of white people to public functions, public parks, and the best schools . . . Their vote selected public officials and while this had small effect upon their economic situation, it had great effect upon their personal treatment and the deference shown them . . . [they] saw in every advance of Negroes a threat to their racial prerogatives.[22]

A SPECIFIC KIND OF RACISM

Southern slavery and the Jim Crow regime of rigorous apartheid instituted at the beginning of the 20th century were characterized by a specific kind of racism. Xenophobia, the term used by the ancient Greeks to explain a "reflexive feeling of hostility to the stranger or Other," can be a starting point for racism. But racism is more than a blatant dislike of a certain group of people and it is also distinct from intolerance, which criticizes and perse-cutes others for what they believe. Instead, racism attacks people for "what they intrinsically are." Stanford scholar George M. Fredrickson says racism is about the establishment of "a racial order, a permanent group hierarchy" that believers see reflecting the natural order or the will of God above.[23] The white supremacism of the South stigmatized African Americans as subhuman. Before and after slavery, Southern whites were taught from childhood that blacks were morally, intellectually, and biologically infe-rior and "suited only for manual work."[24] African Americans learned from childhood that whites regarded them as subhuman and their role was to defer and serve the master race. Blacks were understood to have a tendency toward childlike behavior and an inclination to laziness and criminality.[25]

In Germany, the racism against Jews was different. Assimilated into German society, Jews were not viewed as incompetent. No longer confined to the ghetto, Jews competed and succeeded as middle-class professionals. American blacks never had this chance because the racial hierarchy of the South depended on poor whites taking out their anger on the lowest caste—blacks—instead of the planter class. Forced illiteracy and lack of economic opportunity, as well as the harsh enforcement of Jim Crow norms of subservience, meant generations of African Americans lived life at the bottom of an impoverished region. Almost never were blacks in a position to "exert authority over whites."[26] In Germany, anti-Semitism became virulent, in part, because middle-class Germans resented the success Jews demonstrated at business and the professions. According to Fredrickson, "Germans feared that, under modern competitive conditions, which alleg-edly reward the clever and unscrupulous, Jews might be their superiors. Dis-crimination was justified, therefore, as a means of self-preservation. Most white Americans, on the other hand, believed that blacks were innately incompetent in all ways that mattered. The danger that they represented for extreme racists was the disease, violent criminality, and sexual contamination that a large population in the process of degenerating, or 'reverting to savagery,' could present to their white neighbors."[27] In the United States, it was racism of inclusion (in limited fashion) and domination. In Germany, it was racism of exclusion and extermination, the belief that it was impossible for Germans and Jews to "coexist in the same society." Jews were too dangerous, hence the Final Solution. In both cases, racism was based on a "belief in permanent, unbridgeable differences" between the racists and their target.[28]

SEEKING ALLIANCE WITH NORTHERN BUSINESS ELITES

At the end of World War II, seeing the nascent civil rights movement given support by President Harry Truman, South Carolina's Strom Thurmond led the 1948 Dixiecrat revolt against the Democratic Party. Charles Wallace Collins, the leading Southern public intellectual of the time, argued for an alliance of Southern white supremacy and Northern economic conservatism. Foreshadowing the Gingrich-Trump alliance, in *Whither Solid South?: A Study in Politics and Race Relations* (1947), Collins proposed a realignment of national politics that would place Southern Democrats and right-wing Republicans in one party (today's GOP) and New Dealers and racial liberals in the other (today's Democratic Party).[29]

By 1952, Collins and the Dixiecrats were anxious to take their argument to the national level; in doing so, they understood that a straightforward defense of racism might be a tough sell.[30] In the U.S. Senate, Mississippi's John Stennis arrived in Washington in 1948 to fill the seat of Theodore Bilbo, a notorious white supremacist. Stennis was in fundamental agreement with Bilbo's views on race relations, but the former circuit judge took a new approach that focused on building bridges with conservative whites in the North. Like Collins, Stennis understood that "nationalizing the problem" required that "Southerners downplay regional appeals and racist rhetoric."[31] The best hope for white Southerners, argued Stennis, was to stress personal liberty and the principles of American constitutional government.[32] Retreating from a direct argument in favor of white supremacy, the Dixiecrats adjusted their rhetoric to speak about "a national revolt" against the "overreach" of the New Deal state.[33]

GEORGE WALLACE AND
RAGE AGAINST GOVERNMENT

In the 1960s and early 1970s, Alabama governor George Wallace demonstrated to the nation just how Southern illiberalism could survive and thrive in a world that had bid Jim Crow segregation goodbye. In his presidential campaigns of 1968 and 1972, Wallace took the "defeated" planter ideology of the Southern oligarchy to a national audience—with devastating effect. Neither an intellectual nor a restrained Washington politician, Wallace, in his combative, flamboyant way, spoke the language of the white working class, first in the South and then across the nation. In doing so, Wallace perfected an angry rhetoric that was implicitly racial while being explicitly critical of the federal government and the "liberal elites" who dominated Washington. No one who heard Governor Wallace missed his message. More than anyone else, the defiant Wallace fashioned the antigovernment rhetoric that infiltrated America's national politics; he paved the road for Newt Gingrich and the Tea Party right. For decades, journalists and political observers spoke admiringly of the "Southern strategy" that Presidents Richard Nixon and Ronald Reagan employed to win over the previously solid Democratic South.[34] But the more important change was Southern influence moving north, led by Wallace, a brilliant change agent, and his protégés—political strategist Lee Atwater and talk radio pioneer Rush Limbaugh.[35]

Over the past fifty years, in a critical shift pioneered by Wallace, the animosity that Southern whites once expressed toward blacks has been sublimated and nationalized as rage against government.[36] To verbally abuse African Americans with vicious slurs—as illustrated in the movie *42*, Hollywood's 2013 version of Brooklyn Dodger Jackie Robinson breaking the color barrier in major league baseball—was no longer acceptable. But rage against government—as an autonomous, powerful force that might impose arbitrary rules and regulations made by Washington bureaucrats (who could not park their bicycles straight, according to Wallace)—is perfectly legitimate.

Merging with the radical libertarian message that government endangers liberty and interferes with the market, rage against government quickly became the stock rhetorical ace in the hole for the Republican right. From Wallace and Vice President Spiro Agnew to contemporary Republicans, government became the whipping boy of illiberals. A fiery and charming speaker too crude, too blunt, and too Southern to be elected president himself, Wallace took the antigovernment message of the South to the nation and, in so doing, accelerated and reinforced the right turn that Goldwater and the Birchers represented in the Republican Party.[37]

A protégé of Governor Jim Folsom, Wallace was a populist by nature; his ability to go to college was due in part to his mother securing a job as a sewing supervisor in a New Deal job-training program after his father died at age forty.[38] The towering 6-foot-8 Folsom demonstrated that it was possible to be elected in the South without racist bile. A hill country politician, "Big Jim" refused to play the race card. Whenever he finished a stump speech, Big Jim would seek out a black person and shake their hand.[39] By contrast, Wallace's racial attitudes were typical of his generation of white Southerners. Based in the Pacific theater during World War II, Wallace told his Northern B-29 crewmembers, "I don't hate them . . . The colored are fine in their place, don't get me wrong. But they're like children, and it's not something that's going to change. It's written in stone."[40] Wallace had what *New York Times* journalist Tom Wicker called the "traditional Southern attitude toward Negroes—a mixture of contempt, distaste, amusement, affection, and appreciation for a valuable servant."[41] After the 1954 Supreme Court decision in *Brown v. Board of Education*, an intense backlash of white opinion called for massive resistance. Seeing the winds shift, Wallace broke with Folsom.[42] But his switch was not enough to ensure his victory in the governor's race in 1958. His opponent, a staunch segregationist, had driven the NAACP out of Alabama; attacked for being soft on segregation, Wallace lost. Afterward, he told his inner circle, "no other son-of-a-bitch will ever out-nigger me again."[43]

The year 1963 was notable for its soaring rhetoric about civil rights. Martin Luther King gave his "I Have a Dream" speech and President Kennedy framed civil rights as a moral issue for the nation as a whole. In Alabama, George Wallace issued a stirring illiberal battle cry. In his inaugural address, he famously said "*segregation now, segregation tomorrow, segregation forever.*[44] Speechwriter Asa "Ace" Carter, a former radio announcer, service station owner, and Ku Klux Klan organizer with a history of violence against blacks, had told Wallace, "Here's the lines that are gonna catch everybody," and he was right.[45] Wallace instantly made himself the champion of the embattled white South.

"Segregation now" is the line people remember, yet the importance of the speech lies in the pivot Wallace makes from the traditional hatred of blacks to a hatred of government. Reaching beyond his Alabama audience to speak to the white majority across the nation, Wallace and Asa Carter avoided race and instead declared war on the federal government and the liberal elite. In a voice halfway between a snarl and a defiant shout, Wallace warned his audience, "Then this government must assume more and more police powers and we find we are becoming government-fearing people, not God-fearing people. We find we have replaced faith with fear, and though we may give lip service to the Almighty, in reality, government has become our god. It is, therefore, a basically ungodly government and its appeal to the pseudointellectual and the politician is to change their status from servant of the people to master of the people, to play at being God, without faith in God, and without the wisdom of God."[46] Wallace asserted that the South, in defying court orders to end school segregation, was not defying the law: "We have witnessed such acts of 'might makes right' over the world as men yielded to the temptation to play God, but we have never before witnessed it in America. We reject such acts as free men. We do not defy, for there is nothing to defy, since as free men we do not recognize any government right to give freedom, or deny freedom. No government erected by man has that right."[47]

Beginning in his inaugural address and continuing across his presidential campaigns, Wallace succeeded in a masterful inversion that continues to have ramifications today. He convinced whites—first in Alabama and then across the nation—that "everything they believed in was being swept away by an overbearing and oppressive federal government, that *they*—not blacks—were victims of oppression."[48] In asserting states' rights in a way that echoed the argument Southerners made against Reconstruction, Wallace made the argument that the South should be able to practice its own customs and follow its own unique way of life: "This nation was never meant to be a unit of one, but a united of the many." Wallace concluded his address with a call to the freedom favored by illiberals. He asked his audience to "Stand up for Alabama" in "this fight to win and preserve *our* freedoms and liberties."[49]

WALLACE ON THE STUMP

The Yellowhammer state was the citadel of Southern resistance to the civil rights crusade. Witness the epic struggle: Rosa Parks and the Montgomery bus strike, Wallace blocking the entrance to the University of Alabama in Tuscaloosa, Eugene "Bull" Connor and the Birmingham police force unleashing fire hoses, dogs, and billy clubs on nonviolent marchers, the Ku Klux Klan bombing of the 16th Street Baptist Church that killed four little girls, the assassination of NAACP leader Medgar Evers, the 1965 confrontation on the Edmund Pettus Bridge outside Selma, Martin Luther King's letters from the Selma jail, and the climactic march from Selma to Montgomery led by King.

King recognized Wallace as his most cunning and determined foe, viewing him as "perhaps the most dangerous racist in America today . . . I am not sure he believes all the poison he preaches, but he is artful enough to convince others that he does."[50] Before national audiences, Wallace was combative, but careful to frame his argument around an attack on an intrusive federal government and the public's fear of disorder. However, during a meeting with President Johnson at the White House in 1965, the president asked, "George, why are you doing this? You ought not. You came into office a liberal—you spent all your life wanting to do things for the poor. Now why are you working on this? Why are you off on this black thing? You ought to be down there calling for help for Aunt Susie in the nursing home."[51] Johnson was right. Wallace began his political career as a New Deal liberal who believed in government activism and programs and, as governor, he did not waver. As Alabama's chief executive between 1963 and 1967, just as he declared rhetorical war against big government, Wallace erected fourteen new junior colleges and fifteen trade schools, initiated a $100 million public school–building program, provided free textbooks to all Alabama schoolchildren, and oversaw the largest road-building program in the state's history.[52] He was the Pat Brown of the South.

Yet Wallace found that speaking about activist government did not generate nearly the crowd reaction as when he spoke about race directly or used code words to attack the racial liberalism of Great Society Democrats. Stung by a confrontation with a longtime supporter upset by his turn to raw racism after his lost gubernatorial bid in 1958, Wallace responded, "I started off talking about schools and highways and prisons and taxes—I couldn't make them listen. Then I began talking about niggers—and they stomped the floor."[53] During his successful run for governor in 1962, Wallace worked hard to connect with his audience. Asa Carter became his favorite speechwriter, and to him he would say, "Ace, write me something that is a little fiery."[54] At each campaign stop, Wallace would try something new; his staff watched for reactions and told him what was working, what was getting people excited.

Journalist Wayne Greenhaw described Wallace on the stump in 1962: "He stood flatfooted on the back of the truck. He hollered into the microphone about the outside evils encroaching on these good peoples' everyday lives, and when he got that bait planted real good and solid, he'd jerk the old fishing pole. 'First thing you know, the federal courts'll be telling you who you can invite over for Sunday dinner and who you can't,' he allowed. They whistled and clapped. They liked that. They'd punch each other in the sides with their elbows and nod and grin. 'Ol' George'll tell 'em,' they said. He would rock forward on his toes and back on his heels. 'The federal government up in Washington is breathin' down our backs, and we got to fight 'em off! You elect me yo' governor and I'll fight 'em!' And they knew he would."[55]

An invitation to speak in Wisconsin transformed Wallace from a Southern obstructionist into a national political force. Addressing white ethnics on Milwaukee's south side in March 1964 shortly after announcing his bid for president, Wallace discovered his audience responded enthusiastically to his message. How could a deep South segregationist connect with an audience of Poles, Czechs, Hungarians, and Serbs? "My message is for all," Wallace told them nervously as he began to speak. By the time he finished with, "a vote for this little governor will let the people in Washington know that we want them to leave our homes, schools, jobs, businesses and farms alone," his audience was standing on its feet, cheering and clapping. Discovering that he had an "absolute rapport"—thirty-four ovations during a forty-minute speech—with a Northern working-class audience was an epiphany for Wallace.[56]

In July 1964, President Johnson signed the historic Civil Rights Act. Forty-eight hours later, Wallace addressed a rally in Atlanta. In the sweltering heat, he brought the crowd to its feet declaring that the President of the United States had just signed into law "the most monstrous piece of legislation every enacted . . . a fraud, a sham and a hoax, this bill will live in infamy . . . liberal left-wingers have passed it. Now let them employ some 'pinknik' social engineers in Washington to figure out what to do with it . . . we must destroy the power to dictate, to forbid, to require, to demand." Greenhaw watched the governor with a mixture of awe and alarm. Having just delivered one of the most powerfully racist speeches Greenhaw had ever heard, Wallace had "never uttered the 'n-word.' Instead, his code phrases included: 'the boot of tyranny,' 'the power to dictate,' 'the framework of our priceless freedoms.'" Greenhaw asked, *whose* priceless freedoms?[57] Dan Carter, Wallace's biographer, knew: "Those of the white people of a collapsing social order." The governor understood their pain and spoke for them.[58]

You can hear the echo of Wallace's battle cries, "Stand up for Alabama" and "Stand up for America" in Donald Trump's slogan, "Make America Great Again." What Wallace stood up for was the caste structure, inequality, and privilege of the traditional South and America's original sin. Running for president, Wallace was a political revivalist offering a primal, seductive message about a return to an older, more secure world to a white audience traumatized by the turmoil and social upheaval of the 1960s and '70s. Speaking to rallies across the country, Wallace understood and gave voice to millions of whites of unexceptional circumstance who longed for "a stable world in which work was rewarded, laziness punished, blacks knew their place, men headed the household, women were men's loyal helpmates, and children were safe from vulgar language."[59]

Wallace insisted that the civil rights struggle was part of a larger debate about the power, size, and purpose of government. Earlier populist crusaders had made big business and Wall Street the target of their wrath; Wallace pounded on Washington. Instead of the wealthy elite, his targets were the liberal intellectuals, "the briefcase-carrying bureaucrats," who flocked to Washington to try out their public policy designs, their aspirations for "utopia." He focused on liberal politicians and "elitist" bureaucrats to personify the wicked abstraction called *Washington*.[60] For Wallace and his imitators, this hatred of government cloaked a hatred for minority groups and the poor who, according to this narrative, were suddenly given an unwarranted privileged status by liberal elites social engineering a society that did not need fixing.

Wallace was *the* transitional figure in the linguistic shift from rage against the black man, which was perfectly acceptable in the Old South, to rage against the government, central to the illiberal right's contemporary message. His slashing attacks on government and liberal technocrats anticipated the politics of the present. On the campaign trail, Wallace discovered a large audience of whites outside the South who held racist attitudes and benefited from the psychic wage of "whiteness." Playing the old planter trick of divide and conquer with fiendish dexterity, Wallace sowed the seeds of hate in the hearts and minds of middle- and working-class Americans. He played on their insecurities by telling them that he understood their feelings of powerlessness and would protect them against the liberal elites out to ruin America. Audiences responded as passionately to Governor Wallace in the 1960s and '70s as they do to President Trump at his rallies; both defend the psychological and emotional benefits that whites receive from a racial caste system.

8

Zealots in Charge

In the mid-20th century, the Republican Party had four distinct wings: Progressives such as New York governor Nelson Rockefeller with a lineage back to Theodore Roosevelt, moderates such as President Dwight Eisenhower, staunch traditional conservatives such as Ohio senator Howard Taft, and a right-wing fringe (animated by Senator Joseph McCarthy's anticommunist crusade) chasing the minimalist government vision championed by libertarian economists such as F. A. Hayek and Milton Friedman.[1] Only one of these was strongly reactionary.

Before the 1960s, the idea of purging the Republican Party of heretics who did not pass an ideological test would have been rejected as absurd. Aspects of the progressive and moderate approaches to public policy struck Taft conservatives aligned to the right of Eisenhower as wrongheaded, but these conservatives knew that broad coalitions won elections. While some Taft conservatives edged toward *paleoconservative*—skeptical about foreign trade, overseas military alliances, and nativist when it came to immigration policy—most understood that postwar America was a melting pot of different ethnicities, regions, and industries that needed political bridge builders, not purists. Yet excommunicating nonbelievers is just what "movement conservatives" did after they succeeded in nominating Senator Barry Goldwater as the GOP's standard-bearer in 1964. Instead of viewing progressive, moderate, and conservative Republicans as team members who were slightly misguided, the New Right labeled them traitors to be eliminated, and, led by brass-knuckle operatives such as F. Clifton ("Clif") White, they borrowed political techniques from the communist left to do just that.

> White . . . wanted to emulate the Communists. He saw in their example the methods by which a small, disciplined minority, uninhibited by bourgeois scruples over fair play or tradition or truth, could defeat a majority and bend an organization to its will.[2]

The push for illiberal purity came as presidents John F. Kennedy of Massachusetts and Lyndon Johnson of Texas turned against the segregationist wing of the Democratic Party and together with a majority of the Republican Party passed the landmark Civil Rights Act of 1964 and Voting Rights Act of 1965.[3] The second Reconstruction put an end to American apartheid 100 years after the end of the Civil War. In response, GOP presidential candidates Richard Nixon and Ronald Reagan signaled a rightward shift on race by taking stances against busing and affirmative action and speaking about mythical "welfare queens" driving Cadillacs.

As the GOP became a party increasingly anchored in the South, conservatives in the mode of Robert Taft in the 1950s, Howard Baker in the 1970s, and Bob Dole in the 1990s—who had long dominated the Republican Party—lost power and stature. The GOP's Southern wing pushed for the protection of white privilege and the patriarchal traditional family, while illiberal business elites pressed for economic policies that strongly favored the wealthy. Instead of policies focused on assisting the middle class and businesses on Main Street, Republican economic policy became a servant to the plutocrats of the postindustrial finance era. Between the Eisenhower administration and the George W. Bush years, a pronounced shift took place toward economic policies that favored the wealthiest instead of the broad middle.[4]

THE IMPORTANCE OF WILLIAM F. BUCKLEY

A rebel with a cause—defending wealthy white elites against the onslaught of New Deal liberalism that was "destroying America"—the witty, urbane William F. Buckley Jr. pioneered the illiberal style of going for shock in the 1950s. His message to future provocateurs on the right: "be bold, shocking, daring, and rebellious." The Catholic, well-to-do Buckley would seem to have little to complain about except that he attended Yale College post–New Deal versus the 1880s when Charles Sumner was preaching social Darwinism. In *God and Man at Yale* (1951), Buckley unleashed his rancor on the Yale faculty he believed taught atheism as well as Keynesian economics. In an audacious and rather silly argument, Buckley said academic freedom was an impediment to learning and that those professors who did not foster a belief in God and free enterprise should be fired. The book was a sensation and while his message was different than Jack Kerouac or C. Wright Mills, Buckley anticipated the radical '60s and ushered in a style that would change American culture. After defending Joseph McCarthy in a second book, Buckley founded *National Review* in 1955 and surrounded himself with thinkers such as Whittaker Chambers, Frank Meyer, Brent Bozell, and Russell Kirk. Buckley and the magazine embodied radical libertarianism, devotion to religion, and aggressive anticommunism. As editor, Buckley's goal was to explode the stereotype that conservatives were dull. Indeed, *National Review* exhibited an adolescent youthful spirit as it sought to identify New Deal liberalism as a stalking horse for Lenin and Stalin.[5] For Buckley and his followers, liberals were unfit for the leadership of a free society because they are intrinsically incapable of offering serious opposition to the Soviet and Chinese communists.[6] Buckley and his colleagues loathed Eisenhower, Senator Taft, and middle-of-the-road Republicans who accepted and supported the New Deal. The New Right rejected the premise that government could legitimately cushion the harsher features of capitalism.

For moderate Republicans, liberalism was not the enemy; instead, liberals were allies in the fight against fascism and Soviet communism. To Eisenhower adviser Arthur Larson, Roosevelt's New Deal, while imperfect, was a reform movement that prevented what could have been a revolution from the left or the right.[7] The Burkean Republicanism that President

Eisenhower preached and that Larson championed in *A Republican Looks at his Party* (1956) espoused balance, reason, prudence, and common sense and sought to rationalize and reform the New Deal rather than repeal it. Eisenhower balanced the budget three times in eight years, cut federal employment, and famously warned of a growing "military industrial complex" while supporting public housing, conservation, the extension of Social Security, and the creation of the national highway network. Unlike the Republican presidents who followed Richard Nixon, Ike did not radically cut taxes on the rich.[8]

In contrast, Buckley, Meyer, and the *National Review* circle viewed the world as Hayek did—there were only two roads forward: a radical minimalist government presiding over a free-market economy or the slippery slide to a totalitarian nightmare. *National Review* viewed moderate Republicans, liberal New Dealers, and left-wing Progressives of the Henry Wallace camp as bunkmates of the communists on a downward plunge. The right also broke with mainstream Republicans on the issue of race. In a 1957 editorial, *National Review* sided strongly with white Southerners:

> The central question that emerges . . . is whether the White community in the South is entitled to take such measures as are necessary to prevail, politically and culturally, in areas where it does not predominate numerically: The sobering answer is *Yes*—the White community is so entitled because, for the time being, it is the more advanced race.[9]

Buckley famously purged the John Birch Society and its founder, Robert Welch, from the conservative movement for trafficking in wild conspiracy arguments—one of which was that President Eisenhower was controlled by the Kremlin. He correctly understood that if the illiberal right was to make headway in becoming a dominant political force it was best if the most embarrassing characters were hidden from view. But just because Buckley tried to police the outright wackos on the illiberal fringe does not mean he was a moderate. He was not. He was a true believer in the reactionary cause across a life "noteworthy for its constancy."[10] At first blush, it seems a stretch to say that William F. Buckley and Ann Coulter are cut from the same cloth. But, as the first conservative pundit on television when his *Firing Line* premiered in 1966, Buckley demonstrated that right-wing conservatives could command a large audience. A verbal virtuoso with eyebrows arched and pencil in hand, Buckley set the mold for the more outrageous and confrontational personas of the cable-digital era.[11]

FROM REAGAN TO GINGRICH

President Reagan was one of the founders of the modern right. Yet in his political career he straddled the liberal/reactionary divide. The irony of Reagan's presidency is that while he did more than anyone else to link the Old South to the New Right and thus create the current supercharged illiberal right, he himself remained something of a Lockean liberal. By the 1960s, intellectually Reagan was a man of the hard right—he read libertarian economists Ludwig von Mises, Hayek, and Milton Friedman—and, as a General Electric spokesman in the 1950s, he spent time in the segregated South. But the Illinois native was not racially prejudiced (his parents raised him to be colorblind) and he worshiped President Franklin Roosevelt for more than half his life. Reagan continued to admire FDR after he began to question the size and expense of big government. During the Great Depression, Roosevelt's Works Progress Administration had employed Reagan's father, and the son identified with the basic Jeffersonian values of liberty, equality, and fair play. A self-made man, Reagan identified with strivers and entrepreneurs, rather than those born to privilege. His sunny personality and pragmatism, in terms of taking half a loaf in legislative battles, contrasts sharply with the zealotry of post-Reagan leaders such as Newt Gingrich, Paul Ryan, Ted Cruz, and Mitch McConnell. Reagan had no trouble negotiating and cutting deals with progressive Democrats, both as governor of California and as president working closely with Democratic House Speaker Tip O'Neill; he understood the difference between rhetoric and governing as well as the necessity of operating in the liberal framework established by Jefferson, Madison, and the founders, and modernized by Lincoln and FDR.[12]

A champion of the right, Reagan was not a prisoner of its worst tendencies. An exceptional leader, Reagan both harnessed and tempered the energies of the right; intellectually he was an ideologue, temperamentally he was not. Rhetorically conservative and illiberal, Reagan was a pragmatist in terms of policy and believed in dialogue and compromise, unlike much of the right today. He worked hard to achieve as much as possible for his strong conservative beliefs, but understood that give-and-take is how public policy gets made. As governor, he learned to negotiate with progressive liberals; he did not consider them terrible people, just elected officials who had a different view of the role government should play. Reagan succeeded Pat Brown, a leading example of New Deal activism. Conservative Southern California suburbs outside Los Angeles that became "Reagan country" benefited from government spending. Reagan knew this and did not attack most public achievements as creeping socialism or the leading edge of totalitarianism. Famously against taxes, he raised them often during his time as governor. And while Reagan thought much of Lyndon Johnson's Great Society was misguided, he had great respect for Roosevelt and the New Deal. Both as governor and president, Reagan sought to slow the growth of government and curb domestic programs, but his actions belied an intention to seriously reverse or roll back the welfare state. In the 1980s, when illiberals such as direct mail pioneer Richard Viguerie implored, "Let Reagan be Reagan," this was understood as a message to James Baker and Michael Deaver in Reagan's inner circle not to block the president's illiberal tendencies. The right wanted to believe that Reagan was a pure illiberal in the way they were; fortunately for the rest of the nation, he was not.

If Reagan had an illiberal head and a Lockean liberal heart, this has not been true of Speaker Gingrich and the Republican leaders who have followed him. More than for his brief House speakership during the Clinton presidency, Newt Gingrich will be remembered for how he dramatically changed the political culture of the House of Representatives and engineered the 1994 midterm election victory that gave Republicans control of the House of Representatives for the first time in 40 years. A former history professor, Gingrich adopted a slashing take-no-prisoners style. Among the pyrotechnic gems Gingrich's political vocabulary made possible: "Corrupt liberal bosses cheat, lie, and steal to impose their sick pathetic cynicism and bizarre radical stagnation in order to destroy America." Injecting the confrontational style of the 1960s into the political realm, Gingrich pioneered the politics of character assassination against his liberal opponents and against liberalism as a whole. As he plotted his rise to power in the

1980s, Gingrich castigated Democrats around the clock on C-SPAN and recruited Republican candidates across the country. Memos to his troops included the language to use against liberal opponents: *betray bizarre bosses bureaucracy cheat corrupt crisis cynicism decay destroy disgrace impose incompetent liberal lie limit(s) obsolete pathetic radical shame sick stagnation status quo steal taxes they/them threaten traitors unionized waste welfare.*[13]

Gingrich understood that politics was performance art and rather than be a legislator seeking to build coalitions and do the hard work of passing bills, he focused on framing simple, easily understood messages for a mass audience. Along with other illiberal entrepreneurs—Rush Limbaugh on talk radio, Roger Ailes (who learned the politics of resentment from Richard Nixon) on Fox News, Grover Norquist and his anti-tax pledge, and Coulter in the book world—Gingrich ushered in the modern world of radically polarized politics in which Republicans strive to win and govern by themselves.

Gingrich's distinctive combination of ideological commitment and partisan animosity, gift for saying outrageous falsehoods as if they were as true as the sun rising in the east, and zeal in driving home a malevolent message had a transformational impact on the Republican Party. Many observers hold Gingrich responsible for popularizing the view that the federal government is fundamentally corrupt and that any and all liberal ideas should be treated like the plague. While Republicans love to worship the optimistic, good-natured Reagan, Gingrich's mean-spirited approach to politics is the one they have adopted.[14] For more than thirty years, the right has followed Gingrich in demonizing not only its opponents, but also the entire federal government.[15]

The shift from Ronald Reagan to Newt Gingrich was powered, in part, by evangelical Christians joining the Republican Party en masse and the activism of New Right strategists Paul Weyrich and Richard Viguerie. These two conservative Catholics saw the Republican Party as a vessel for the right's political vision and understood that a focus on issues such as busing, abortion, and gun rights would bring evangelical white Christians—a large voting bloc in the South and the Sunbelt—increasingly to the GOP fold. The energetic partisanship of white evangelicals, both in and out of the South, was crucial to Reagan's two presidential victories and the ensuing illiberal transformation of the GOP.

In the 1920s, the cultural disruptions of modernity—urbanization, youthful hedonism, Freud and the loosening of sexual mores, the challenge of science to a literal reading of the Bible, and the flood of Catholic and Jewish immigrants to northern cities—made fundamentalists fear that the United States was losing its identity as a white Protestant nation and becoming a modern Babylon—the wicked city of the Old Testament.[16] But the political power of fundamentalists was split between the two parties.[17] In the 1930s, Southern Baptists as Southern Democrats supported FDR's New Deal as northern fundamentalists criticized the increase of federal power. In the 1940s, the conservative Protestants who created the National Association of Evangelicals dropped the label "fundamentalist" in favor of the more upbeat "evangelical," and in the 1950s President Eisenhower and Congress added the phrase "under God" to the Pledge of Allegiance as the idea of America as a fundamentally Christian nation was enlisted in the battle against Communism.[18]

Both aspects of American illiberalism helped create the religious right of the last half century. As Princeton historian Kevin Kruse shows in *One Nation Under God: How Corporate America Invented Christian America*, right-wing business elites enlisted conservative evangelical pastors to fight the "slavery" of FDR's New Deal. Their mutual fear of Soviet Communism helped elect Eisenhower and shift evangelicals to the Republican Party.[19] The shift was solidified after the Civil Rights revolutions prompted many Southern whites to abandon the Democratic Party. One of the leaders of this political realignment was the founder of the Moral Majority, Reverend Jerry Falwell. Like many white Southerners at the height of the civil rights struggle, Falwell was an outspoken segregationist. Billy Graham, a North Carolina native, straddled the racial divide by supporting *Brown v. Board of Education* while criticizing Martin Luther King Jr. By contrast, Falwell passionately objected to any change in the racial caste system of the South. As the young pastor of a fast-growing fundamentalist Baptist church in Lynchburg, Virginia, Falwell told his congregation, "The true negro does not want integration. He realizes his potential is far better among his own race. Who then is propagating this terrible thing? . . . We see the hand of Moscow in the background." Falwell concluded his 1958 sermon by assuring his white audience that racial integration was the product of the "Devil himself."[20] Following the passage of the Civil Rights Act of 1964,

Falwell started Lynchburg Christian Academy when the town's schools integrated in 1967. Because the *Brown* decision did not apply to private schools many private Christian schools in the South—sometimes called "segregation academies"—became a refuge for well-to-do whites.[21] In 2012, decades after the civil rights revolution, *The Atlantic* reported that in many of these private Christian schools, not one black person could be found.[22]

Long wary about direct involvement in politics, Falwell was recruited by Weyrich to launch the Moral Majority in 1979. Falwell, Pat Robinson, and other evangelical leaders saw an opportunity to "change the nation's government by forming a comprehensive political movement allied with the New Right."[23] Courted by Ronald Reagan during the 1980 campaign, Falwell helped shape a Republican platform that included endorsements of prayer in school, prohibition of abortion, and a denunciation of the Equal Rights Amendment (ERA) that the GOP had supported for four decades. With Reagan at the top of the ticket sending a message that he was conservative on race, white Southern Baptists abandoned the Democratic Party and reshaped the South into a Republican stronghold. Adopting culture war rhetoric and Willie Horton–type racial campaign attacks when necessary, the Republican Party of Reagan and Gingrich presented Democratic appeals to fairness as a commitment to favor minorities over whites. Republican voters increasingly viewed public policy through a racial filter. The push for welfare reform by Republicans appealed to voters "who believed not only that the poor were often undeserving, but that the undeserving were often black."[24]

At war with both liberalism and traditional conservatives, the New Right had a vision "less of party than of *partisan majority*," with the Republican Party being a bottle for illiberal drink.[25] The goal was power and Weyrich excelled at developing and executing a strategy to push the GOP rightward by mobilizing voter groups that could supersede the fraying New Deal coalition. A "rejection of limits and the absence of internal checks on extremism" was intrinsic to the New (or illiberal) Right.[26] Blue-collar Wallace voters animated by coded racial appeals became a core voting bloc for the New Right's majority coalition. Between 1973 and 1976, direct-mail wizard Viguerie took on Wallace as a client and raised approximately $7 million for the Alabama governor. Viguerie understood that Wallace "was not a 100 percent conservative. He had a lot of populist, non-conservative ideas. But he and I agreed on about 80 percent of the important issues, social issues such as busing and law and order . . . So we struck a bargain."[27] The New Right alliance with Wallace helped set the stage for the later populism of Pat Buchanan and Donald Trump. The New Right also played a key role in the emergence and success of Gingrich, who had been a moderate Republican growing up. Meeting Weyrich at a campaign school in 1975, Gingrich became Weyrich's protégé and quickly grasped that politics was all about winning the majority and that "party mattered only if it would aid in that essential task." In 2005, Gingrich looked back on his House career and wrote, "All of our work was done against the active, continuing opposition of the traditional party" and Burkean-Eisenhower style establishment conservatives.[28]

In the post-Gingrich era, conservatism remains alive in the writings of George F. Will and other conservative pundits such as *Weekly Standard* founder William Kristol, but among Republican elected officials, classic conservatism has become a relic, like a dinner jacket from the 1950s. Under siege over the past thirty years, traditional GOP moderates and conservatives faced a choice—shift right or face political excommunication and exile. They could stay true to their beliefs and exit the political stage or join, and swear allegiance to, the right—similar to the crypto-Jews or *conversos* who became Catholic during the Spanish Inquisition.[29] President George H. W. Bush, Arizona senator John McCain, and Senate Majority Leader Mitch McConnell all faced an existential choice. Bush 41 famously toed the illiberal line of "no new taxes" during his 1988 campaign only to break that pledge while in office. His mistake was not in his prudent decision to raise taxes to escape endless deficits, but in making the pledge. McCain touted his moderate side when teaming with liberal Minnesota senator Russ Feingold to lead the way on the McCain-Feingold Act, the 2002 campaign finance reform law, and on supporting comprehensive immigration reform, but under pressure in his 2010 Republican primary, he moved right and in 2016 gave a lukewarm endorsement of Donald Trump. McConnell avoided the troubles that the right made for President Bush and Senator McCain by sliding steadily to the illiberal pole and during the Obama presidency acted as the GOP's obstructer-in-chief. In deciding that the Senate should ignore its constitutional responsibilities and stonewall a vote on Justice Scalia's replacement on the U.S. Supreme

Court—even though past presidents had seen twenty-one of twenty-four judges nominated in the fourth year of a presidential term approved by the Senate—McConnell played the nullification card and revealed his Southern roots.[30]

THE REACTIONARY SIDE OF CONSERVATIVE INTELLECTUALS

In the early '60s, illiberals on the right appropriated the term "conservative" and declared victory over Eisenhower's center-right approach to American politics. Self-described "movement conservatives" believed the New Deal was alien to the American experience, Social Security a tragic mistake, and Lyndon Johnson's Great Society a fiasco of personal liberation and government dependency run amok.[31] These positions remain a tenet of faith for many on the right; the unrelenting attack on the Affordable Care Act is nothing new. By their steadfast insistence that the New Deal state is somehow illegitimate, intellectuals on the right contributed to the reactionary zealotry of the Republican base. Some conservative writers (such as *New York Times* columnist David Brooks) focus primarily on cultural issues and endorse the Burkean tradition of thinking about society as a complex web of interconnections and customs. But other prominent conservatives focus their fire on the liberal state and wish the Reagan Revolution had been more successful in rolling back the size and intrusiveness of the federal government.[32] Serious intellectuals (columnist George F. Will and Claremont McKenna College professor Charles Kesler are two examples) join Hayek when they oppose the New Deal state and Progressive Era reform.[33] Viewing the American founding, and especially the Constitution, as sacrosanct, there is a utopian, reactionary aspect to their thinking. In *The Conservative Sensibility* (2019), Will writes:

> "It has been our fate as a nation," the historian Richard Hofstadter said, "not to have ideologies but to be one." This sentence sacrifices accuracy for felicity. Writing in the middle of the twentieth century Hofstadter surely understood that the United States had long ceased to be a nation embodying only

one ideology. Since early in that century, and especially since the New Deal, there have been two political philosophies contending for supremacy. The original one, the Founders' natural rights philosophy, began to lose ground to progressivism more than a century ago and today is seeking to regain lost ground. What progressives aimed for, and largely achieved, was a second American Founding, this one taking its bearing not from unchanging nature but rather from history, which is a river of change.[34]

For these thinkers, the expansion of the federal government at the start of the 20th century is a wrong turn that deserves to be reversed.[35] Sam Tanenhaus, a former *New York Times Book Review* editor, makes an important distinction between revanchist and conservative in his book *The Death of Conservatism* (2009).[36] Derived from the French word for revenge, revanche is defined by Webster as a "political policy designed to recover lost territory or status." In the decades before the Reagan Revolution and subsequently, Republican intellectuals have championed a bucolic dream that the United States could have a dynamic world-leading corporate economy, a superpower defense budget, and a national security state while returning to the limited federal government of the 1890s. This is a chimera. But Will and other conservatives believe we should stay true to the "founders' revolutionary vision of limited government, separation of powers, maximal federalism, and inviolable individual freedom."[37] By falsely insisting that modern liberalism stands in opposition to the founders' vision for America, otherwise sane intellectuals have played a significant role in encouraging and enabling rabid illiberals more radical than they. Making things worse, over the past quarter-century center-right intellectuals—Max Boot and Michael Lind are two prominent examples—have been disavowed and excommunicated as the Republican Party has become increasingly reactionary.[38]

THE TEA PARTY'S RISE: THE BASE SHIFTS RIGHT

After Barack Obama's 2008 victory, the GOP—led by then House Majority Leader Eric Cantor along with former Speaker Paul Ryan and congressman Kevin McCarthy—had a plan. They sought to recruit:

a new generation of highly ideological and uncompromising conservative candidates for the 2010 elections, provide them with money and technical support, and keep the focus on fiscal issues. The fiscal issues served two goals: to reinforce voters' unhappiness with Washington and the economy, and to accomplish a greater end by decreasing—*by any means necessary*—the size of government to pre-1960s Great Society levels.[39]

Early in 2010, I was one of a group of *Time* correspondents reporting on the emerging Tea Party movement.[40] One of the things I discovered during a Tea Party rally in Scottsdale, Arizona (one of a series of regional reports for *Time's* March 1, 2010, cover story—"Tea Party America") was that the gathering included the statewide organizer for Americans for Prosperity (AFP). A professional political activist, Tom Jenney said he coached the local Tea Party groups in Arizona and that the goal of Americans for Prosperity was "to become the NRA of fiscal conservatism. We want people who cling to their guns to cling to their wallets and pensions with the same passion." He would not say who funded AFP. Research revealed that the low-tax libertarian advocacy group was sponsored primarily by the wealthy Koch family of Wichita, Kansas. Like its sister organization FreedomWorks, run by former House Majority Leader Richard Armey, AFP nurtured the Tea Party in its early days, offering training and logistical support. The Koch brothers wanted to have a grassroots movement, and not just corporate lobbyists working on issues for the right.[41] Honey E. L. Marques, the group's leader, told me, "Government has taken too much control. We want to take back our country. Look at the 35-plus czars in the White House, 99.9 percent of them are communist, socialist, Marxist theological ideologues." The then thirty-four-year-old physician's assistant, who discovered Rush Limbaugh while a teenager in Hawaii, said, "Obama wants to fundamentally transform the country and put a whole new system in place—call it socialist." Marques said that, along with activists from around the country, she had attended a Tea Party training seminar on the East Coast. There she learned that the big problem was the Progressive Era reforms put in place at the beginning of the 20th century. If only we could go back to the late 19th century, that was the golden age before big government made things terrible. A tried and true libertarian,

Marques declared, "the pure unfettered free-market system provides the best system possible—competition and choice for all."[42]

Across history, reactionary movements tend to be populated by educated, skilled, successful middle-class people who see a threat to their position and status and rally to defend privilege, hierarchy, inequality, and exclusion. The emergence of the Tea Party drew different reactions from observers. Some conservative authors argued that the Tea Party is simply a reaffirmation of basic conservative principles: limited government, national sovereignty, and constitutional originalism.[43] Other scholars saw the Tea Party expressing a reactionary strand of American political thought with roots tracing to the Ku Klux Klan and the John Birch Society. According to political scientists Christopher Parker and Matt Barreto, President Obama and his policies threatened Americans who view the world through the lens of "white, middle-class, middle-aged, Christian, heterosexual, mostly male identity."[44] Studying race and politics in seven states, including six of the 2008 battleground states, Parker and his University of Washington colleagues probed the differences between strong Tea Party supporters with the attitudes of all whites. Countering the claim of those who argue that Tea Party supporters are "principled conservatives" simply championing a smaller government, fiscal discipline, and free markets, Parker's data showed:

> that when you account for/control for conservatism, and partisanship . . . there's still *a strong connection between support for the Tea Party*—rather than conservative politics generally—*and racial resentment*. Indeed, ideology does matter: If one is conservative, he or she is 23 percent more likely than a liberal to hold racially resentful attitudes . . . (believing) that blacks simply need to work harder, and that the legacy of slavery and discrimination has no effect on blacks' current condition in American society.[45]

The emergence of the Tea Party movement in the United States can best be understood as an outgrowth of the increased illiberalism of the Republican electoral base. Drawing on evidence from American National Election Study surveys, Emory University political scientist Alan Abramowitz says that while only a small percentage of the Republican base participated in Tea Party protests, "the expansion of the activist conservative base of the

Republican Party has produced a large cadre of politically engaged sympathizers from which such participants can be recruited." Critically, over the past thirty years "there has been a marked increase in the size of the activist base of the Republican Party," Abramowitz says. Moreover, as the GOP's activist base swelled, it was also "becoming increasingly conservative [read: illiberal] . . . Rank-and-file Republicans have been following their party's leaders to the right . . . While the increase in conservatism was fairly modest among inactive Republicans, it was *very substantial* among the most active group—those engaging in at least three [campaign] activities."[46]

Along with their shift to illiberalism, Republican activists on the right have continually outworked the business class, traditional conservatives, and moderates.[47]

AN INTENSE MINORITY

Traditionally, political scientists and statesmen who care about the health of America's democratic system are concerned about minority rights.[48] Yet the cause of America's current crisis involving a renegade right is not the majority ignoring the rights of the minority. Instead, an intense minority, the reactionary right—standing well outside the Lockean liberal mainstream—aggressively seeks to impose its beliefs and values on a relatively apathetic majority. Our situation is, oddly, the reverse of the one over which James Madison and Robert Dahl lost sleep; it is more analogous to the Civil War era in which an intense minority—a small group of plantation owners who owned a majority of the black slaves in the South—sought to impose its economic and social system on the rest of the nation. The population of the South in 1860 was just 9.0 million, including 3.5 million slaves, across eleven states. In contrast, the North held nearly 21 million people living in twenty-three states.[49] Similarly today, illiberals are numerically a minority in the United States population even as they are a controlling influence inside the Republican Party. An intense, militant minority acting as a vanguard—Lenin's evocative term—often can have political influence that far surpasses its actual numbers.[50] Eccentric extremists, a few "wacko birds," as Senator McCain called them, always exist in politics and make good copy for journalists. However, trouble brews when a large number of legislators hold views that sharply clash with America's Lockean tradition.

Why does an intense illiberal minority control the Republican Party and Congress? In the years since the George W. Bush presidency, illiberal groups such as the Tea Party, the Club for Growth, and Koch's Americans for Prosperity, have challenged more mainstream Republicans in GOP primaries. In these situations, it is relatively easy for energized illiberals to mobilize and amass enough votes to win the Republican nomination. This happened all over the nation in the 2010 midterms when the emergence of the Tea Party stunned the Obama administration. In the Delaware Senate primary, the highly respected two-time governor and longtime Republican congressman Mike Castle was defeated by Christine O'Donnell. *Washington Post* columnist E. J. Dionne wrote, "After two decades in which the moderates fled a party increasingly dominated by its right wing, the Republican primary electorate has been reduced to nothing but its right wing." O'Donnell, an eccentric character who had trouble paying her rent and who spoke of believing in witchcraft, "pulled off her revolution with a little more than 30,000 votes. That's all it took," wrote Dionne, "to seize control of a once Grand Old Party in which the center no longer has the troops."[51] In Florida, Governor Charlie Crist, enjoying an approval rating of nearly 70 percent, seemed on cruise control to become the state's next Republican senator. There was one problem: Marco Rubio, the House Speaker of the Florida legislature but little-known outside of his Miami district, refused to quit the race when Texas senator John Cornyn, head of the National Republican Senate Campaign (NRSC), threw its weight and fundraising prowess behind Crist. Miffed, Rubio jumped on social media, positioned himself as a Tea Party crusader with the help of then South Carolina senator Jim DeMint, and used fury on the right around healthcare, President Obama, and the complacency of the Republican establishment to race past Crist in the polls and force the governor to run as an independent, before winning the general election in a walk.[52]

In Arizona, Democratic representative Gabrielle Giffords narrowly fought off a strenuous 2010 challenge by Jesse Kelly, a 6-foot-8, fire-breathing former Marine. When I interviewed Kelly for *Time*, he told me he decided to run for Congress against Giffords "because Barack Obama is ripping up my country." To face off against Giffords, Kelly had to first defeat front-runner state representative Jonathan Paton. Full-throated in their rejection and abhorrence of liberals and centrists of all stripes, Kelly, campaign manager Adam Kwasman, and their Tea Party colleagues viewed the conservative Paton as part of the problem. Libertarian free-market purists, Kelly and Kwasman said they believed the 2008 Wall Street collapse was caused by government interference. At a February Republican primary debate, 700 people jammed into an auditorium to hear Kelly say that the United States needed to cut taxes and that "if 10 percent was good enough for Jesus Christ it should be good enough for us." A Giffords staffer who watched the GOP debate said, "The crowd was so agitated and energized that I could see this could be a very tough campaign." In the triple-digit Tucson heat in June and July, Kelly's fundraising surged as his volunteers swarmed the district. At the end of August, Kelly won the Republican Primary, beating Paton soundly—49 to 41 percent. As the fall campaign began, Giffords noted that her opponent had said some remarkably harsh statements, such as, "Hopefully, there will be no Democrats left in Congress after the election," and that Kelly wanted to "crush liberals." An earlier campaign event ad produced by the Kelly team urged voters to: "Get on Target for Victory in November. Help remove Gabrielle Giffords from office. Shoot a fully automatic M16 with Jesse Kelly."

In Texas, 2014 primary headlines heralded incumbent senator Cornyn easily beating back Tea Party challengers. Yet the real story was the continued ascendancy of the party's right wing. As reported by Dan Balz of the *Washington Post*, GOP candidates bonded with the illiberal base:

> With no worries . . . about winning general elections, all the incentives push them to the right. Their impulse is to out-conservative their opponents . . . Call this tea party Republicanism or *a purer strain of conservatism*. The construct that this (the primary election season) was a true test of the GOP establishment vs. the tea party misses the point. As a new generation of leaders rises in the Lone Star State, there are few dissenters from the views of the party's most conservative wing.[53]

Mark Jones, a political scientist at Rice University, explained. Senator Cruz's 2012 campaign as a Tea Party icon "scared the daylights out of center and center-right conservatives to the extent that they do not feel comfortable enough to run on their true positions and feel compelled to cater to the most conservative elements of the Texas Republican primary electorate."[54]

PAUL RYAN AND TED CRUZ:
THE LEGACY OF RAND AND HAYEK

The radical anti-statist philosophy of the contemporary Republican Party comes to us via Spencer, Rand, and Hayek—three European intellectuals reacting to Marx.[55] The fear of a communist revolution may have made sense in Europe. However, it had no grounding in the United States; a Marxist-Leninist left never took root in America. Yet, to resist the liberal reforms of the Progressive and New Deal eras, American illiberals insisted on grafting this anti-Marxist ethos onto the small-government tradition of Thomas Jefferson. In doing so, however, modern-day radical libertarians such as Texas senator Ted Cruz and former House Speaker Paul Ryan confront a serious problem. Jefferson's ideals were intimately tied to an agrarian vision of preindustrial America filled with yeoman farmers of independent economic means. Jefferson believed a rural economy, as opposed to Hamilton's dream of factories and manufacturing, would maintain the civic virtue, equality, and community spirit necessary for town hall democracy to flourish in a decentralized nation-state.[56] But when the Industrial Revolution followed the Civil War and large corporations became pillars of the national economy after 1900, Jefferson's bucolic vision became a relic of the past. Modern liberals recognize that there is good reason why the power and influence of the wealthiest needs to be limited in its reach; if not, privilege, hierarchy, and inequality will grow and a dangerous class division will widen and eventually endanger democracy.

Wisconsin-friendly Ryan and Texas firebrand Cruz personify the hard-edged libertarian wing of the modern Republican Party. Their agenda: dismantle the New Deal state, cut taxes for the wealthiest, eliminate environmental regulation, shred workplace protections, and obliterate any and all government programs for the poorest and neediest. Weaned on the libertarian gospel of Rand and Hayek, their public policy is all about helping the 1 percent and the financially successful gain yet more power and wealth while eliminating much of the nation's modest social safety net. Ambitious and talented, Ryan and Cruz leapfrogged ahead of others to claim the mantle of leadership on the ideological right and the party as a whole. The former speaker of the House, Ryan straddled the "establishment" and Tea Party divide and thus positioned himself to be the consensus candidate who replaced John Boehner as the leader of a fractured Republican House caucus. Hamstrung and continually embarrassed by President Trump, Ryan achieved his treasured tax cut for corporations and the wealthiest Americans—the ten-year cost to the U.S. treasury is approximately $2.3 trillion—and then announced his retirement seven months before the 2018 midterms.[57] Cruz loves throwing rocks. Abrasive and confident in his intellectual prowess and debate skills, he made himself the darling of the Tea Party right by being a one-man wrecking crew in Washington, D.C., thereby launching his 2016 presidential campaign in which he finished second to Trump. Few politicians can claim credit for bringing the entire federal government to a standstill, but this is what Cruz accomplished when he led the right's sixteen-day government shutdown in October 2013.[58] Quite different in their personalities, Ryan and Cruz drink from the same well. Unlike President Trump, they articulate a coherent philosophy with an intellectual pedigree rooted in Rand's strident novels, the free-market mantra of Hayek and his University of Chicago disciple Milton Friedman, and the original libertarian—the 19th century social Darwinist Herbert Spencer.

A lack of realism, an absence of empathy, and a meanness of spirit color the libertarian position. Libertarians such as Speaker Ryan and Senator Cruz claim to be the true defenders of liberty. The question is, *whose* liberty? As radical libertarians, they defend the liberty of supercapitalists to do as they choose, no matter the consequence to others.[59] In the 21st century, corporate capitalism unregulated and unimpinged leads to two inevitable outcomes—both negative. First, laissez-faire corporate capitalism leads to a steady expansion and acceptance of hierarchy, privilege, inequality, and exclusion across society. French economist Thomas Piketty's massive cross-national study, *Capital in the Twenty-First Century* (2013), proves that the tendency of returns on capital to exceed the rate of economic growth generates extreme inequalities.[60] Second, capitalism without rules or regulations results in regular financial meltdowns, such as the Wall

Street crash of 2008; such massive economic retrenchments devastate middle- and working-class families lacking the financial resources of the wealthy elite. Still, Cruz and Ryan spout a rhetoric that many Americans buy. Cruz speaks volumes about freedom and "opportunity conservatism"; similarly, "upward mobility" is a vital concept for Ryan. In portraying his radical budget plan for the nation, Ryan said,

> We believe that Americans are better off in a dynamic, free enterprise–based economy that fosters economic growth, opportunity, and upward mobility instead of a stagnant, government-directed economy that stifles job creation and fosters government dependency.[61]

Growing up in Houston, Ted Cruz had two formative influences in his life. One was the fierce anti-communism of his father, Rafael, who fought alongside Castro's revolutionaries against the dictatorship of Fulgencio Batista only to see Castro become a full-fledged Communist. The other was the time spent as a teenager with the Free Market Education Foundation, an after-school program designed to instill free-market values in young people; here, he read and gave speeches about the radical libertarian economists—Hayek, Mises, and Friedman. In a spinoff group, the Constitutional Corroborators, the young Cruz learned to read the Constitution in a literal, originalist way.[62] A Supreme Court clerk to Chief Justice William H. Rehnquist, Cruz holds constitutional views that complement his antigovernment, free-market rhetoric. Walter Dellinger, the former acting solicitor general in the Clinton Administration, says, "The only problem is that Ted's view of the Constitution—based on states' rights and a narrow scope of federal power—was rejected at the Constitutional Convention in Philadelphia, and then was resurrected by John C. Calhoun, and the Confederates during the Civil War, when it failed again."[63] In the 2016 Republican nomination contest, Cruz won nearly 700 delegates and defeated Donald Trump in a number of states, something no other GOP candidate did. Widely disliked in Washington, D.C., Cruz correctly anticipated the rightward tilt of the Republican Party in 2016.[64] Positioned further to the right than Barry Goldwater, Cruz is a true believer, a zealot on a crusade, and an apostle of Hayek and Friedman.[65] He appears to accept

Friedman's premise that only public safety, national defense, and the courts are "legitimate functions" of the federal government.[66]

Ryan—former House Speaker and Mitt Romney's 2012 vice-presidential running mate—has a longstanding love affair with Rand's ideas and, in turn, with Nietzsche's dark philosophy.[67] In 2005, the congressman spoke to a "Celebration of Ayn Rand" event and said, "I grew up reading Ayn Rand" and she "inspired me so much that it's required reading in my office for all my interns and my staff. We start with *Atlas Shrugged* . . . we go to *Fountainhead*, but then we move on, and we require Mises and Hayek as well." Ryan continued:

> "But the reason I got involved in public service, by and large, if
> I had to credit one thinker, one person, it would be Ayn Rand.
> And the fight we are in here, make no mistake about it, is a fight
> for individualism versus collectivism . . . you can't find another
> thinker or writer who did a better job of describing and laying
> out the moral case for capitalism than Ayn Rand."[68]

Like his heroine Rand, Ryan is all about celebrating and defending the new aristocracy of money while denigrating the poor and the working class.[69] Democrats found it particularly galling that editorial boards regularly praised Ryan for his "courage" to tackle the deficit by proposing $700 billion in cuts to Medicare, which protects the most powerless people in society, while reducing taxes on corporations and the wealthiest Americans. To Ryan's delight, when the Tea Party congressional class came to Washington in 2011 he found the freshmen dedicated to slashing domestic spending and "required very little persuasion when the topic turned to Medicare and Medicaid." Ryan and House Whip Kevin McCarthy celebrated: "Wow. We can go further on entitlements."[70]

Unlike Cruz, Ryan strove to appear reasonable and moderate. But he spent the George W. Bush years calling for larger, more regressive tax cuts than a president who succeeded in radically reducing taxes for the wealthiest Americans. As chair of the powerful House Budget Committee, Ryan produced a series of budgets that twenty years prior would have been outside the bounds of mainstream political discussion.

Of Ryan's annual budget, Robert Greenstein, a respected left-of-center budget analyst who heads the Center on Budget and Policy Priorities in Washington, wrote:

> [this] is a remarkable document . . . *It would likely produce the largest redistribution of income from the bottom to the top in modern U.S. history* and likely increase poverty and inequality more than any other budget in recent times (and possibly in the nation's history) . . . Specifically, the Ryan budget would impose extraordinary cuts in programs that serve as a lifeline for our nation's poorest and most vulnerable citizens."[71]

A Congressional Budget Office (CBO) analysis of the budget plan, which Ryan himself requested, indicated its implementation would set the nation on the path to end most government programs other than Social Security, healthcare, and defense by 2050. The CBO analysis indicated that after several decades, the Ryan budget would so shrink the federal government that "most of what it does outside of Social Security, healthcare, and defense would *essentially disappear.*"[72] Along with extraordinary budget cuts—which would cut everything from veterans' programs to medical and scientific research, highways, education, national parks, border patrols, protection of food and water supplies, the EPA, law enforcement, and nearly all programs for low-income families other than Medicaid (which would radically shrink due to the drop in the amount of money the federal government would offer each state)—the Ryan budget featured tax cuts for the wealthiest Americans that would cost $4.6 trillion in lost federal revenue over a ten year period.[73]

Ryan's budgets from 2012 to 2018—and the Trump administration budgets prepared by Office of Management and Budget Director Mick Mulvaney, a founding member of the reactionary House Freedom Caucus—amount to a withering assault on the New Deal state and an effort to increase economic inequality to protect the privileged status of the well-to-do and the powerful. The Trump/Mulvaney plan proposes unprecedented cuts to programs for poor and working-class families over the next decade. Medicaid would be cut by $800 billion, the Supplemental Nutrition Assistance Program (SNAP or food stamps) would be cut by $192 billion, and disability benefits would drop by $72 billion. The Republican rationale is that the cuts would force "freeloaders" to return to the workforce. But three-quarters of SNAP recipients work full time or more than part time and the remainder are disabled or elderly. Instead of causing people to go back to work, the proposed cuts would cause people to go hungry.[74]

THE ATTACK ON GOVERNMENT

When Abraham Lincoln helped create the Republican Party in the decade before the Civil War, his aim was to promote economic opportunity for all Americans. For more than 100 years—from Lincoln to Gerald Ford—the Republican Party championed broad middle-class equality. Lincoln, Teddy Roosevelt, and Eisenhower each believed government should not privilege any sector of the population; it must neither bias the system to benefit the rich nor redistribute wealth to those at the bottom.[75] President Eisenhower guided the United States during a postwar boom. In the 1950s, an era to which many illiberals would like to return, progressive taxes on the wealthy were high, unions were strong, a majority of Americans enjoyed economic prosperity, the federal budget was balanced, and the president restrained military spending while investing in research, science, education, and infrastructure. Since the Reagan revolution, however, the growing power of reactionaries has thwarted attempts by moderate Republicans to use the power of government to increase economic opportunity, promote the interests of a growing and vibrant middle class, and build the nation's infrastructure and education system.

Americans are schizophrenic about how they feel about government.[76] For five decades, public opinion has shown a persistent pattern: voters express a desire for small government in theory while at the same time saying that they value specific government programs—from college loan assistance to Medicare, from small business loans to the Federal Emergency Management Administration. When the Gingrich Republicans came to Washington in the 1990s saying they wanted to cut government, President Clinton responded by agreeing in the abstract—the "era of big government is over," he said—while defending against the "deep" and "unwise" cuts that the Republicans proposed to "Medicare, Medicaid, education, and the environment." Clinton won the battle. Fast-forward to the Obama years and Republicans storming Congress in 2010 by arguing that the Affordable Care Act was going to socialize medicine and take away freedom of choice. When President Trump took office in 2017 and the Republicans gained control of both the House and Senate it seemed a slam dunk that the GOP would live up to its longstanding promise of repealing Obamacare. The political winds shifted radically, however, when the Congressional Budget Office reported that 23 million Americans would lose their health insurance plans and those with preexisting conditions might again face astronomical premiums to gain healthcare coverage. Suddenly, it was Republican lawmakers facing angry town hall crowds.

It is a fallacy to say that true conservatives want to eliminate the New Deal state and return to the 1890s; they do not. As presidents Eisenhower, Nixon, and Ford understood, in an age when America is the world's superpower and the U.S. economy leads the world, it is simply not possible to return to the small government that the Reagan-Gingrich-Tea Party revolutions promised. The issue is not big government versus small government. The real question is: toward what ends and whose interests should a large and powerful national government be driven?[77] Hamiltonian big government is the vital center of 21st century American politics.[78] The illiberal mantra about the virtues of small government and loss of individual liberty to Washington bureaucrats blinds us to the fact that under Republican administrations—from Reagan to George W. Bush to Donald Trump—federal power has reached new heights and the cozy relationship of the GOP to the economic elite has fueled staggering levels of inequality that leap beyond anything in American history. Plutocrats benefit greatly from big government, they just want to dominate and control it; witness the Republican tax bill rushed to passage at the end of 2017.[79] The public has clearly said it wants a government with the capacity and brainpower to soften economic downturns and save the economy in case of a catastrophic financial crash as occurred in the Great Depression and recent Great Recession. People depend on Social Security, Medicare, Medicaid, and Obamacare for retirement assistance and affordable medical care, and are grateful for unemployment and disability insurance when they need it. In addition, the public supports programs that promote economic growth and assist the middle class, such as infrastructure spending, scientific research, student loans, and home mortgage programs. Today, environmental protection, the Centers for Disease Control and Prevention, FEMA, the National Park Service, and fire crews are all seen as essential services, as are the military and Homeland Security. One can enumerate additional federal programs that a broad majority of the public believe to be essential. Few Americans aspire to the illiberal libertarian heaven of a government limited to first responders, the military, and the courts. Only the most hard-core reactionaries want to walk that road.

There is, of course, a racial aspect to the illiberal attack on government. The facts are clear—an activist national government remained highly popular as long as the focus was on programs and policies that primarily benefited whites. As Ira Katznelson shows in *When Affirmative Action Was White* the key programs passed during the New Deal and Fair Deal era of the 1930s and 1940s were created in a deeply discriminatory manner.[80] The pushback by the right against the liberal state only gained traction when the Johnson administration pressed hard to expand the benefits of the New Deal to Americans of all ethnicities and both genders.

Curiously, the "fear of government" storyline is always directed at the federal level. But if one truly cared about individual freedom, as those on the right insist they do, one would worry about the disgraceful record many states have when it comes to individual rights and personal freedom. Americans say they do not want government meddling with their lives, but state governments have repeatedly imposed majority views about religion, marriage, race, abortion, and schooling on their neighbors and, shockingly, it was only in the 1960s when the Bill of Rights was finally applied to the states. Many people remain unaware of this. To think, as many illiberals do, that rights are best secured by getting government out of the picture and "off our backs" is ignorant at best.[81] The abuse of power by the federal government pales in comparison to the record of the states.[82] The United States is a nation that famously promises individuals great freedom, but until the 1960s it allowed the states—the places where people actually lived and worked—vast unchecked powers of coercion, intimidation, and punishment.[83] At the founding, Madison wanted to apply the Bill of Rights to the states but was unable to get the support of his colleagues. It was only fifty years ago that the Supreme Court finally made the Bill of Rights the law of the land and ended the long tradition of "states' rights" that enabled discrimination at will and the trampling of personal freedom. It was the activist, liberal Warren Court that took government "off the backs" of the people—across a range of issues from voting rights, marriage, and criminal justice to sexuality, education, and religion.[84]

9

Donald J. Trump:
Revival of the Southern Demagogue

onald Trump stands as the embodiment of reactionary America. He is both a hard-right capitalist and a man who believes that his whiteness and maleness give him the right to hold others who are neither in contempt. We have had other modern presidents and presidential candidates who displayed elements of the reactionary mindset. Barry Goldwater and Ronald Reagan were Hayek true believers who understood Southern racism and used it to their electoral advantage. Richard Nixon was an Eisenhower moderate on domestic policy, but reached out to Strom Thurmond and developed a Southern strategy to head off the challenge from George Wallace. Wallace, of course, pioneered racial resentment on the national stage. Bush 41 and Bush 43 were moderates on race and immigration but George W. Bush, once president, followed Reagan on tax cuts for the wealthy and targeted Social Security for privatization. His father, George H. W. Bush, spoke of a thousand points of light and governed in the prudent tradition of Eisenhower, but played the Willie Horton card to defeat Michael Dukakis. Presidential candidates Mitt Romney, John McCain, and Bob Dole all struggled to moderate the reactionary forces in the GOP.

In a league of his own, Trump has embraced the illiberal tradition to a degree far beyond any prior president or presidential candidate. His bravado and snarls follow seamlessly George Wallace's illiberal rage and Ayn Rand's insistence that the rich live by their own rules. On the libertarian side, Trump has displayed unorthodox views on trade versus more mainstream libertarian billionaires, but his tax and regulatory policies adhere to the Paul Ryan-Milton Friedman playbook. Trump regularly declares himself a genius and appears to believe that as a Randian superman figure he can play by his own set of rules.[1] As one of the greatest presidents in American history, why should he be restrained by the Constitution, the separations of power and checks and balances, laws, democratic norms, or basic morality? He is above that; they're merely hindrances to action and apply only to lesser beings. On the other side of the reactionary coin, Donald Trump's brand of demagoguery has deep Southern roots. It features Wallace-style rhetoric to gin up the passions of whites angry at "line cutting" by minorities and a "rigged system" that treats them unfairly. *"You're watching the world take our country away from us,"* says Trump addressing his rallies.[2]

A consummate performer and expert at saying the outrageous to attract media attention—Trump relishes the lead in this illiberal opera.[3] The president is first and foremost a crude and vulgar entertainer who prides himself on ratings—they literally mean everything to him.[4] The real estate tycoon and reality television star turned president struts the role of the rich, powerful Anglo adored and envied by his supporters for his ability to freely insult and criticize immigrants, minorities, uppity women, liberals, the media, coastal elites—as well as Democrats and fellow Republicans. A gifted rabble-rouser, Trump freely employs racism when it suits his purpose. He first emerged as a national political figure—as opposed to a rich businessman hosting a reality television show—by becoming the leading spokesman of the "birther movement," which claimed that President Obama's birth certificate was falsified and that the former president had no right to be chief executive because he was born outside the United States, possibly in Africa. During the 2016 campaign, 66 percent of Trump's Republican support nationally continued to believe the right-wing myth that President Obama was a Muslim, with 61 percent believing he was an illegitimate president because he "was not born in the United States."[5] Exit polls of Trump's South Carolina primary voters were revealing: 33 percent said Islam should be illegal, 32 percent believed Japanese internment during World War II was a good thing, and nearly 40 percent wished the South had won the Civil War.[6] When President Trump sent a racist tweet telling four minority Democratic congresswomen to "go back" to the countries "from which they came," Trump voters were not surprised.[7] They know that he speaks for them.

Almost four years to the day after he rode down the escalator at Trump Tower in New York City to announce his long-shot candidacy for president, Trump kicked off his reelection campaign with a massive June 2019 rally in Orlando, Florida. Addressing a raucous crowd, the president said, "Our political opponents look down with hatred on our values and with utter disdain for the people whose lives they want to run . . . They called us deplorables . . . That was a big mistake." Standing in front of thousands wearing his trademark red "Make America Great Again" hats, Trump raised fears about immigrants and said the Democrats "want to destroy you and they want to destroy our country as we know it." Presenting his stark vision of a nation under assault, he accused the Democrats of supporting "open borders" and unrestricted immigration. Blaming the left for allowing "aliens" into the country, he said the Democrats had betrayed the American middle class. Bonding with the crowd, Trump declared, "They tried to take away your dignity and your destiny. But we will never let them do that, will we?" Previewing his reelection strategy, he made a direct link between the investigations that have plagued him and his supporters: "They went after my family, my business, my finances, my employees, almost everyone I've ever known or worked with, *but they are really going after you*," he said. "That's what it's all about, not about us. It's about you." The list of grievances was familiar: immigration, fake news, Democrats, Hillary Clinton, the Russia investigation and Special Counsel Robert S. Mueller.[8] His warning to Trump nation: "The establishment will stop at nothing to rob you of another four years." The seventy-six minute speech was vintage Trump; "a torrent of attacks, falsehoods, exaggerations, and resentments" reported the *New York Times*.[9] Both the *Washington Post* and CNN reported that the speech contained more than fifteen falsehoods, many of which were repeated by the tweeter-in-chief.[10] But the media's focus on Trump's misstatements and lies misses the emotional connection Trump forges with his audience.

Afterward, his supporters spoke of the president in glowing terms when asked questions by *New York Times* reporter Maggie Haberman: "I was a delegate for Ted Cruz but he's earned my support by appointing conservative judges," said one man. "I'm ecstatic with the last two and a half years," one woman said. "He speaks for the blue collar and the middle-class America and he says all the things that we've been wanting to say, doing the things that we saw needed to be done, and if Congress would get its act together, he could do a lot more." Asked how he could be happier, a second man said, "If immigration were stopped, if immigrants [were] out, build a wall, and other than that I'm satisfied." Another supporter said he was unsure about Trump in 2016. "I did not support him because I did not think he was being truthful," he said, but once in office the president proved he was "pro–Second Amendment" and "he's appointing pro-life judges, doing the things that I support."[11]

POPULISM—OR PLUTOCRACY AND RACISM?

In taking traditional GOP positions on abortion and gun rights and in appointing reactionary judges, the president has maintained Republican Party orthodoxy. However, in pitching himself as a serious populist who would use the tools of government to help the working class, Trump emerged an empty suit.[12] UC Berkeley political scientist Paul Pierson writes, "Trump has continued to present himself in populist garb, but it has rarely carried over to policy . . . on the big economic issues of taxes, spending, and regulation—ones that have animated elites for a generation—he has pursued, or supported, an agenda that is extremely friendly to large corporations, wealthy families and well-positioned rent-seekers." Instead of governing as a populist, enacting policies that would benefit the working and middle classes, Trump doubled down on the "long-standing Republican commitment to a radically inegalitarian brand of market fundamentalism."[13]

On the campaign trail in 2016, Trump blended xenophobia and racism with the promise to help white middle America with generous social programs and a return of manufacturing jobs. But after taking office, Trump produced a mean-spirited budget with huge cuts to social programs and crafted a 2017 tax cut that was a massive windfall for corporations and business owners while containing only small change for average Americans.[14] The manufacturing share of U.S. employment has been on a steady decline for seventy years: it was 31 percent in 1950, 25 percent in 1970, 20.7 percent in 1980, 13 percent in 2000, 8.8 percent in 2010, and basically has been flat since—standing at 8.5 percent in 2018, ticking up slightly from 8.4 percent in 2017.[15] In Michigan, manufacturing jobs continue to disappear at an alarming rate. From January 2017 to December 2018, Eaton County *lost nearly 9 percent of its manufacturing jobs*, and "17 other counties in Michigan that Mr. Trump carried have experienced similar losses," according to an analysis of employment data by the Brookings Institution.[16] No matter what Trump says, manufacturing jobs in the United States are not "roaring back," to use Vice President Mike Pence's phrase.[17]

Fake populism and explicit misogyny and racist demagoguery is what powered Trump and Republicans to victory in 2016. In this regard, Trump has acted as a big-league grifter, the type who excels at separating suckers from their wallets; he bears a resemblance to Mark Twain's famous fraudsters in *The Adventures of Huckleberry Finn*. On their trip down the Mississippi, nearly everyone that Huck and Jim encounter is an unsavory character in some way or another. Similar to Twain's con artists—the duke and the dauphin (supposedly the lost son of King Louis XVI of France)—Trump talks a big game and promises his audiences their dreams. In Twain's telling, when the thespians unveil an inept and shockingly short performance of "The World-Renowned Tragedians" the audience of "Arkansaw lunkheads" quickly understand that they have been ripped off ("What, is it over? Is that *all*?"). They then decide to protect their honor by making certain that *everyone* in the town gets swindled. Those in attendance conspire to tell everyone the play is wonderful:

> "We are sold—mighty badly sold. But we don't want to be the laughing-stock of this whole town, I reckon, and never hear the last of this thing as long as we live. *No.* What we want, is to go out of here quiet, and talk this show up, and sell the *rest* of the town! Then we'll all be in the same boat."[18]

The second night, after a capacity crowd watches the show, the rapscallions escape with winnings in hand.

Trump supporters do not demand that he fulfill his campaign pledges—tax reform tilted not to business executives but to the working class, the magical return of industrial jobs and coal mining, a border wall paid for by Mexico, and a new healthcare law that results in all the benefits of Obamacare but delivered at a lower cost. Instead, reactionary radio host Michael Savage (an early supporter of Mr. Trump going back to 2011) says of his listeners, "I don't think they care very much about issues. They'll vote for him no matter what because he's not 'them.' I think it comes down to 'them' or 'us.'"[19] Like the small-town audience in *Huckleberry Finn*, Trump supporters are satisfied with attitude, bluster, and the scapegoating of those who dare criticize the president—and insist that *yes*, so long as Trump and the Republicans are in charge, America *is* great again. The deep draconian cuts the Trump administration proposed for Medicare (of $800 billion in the Republican healthcare plan and another $600 billion in the budget) and other programs that candidate Trump promised to maintain may have come as a surprise to his more attentive working-class supporters. They will suffer greatly along with poor minorities. But the severe Republican budget (call it the Trump-Ryan-Freedom Caucus budget) is no shock to those who understand that the No. 1 priority of the reactionary right is to gut the New Deal state and provide massive tax cuts to the millionaires and billionaires who fund the party.

Our problem is not President Trump, but his supporters. If nothing else, successful politicians are weather vanes. Trump is a chameleon who panders to what his audience demands. What matters are the political beliefs and loyalties of the Republican base. What *is* disturbing is that a majority of the Republican Party—a party of the middle and upper-middle classes and the wealthy, with increasing working-class support, whose ethnic makeup is nearly all white—has shifted, markedly, to the right. The essence of the Trump presidency mirrors the illiberal impulses that drive contemporary Republican politics: misogyny and racism in the defense of white male privilege combined with a hard-right economic agenda that is all about benefiting the wealthiest Americans. Republican strategist Kevin Phillips famously said the key to politics is the exploitation of resentments and ill-feelings—of "knowing who hates who."[20] We live in an era when being a Democrat or a Republican has become markedly associated with other noteworthy social and political divides in American society, especially race and religion. As a result, political scientist Alan Abramowitz writes, "supporters of each party perceive supporters of the opposing party as very different from themselves in terms of their social characteristics, political beliefs and values and to view opposing partisans with growing suspicion and hostility."[21]

In our strongly polarized politics, President Trump's firm hold on the Republican Party has been accomplished because of the rise of what political scientists call "negative partisanship." This occurs when political actions and beliefs are shaped more by antipathy for the opposition than by positive feelings for one's own party or leadership. Some Republicans have misgivings about President Trump's qualifications, competence, and ethics, yet a steady 90 percent of Republicans support the president, in part, because of their utter fear (stoked by their illiberal beliefs and the right-wing media) of liberals whether they be Bernie Sanders, Barack Obama, Joe Biden, Hillary Clinton, Elizabeth Warren, or Amy Klobuchar. A female Trump supporter in Arizona told the *Los Angeles Times* in 2019: "Sure he has a so-called unpredictable, so-called unpresidential manner of speaking, but his very explosive rhetoric is very effective to stop this toxic metastasizing political power that the Democrats, even more left of [President] Obama, represent at this time."[22] Put dryly by Abramowitz, "in a two-party system strongly negative feelings toward one party leave voters with only one choice—supporting the other party."[23] Hence, President Trump's apparent ability to do pretty much anything he wants—flagrant examples of self-dealing, constantly breaking the democratic norms that protect constitutional democracy, violations of federal law, abuses of power, breaching his oath of office to "preserve, protect and defend the Constitution," and his attempted bribery of a foreign government in the pursuit of manufactured political dirt against one of his leading political opponents in the upcoming 2020 presidential election. Because of the deep antipathy with which Republicans hold Democrats, Republicans have remained steadfastly loyal to their man in the White House, no matter what. This could change, but it probably will not.

TRUMP'S REVIVAL OF THE
CLASSIC SOUTHERN DEMAGOGUE

By the second decade of the 21st century, most Southern whites had moved decisively to the Republican Party. As a result, the Southern Democratic Party became a predominately black party and the biracial governing coalitions of the Carter and Clinton years became unattainable. "White Democrats in the South are gone," says Hodding Carter III, a journalist who was assistant secretary of state for President Jimmy Carter and whose father was a crusading Mississippi publisher and one of the South's great liberals in the civil rights era.[24] With the advent of the Tea Party, the dog whistle perfected by generations of Republican leaders became loudly audible. With the election of Donald Trump, racism and sexism have become explicit. But they never really went away.

It takes only a short flight of the imagination to picture Donald Trump as a plantation master in the antebellum South. There he stands, red-faced and tinsel-haired under a broad-brimmed white hat, issuing orders to his underlings and slaves, pontificating to his planter neighbors about how the emerging Confederacy would be better off with a President Trump instead of that buffoon, Jefferson Davis. The long history of slavery and the failure of Reconstruction hangs heavily on contemporary American politics. For decades, Trump was known as an egocentric, bombastic New Yorker who loved the spotlight. However, his stunningly successful campaign to capture first the Republican nomination and then the White House was less New York chutzpah and more Southern demagogue of the blatant white supremacist variety.

Donald Trump is not only a successor to George Wallace, but more importantly, he reincarnates the earlier more savage, more racially explicit and extreme Southern demagogues who ruled the Jim Crow South when American feudalism was alive and well. Announcing his candidacy in the summer of 2015, Trump declared, "When Mexico sends its people, they're not sending their best . . . They're bringing drugs. They're bringing crime. They're rapists."[25] He campaigned as an old-fashioned Southern demagogue—all ethos (*trust me*) and pathos (*fear them*) and little Logos or argument.

In the Old South, racism was *the* key to preventing an alliance of poor whites and poor blacks that would threaten both white supremacy and the continued power of the planter aristocracy. This was especially true after the Populist revolt of the 1890s when, for a brief period, poor whites and poor blacks united in a common cause against the upper crust. The response by the Southern oligarchy was twofold. First, the white elite disenfranchised nearly all blacks and a good portion of the white working class with a variety of political and economic devices including the infamous poll tax, while changes in the system of land tenure caused white smallholders as well as blacks to become sharecroppers. Second, planters and their urban business partners developed and perfected a brand of politics based on turning poor whites against blacks to head off the biracial coalition of working-class blacks and whites that could again threaten the power of the bourbon elite. By 1910, virtually all black elected officials were expunged from the states of the former Confederacy, along with nearly all black voters.[26]

More than a century after the destruction of the original Reconstruction, Trump and the GOP have returned to the same dual strategy of voter suppression and the politics of racial resentment to block liberal advancement or biracial coalition. Before, it was the Populist revolt; this time, the backlash is against the success of the second Reconstruction and the danger of a biracial, cosmopolitan coalition digging the grave of the Old South. The epitome of an affront to the America of white supremacy was the election of the nation's first black president, Barack Obama. "By 2010, there was full horror that a black man was now president and a full-fledged liberal," says Hodding Carter, now a professor at the University of North Carolina. "Obama was at the door and soon in the bedroom. It brought back all the atavistic, Old South fears."[27] Of course, before Trump began bashing immigrants, he promoted the canard that President Obama was born in Kenya, a lie that sent exactly the right signals to the base.

In 1968, Wallace helped deliver the White House to Richard Nixon when the former Democrat headed the American Independent ticket and garnered 13.5 percent of the vote and 46 ballots in the Electoral College. Wallace stunned political observers by showing surprising strength in the blue-collar North. His support among the working class cost Democrat Hubert Humphrey dearly in such states as Ohio, Michigan, Pennsylvania, and Illinois, where Wallace votes exceeded Nixon's margin over Humphrey. A September 1968 AFL-CIO poll indicated nearly one in three union members supporting Wallace, and a *Chicago Sun-Times* poll showed Wallace with the support of 44 percent of Chicago's white steelworkers.[28] The Wallace campaign, its appeals, and its nascent coalition foreshadowed 2016. "Trump's voters are the sons and daughters, mostly the sons, of the Wallace voters," says Ferrel Guillory, a veteran journalist and director of the Program on Public Life at the University of North Carolina at Chapel Hill.[29] Every modern Republican presidential candidate starts with a white base in the South. Novel was Trump's audacious attempt to take the white politics of the South national—via an aggressive demonization of immigrants, Muslims, women, blacks, and minorities of all stripes.

Donald Trump has "a train horn appeal—not a dog whistle—and many are responding," said *Washington Post* op-ed columnist Eugene Robinson.[30] When the South was the Democratic South in the 1920s '30s, and '40s, politicians such as Mississippi's Theodore Bilbo, South Carolina's "Pitchfork Ben" Tillman, and Georgia's Eugene Talmadge and their ilk were far more blatant and direct than George Wallace in the 1960s in demeaning blacks. Like Trump, they insulted and belittled their targets explicitly and relished the fact that they were not about issues—for issues (other than race) mattered little in traditional Southern politics. Instead, they concentrated on providing a venomous, racist form of entertainment for the white working and middle classes, which is exactly what President Trump, a reality television star now on the biggest stage, provides for his audience on nearly a daily basis. By contrast, for all of his coded hostility toward the federal government (which was entirely about race), at heart Wallace remained a New Deal Democrat and, by allocating tax dollars to ambitious public works, governed as one.

POLITICS WITHOUT ISSUES

In the Southern feudal order, blacks were of the lowest caste. But even as they were denied the basic rights of citizenship, including access to the ballot box and equal justice under the law, they played the lead role in the Old South's political drama. Blacks were blamed for all the shortcomings and sins of the South, and race-baiting—vicious verbal attacks on African Americans meant to stoke the anger of whites of all classes—was a verbal art form in the pre-1965 South.[31] Mississippi senator Bilbo and three-term Georgia governor Talmadge were part of a breed of Southern demagogues who fueled racial hatred to build followings. While running for reelection in 1942, Talmadge bragged that he had once personally whipped a black man for eating apples out of the same sack as a white woman. The woman was from the North and the African American was her driver:

> "I jus' picked up mah buggy whip an' I walked down to the nigger an' that red-headed woman an' I stopped 'em. I cut that big nigger with that whip, an' yknow th' impudent sonuvabitch wanted to fight me. Jus' shows how Yankees mistreat niggers. So I jus' [drew] my gun on him an' let 'im have that whip til he hollered Sweet Jesus. It was the funniest thing y'ever saw . . . They still tell down there how fast that big nigger an' that red-headed woman got that old automobile out'a Jawjuh [Georgia]."[32]

Mississippi's James K. Vardaman, both governor and U.S. senator between 1904 and 1919, famously declared, "If it is necessary every Negro in the state will be lynched; it will be done to maintain white supremacy."[33]

Blacks were the object of "derision, discrimination, loathing," and fear and this allowed Southern politicians to skip serious discussion of public problems. Issues played a very limited part in electoral politics. Said one Southern judge, "Issues? Why, son, they don't have a damn thing to do with it [getting elected]."[34] University of Florida political scientist Richard K. Scher explains:

> Since it was possible, indeed legitimate and necessary, to blame blacks for the ills of the South, the politician need not then bother with serious discussion of public problems. Issues were of little or no significance, since the causes of southern problems were not a colonial economy and maldistribution of resources leading to poor education, ignorance, poverty, and disease. Rather, they were the consequence of a large black population that sucked energy and resources from whites in the region.[35]

The idea of an issueless campaign was adopted by Donald Trump in 2016. It did not seem to matter that the future president was all over the map on the issues. One week he was anti-banker, the next he reassured all the bankers with whom he worked. He liked Planned Parenthood, then he did not. But just as "issues" did not matter to whites who clearly got the message from Talmadge, Bilbo, et al. that they were defending the white race against blacks, the Trump constituency gets the deeper message. It is not about issues as conventionally understood; it is very much about white power and privilege, maintaining patriarchy, the sense of unresolved grievance on the part of economically strapped whites, and the scapegoating of blacks, Latinos, and immigrants. It's about the economic stagnation of working-class people in the global economy and the feeling of whites that their hard work goes for naught while minorities and women are allowed to line-cut in front of them.[36]

In the pre–civil rights South, using the government to improve public welfare would have increased the health and well-being for many of the South's impoverished population—both black and white. But to do so was unacceptable because it would have led to greater equality between the races. Elected governor of Mississippi in 1903, Vardaman was emblematic of the South's white populism and racist politics. As he explained, "Why squander money on [black] education when the only effect is to spoil a good field hand and make an insolent cook?"[37] Real issues have the potential of arousing the public, causing people to pay attention, ask questions, and demand that their leaders solve problems. Thus, it was in the interest of the political pros of the Old South—the demagogue, the upper-crust planter gentleman, the courthouse crowd—to feed the public fiction about the cause of their problems. When their constituency was "poor, frustrated, ignorant, and racially bigoted," and desiring free public entertainment, it made sense for these politicians to make their racial lies as "vivid and outrageous as they wished."[38] President Trump follows this script by feeding his audience fiction about Muslims, an "invasion" at the Southern border, Russian interference in U.S. elections (it could have been a 400-pound hacker sitting on a bed), trade with China, NATO, and various authoritarian heads of state.

And, in a grotesque way, Donald Trump again emulates the Southern demagogues of yesteryear when he spouts lurid, sensational falsehoods that are meant to slander and defame: such as his claim that Muslims across the

East River celebrated when the Twin Towers crashed down on 9/11, the birther lie that Barack Obama was not born in Hawaii, his insinuation that Ted Cruz's father was somehow involved with Lee Harvey Oswald and the John F. Kennedy assassination, and his endless assertions as president that immigrants are dangerous criminals. The difference, of course, between President Trump and the older Southern demagogues is that he has expanded the target list of "others" beyond black Americans to a sitting president; immigrants from Latin America, Asia, and the Middle East; Muslims; women; all people of color; and whoever his current political opponent happens to be.

THE SOLID SOUTH AND THE ATTACK ON THE SECOND RECONSTRUCTION

The South, like it or not, is the key to American politics. The Tea Party right of the Republican Party is most strongly anchored in the South; it is the South that drives the party. And during the 2016 Republican primary campaign, apart from Texas, where he was beaten by the Lone Star State's Ted Cruz, Trump triumphed across the entire old Confederacy. Southern whites—especially over the past fifteen years—have sought to defeat the second Reconstruction of Lyndon Johnson and Martin Luther King by constructing a new racial Maginot Line that allows them to control the Republican Party and much of the nation's politics. North Carolina congressman David Price, one of the few moderate Democrats still serving in Congress from the states of the old Confederacy, says there is a "backlash against the second Reconstruction and Trump is taking it a few steps further."[39] The goal of Southern white reactionaries is to "lock up and lock down the South," says Reverend William Barber II, president of the North Carolina NAACP and founder of the "Moral Mondays" movement. With the South once more the white Solid South, the eleven former Confederate states have an outsized hold on national politics.

In national elections where Republicans win every Southern state, the GOP secures 160 Electoral College votes and needs only 112 more for the Republican nominee to win the presidency; it gains 22 Senate seats and requires only seven more to have a majority, and controls 131 House seats and needs fewer than 90 congressional seats in the rest of the nation to have a majority. Add to this 11 Republican governors setting the policy agenda for state legislatures where the GOP often holds supermajorities, and Democrats become superfluous. For good reason: Reverend Barber says that Southern Republican thinking is, "if we hold these eleven states, we can control the rest of the nation's politics."[40]

Trump's focus on white working-class voters *nationally* in the 2016 campaign was the logical culmination to the GOP's Solid South strategy where Republicans regularly captured 70 to 80 percent of the white vote across the old Confederacy. As George Wallace understood in 1964, once you have the South locked up you can "concentrate on the industrial states of the North and win." Wallace shocked liberals by doing well in the industrial heartland of the Midwest; Trump stunned the Hillary Clinton camp in 2016 by campaigning hard in states such as Wisconsin, Michigan, Indiana, Ohio, and Pennsylvania based on similar rhetoric and resentments.[41]

As recently as the turn of the current century, scholars were celebrating the success of the second Reconstruction, which emerged from the coalition of Democratic presidents (Truman, Kennedy, and Johnson) working with civil rights leaders and activists.[42] It is clear that the celebration was premature. In the post-Gingrich era, the GOP has become a traditional white Southern party, much more so than in the Nixon and Reagan eras. The 1970s–1990s governing coalition of blacks, racially liberal whites, and moderate business leaders that elected Southern governors such as Jimmy Carter, Bill Clinton, and Ray Mabus of Mississippi has been overtaken by a Republican governing coalition of neo-segregationists, antigovernment libertarians, and right-wing business leaders. Outside black majority districts (into which African American voters have been packed to weaken their voting strength elsewhere) in the states of the old Confederacy, the white Republican Party has a stranglehold on governorships, state legislatures, and nearly all congressional seats. "There are very few biracial coalitions left at the state level," says North Carolina Democratic representative Price.[43] As Republicans more flagrantly have become members of a white party, Democratic statewide candidates—be they white or black—have been unable to "attract sufficient white votes to marry to the united support provided by African American voters."[44]

The parallels between the attacks on voting rights in the first and the second Reconstructions are striking. Between 1890 and 1910, the black electorate was radically reduced by a combination of poll taxes, literacy tests, residency requirements, and early registration months before the election as well as inconvenient hours, harassment, and sheer intimidation.[45] In the midst of the second Reconstruction we see a new wave of voter suppression techniques. Over the past decade, abetted by a partisan Supreme Court, Republicans have moved with strategic intensity to limit the vote of key Democratic constituents—the elderly, minorities, and the young.[46] In 2013, the illiberal judicial attack culminated with the 5–4 Supreme Court decision in *Shelby County v. Holder*, effectively gutting the Voting Rights Act; this allowed legislative action by former Confederate states to restrict voting without fear of federal government supervision. Only hours after the high court struck down key provisions of the Voting Rights Act, Republican legislatures in Texas and North Carolina launched attacks on voting rights. One conservative North Carolina lawmaker expressed relief that the "headache" of the Voting Rights Act was gone.[47]

Forty years ago, there was broad hope that the New South was becoming more like the rest of America. President Trump's appeal suggests that the United States in the post-Obama years is becoming uncomfortably like the Old South. There is a Southern saying that Rev. Barber likes to recall: "A dying mule kicks the hardest." He says white reactionaries know they will ultimately lose. In the next decade, the Democratic Party has the opportunity of breaking the Republican lock on the South, starting with Florida, Virginia, and North Carolina, with Georgia and Texas—as evidenced by the strong showings of Stacey Abrams and Beto O'Rourke, respectively, in 2018—on track to go from purple to blue in the future. Doug Jones's dramatic victory over Roy Moore in the 2017 Alabama senate contest demonstrates that, at least occasionally, the Democratic biracial coalition *can* win in the deep South.

FROM GOLDWATER TO TRUMP: THE ILLIBERAL DYNAMIC

How did we get from Barry Goldwater and Ronald Reagan's GOP to the Republican Party in the Trump era?[48] In essence, it is the snowball effect.[49] A certain trend gains size and speed as it picks up momentum and demolishes the obstacles that stand in its path. Since the Nixon presidency, Republican political actors at crucial junctures have faced a choice of whether to please the reactionary side of the party or to tack in a more moderate direction. Again and again, decisions have favored the right side of the party. As moderates have lost numbers and clout, reactionaries have taken greater control. Having been Eisenhower's vice president, President Nixon was a moderate liberal on domestic policy. But facing the Wallace challenge, he honed a Southern strategy on race, busing, and affirmative action. In doing so, he assiduously courted Senator Strom Thurmond, the 1948 Dixiecrat presidential nominee, and abandoned the innovative idea of a "guaranteed minimal income" championed by Daniel Patrick Moynihan as a Republican solution to poverty. Ronald Reagan famously ran against "welfare queens" and then clamped down on domestic spending as he dramatically cut taxes and increased military spending. Reagan's "cut taxes, shrink the government" message became the GOP gospel. According to Reagan, "government was the problem," not the solution, and the unleashed market would result in the growth of both income and personal freedom. It was Hayek's mantra of "minimal government and free the market" as national policy. Of course, the Reagan version of Hayek includes corporate welfare, or "the predatory state" in economist James K. Galbraith's phrase, wherein the wealthy benefit from the government much more than regular people, but Republicans do not advertise this reality of reactionary politics.[50] Reagan succeeded in reducing taxes for the wealthy and increasing defense spending but he put nary a dent in the size, scope, and cost of government. He persuaded a large swath of the electorate that taxes were too high, regulation excessive, and that many government programs were inefficient and wasteful.[51]

Between 1980 and 2010, the conservative wing of the Republican Party lacked a strong, dynamic, charismatic leader. Senator Dole was past his prime and easily defeated by President Clinton when he ran for president in 1996. Senator McCain had courage and foreign policy gravitas but, like George H. W. Bush, he lacked a compelling domestic message. Rep. Jack Kemp had one, and inspired younger politicians such as future House Speaker Paul Ryan, but Kemp never became the GOP presidential nominee. After Reagan left office, "movement conservatives" distrusted George H. W. Bush's resolve; after all, Bush had labeled Reaganomics

"Voodoo Economics" on the campaign trail. Then, when in the face of a rising deficit, President Bush broke his no new taxes pledge, the right was furious. In managing the end of the Cold War and in winning the first Gulf War, Bush 41 succeeded magnificently, but on domestic policy he lacked dexterity. His ill-advised pledge to not raise taxes backfired; the result emboldened reactionaries and seriously weakened traditional conservative Republicans such as senators Dole (Kansas) and Richard Lugar (Indiana), and House Minority Leader Robert Michel (Illinois), who began to lose power inside the party.

In President George W. Bush's administration, we see another key turning point. Newt Gingrich had led the Republicans to a landmark victory and the control of the House of Representatives in 1994 but then, as speaker, overreached, alienated his followers, and lost power. More than his father, George W. Bush had the political skills and the broad-based support to shift the party toward the political center instead of toward the right; with the radical Gingrich off the Washington stage, Bush campaigned as a "compassionate conservative" and began his presidency following this path. An event and a strategic decision shifted his presidency to the right. The 9/11 attacks shocked the nation and propelled President Bush into his wars in Afghanistan and Iraq and a global war on terror. Simultaneously, Karl Rove, Bush's political strategist, decided to pursue a reelection strategy focused on rousing the Republican base and ignoring moderate voters in the middle. Rove's decision dovetailed with a shift to political rhetoric. With the evil empire gone, reactionaries spoke of American liberals as the new enemy. Neoconservative icon Irving Kristol wrote that with the Soviet Union gone, conservatives should begin a crusade against liberals in America, the true, "internal enemy."[52]

In pursuing education reform with Senator Edward Kennedy and comprehensive immigration reform, Bush was a traditional conservative. But his reactionary colors shown bright when he started his second term with a radical effort to privatize Social Security.[53] If, on the surface, it appeared Bush 43 had the opportunity and possibly the motivation to take the GOP back toward the center, in reality, the die was cast. The right already had control of the Republican Party by 2000 and Bush, Cheney, and Rove were happy running to the right. In large part, this was because of the growing power of the Republican base, as described here in 2005:

The base is the party's most committed, mobilized, and deep-pocketed supporters: big donors, ideological activist groups, grassroots conservative organizations, and increasingly, party leaders themselves. The base has always had power, but never the kind of power it has today. With money more important in campaigns than ever, the base has money. With the political and organizational resources of average citizens in decline, the base is mobilized and well organized. With most congressional seats safe for one party or the other, the base has the troops to influence the typically low-turnout primaries that determine who goes to Washington.[54]

Not all of the GOP was happy; conservative moderates such as Treasury Secretary Paul O'Neill, EPA Administrator Christine Todd Whitman, and head of the Office of Faith-Based Initiatives John Dilulio felt abandoned and marginalized. After leaving the Bush administration, Whitman wrote:

The Republican Party at the national level is allowing itself to be dictated to by a coalition of ideological extremists . . . groups that have claimed the mantle of conservatism and show no inclination to seek bipartisan consensus on anything.[55]

Weakened by his unsuccessful war efforts in the Middle East and the FEMA fiasco in the aftermath of Hurricane Katrina, Bush became an embattled, feeble president. His electoral decision to energize the base and demonize the Democrats paid off in the short term, but his inability to curb the federal deficit, in part because of expensive fixes to the Medicare prescription program, angered conservatives concerned with the federal debt. In the end, in the wake of the 2008 financial crash, Bush was a pariah to both liberals and the right.

The Tea Party victory in the 2010 midterm elections cemented the right's control of the Republican Party. After Barack Obama defeated John McCain in 2008, the Great Recession allowed reactionaries to rally as the "Tea Party" in 2010 and win sixty-three House seats. The real story of 2010 was a multitude of primary fights inside the Republican Party. The ideological shift among the Senate Republican caucus was stark: Utah's Robert

Bennett, a respected three-term senator, lost his primary and was replaced by Tea Party zealot Mike Lee; in Kentucky, Senator Jim Bunning stepped down after two terms and the seat was won by libertarian Rand Paul; in Texas, Senator Kay Bailey Hutchinson, an establishment Republican, stepped down after two terms and was replaced by Tea Party firebrand Ted Cruz; and in Delaware, Tea Party radical Christine O'Donnell defeated former Governor Castle in the primary before losing the general election. The 2010 Tea party victories in the House and the Senate suddenly gave reactionaries a source of power inside the government they had never had before.

Finally, Mitt Romney battered his Republican opponents with a hard line on illegal immigration in his presidential bids of 2008 and 2012, and Iowa congressman Steve King and Senator Cruz whipped the sentiment into a fury to defeat immigration reform when it was championed by Florida senator Marco Rubio in 2013. Speaker Boehner played it safe and did not commit to pushing for immigration reform, something he now regrets. As with the politicians who preceded him, "Boehner's quandary boiled down to a choice between protecting his right flank and doing what he thought was best for the country. He chose the former."[56]

THE IMPORTANCE OF PAT BUCHANAN
AND SAMUEL FRANCIS

Pat Buchanan's presidential campaigns of 1992 and 1996 anticipated Trump's road to the White House. In the 1992 primaries, Buchanan received three million votes by challenging President George H. W. Bush as weak on taxes and soft on moral issues. When polled, viewers of Pat Robertson's evangelical television program, *The 700 Club*, supported Buchanan over Bush by a 2 to 1 margin.[57] Buchanan shook the 1992 Republican National Convention in Houston when he declared there was a "culture war" taking place for the soul of the nation, condemning the Democratic Party and the Clintons for supporting abortion, radical feminism, environmental extremism, and the "homosexual rights movement."

My friends, this election is about much more than who gets what. It is about who we are. It is about what we believe. It is about what we stand for as Americans. There is a religious war going on in our country for the soul of America. It is a cultural war, as critical to the kind of nation we will one day be as was the Cold War itself.[58]

A bad-boy Scots-Irish Catholic who grew up in then-segregated Washington, D.C., and a gifted phrasemaker as an editorial page writer, Buchanan became a key aide and speechwriter to President Richard Nixon. He remained in the public eye as a columnist and a regular on one of the leading political television shows of the period, CNN's *Crossfire*. Pugilistic in life and in print, Buchanan tested the boundaries of the conservative establishment. When Bush 41 raised taxes he faced a rebellion on the right headed by Newt Gingrich and Buchanan. Buchanan's critique was more radical because he broke with GOP orthodoxy by questioning free trade. With roots in the "America First" Old Right of the 1930s, Buchanan flashed the "right-wing Catholic and neo-Confederate strands of the New Right."[59] Growing up with a father who adored Senator Joe McCarthy and Spanish dictator Francisco Franco, Buchanan gave a pithy description of his worldview in his 1988 autobiography, *Right From the Beginning*: "Segregation in the '50s was truly the biggest thing wrong with a country about which so very, very much was right."[60] Buchanan was not comfortable in the post-'60s world. His friend, the liberal columnist Mark Shields, said, "To Pat, the diversity of America is not a strength."[61]

Beneath Buchanan's populism was the intellectual tradition of paleoconservatism, a politics that rejected the economics-centered conservatism of Reagan, Jack Kemp, Gingrich, and Ryan in favor of traditional values of small towns in the Midwest and the South. Some paleoconservatives shared views with the far right, recalled the Confederate cause with affection, and viewed the white race as being under attack; other paleos talked about race but without emanating "hostility or bitterness" toward minorities.[62] Writing in the *Weekly Standard* about Buchanan's 1996 presidential run, David Brooks concluded: "Blood and soil are central to their creed."[63] In a 1988 interview, Buchanan was asked to draw the line between the right and the extreme right. He joked, "It's about two inches off my right shoulder."[64]

Two intellectuals helped shape Buchanan's worldview and prepared the GOP for the coming of Trump. In the 1940s, James Burnham, a one-time Trotskyite and a philosophy professor at NYU disillusioned with the Leninist left, framed a contrasting vision of the world. For Burnham, power in the 18th century lay with aristocrats and in the 19th century with capitalists, but in the modern age it was wielded by the managerial elite who ran the complex institutions that dominated society. Burnham's *The Managerial Revolution* (1941) was an unlikely bestseller and the author later joined Buckley's *National Review*. Fast forward to the 1990s and Buchanan was close to a right-wing intellectual named Samuel Francis who agreed with Burnham that the New Deal ushered in a government and corporate elite that ran the country's institutions and operated its foreign policy. Echoing his intellectual mentor, Francis wrote,

> Between approximately 1930 and 1950 the United States experienced a social and political revolution in which one elite was largely displaced from power by another. The new elite, entrenching itself in the management of large corporations and unions, the federal bureaucracy, and the centers of culture, education, and communication, articulated an ideology that expressed its interests and defended its dominance under the label of liberalism.[65]

While liberalism opposed communism abroad, Francis argued it expressed the basic utopian Marxist premise that "human beings are the products of their social environment and that by rational management it is possible to perfect or ameliorate significantly the human condition and indeed man himself."[66]

Armed with a history doctorate from the University of North Carolina, Francis was a serious political intellectual. "Perhaps the brightest and best thinker on the right," said Buchanan.[67] In 1969, Kevin Phillips wrote *The Emerging Republican Majority* mapping how this would happen if the formerly Democratic South joined the Republican Party. In similar fashion, Francis sought to identify the social forces that could challenge the modern administrative state run by a cosmopolitan meritocracy. He differed from more prominent Republican intellectuals because he "emphasized Catholic and neo-Confederate lineages in right-wing politics so often left out of the dominant narrative."[68] Forty years after *Brown v. Board of Education*, he described the historic ruling as "the most dangerous and destructive Supreme Court decision in American history."[69] Suspicious of the neo-conservative movement because of the elitist credentials of many of its members and critical of the Reagan Revolution as being incomplete, Francis sought to develop an ideology for "flyover country."

A fan of Antonio Gramsci, the Italian communist who died in a Mussolini jail, Francis believed elites rule via cultural hegemony—their dominance of culture and the realm of ideas. For Francis, what counted was identifying the "social forces such as class and region and ethnic identity"— significant sets of interests to which ideas could attach themselves. He sought to radicalize "the Middle American core" of American society against the "incumbent regime."[70]

> For reasons he never quite explained, [Francis] insisted that the cosmopolitan elite threatened the traditional values cherished by most Americans: 'morality and religion, family, nation, local community, and at times racial integrity and identity.' These were sacred principles for members of a new 'post-bourgeois proletariat' drawn from the working class and the lower ranks of the middle class. Lacking the skills prized by the technocrats, but not far enough down the social ladder to win the attention of reformers, these white voters considered themselves victims of a coalition between the top and the bottom against the middle.[71]

The connection between Nixon's silent majority and these voters is clear to see. Francis saw the United States in the midst of social and regional frag-mentation which was the result of the 1960s giving identities to a number of groups—blacks, women, youth, students, Native Americans, ethnics of one shade or another, and homosexuals—identities that separated them from mainstream American culture.[72]

Francis is a controversial figure because he took the politically incorrect step to argue that America's managerial revolution—exemplified by cos-mopolitan success stories such as Barack Obama—jeopardized the nation's traditional racial hierarchy.[73] To his critics:

Whereas mainstream conservatives depicted the U.S. as a nation whose diverse population was linked by devotion to its founding principles, Francis viewed it as a racial project inextricably bound up with white rule. The managerial revolution jeopardized this racial hierarchy, and so it must be overthrown.[74]

With conventional conservative doctrines—mainstream conservative, neoconservative, and libertarian—political dead ends for the "simple reason that the social groups that found them expressive of their interests and values no longer exist or no longer are able to command a significant political following," Francis saw the Buchanan candidacy showing the path forward. The goal was to capture the large white middle-class and working-class votes in the heartland.[75]

Liberal political analysts such as Ruy Teixeira, Joel Rogers, and John Judis also saw the white working class in play as both parties were failing to address the needs of this forgotten majority that constituted roughly 55 percent of the electorate in 2000.[76] Political opportunity existed if the Republicans shifted away from pro-corporate free-market economic policies, or if the Democrats moderated their cultural liberalism by signaling respect for white workers. Francis and Buchanan did not oppose the New Deal state, per se; instead, they stood against the liberal tradition and the cultural snobbery of the transnational MBA crowd, technocrats, digital billionaires, and Washington policy wonks and lawyers.[77]

Buchanan and Francis were building on the political model that powered Richard Nixon in the 1960s and '70s—a politics of resentment against the upper crust. This came naturally to Nixon, a kid from small-town Whittier, California who was accepted to Harvard College on the basis of grades but who could not go because his family lacked the money. As Rick Perlstein explains in *Nixonland*, Nixon represented the uncool average kid as opposed to the smoothly entitled rich, such as the Kennedys (who, of course, had resented the Boston Brahmins before them).[78] Nixon's politics were more about class than race; with Buchanan and Francis the reverse was true—sons of the South, they both thought of Middle America largely in terms of white identity politics that morphed into a nationalist politics celebrating the white Protestant nation of yesteryear.

Viewed by some as a founder of the alt-right, Francis followed in the footsteps of Charles Wallace Collins; he too had an illiberal neofeudal vision of America's future.[79] If Republican candidates were to side with workers as opposed to the corporate elite, a new GOP—recast as a nationalist party—could become the clear majority party. The secret to politics, said Francis, was something successful politicians from Adolf Hitler to Franklin Roosevelt to Lyndon Johnson understood. "The political masses are motivated largely by slogans, programs, and policies that revolve around the sentiments of 'us against them' and 'something for nothing.'"[80] In 2016, Donald Trump understood this well. Breaking with the idea that the United States should remain the superpower of the West, Francis wrote, "It may be that the United States will decide that it does not want a 'dominant position' in international affairs, that its own interests can best be served in a multipolar world with many different, sometimes competing, sometimes cooperating, centers of power."[81]

Francis argued that the liberal elite, or "the Ruling Class," which "uses and is used by secularist, globalist, anti-white, and anti-Western forces for its and their advantage" was increasingly vulnerable. To Francis, Buchanan's "America First" foreign policy was more than 1930s isolationism because it broke with conservatism by "giving priority to the nation over the gratification of individual and subnational interests." In contrast to large-state nationalists of the European model or American Hamiltonians, Buchanan and Francis saw the nation primarily as a "social and cultural unit" a vessel for a nation's traditional values. In late 1992, as Buchanan was about to continue his insurgent campaign against President Bush, Francis told him: "Go to New Hampshire and call yourself a patriot, a nationalist, an American Firster, but don't even use the word 'conservative.'"[82]

> Francis urged Buchanan to no longer police his ranks for the occasional racist or conspiracy theorist but instead to challenge the authority and legitimacy of the media and elites who demanded he do so. Francis's strategy was a hard right version of 'permanent offensive.'[83]

Upon gaining power, Francis had a radical vision of the presidency—one that was unnervingly prophetic about the Trump White House.

> The New Right, therefore, should make use of the presidency as its own spearhead against the entrenched elite and should

dwell on the fact that the intermediary bodies—Congress, the
courts, the bureaucracy, the media, etc.—are the main supports
of the elite. The adoption of the Caesarist tactic by the New
Right would reflect the historic pattern by which rising classes
ally with an executive power to displace the oligarchy that is
entrenched in the intermediate bodies. [84]

In the end, Francis's idea of a political coalition centered on the nation's
middle class is self-limiting because he thought of Middle America in
racial terms. A Southerner born in Chattanooga, Tennessee in 1947,
Francis came of age when the racial caste system of rigid segregation
and explicit racism ruled. The norms of his youth stayed with him. A
columnist and editorial page writer for the conservative *Washington Times*,
he attended a white nationalist conference in 1994 where he openly
expressed his racial views. We must, he said, "reassert our identity and
our solidarity, and we must do so in explicitly racial terms through the
articulation of racial consciousness as whites . . . The civilization that we
as whites created in Europe and America could not have developed apart
from the genetic endowments of the creating people, nor is there any
reason to believe that the civilization can be successfully transmitted to a
different people."[85] When his remarks came to light, he was fired by the
Times. Afterward, he was more open about his racial politics. He joined
the Council of Conservative Citizens, an anti-black, anti-immigration
group, was a regular contributor to *Chronicles*, a conservative intellectual
journal "with a focus on defending the traditions and history of America
and the West" that does not accept explicit racial material, and was associate editor of *The Occidental Quarterly*, which the Southern Poverty Law
Center describes as "a racist journal devoted to the idea that as whites
become a minority 'the civilization and free governments that whites have
created' will be jeopardized."[86] According to his defenders, "Sam never
penned a single line of racial hatred, but sought simply to protect and
conserve his own people and culture."[87]

Francis, who died in 2005, was the "philosopher king of the radical
right," says Leonard Zeskind, author of *Blood and Politics: The History of the
White Nationalist Movement from the Margins to the Mainstream* (2009).[88]
Together, Francis and Buchanan helped propagate the idea that a "coastal

liberal elite" run the country while leaving the rest of the nation behind to rust and rot as "American carnage."

ANY WARM BODY WILL DO

With traditional conservatives marginalized, radicals on the right pursue their twin passions: reshaping the power and reach of the federal government to benefit the elite—in Mr. Trump's case, himself—and protecting the power and privilege of white male America. The passion of conservatives for responsible government focused on solving pressing public problems has been abandoned as frivolous and unnecessary. Once upon a time, Republicans were careful to nominate and elect "serious" people for the presidency. Now it seems that any warm body will do as long as it is not a Democrat. Anti-tax zealot Grover Norquist, one of the right's leading strategists, explicitly articulated this strategy when addressing the American Conservative Union in 2012:

> We are not auditioning for fearless leader. We don't need a president to tell us in what direction to go. We know what direction we want to go. We want the Paul Ryan budget that cuts spending by $6 trillion dollars . . . *We just need a president to sign this stuff.* We don't need someone to think it up or design it . . . The leadership now for the modern conservative movement for the next 20 years will be coming out of the House and the Senate . . . So *focus on picking a president with enough digits to handle a pen to become president of the United States.*[89]

This is a profoundly disturbing development. During the Cold War era, Republican presidential nominees such as Dwight Eisenhower, Richard Nixon, George H. W. Bush, and Ronald Reagan were either steeped in domestic and foreign policy knowledge or, in the case or Reagan, maintained a clear vision on both domestic and foreign policy and had a two-term stint running the nation's largest state. In backing Donald Trump, the GOP decided to risk electing an intellectually and emotionally challenged man to the toughest job in the world, because, how difficult can it be? Less than six months into the Trump presidency, George F. Will wrote, "It is urgent for Americans to think and speak clearly about President Trump's inability to do either."[90] During his 4th of July address in 2019, President Trump said:

> The Continental Army suffered a bitter winter of Valley Forge, found glory across the waters of the Delaware and seized victory from Cornwallis of Yorktown. *Our army manned the air, it rammed the ramparts, it took over the airports*, it did everything it had to do, and at Fort McHenry, under the rocket's red glare, it had nothing but victory.[91]

Supporting someone radically inexperienced in government and whose capacity for reasoned judgment is in serious doubt is possible only because the reactionary right has fomented such contempt for government that many Republican voters simply wish Washington would disappear. The whole philosophy of the post-Gingrich Republican Party is to play wrecking crew to government so it does not matter if the president and his administration are massively incompetent. Why would the reactionary right want the national government to work?[92] Historically, nihilism was the doctrine of an extreme Russian revolutionary group in the mid-19th century that found nothing to approve of in the existing social order. These Russian rebels, the "new people" (as they called themselves), repudiated all the norms and institutions of the prior generation. Dedicated reactionary revolutionaries take the same stance today.[93]

In a 2012 interview that coincided with the 225th anniversary of the Constitution, former U.S. Supreme Court Justice David Souter gave a PBS *NewsHour* interview in which he spoke about the importance of an educated, thoughtful, civically engaged public. Justice Souter said republican government wasn't threatened by foreign invasion or a military coup, but by civic ignorance. "What I worry about is, when problems are not addressed and the people do not know who is responsible . . . some one person will come forward and say, 'Give me total power and I will solve this problem,'" he said. "That is how the Roman Republic fell . . . That is the way democracy dies."[94]

IO

America's Reactionary Revolution

I n his classic *The Anatomy of Revolution*, Crane Brinton saw the British, French, and Russian revolutions following a pattern that began in "hope and moderation," reached a crisis in a reign of terror which purged first the moderates, then the less extreme radicals, and finally the most fanatic, before sliding into a Thermidorean period that retreated from the revolution's most radical goals, and ended in the dictatorships of Cromwell, Napoleon, and Stalin.[1] The American revolution did not follow this pattern. Why? The newly formed United States did not have a group of Jacobins led by Robespierre and Danton eliminating the moderates and driving the revolution into a more militant phase. Compared to the other great revolutions, the American Revolution was relatively bloodless and radically incomplete. Our aristocracy was neither killed nor driven out of the country; the Southern slave aristocracy helped lead the revolution, with the Virginians Thomas Jefferson, George Washington, and James Madison at the forefront. The power of the slave owners was not challenged because the War of Independence would have failed without Maryland, Virginia, North Carolina, South Carolina, and Georgia joining the rebellion.[2]

In fledgling America, there was nothing for would-be reactionaries to react against because the most radical aspects of the American

Revolution—that all people are created equal and that ordinary people would no longer defer to a social elite—were delayed. The radical ideology of the revolution remained a latent promise. In *On Revolution* (1963), Hannah Arendt praised the relative lack of violence in the American Revolution while condemning the bloodletting in the French cataclysm. But the bloody phase of the revolution took place in the Civil War when Lincoln and the abolitionists pushed the Declaration's announcement of equality for all toward its logical conclusion. It was only then that America's landed aristocracy was challenged and its power reduced.

In the 19th century United States, only the Southern slaveholders looked back at the feudal order with envy. In the North and the West, areas of the nation that Tocqueville celebrated, Americans were thrilled to be free and wanted nothing to do with slavery, serfdom, or the old regime. By the Jacksonian period, it was clear that the democratic elements in American culture had pushed aside the political and financial elite who had framed the Constitution as a conservative, cautious document. The Constitution's design reveals how Madison, Hamilton, and the founders were Burkeans at heart who viewed government as a necessary and good thing, best trusted to those with the necessary wisdom and training to direct the state.[3] Their republicanism was permeated with a philosophical conservatism that sought stability.[4] As time went on, being a conservative in the United States took on a different meaning when compared to older nations. In America, conservatives must protect and preserve not only property, but also the founding liberal principles and spirit of democracy. In the liberal theology championed by Paine, Jefferson, Lincoln, and John Dewey, the United States established a new world in which persistent privilege, hierarchy, inequality, and exclusion were viewed as a violation of the nation's liberal democratic ideal. Achievement and distinction are recognized, but a permanent elite is not inherently favored from birth and the liberal theology preaches that no one should be excluded from the possibility of enjoying a rich and rewarding life.

The American Revolution remained moderate in temperament and its leaders pragmatists instead of zealots, but its goals ring radical when viewed from the perspective of human history. American liberals not only invented a new political order by pioneering modern representative government, they sought to cultivate and instill democratic norms in the society at large. Tocqueville and Dewey knew that institutions without robust democratic habits of action stand hollow and can easily topple when challenged by contemporary aristocrats dressed in new clothes. This is why Dewey spoke of democracy not as elections but as a "way of life" and Tocqueville argued that "habits of the heart" are more important than laws or constitutions. Widely regarded as the leading American philosopher of the 20th century, Dewey's ambitious philosophical project—from *The School and Society* (1899), *How We Think* (1910), *Democracy and Education* (1916), and *Reconstruction in Philosophy* (1920) to *Human Nature and Conduct* (1922), *The Public and Its Problems* (1927), *The Quest for Certainty* (1929), and *Liberalism and Social Action* (1935)—can be read as his attempt to create an education system and a society untainted by the feudal norms of hierarchy and class. Against the selfishness of the right, liberals champion an ethic that is more communal. Echoing Tocqueville, modern liberals believe in "self-interest properly understood." Liberals such as Barack Obama and Elizabeth Warren believe the United States should be defined as much by democracy as it is by capitalism.

The nation's ongoing liberal revolution has its roots in the commonsense, empowering, pragmatic philosophy of Locke. Proclaiming the dignity of every individual and discrediting the idea of aristocracy based on class-based intellectual differences, Locke did not see the need to put forth a model of the perfect republic as did Rousseau in *On the Social Contract*. Both the French and Russian revolutions quickly sped into radical phases due, in part, to the utopian visions that Rousseau and Marx provided to Robespierre and Lenin. By contrast, thanks to America's liberal origins and intellectual inheritance from Locke, our revolution has remained moderate and gradual. Using the Declaration as our lodestar, we have followed a "persistently nonradical road toward a radically new multicultural social order," writes historian William Freehling.[5] Largely peaceful, it has been fought in courtrooms and on picket lines, by nonviolent resistance and restrained demonstrations, not street battles. The notable exception was the Civil War—sparked by the South's desire to extend slavery westward and the Confederacy's secession from the Union following Abraham Lincoln's election in 1860.

Still, the moderate nature of our ongoing liberal revolution was clearly demonstrated in Lincoln's decision not to punish the Confederate elite after a horrific North-South sectional struggle that left 750,000 dead.[6] In a more radical revolution, General Lee, President Jefferson Davis, and many of the Confederate military leaders whose statues continue standing in the South would have been tried and executed. Lincoln and the great reform presidents who followed him—Theodore Roosevelt, Woodrow Wilson, Franklin Roosevelt, and Lyndon Johnson—are not anyone's idea of radical revolutionaries. The liberal presidents of the 20th century confronted the reactionary elements blocking liberal advance and defeated them at the ballot box and in the legislative arena. Some might argue that the 1960s exemplified the American Revolution's liberal excessive phase and the Reagan revolution represented the moderating Thermidorean correction. But such an appraisal is wrong; to see Lyndon Johnson and Martin Luther King as Robespierre and Danton is misguided.

A DELAYED COUNTERREVOLUTION AGAINST THE FOUNDERS

Since the 1990s, the reactionary push coming from the Republican Party can best be viewed as a delayed counterrevolution waged against the liberal ideas of John Locke, the founders, Alexis de Tocqueville, and Abraham Lincoln. Most revolutions spark a reactionary response at the time the revolt takes place. The French Revolution, for instance, witnessed a counterrevolution first in the provinces outside Paris, and then in the Thermidorean reaction that toppled Maximilien Robespierre and the Jacobins from power in 1794. The birth of the United States did not set off a counterrevolution, in part because the American Revolution was not a social revolution in which the upper class in the colonies lost power. But our Lockean foundation—given poetic intensity by Jefferson and Lincoln—with its focus on equality and individual rights, generated a political logic that unleashed an ongoing political and social revolution over the course of several centuries. This stands in sharp contrast to the classic revolution compressed into one or two decades. In a very real sense, America's liberal revolution continues: groups at first marginalized, discriminated against, and excluded demanded inclusion and full recognition as equal citizens in a republic where from the early decades of the 19th century white males enjoyed unprecedented equality of status, political rights, and individual freedom. This has been a recurring theme across American history. Yet this march toward inclusion, which increased in its intensity and power beginning in the 1960s and produced the presidency of Barack Obama, spawned a reaction. Since Newt Gingrich's speakership, liberal America has confronted a fierce right-wing counterrevolution that is antidemocratic, anti-liberal, and anti-American and is driven by white fear of losing status, power, and position in a diverse, cosmopolitan country.[7]

Both in its liberal origins and reactionary dimension, the United States is politically unique. The United States never had to contend with an old aristocratic order connected to monarchy and formal feudal rank. In post-revolutionary Europe, surviving remnants of the aristocracy openly championed the old order. Some saw democracy as a moral affront to the natural order of the elite and subordinate. Others, such as the early 20th century British elite that pursued appeasement with Hitler and the Nazis, revealed a comfort with the forces of reaction that sought a slowdown of and possibly a reversal in the increasing power of the laboring classes. The reactionary movement in the United States is not a classic Thermidorean response to curb the violence and excesses of the revolution because the American Revolution of 1776 never became radical with extremists leading the charge. Nor is it the traditional reaction found across 19th century Latin America and some European states in which a powerful landed elite teamed with an emerging urban capitalist class to stop liberal and democratic reform from gaining traction and becoming accepted and a permanent part of the political culture. Nor has America experienced a reactionary right comparable to that of post–World War I Europe, in which the surviving elements of the aristocracy teamed with fascist thugs to eradicate fledgling democracies in Spain, Italy, and Germany.

The United States was spared both the necessity of waging a battle against the forces of repression across the whole of society at the nation's beginning (as in the French Revolution) and the agony of dealing with the nostalgia of a failed aristocracy that despised democracy and dreamed of restoration (as in the Europe of Hitler and Mussolini in the 1930s). The world is filled with infinite variety so, of course, American authoritarianism is unique compared to other nations. In the United States, the reactionary assault is the result of our original sin: allowing a feudal aristocracy to dominate the South and generate a potent illiberal ideology that only recently partnered with hard-right elements of the business class. We eliminated slavery in the Civil War, but the planter class survived, the slaves were converted into landless, uneducated sharecroppers ever in debt, with little chance of advancing. America's gaping racist wound festered as the Southern elite used the "race card" to perpetuate their power and Northern whites demonstrated their own "white rage" with intimidation, race riots, and systemic police brutality.[8]

My argument that we are experiencing a reactionary revolution owes a debt to Gordon Wood's claims about the radicalism of the American revolution.[9] What occurred then and now are ideological shifts in the American political mind of real consequence. At the dawn of the 19th century, Americans gave up on the civic republican conception of a leisure class gentry being the leading political actors and embraced mass democracy. Two hundred and twenty years later, reactionaries, once divided and housed in different political parties, are now united inside the Republican Party. Illiberals *united* versus illiberals *divided* represents a quantum leap in the danger that the reactionary rejection of America's founding principles will become majority sentiment. Today, traditional conservative politicians have been largely purged from the GOP and the party is powered by radical libertarians determined to dismantle the New Deal state and "cultural conservatives" who fear an increasingly diverse world in which the historic advantages of being white and male are under assault. The illiberal "movement conservatives" who supported Reagan, George W. Bush, and Trump (as opposed to traditional conservatives who backed Eisenhower, Nixon, Ford, and George H. W. Bush) saw their mission as waging war against the New Deal state. Sometimes this ideological campaign was "too urgent to be trusted to the traditional channels of governance" and resulted in conduct (Watergate, Iran-Contra, aspects of the war on terror, the Ukraine scandal) widely viewed as illegal. Sam Tanenhaus writes that "adherents of revolutionary movements, right and left, can be described as people who 'will not take No for an answer.' This adamant refusal is the essence of movement conservatism"—which has metastasized into a counterrevolution against the founders and America's liberal ideal.[10]

The fate of the landed elite holds the key to whether a nation will continue as a stable democracy or will, at some point, follow the authoritarian road. But the challenge to liberal pluralist democracy lurks not only when the landed nobility has power, as with the Prussian Junker class and Hitler. It also exists when the anti-liberal, antidemocratic, and quasi-feudal ideas of a landed elite live on in DNA of generations far removed from both slavery and segregation. This is the experience of the United States and the result is a potent force in mass democratic politics—as witnessed in Donald Trump's unorthodox, triumphant 2016 campaign. Across class lines—from blue-collar workers to Wall Street investment bankers—the white males who make up a strong majority of the GOP understand that voting Republican is a vote to maintain, preserve, and perpetuate their social status, economic power, and privileged standing in society. They appreciate the benefits bestowed by patriarchy and "whiteness."

As the planter class was happy when flamboyant demagogues would excite white voters with racial lies, so too today's Business Roundtable understands the valuable and useful role that a modern demagogue such as President Trump plays in deflecting attention from the corporate elite. Most sophisticated Republicans would rather have a President Reagan on the stump than President Trump. Charismatic in a completely different way, Reagan made the college-educated proud in a way that is just not possible with Donald Trump. But the GOP has changed and the moderate Midwestern and New England wing no longer exists. When Reagan was president, the racist South was a piece of the Republican coalition, much in the same way that the Old South had been part of FDR's New Deal coalition. In both cases, it was possible, to some degree, to keep the white supremacists at bay because the parties had significant moderate ballast. Neither the racial nor the authoritarian tendencies of the Old South were given full voice in Reagan's Republican Party or Franklin Roosevelt's Democratic Party. But they have been amplified in the post-Gingrich GOP, powered by unreconstructed whites and a reactionary business elite; rarely have politics at the national level been this polarized and venomous. Traditional business Republicans remain in the party because of the GOP's commitment to lower taxes and less regulation than the Democrats, but they are merely passengers, not the engineers driving the train. In an important sense, the center-right Republican business class is the key to America's political future. If small business owners, middle management executives, and CEOs sense the danger that Trump and the reactionaries represent, then they can voice their conservative conscience. They can say, "No—this is not right," and reject the party of Trump. Nothing sends a signal to politicians like losing an election. A lifelong Republican and now a man without a party, Max Boot writes:

> I am now convinced that the Republican Party must suffer repeated and devastating defeats . . . Only if the GOP as currently constituted is burned to the ground will there be any chance to build a reasonable center-right party out of the ashes.[11]

However, it is unclear whether the business class cares enough about the Constitution, a free and fair press, democratic norms, and having a national government that is staffed and works to notice that the Trump Administration is conducting a counterrevolution from within against American democracy and the "liberal project" of the founders and Lincoln.

As the radical phase of our reactionary revolution accelerates, we may reach a point where a portion of the population that has supported the Republican Party rejects the chaos, instability, dishonesty, and attack on basic American values that the Trump Republican Party has come to represent. Revolutionary excess takes its toll. Exhausted, the public may push the pause button on the frenetic activity and radical policies that in a normal time would be rejected out of hand. To many observers, the Trump presidency does not seem sustainable. But, of course, many so-called political experts were shocked when Donald Trump won the 2016 presidential election. It is unclear whether this revolution's Thermidor is approaching. On the one hand, either singularly or jointly, President Trump's impeachment by the House of Representatives in the wake of the Ukraine scandal involving the 2020 presidential election (building on the Mueller investigation into the Trump administration and Russian interference in the 2016 election) and trial in the Senate, or a Democratic victory in the 2020 presidential election may result in reactionaries losing energy and zeal. On the other hand, we may be nowhere near the end of the reactionary surge that has reshaped American politics. What appears to some to be the last phases of the radical period may, in fact, be the beginning stage of a thoroughgoing reactionary reconstruction of American society that rejects the 1960s and New Deal eras as profound mistakes.

WHITE PATRIARCHY AND THE "AUTHORITARIAN LANE"

Some say that working-class angst, deindustrialization, and resentment of coastal elites powered Trump's 2016 victory. The evidence says otherwise. The blue-collar vote was but a modest percentage of Trump's electoral coalition. It is true that the president's strength among white working-class voters, especially men, proved to be the margin of victory in the decisive battleground states of Pennsylvania, Wisconsin, and Michigan. But, according to a 2018 study by the Pew Research Center, just 33 percent of Trump's supporters were white men without a college degree.[12] And data from the American National Election Survey show that white non-Hispanic voters without college degrees and earning a below-the-median-household income made up a scant 25 percent of Trump voters. Downscale working-class whites surely helped put Mr. Trump in the White House, but a majority of Trump voters are middle-class or affluent.[13] His electoral coalition was similar to that of the three previous GOP presidential nominees: Mitt Romney, John McCain, and George W. Bush. Giving the white working class the credit—or the blame—for President Trump's election is entirely too modest.

> Trump's dominance among whites across class lines is of a piece with his larger dominance among whites across nearly every white demographic. Trump won white women (+9) and white men (+31). He won white people with college degrees (+3) and white people without them (+37). He won whites ages 18–29 (+4), 30–44 (+17), 45–64 (+28), and 65 or older (+19) . . . Trump's white support was not determined by income. According to Edison Research, Trump won whites making less than $50,000 by 20 points, whites making $50,000 to $99,999 by 28 points, and whites making $100,000 or more by 14 points . . . the focus on one subsector of Trump voters—the white working class—is puzzling, given the breadth of his white coalition.[14]

The idea that Trump's political strength is primarily rooted in cultural resentment of liberal elites and economic reversal is a convenient narrative that protects white America from looking in the mirror. Americans are far more comfortable speaking about class than they are of race. When the "broad and remarkable white support for Donald Trump can be reduced to the righteous anger of a noble class of smallville firefighters and evangelicals, mocked by Brooklyn hipsters and womanist professors into voting against their [class] interests, *then the threat of racism and whiteness . . . can be dismissed.*"[15] While many in the media and the public sought to find alternative explanations for Trump's success—Rust Belt anger about jobs lost to China and Mexico, frustration with Washington, D.C., and traditional politicians, Hillary Clinton's baggage—a defense of white America lies at the core of his appeal. Trump's base—hovering always between 38 to 46 percent of the voting age public—stays with him. And, as a result, this president has received "blanket support" from Republicans in Congress.[16] For at least part of the Republican electorate, he is what they have "always wanted: a president who embodies the rage they feel toward those they hate and fear, while reassuring them that that rage is nothing to be ashamed of."[17] Trump acts as the Freudian id—instinctual, primitive, aggressive, and selfish—of the White Republican Party. This allows other Republicans to tout their superego morality and to deny that racism or sexism have anything to do with their support of a man whose only consistent ideology is white supremacy and the patriarchy.[18]

In using the term "reactionary revolution," I am not arguing that the United States is experiencing a massive violent social revolution. That is obviously not the case. Instead, racially "conservative" whites finding common cause with moneyed libertarians atop the world's most powerful corporate culture has created an "authoritarian lane" in American political culture; it is the one on which President Trump is driving. As the GOP has abandoned conservatism and adopted a reactionary stance many Republicans have become increasingly reticent about standing up for the rule of law. Showing more loyalty to party than country, their allegiance to the Constitution and America's ideals suddenly is in doubt. Some will argue that this portrait of contemporary American politics is overblown and that what we are experiencing is similar to the 1960s and Watergate when political passions ran hot. Harvard political scientist Samuel Huntington argued that such periods of high emotion and extreme rhetoric are episodes of "democratic distemper" that pass.[19] This point of view thinks of American politics as being solidly grounded in the consensus middle and that if one party swings to the left, as the Democrats did with presidential nominee

George McGovern in 1972, or to the right, as the Republicans did with President Donald Trump in 2016, the pendulum swings back and the nation returns to the "politics of normalcy" as President Warren Harding called it.[20] While this may be true and the Trump presidency may be but a brief chapter in our politics, there is also good reason to believe that the tectonic plates undergirding American politics have shifted and that the United States is now more open to reactionary politics than in the past.

FEAR OF FALLING

Reactionary politics is powered by a fear of losing status, power, and position. Illiberals may tout free-market competition, but they are heavily invested in making sure that they have a privileged and advantageous position from which to start. Reactionaries want to maintain their position in the hierarchy created by capitalist competition and they continuously look for ways to protect and preserve their power and stature in society; they want to fortify and strengthen their class position—and this applies both to the financial elite and Wall Street barons as well as to people in the middle and upper-middle classes. While they may speak about a rising economy lifting all boats, reactionaries do not want lesser boats rising faster than they are. The class structure, as it is, is to be perpetuated. People who were subordinate in the past should remain supporting players, not leading actors.

More than sixty years after *Brown v. Board of Education*, the United States continues to be a caste society in which race often functions as class. William Julius Wilson wrote *The Declining Significance of Race* (1978) at a hopeful moment, but the thinly veiled racism and immigrant-bashing of the contemporary Republican Party is a calling card that unites reactionary whites and rallies the base. Yes, many people of color have joined the middle class and managerial professions and scores of women have risen to positions of authority and power formerly reserved for white men, but as long as these numbers are modest the earlier structure remains altered, not transformed. Women now make up 51 percent of students entering law school, but only 19 percent of equity partners at the nation's major law firms.[21] Barack Obama was twice elected president of the United States, but the number of African Americans and Latinos emerging from the nation's top law, business, medical, and graduate schools remains a fraction of what it might be. Why? In large part because an increasingly white male Republican Party thwarts attempts to confront issues such as school and housing segregation and gender discrimination. Looking back fifty years, the right's attacks on Lyndon Johnson's Great Society and metropolitan busing to achieve racial desegregation were unrelenting. Similar to the post–Civil War era when former slaves were granted political rights, political equality for people of color became a reality in the 1960s (as for women in the 1920s), but economic power largely remained with white males. Black and Latino unemployment has always been double that of whites. Today, the plight of white working-class America is a subject of concern. But this only demonstrates that deindustrialization and the pathologies of chronic unemployment have crossed the color line.

The fear of falling from one social class to a lower one has always driven reactionary movements. When the economic floor opens up and people begin a free fall they cast about for a savior. In Germany, the astronomical inflation and soaring unemployment of the early 1930s decimated the middle class, fueling the rise of Hitler and his National Socialist Party. In the 2016 presidential election, working-class voters heard Trump's message about "bad" trade deals and how he would bring manufacturing jobs back to the United States. Reactionary politics is also powered by the upper middle class calmly taking self-interested actions to solidify and enhance their economic position. From Reagan to Trump, the Republican Party has diligently pursued public policies to protect and enhance the financial portfolios of America's managerial and investing classes. While the middle class fears financial ruin due to a capricious economy, the elite know they can weather a financial storm, and even a hurricane. The fear of falling for the wealthy is different from that of the middle class. What scares the financial elite is class warfare powered by the left. While the middle class loses sleep in an economic downturn, the upper crust has nightmares about a charming Reaganesque all-American 21st century New Dealer making believers out of a majority of the electorate.

The psychology of the wealthy meshes with Hayek's either/or worldview. Framing the choice as minimal government or full-scale socialism with a Leninist vanguard is beautiful politics for plutocrats. In tandem, the upper middle class and the wealthy fear a more equitable progressive tax code fueling demands for more and greater government programs such as the Affordable Care Act or student loan forgiveness and very low tuition for public higher education in the manner of Pat Brown's California. Ambitious programs designed to help America's middle and working classes succeed could send the United States down a slippery slope that leads not to the Soviet Union, but to Denmark, Germany, Sweden, and Japan. In these countries, the wealthy may be richer than others, but taxes on the very rich are steeper than in the United States and CEOs, on average, enjoy less extravagant pay and perks.

In the United States, the fear of falling for whites has always been cushioned by the knowledge that they cannot fall all the way to the bottom. From colonial Virginia to the present day, the basement of American society has been occupied by poor blacks: first as slaves, then as landless peasants in the sharecropping South of Jim Crow segregation and lynching, and now in the toughest northern ghettos.

> I knew that West Baltimore, where I lived; that the north side of Philadelphia, where my cousins lived; that the South Side of Chicago, where friends of my father lived, comprised a world apart. Somewhere out there beyond the firmament, past the asteroid belt, there were other worlds where children did not regularly fear for their bodies . . . When our elders presented school to us, they did not present it as a place of high learning but as a means of escape from death and penal warehousing.[22]

In the Old South, the psychic wage that every white sawmill worker earned was the emotional assurance that no matter how bad things got economically, no matter how much he was squeezed by his boss or local banker, he always stood head and shoulders above any black man or woman.[23] The psychic wage remains at work from Baltimore to Portland. Part of the unspoken fear of whites is that in a cosmopolitan, fully integrated, mixed-race America—an advanced version of where California is today—blended ethnic and racial identities could doom whiteness. Without the power of white racial identity, this nightmare warns, lower-class whites who cannot compete in today's economy would be as likely as poor African Americans to be on absolute bottom rung of society, struggling and dying in dysfunctional, crime-ridden neighborhoods where opportunities are scarce.

THE REACTIONARY REVOLUTION IN AMERICA

The contemporary Republican Party can be viewed from the standpoint of conservative, reactionary, and counterrevolutionary.[24] Conservatives defend the status quo, believe in stability, and are open to incremental reform. Reactionaries scorn the present, dream of the way things were, reject efforts at reform, and want to retreat to a mythical past. The goal of the reactionary is to preserve a hierarchical order of privilege.[25] More extreme, counterrevolutionaries wish to blow up the society in front of them and start anew. In style, method, and appearance, they often make a break with the politics of compromise and incrementalism that is radical indeed. Both traditional conservatives and reactionaries find themselves outflanked and stymied by the counterrevolutionary focused on personal power, not ideology. In a reactionary revolution, traditional conservatives who defended the status quo are overwhelmed. This happened when apartheid-like Jim Crow laws were instituted in state after Southern state after 1900 as conservative politicians were pushed aside by the reactionary Redeemers playing the race card, it happened in Europe during the 1920s and '30s when conservatives were outmaneuvered by the fascists and Nazis, and it has happened again in the post-2000 United States.[26]

As Brinton explains in some detail in *The Anatomy of Revolution*, in the middle of a revolutionary situation, radicals have greater power than do moderates.[27] This is the lesson of the English, French, and Russian revolutions, and this dynamic is at play in the American counterrevolution as well. If John McCain and President George H. W. Bush represented conservative Republicans, then politicians such as senators Ted Cruz of Texas and Mike Lee of Utah and retiring North Carolina congressman Mark Meadows stand as reactionary leaders who seek to raze the liberal New Deal state. President Trump is an example of a counterrevolutionary leader who is scorned, not only by liberals, but by the conservative establishment, and insists on playing politics by his own rules.

The reactionary revolution in the United States is distinctive in at least three respects when compared to the European experience. First, in contrast to the classic revolution compressed into one or two decades that was the experience of England (1640–1660), France (1789–1799), and Russia (1917–1938), America's revolutionary and counterrevolutionary experience has played out across centuries. The reactionary revolt in America is long delayed, in part, because the idea that "all men are created equal" *applying to everyone* regardless of race, national origin, or gender became widely accepted only within the past fifty years. Until recently, it would have been impossible to conceive of Barack Obama (with a black Kenyan father and white Kansas mother) and Hillary Clinton (a graduate of Wellesley College) as president and secretary of state. Many white Americans enjoy the benefits of a white-dominated society and the psychic wage it confers on them even as they insist they are not racists. And most are not.[28] Still, seeing the future, some fear the day that they and their families will live in a nation that is majority minority.

Second, if America's liberal revolution has been gradual and moderate in nature, the reactionary revolt against it appears disproportionate and exaggerated. The intense hatred of liberalism and the modern New Deal state makes little sense until we understand that Spencer, Hayek, and Rand had a fear of Marx based on the European experience. Additionally, white resentment of minorities and immigrants has been supercharged by globalization, deindustrialization, and the wage stagnation of the past thirty years. Ironically, if the libertarian wing of the GOP had not been so successful in fighting organized labor, the white working class would be less opposed to immigrants, minorities, and women trying to improve their lot.

Finally, the United States flips the classic revolution on its head. The American counterrevolution is not a Thermidorean reaction taking place because of radical excess. Instead, it is a full-scale *revolution* in the sense of Brinton's four stages. Paradoxically, in the United States, while liberals are moderates, reactionaries *are* radical revolutionaries seeking to overthrow the liberal-conservative worldview that has guided the nation for nearly 250 years. In calling for a dedication to revolutionary principles and purity, Barry Goldwater ("extremism in the defense of liberty is no vice") played, as did Newt Gingrich and now Ted Cruz and others on the right, the role of Robespierre, Marat, and Lenin. For the reactionaries who now dominate the Republican Party—such as Senate Majority Leader Mitch McConnell, White House Chief of Staff Mick Mulvaney, Utah senator Mike Lee, and Rep. Mark Meadows (leader of the radical Freedom Caucus in the House)—the Old Order consists of the Progressive-New Deal state that they are trying their best to overthrow. The moderate phase took place when the Reagan revolution halted the liberal New Deal era; the radical phase began when Republicans captured the House of Representatives in 1994 and Gingrich became House Speaker, and only became more extreme with the emergence of the Tea Party and the white backlash against the Obama presidency. With the Trump presidency, to extend the comparison with the French Revolution, we now have entered a metaphorical "reign of terror"—a period in which every liberal premise and program is under assault and democracy imperiled trembles. As the counterrevolution has escalated, violence from the right has increased: witness Charlottesville, the uptick in hate crimes reported to the FBI, and horrific mass shootings targeting schoolchildren, African Americans, gays, Latinos, and Jews. At the same time, Trump and his White House have launched daily attacks on journalists, the administration of justice, the rule of law, and Congress and the Supreme Court as coequal branches of government with hardly a word of protest from congressional Republicans. Needless to say, the liberal and conservative commanders in chief who preceded the current president in the Oval Office never behaved in such openly authoritarian ways.

Classically, revolutions eat their young. Here again, the counterrevolution in the United States fits the pattern and in so doing demonstrates that it is truly radical. Examples include Speaker John Boehner, a supporter of the Gingrich revolt inside the GOP, ousted for being too moderate; Tea Party House Minority Leader Eric Cantor, "primaried" by a libertarian purist; Speaker Paul Ryan being continually whipsawed by the Freedom Caucus and President Trump; and, more recently, Arizona senator Jeff Flake, a strong conservative who dared criticize President Trump's behavior in office, forced to resign rather than face certain defeat in the Arizona GOP primary. One could argue that the radical side of the illiberal reaction within the GOP is no more radical than the Students for a Democratic Society (SDS) and the Black Panthers in the 1960s. But such a comparison fails because when Tom Hayden penned *The Port Huron Statement* in 1962 the SDS was inspired more by Jefferson and America's lofty democratic ideals than Marx, and the Black Panthers took up arms in self-defense against racist police departments.[29] Both groups became more radical as the 1960s proceeded and a tiny fringe of the radical left, represented by the Weather Underground, turned violent. But neither the SDS nor the Black Panthers nor any of the other left-wing groups pushing for radical change became a dominant force in the Democratic Party; instead, they and a multitude of less strident liberal activists campaigned from the outside. The Democratic Party changed when it increased the representation of women and minorities at its national convention starting in 1972. But the minuscule hard-Leninist left of the 1960s, consisting primarily of people under thirty protesting against "the system," in no way came to dominate and steer the Democratic Party of Jimmy Carter, Bill Clinton, or Barack Obama. For example, Bill Clinton came of age during the '60s and was a political activist who worked on the McGovern campaign in 1972 but he was not a Maoist radical and as president governed within the Reagan paradigm. In sharp contrast, the hard-right reactionaries who make up the "conservative movement," the Tea Party, the Freedom Caucus, and the Trump base, joined by billionaires such as the Koch brothers and Mercer family, in fact, do dominate and control today's Republican Party.

FATE OF THE LANDED ELITE—THE LOGIC OF REACTIONARY PERIL

The nuptial of racially reactionary whites and moneyed libertarians is no ordinary political alliance. Southern neofeudalism married to the libertarian dream of destroying the government's taxing and regulatory authority constitutes a grave threat to America's future. The experience of other nations allows us to grasp why. In a landmark book that remains a classic in the field, *Social Origins of Dictatorship and Democracy* (1966), Harvard sociologist Barrington Moore Jr. investigated how the world's leading nations navigated the transition from an agrarian society to the modern industrial and postindustrial world. Moore discovered that the fate of the landed elite—the most powerful antidemocratic element in nations such as Great Britain, France, Germany, and the United States—is *the* central factor determining whether a nation becomes a strong and stable democracy or is susceptible to the siren call of authoritarians.[30] What Moore learned speaks forcefully today. Unless crushed, eliminated, or transformed, the venomous ideology of the landed elite lurks in the background of the political landscape, waiting for its chance to poison liberal democracy.

As a result of the American Revolution, the United States became strongly liberal and robustly democratic, and in the climactic struggle of the 19th century—the Civil War—the Northern capitalists and Southern landed elite were on opposite sides. In Europe and Latin America, by contrast, a political alliance between capital and the landed elite (the marriage of "iron and rye" in imperial Germany) often blocked efforts to build a modern liberal society, replete with democracy and civil rights. Absent a strong cultural tradition supporting liberalism and democracy, the transition to democracy was incomplete—sometimes with tragic results as in the Weimar Republic, the short-lived democratic government in Germany that preceded Adolf Hitler.

In America, things were different—until now. But the Northern victory of Lincoln and Grant did not eliminate the possibility of the reactionary partnership between capital and the landed elite emerging at some future date in a novel form. The Southern aristocracy—this nation's landed elite—could not win the Civil War, but the planter class and its large estates survived and dominated the South for the next 100 years. The plantation owners may be gone, but their reactionary ideas live on, having resurfaced with a vengeance during Barack Obama's presidency.

Europe's three major countries—Great Britain, France, and Germany—followed separate paths out of feudalism. In Great Britain, the landed class gradually aligned itself with the new commercial elite and accepted both the Industrial Revolution and the gradual expansion of suffrage to the middle and working classes. With strong class distinctions, enforced by the sharp differences between the wellborn schooled at Oxbridge and the blokes shoveling coal, marching in the infantry, and drinking at the pub, Great Britain was governed by an elite that strongly identified with constitutional government and had long experience with a gradually expanding electorate participating in elections for Parliament. In France, early in the French Revolution portions of the aristocracy had a chance to make an alignment with the rising bourgeoisie and join the tide of history that was pulling away from Louis XVI, the Church, and the nobility. In the first year of the Revolution, the goal was a constitutional monarchy similar to that of Great Britain. But opportunities were missed, history accelerated, and the great Revolution of 1789 swept the king, the aristocracy, and the feudal order to their doom.[31] Britain and France, following radically different paths, arrived at the same endpoint: the landed elite no longer blocked modernization premised on industrial capitalism and liberal democracy.[32]

In Germany, however, it was different. The wealthy landed families of Prussia never were challenged. The power of the feudal Junker class remained intact when the fragile Weimar Republic was born following World War I. A decade later, in the economic chaos of the Great Depression, the Junkers' authoritarian, illiberal views led them to abandon democracy and throw their support behind Adolf Hitler and the Nazi Party. The consequences for millions of people were horrific.[33]

In the United States, the planter elite presented an obstacle to democracy and Lockean ideals but was no fetter to industrial capitalism. The South supplied cotton and other raw materials to the North's factories, and American slavery, on the eve of the Civil War, was a rousing economic success.[34] The price of slaves rose in the 1850s, responding to strong demand as plantations spread westward. The crisis that doomed antebellum slavery was political, not economic.[35] If the South had won the Civil War and the Southern plantation system had established itself in the West, the United States would have emerged a far different nation in the 20th century. A United States of the Confederacy very likely would have been similar to many developing countries such as those in Latin America in the 20th century—"a latifundia economy, a dominant antidemocratic aristocracy, and a weak and dependent commercial and industrial class, unable and unwilling to push toward political democracy."[36] Lincoln is viewed as America's greatest president, for good reason. Under his leadership, the Union defeated the Confederacy, abolished slavery, and ended the danger that the slave economy would dominate national development. Unfortunately, slavery was replaced by a caste system and economic bondage based on sharecropping. Most of the plantation elite survived the ordeal of war and reconstruction and the mass of newly freed blacks became a dependent, propertyless, and nearly penniless peasantry.[37]

It is not a mandate of heaven that the United States remains a constitutional democracy. The decision, instead, is ours to make. America could, in fact, abandon its liberal tradition and choose the authoritarian road. Since the American and French revolutions taught the world that it is possible to construct societies based on liberty, equality, and democracy, reactionary politics has shown its ugly face in country after country. In numerous nations, the reactionary, anti-liberal, and antidemocratic views of neofeudal land owners and conservative elements in the rural areas found support among elements of the urban business class anxious to block liberal reform and working class progress. This reactionary coalition benefited from the investments of multinational corporations happy to profit under authoritarian regimes. This happened in much of Latin America where the landed elite maintained its power well into the 20th century. And it happened in Germany, where the great Junker landlords of Prussia backed Hitler's storm troopers and were joined by a supporting cast of corporate icons. Among the famous companies that either supported or, at minimum, profited from the Third Reich: IBM, Volkswagen, Coca-Cola, Hugo Boss, the Associated Press, Kodak, Bayer, BMW, Siemens, Ford, and Koch Industries.[38]

Spurred by the anti-liberal, antidemocratic elements, Italy followed one reactionary path with Mussolini and the Italian fascists marrying state power to the needs of the capitalist class. Spain and Latin America charted another route. There, dictators such as Generalissimo Francisco Franco—victor in the savage Spanish Civil War in which American and English volunteers to the Spanish Republican cause, such as George Orwell, were later labeled "premature antifascists"—focused on the military and kept the state relatively small. In much of Latin America, with Chile the major exception, democracy was a rare occurrence during the 20th century; elite latifundia families held the levers of power as generals played enforcers and chiefs of state.

In the United States, by contrast, the recipe for classic reactionary politics never existed. During the late 19th and first half of the 20th centuries—the period of William Faulkner's novels—the planter elite and its profoundly illiberal ideology were largely isolated from the rest of America. The slave owners were buried, but their ideological and political heirs dominated the former Confederacy for a century. As a result, the one-party South remained the most anti-liberal, antidemocratic region of the nation. Its political habits and norms were predicated on white supremacy, and generation after generation the authoritarian, illiberal, racist planter mentality endured. Things were different north of the Mason-Dixon Line. The North and the West prospered thanks to both a booming industrial economy and government programs that expanded the middle class and assisted with income stability. In the North, reacting to the inequalities and injustices of the robber barons, many farmers and small business owners joined laborers and middle-class reformers pushing for change. Their efforts culminated in Woodrow Wilson's Progressive Era reforms and Franklin Roosevelt's New Deal. As 20th-century liberalism powered a massive expansion of the middle class, millions of American families benefited from Social Security, Medicare, public schools and universities, and home and small business loan assistance as well as a host of other programs.

Yet embers of defeat sometimes hide the seeds of resurrection. The 1960s' civil rights and anti-war protests, the second feminist wave, the passage of the Civil Rights and Voting Rights acts, and President Johnson's liberal Great Society propelled a union between the ideological descendants of the plantation elite and the most reactionary portion of the capitalist class. It seems an odd alliance, except when we recognize their common hatred of the egalitarian ideals of the Declaration.

THE UTILITY OF RACISM FOR MODERN PATRICIANS

Some may read this book and see it as an attack on the South and free market capitalism. That is not my intent. To understand illiberalism in America one must grapple with the legacy of slavery and segregation on one side, and the power of right-wing capital on the other. Subtle and blatant racism, both personal and institutional, pervades American society. While Colin Powell has been the chairman of the Joint Chiefs of Staff and Barack Obama has been president, the United States in 2020 is hardly a color-blind society. Racism infected the nation writ large—think of the virulent racism displayed in Boston and Chicago during the 20th century, for example. In both cases, it was people with my ancestry, Irish Catholic, who played a leading role in keeping black Americans in their place.

> The Irish came to America in the eighteenth century, fleeing a homeland under foreign occupation and a caste system that regarded them as the lowest form of humanity. In the new country—a land of opportunity—they found a very different

form of social hierarchy, one that was based on the color of a person's skin. *How the Irish Became White* tells the story of how the oppressed became the oppressors; how the new Irish immigrants achieved acceptance among an initially hostile population only by proving that they could be more brutal in their oppression of African Americans than the nativists.[39]

But American racism has its origins in the South, so it is important to understand that history and its political dynamics.

What function does racism play in the 21st century, more than a half century after the civil rights revolution and a decade after the United States elected its first black president? Why does America enable current newcomers of different ethnicities, religions, and shades—the Vietnamese, Latin Americans, Southeast Asians, Iranians, Syrians, etc.—to rise while keeping many African Americans in urban ghettos and rural poverty, even as many blacks have achieved the American dream and professional success? Just as unleashing the intellectual and entrepreneurial talent of women—no longer limited to careers as librarians, schoolteachers, nurses, or stay-at-home moms—makes rational sense in a global economy, it would seem to be in the national interest in our economic competition against China and Germany to minimize the number of people in poverty and maximize the number of educated, energetic workers. Why does a nation with the most successful economy in world history allow poverty, homelessness, and racism to persist decade after decade?

The exercise of power by the planter class in the Old South helps us to understand the utility of race to illiberal America. In a democratic society, the economic elite face a problem. Being a minority of the population, upper-class families require allies if they are to have political power. The patricians of the modern world have every incentive to pit the plebeians against each other and to encourage one portion of the mass electorate to find commonality with the wealthy elite. Different techniques work in different countries. In the United States, racism acts as a power tool in this effort. Bluntly put, racism continues to exist in America because it is a cheap, easy, and effective way for the rich to capture and hold political power. It is also lazy, a gross violation of the Lockean project, and incredibly destructive. (Why, for example, does police violence against African

Americans—often with deadly effect—continue at an astounding rate fifty-five years after the Civil Rights Act was enacted?) The Southern elite long ago demonstrated that employing racism so that working-class whites dislike and resent working-class blacks is a time-tested successful formula at the ballot box. Plain and simple, strategies of racism allowed the Old Southern elite, the plantation families of the Black Belt, to exercise and hold power. Those same strategies of division and resentment—generalized to people of color in general coupled with attacks on women—have enabled a modern economic elite to seize power in the Republican Party. The Spencer-Randian-Romney mantra communicates that society is divided into producers and leeches. When racism is prevalent in a society, people know who the moochers are. As Mitt Romney said in 2012:

> All right, there are 47 percent who are with [Obama], who are dependent upon government, who believe that they are victims, who believe that government has a responsibility to care for them, who believe that they are entitled to health care, to food, to housing, to you name it. That that's an entitlement. And the government should give it to them . . . These are people who pay no income tax. Forty-seven percent of Americans pay no income tax . . . my job is not to worry about those people—I'll never convince them that they should take personal responsibility and care for their lives.[40]

We should recognize that the CEO of a large privately held corporation is, in many respects, the modern counterpart of the landed elite of the pre-industrial era, his voice amplified by mass communications and *Citizens United*.[41] Both the plantation elite of old and the superwealthy of today are members of the same capitalist club. They own the means of production in their respective economies and, being a rather small minority of the total population, both require the support of others to achieve their political goals. To protect their wealth and their liberty to do as they wish, they benefit when working people identify another target other than the rich and the powerful as the enemy. In the Old South, Black Belt plantation whites encouraged poor whites to target the black serfs; in today's world, the modern right designates as villains inner city minorities, liberals, uppity women, people of color, immigrants, and big government.

A business class laser-focused on maximizing returns for Wall Street and climbing the corporate ladder typically pays scant attention to threats to democracy as long as the economy stays healthy. Markets are amoral and indifferent to whether a country is a liberal democracy or a dictatorship. Investors and the business class understand that autocrats and economic growth often go hand in hand, particularly in nations where political institutions and the rule of law are relatively weak.[42] That has never been the situation in the United States. However, in the aftermath of the New Deal, America's powerful anti-statist right has actively sought a return to a minimalist national government that would allow corporations the unfettered freedom to pursue maximum profit by any means, regardless of the cost to society.[43] The strength of libertarian "government is evil" forces has only grown since the Reagan presidency.[44] The tenacity, focus, and resources of the American illiberal right are something to behold. Veteran journalist Thomas Edsall observes:

> While the Democratic Party has an extensive network of defenders in the advocacy community on the left, these center-left groups operate on uncertain terrain. They have to date been less aggressive, less innovative, less resourceful and entrepreneurial, less hardnosed in their media tactics, less effective in influencing the outcome of policy debates, and less systematically focused on the political dimension of their goals than their conservative counterparts . . . these progressive groups . . . now operate with a far more unreliable base of support than similar Republican associations . . . The GOP has achieved a gradual erosion of the popular consensus behind the major progressive and social-egalitarian movements of the twentieth century.[45]

If we are not careful, if we are not vigilant, the day may come when liberals and conservatives wake up to realize that this generation witnessed the death of America. Yes, the nation's borders will still exist, yes, there will still be fifty states, yes, the Dow Jones will still climb, but the Constitution will have been shredded and elections rendered meaningless.

AUTHORITARIAN PSYCHOLOGY

"Authoritarianism is not a momentary madness," say political psychologists Karen Stenner and Jonathan Haidt. People are different and some human beings are vulnerable to the calls of demagogues who want to divide society into "us" and "them." In every liberal democracy, there are people:

> who—by virtue of deep-seated predispositions neither they nor we have much capacity to alter—*will always be imperfect democratic citizens*, and only discouraged from infringing others' rights and liberties by responsible leadership, the force of law, fortuitous societal conditions, and near-constant reassurance.[46]

According to Stenner, the intolerance of differences—expressed as racism, political and moral prejudice, or censorship—is principally caused by two factors: an individuals' psychological predisposition to authoritarianism interacting with societal threats. Stenner's research shows that people with an authoritarian tendency find comfort and pleasure in societies and social interactions that enhance sameness and minimize diversity of people, beliefs, and behaviors.[47] While some people relish freedom, novel experiences, and variety, others are more comfortable in orderly homogeneity and receive pleasure from rituals that reinforce the sense of all of us being part of one community. In normal times, authoritarians are proud democratic patriots, embracing and defending the best traditions of the United States of America, or France, or Germany. However, when they begin to feel at a loss of "who we are" and "our way of life" and become "strangers in their own land," they listen to politicians speaking forcefully to their fears and resentments.[48] Triggered by perceived threats to stability, oneness, or sameness—economic depressions, surges in the immigration by people with different heritages, or rapid cultural change (the acceptance by the courts of gay rights, for example)—their illiberal side comes out in force.[49]

Stenner's findings support the critical distinction between traditional conservatives and illiberals; while conservatives are guardians of liberal democracy, illiberals have the clear capacity to push politics in a fascist direction.[50] The distinction Stenner makes is important. Traditional conservatives of the Burkean variety have an aversion to rapid change; for them, social stability is far more important than striving for oneness and sameness. Conservatives can live with racial diversity, civil liberties, and moral freedom, especially when they are institutionalized and part of a well-established tradition. By contrast, illiberal authoritarians have an aversion to complexity. As a psychological type, they "simply cannot abide freedom and diversity." When their fears are triggered across cultures and political regimes, these people will support and "push relentlessly for restrictions on all manner of difference, even at the risk of tremendous social change and instability."[51] Critically, while conservatives abhor revolution, some illiberals welcome social upheaval and revolution as long as conformity and sameness is the promised outcome.

> The animating spirit . . . is to limit difference in people, beliefs, and behaviors. Across time and space, authoritarianism persists in packaging together the taste for racial discrimination, moral regulation, and *all-out political repression*.[52]

To calm the fears that can trigger an authoritarian response, Stenner recommends liberals and conservatives emphasize and practice civility in public discourse, and speak about their ability to "work across the aisle."[53]

DEMOCRATIC BREAKDOWN AND
SOFT AUTHORITARIANISM

The breakdown of democracy is a step-by-step process. As Republicans scrap democratic norms, deny plain-as-day facts, and engage in winning-is-everything behavior, we are seeing what politics can become in the absence of partisan restraint.[54] Why is this dangerous? Because as Yale University political scientist Juan Linz stressed in his classic study *The Breakdown of Democratic Regimes*, polarization is a central factor in democratic rupture. When politicians begin to see the opposing party as illegitimate, they become increasingly willing to break longstanding political rules to keep their rivals out of power. As the Republican Party has shifted sharply right since the Gingrich speakership, it has "increasingly abandoned established norms of restraint and cooperation—key pillars of U.S. political stability—in favor of tactics that, while legal, violate democratic traditions and raise the stakes of political conflict."[55]

> Democratic legitimacy, therefore, requires *adherence to the rules of the game* by both a majority of the voting citizens and those in positions of authority, as well as trust on the part of the citizenry in the government's commitment to uphold them.[56]

Significant examples abound of Republicans playing a new form of political hardball that slides the nation toward *soft authoritarianism*—a situation in which democratic institutions continue to exist and function yet the party in power employs and abuses state power to the disadvantage of the opposing political party and its political opponents in general. A small but telling example is the Trump administration's egregious violation of the Hatch Act—the 1939 law that prohibits federal employees from engaging in political activities in the course of their work. A report from the Office of Special Counsel, a watchdog agency that enforces civil service laws, found that White House adviser Kellyanne Conway violated the Hatch Act on numerous occasions by "disparaging Democratic presidential candidates in her official capacity during television interviews [often with the White House as a backdrop] and on social media." The report, submitted to President Trump, asked that she be fired because of "persistent, notorious and deliberate Hatch Act violations." Examples cited included Conway's attacks on former Vice President Joe Biden and Senators Elizabeth Warren and Cory Booker.[57] Other administrations have occasionally stepped over the line in regard to the Hatch Act; the difference with the Trump administration is its open defiance of federal law.

Authoritarians consolidate power when others play by the rules and they do not. When actions that once provoked outrage become casually accepted, a free democratic society becomes increasingly fragile. Instead of being shrewd, evil masterminds, modern authoritarians and dictators often are poorly educated men of average or below-average intelligence who use the blunt instrument of their ignorance to propel themselves to power. Unable to navigate the real world's complexity, they reduce politics to simple, primitive storylines in which they are the hero and those who dare oppose them are the villains to be defeated and, sometimes, eliminated.[58] The question remains: Why the "German catastrophe" of 1933? Why did 20th-century Germany, after a century-long struggle to establish democracy and construct a seemingly sound constitutional structure in the Weimar Republic, capitulate to the challenge posed by Adolf Hitler and the Nazi Party? German historian Karl Dietrich Bracher, author of path-breaking studies on the breakdown of the Weimar Republic and Hitler's road to power, argued that the collapse of democracy in Germany was not inevitable, even in 1932, but that Hitler was constantly underestimated and that the future Führer followed "the tactic of winning power through the unremitting exploitation of the legal and pseudo-legal opportunities offered by a tolerant democratic framework."[59]

A populist autocrat, Trump resembles the Latin American populists who win elections by politicizing feelings of fear and resentment and claim to represent "the people." For Juan Perón of Argentina and Hugo Chávez of Venezuela "the people" were poor and nonwhite. President Trump's "people" are overwhelmingly white, predominantly Christian Americans who view themselves in Randian terms as producing wealth and not living on government handouts. Populism is a strategy to win elections and hold power, says Latin American scholar Carlos de la Torre. Like Perón and Chávez, Trump paints politics as a white and black Manichaean conflict. Authoritarian populists do not face democratic rivals; they confront enemies who must be defeated and destroyed. Populist leaders present themselves as extraordinary leaders whose mission is to save and liberate the people. To gain power, they stoke feelings of fear and resentment; once in government, they view the constitutional framework of democracy as a roadblock unnecessarily constraining their freedom of action. Starkly antipluralist, populists see no need to have a dialogue with those who oppose them because these charismatic leaders claim they embody the will of the people as a whole. Chávez would boast, "This is not about Hugo Chávez; this is about a people." Trump tells his rally crowds, "It's not about me—it's about all of you. It's about all of us, together as a country." Anyone watching a populist soap opera quickly recognizes who qualify as "the people" and who are "the enemies," the latter an essential element in a demagogue's spectacle.[60]

We would, of course, prefer not to recognize the parallels between the president and the fascist dictators of the 1930s—Benito Mussolini and Adolf Hitler. But similarities exist in Trump's love of mass rallies, his endorsement of authoritarians who proclaim that they should be president for life, and the lack of a coherent agenda other than gaining power and having supporters adore him as their leader. Hitler did not care about issues. Neither does Trump—building a wall, bashing China on trade, abolishing the Affordable Care Act are just temporary positions to win votes and please the base. As many have observed, Trump will say whatever he thinks best serves his purpose at the moment. He constantly waves a shiny object in front of the media to distract attention from damaging revelations. Famously impulsive and lacking traditional discipline, he has a sharp instinct for what his audience wants and will buy. Unlike authoritarians in other nations, Trump did not build a party around himself, but once in the White House the president took over the Republican Party apparatus and made it his own. Critically, President Trump has assiduously stroked and maintained strong relationships with the illiberal leaders of the "conservative movement." A 2017 *New York Times* story reported:

> Mr. Trump has strained relations with a lot of people these days—members of his own party in Congress, the 55-plus percent of Americans who say they disapprove of his performance, his attorney general, his recently ousted communications director and chief of staff. But through all the drama and dismay, one group has never really wavered: the leaders of the conservative movement. This is no accident. Mr. Trump and members of his administration have spent their first six months in office cultivating and strengthening ties to the movement's key groups and players with a level of attention and care that stands out for a White House that often struggles with the most elementary tasks of politics and governing.[61]

The Trump presidency brings a dilemma into stark relief: an unpopular president can wield considerable power if his party controls at least one House of Congress and if his party's base is passionately behind him. The illiberals who back President Trump—an intense minority of the nation's voters as a whole—have clearly instilled fear in the party's congressional leadership. While a majority of Americans believe the president is doing a poor job, according to Gallup between 40 and 46 percent of voters—and nearly 90 percent of Republicans—approve of the president's performance.[62] In the face of continual outrageous behavior by the president, precious few congressional Republicans have criticized his conduct.[63]

The Constitution cannot defend itself. The extreme partisanship of Republicans and the deep polarization within Congress and the nation reduces the chances that Congress will constrain Trump's unprecedented behavior. If Congress does not stand up to a renegade president because members fear they will be punished by voters, a president can transgress democratic norms at will and obstruct justice with impunity.[64] Liberals and conservatives would like to think that President Trump, with his chaotic, in-your-face style, is an anomaly. But he is dangerous for who he is—a loudmouthed, racist egomaniac with little knowledge of government, economic policy, or national security—*and* because his presidency opens the door to future elected authoritarians who may pitch a similar message, but in a more sophisticated and calculated way.

Why is a modern postindustrial nation such as the United States vulnerable to illiberal politics and authoritarian leaders? Part of the answer is that many Americans are uninterested in politics and poorly informed about issues and how the government actually works. Instead of thinking about the challenges facing the country and how we might best find solutions to our common problems, these people choose their political party based on group identity and "who they are." By and large, Americans make political decisions based on "emotional attachments that transcend thinking." Group identities can wax and wane. Why, for example, have the industrial states of the Midwest that were once Democratic strongholds become hotly contested swing states? Because along with the decline in heavy industry and manufacturing, union membership has faded and, in the absence of union identity, politicians—including Trump—have made appeals to other identities among the white working class such as race, ethnicity, religion, and gender.[65]

In the post–Cold War world, many nations have experienced a sharp division between citizens who embrace a cosmopolitan future and diversity and those who favor the past while fearing change and *others*. We did not think that a "blood and belonging" mentality could take hold in America, but it has. White ethnic nationalism lies at the core of Trump's appeal to a white Republican Party and those working-class voters who in previous generations voted with the Democrats.[66] This ethnic nationalism is based on finding solidarity and security with people who look, act, and think alike. By contrast, Lockean liberalism envisages the nation as a community of equal citizens united by the shared values of freedom, democracy, and inclusion.[67] In the postwar era from Truman and Kennedy to Reagan and Obama—when, indisputably, the United States was *the* superpower—America's foreign policy was based on the idea that the country would thrive if a majority of the other prominent powers also were cosmopolitan, tolerant, interdependent, and democratic. By contrast, Trump's "America First" policy is explicitly isolationist and exclusionary, focusing on the walling off of the United States—especially the illiberal white GOP base—from the rest of the world except, of course, his authoritarian friends.

A sense of emotional connection is an essential part of politics. Edmund Burke knew this and decried the abstract principles of the French Revolution for ignoring the importance of human sensibilities and belonging. Emotions-centered candidates—and this is what populist demagogues are—understand this, and it is why they connect so well with their audiences.[68] The trick, said Burke, is to understand emotions and prejudice and use them in a way that excites passions toward what is good and noble in a society, not what is base and abhorrent.[69]

CONCLUSION

Liberals Answer Back

Beginning in 2008, the United States entered a period without a dominant president whose influence remains strong long after leaving office, casting a larger-than-life shadow over the political landscape, molding public opinion, and causing both political parties to follow his lead. Such leadership was the natural order as Franklin Roosevelt inspired Democrats from 1932 to the 1970s and Ronald Reagan rallied Republicans in the years between 1980 and 2008. Then the Iraq War, Hurricane Katrina, ethics scandals, and, ultimately, the 2008 financial crash that triggered the Great Recession combined to make George W. Bush's second term an unmitigated disaster. The Bush implosion derailed the free-market ideology of the Republican Party, led to sharp GOP congressional losses in 2006 and 2008, and gave Democrats a once-in-a-generation opportunity to establish a new political order in Washington and the nation. This did not happen. We do not live in an era similar to Roosevelt's America or Reagan's America when a great president provided the master narrative for the nation and his successors. Instead, the United States remains bitterly split in a red-blue divide with no end in sight. Right-wing plutocracy has linked arms with the ideological children of the plantation elite to fracture the liberal-conservative consensus and force an interruption of Madisonian government. Historians of American political speech tell us that "the United States" generally was used as a plural noun before the Civil War, but as a singular one after it.[1] It appears that we have returned to the prior usage; the disunity of the country stares us in the face every day.

Barack Obama campaigned on the theme of "change" in 2008, but the change that occurred on his watch was not the change he intended, nor the change for which most Americans had hoped. Instead, because the Reagan era has ended and Obama was unable to launch a new Democratic era, America has entered a treacherous and perilous time—an interregnum. When Obama won the presidency in a near-landslide, many Democrats saw him as a transformative figure. At the same time, many Republicans hoped the Reagan era would still live. Neither wish came true. Instead, the regular cycle of presidential succession was broken by the events that unfolded during the Obama years. The ground shifted, the age-old pattern of American politics disrupted. At some point, we will return to a time when a presidential superstar sets the agenda for subsequent presidents and Congress, but we are not yet there—and because the transformative opportunity is rare but essential to "normal" American politics, we are stuck in no man's land. As a result, the nation has entered a strange hiatus, with *both* parties energized and presidents of either party having a difficult time leading Washington and the nation.

PRESIDENT OBAMA EXPLAINED

At the end of the Bush years, the Republican brand was toxic and Democrats appeared to have a golden opportunity not only to retake the White House, but to start a new Democratic era. When Obama was elected, there was widespread speculation that he might become a dominant president, a superstar in the way Roosevelt and Reagan had been.[2] On policy, Obama was a remarkable doer, especially in the face of near-unanimous Republican obstruction. But he failed to achieve political success on a scale that broke Republican resistance and convinced moderate voters that the Democrats had the answers to many of the nation's challenges.

In retrospect, it is clear that to succeed in founding a new party era, Obama—early in his first term—would have needed to act in three ways.

First, acquire a Harry Hopkins–like adviser skilled at getting Americans back to work. When Hopkins set up the famed Works Progress Administration (WPA) for President Roosevelt in the 1930s, he placed programs putting people to work in *every county in the nation* within four months.[3] In *The Promise*, a portrait of Obama's first year as president, Jonathan Alter writes:

> [Obama's] advisors rejected WPA-style direct government hiring, an idea that had fallen out of fashion in the 1970s, when the Carter administration's CETA [Comprehensive Employment and Training Act] jobs program ran into trouble and contracting-out became the rage. Government jobs would have attacked unemployment immediately . . . It was true that the twenty-first-century economy was different from the twentieth century's—it contained millions of middle-aged white-collar workers who didn't want jobs picking up trash and weren't qualified to work construction—but there were plenty of Americans who just wanted to work. Unemployment for low-wage workers was 30 percent in some areas; any job would do. The failure to think more boldly about creating jobs fast would haunt the administration.[4]

Second, get tough on Wall Street. At minimum, early in the financial crisis, President Obama should have seized *one* big bank, thus sending a signal—both to the financial community and to the public at large—that the egregious greed and incompetence that brought about the financial crash and the Great Recession would not be tolerated. Third, in no uncertain terms, criticize and repudiate George W. Bush and Ronald Reagan's market mantra. This could have been done with a smile, as FDR and Reagan did with their predecessors, but it needed to be done to drive a stake through the heart of the Republican ideology of deregulation and market perfection.

Unfortunately, President Obama did none of these. He accomplished a great deal in his first two years—some say half a New Deal—as he passed the American Recovery and Reinvestment Act (pumping nearly $800 billion into a staggered economy), signed the Affordable Care Act, championed the Dodd-Frank financial reforms, revamped the student loan program, and saved Detroit.[5] However, he failed to act with the audacity necessary for him to take charge of Washington and become a transformative president. Had President Obama fashioned and communicated an economic rescue plan—*focused on jobs*—and channeled public anger about the economic disaster toward Wall Street, he could have blunted considerably the ability of Republicans to channel the anger of middle- and working-class whites to the Tea Party and then to Donald Trump. Put simply, lacking a champion on the liberal side, the white working class found one in a reactionary spouting a populist program on the right.

Obama twice won the presidency with commanding victories and the Democrats held the Senate as well as the House during his first two years—something Reagan did not achieve during his eight years in office. Even so, the wounded Republican Party remained powerful, capturing the House of Representatives dramatically in the 2010 Tea Party revolt, and after the 2014 midterms it gained control of the Senate and the House as well as numerous state houses across the nation. No longer the dominant sun party, Republicans neither are a distant moon, lost at the edge of the political solar system—as they were in the 1930s and '40s. Republicans would like to believe that President Obama was an interloper, similar to Bill Clinton—a temporary distraction and annoyance in the middle of their political dominance.

In 2016, it appeared that Republicans had reclaimed their status as the dominant party when they regained control of the presidency and won both houses of Congress, as well as held a majority of the nation's statehouses. Yet the uproar over President Trump and his tabloid approach to governing—his childish temper and the coziness with white nationalists, the swirling questions regarding his relationship with Russian president Vladimir Putin and Russia's interference in the 2016 presidential campaign, the theft of the Supreme Court seat from President Obama, the harshness of his policies (especially in regard to immigrants of color), the overall amateur style of the administration, and his authoritarian musings about being president for life—has galvanized Democrats, who won back the House in dramatic fashion in 2018, and raised doubts in the minds of some Republicans.[6] Instead of being president for the entire nation,

Trump has focused exclusively on his illiberal base and the Republican Party—everyone else be damned.

WELCOME TO THE INTERREGNUM

The shift—either from the Reagan era to the Democrats, or to a resurgence of the Republicans—is, as yet, incomplete. Consequently, we hang in limbo between political leaders and historical eras. In our political purgatory, the term interregnum serves to describe the absence of a great president setting the nation's agenda and receiving support from a substantial majority of the country's population. An interregnum occurs when a nation's characteristic pattern of governance is derailed. It is characterized by a period of uncertainty, political turmoil, and sometimes economic peril when a nation struggles to end a protracted (and often bitter) political war and choose a new path forward. During an interregnum (derived from Latin for "between reigns"), regular governing is suspended, the political scene is in flux, and the certitudes of the past no longer hold true. This has been true of American politics over the past decade. The term interregnum is most frequently associated with the English Civil War when King Charles I was executed in 1649 and Oliver Cromwell and his Puritan followers in Parliament ruled without a king for eleven years.

The fragmented nature of the American political system—two houses of Congress, the separation of powers, and federalism—makes it difficult for political leadership to take place on a regular basis. Presidential scholar Richard Neustadt wrote that the powers of the president are those of a "clerk," while the responsibilities of American presidents in the modern era are immense.[7] As a creative response to the difficulty of leadership in our Madisonian system, American chief executives fit together as founders and followers in a series of presidential dynasties. The regular occurrence of a founding president—a larger-than-life transformative figure who captures the political zeitgeist of the moment, fashions a powerful political coalition, and offers a compelling political vision—provides the office the energy necessary to succeed. In this system of succession, not every president needs to be as gifted as a Lincoln, Roosevelt, or Reagan. Instead, a select few are asked to play the role of a great party leader, with the majority of presidents being loyal followers of a political genius.[8]

A presidential interregnum by itself—a failed president not being succeeded by a founding president from the other party announcing a new political order—is not a crisis. One can imagine a presidential interregnum occurring at the beginning or the end of the 19th century and the nation barely noticing. Such an interruption in presidential sequence would be a mere pause in the normal order of political development. The more serious interregnums occur when there is a radical challenge—from the right or the left—to our liberal norms. Such a situation *is* a political crisis; this is why the Trump presidency has set off alarm bells.

An interregnum precipitated by either Marxist-Leninists or illiberal reactionaries represents a frontal assault to the values proclaimed by Jefferson, Madison, and Lincoln. The radical goal is to overthrow the ideology and political structures of Lockean liberalism and create a society based on other values. In the 1920s and the 1950s, the nation suffered through "red scares." The hysteria over communist subversion, however, was exaggerated; a strong, militant Leninist left has never existed in the United States. While some on the left wing of the Democratic Party were sympathetic to the goals of democratic socialism found in Western Europe, a dogmatic, authoritarian Marxist-Leninism was never a serious threat on American soil. But zealotry, an Orwellian relationship to the truth, and a susceptibility to authoritarianism have taken root on the right. This has been the real danger to American democracy: the possibility of a strong, militant, reactionary right. Now that illiberal right has emerged.

WILL REACTIONARY AMERICA GROW STRONGER OR BREAK APART?

Will the power of reactionary America strengthen or ebb? That is the critical question facing the United States over the next decade. A republic is always in danger of corruption and decay. Today, too many Americans do not take politics seriously enough to understand that a man such as Donald

Trump is simply not fit to be president. Today, too many business leaders continue to view the quest to reduce the size and intrusiveness of government, particularly when it comes to their companies and their industries, as the paramount issue. The tacit acceptance of the illiberal revolution by the business community arguably is *the* key reason that the insurrection has succeeded to this point.

The crux of the reactionary position is that the United States is the capitalist economy par excellence, and the liberty of the capitalist class to thrive, build and, yes, dominate society is America's paramount value—its raison d'être. In post-Reagan America, this modern aristocracy values its privilege and access to life's luxuries, its immense power atop the economic and social hierarchy, its outsized share of wealth and income, its use of money to exclude others while dominating the political process, and its ability to insulate itself and exclude the unworthy from its gated communities, private schools, and social gatherings. Here, supercapitalist billionaires, Fortune 500 CEOs, and major investors see eye to eye with Ayn Rand's Nietzschean heroes and the plantation elite of yesteryear. If others—the working and middle classes, poor families, and the elderly living on Social Security—suffer as the top 5 percent (and especially the top 1 percent) of American families skim off more of the surplus value generated by those below, so be it.[9]

By contrast, liberals and conservatives believe in capitalism, but understand two things that illiberals deny. First, even though capitalism is hardly feudalism and constitutes a new and quite distinct form of social organization, it does, inarguably, generate its own set of privileges, hierarchies, inequalities, and exclusions. Second, making capitalism one's highest value is dangerous for the simple reason that capitalism is agnostic when it comes to a choice between liberal democracy and authoritarianism. History exhibits abundant examples of capitalists thriving in authoritarian regimes; Hitler's Germany, the Old South, and modern China and Saudi Arabia all fit this bill. The liberty that capitalists care for the most is the liberty to make money, to keep profit margins high and market shares robust. Everything else is secondary, and this is what worries thoughtful liberals and conservatives aware of history's vicissitudes.[10]

Capitalists can be hugely successful in a variety of contexts; there is money to be made in the Middle East, Russia, Latin America, and

China. What distinguishes the United States in comparison to other nations is a unique political culture that values liberty, equality, and democracy. What is exceptional about the United States is a threefold combination: a can-do individualism and radical freedom to pursue one's dreams; an egalitarian ethos that says everyone is valued and contributes; and a political culture that stresses equality and participation, tied to an idealistic conception of democracy that binds the nation together as one political community.[11] Many, if not most, nations in the world are illiberal and authoritarian. Illiberals often talk about American exceptionalism—which they define as maximum liberty for the business class; this is a difference in degree in comparison to other nations, not a difference in kind.

The other side of illiberalism—our Anglo-Saxon ethnic heritage and America's history of racism—continues to affect not only Southern blacks and whites, but the nation as a whole. Our long history of a slaveholding landed elite in the South remains the major anomaly for America's grand liberal experiment. Critically, our Southern exceptionalism has meant that the United States is not as dedicated to liberal and progressive ideals as it might have been had the South not imported slaves and built its economy on their unpaid labor.[12] As one example, because of our Southern distortion, the American left has always been significantly weaker than the American right. The Southern political economy was not only a curse to black Americans; it was a blight for labor. Nationally, unions are much weaker than they would be if not for the anti-union attitudes of the South and the often-violent resistance union organizers faced below the Mason-Dixon Line during the 20th century. The nonunion aspect of the Southern economy is attractive to transnational corporations; numerous foreign auto companies including BMW, Honda, Hyundai, Mercedes, Nissan, and Toyota have American production facilities in the South.[13] The weakness of unions (in particular) and workers (in general) across the former Confederacy, along with the strident opposition to unionization and modest social welfare reforms by the powerful Southern cadre in Congress (now wearing Republican uniforms), have played a key role in the United States lagging far behind Western Europe in constructing a social safety net, guaranteeing universal healthcare, instituting workplace and environmental protections, and giving workers more power in the corporate arena.[14]

Shortly after 9/11, Philip Roth provided an alternative history of mid-century America. In *The Plot Against America* (2004), the terrorist threat comes from the American right as Charles Lindbergh defeats Franklin Roosevelt in the 1940 election, makes peace with Hitler, and leads a neo-Nazi movement in America. Roth's novel is a nightmare vision of the past and the future. But a similar counterfactual novel could be written imagining American history without racism and slavery; a nation dedicated 100 percent to Lockean ideals. This would be a story—a fantasy if you will—of what could have been.

OUR POLITICAL
CUL-DE-SAC

With the party base and the establishment at odds during the 2016 presidential campaign, the Republican Party appeared headed for a crack-up. But in the first year of Trump's presidency the party's leadership made a pact with the devil and climbed aboard the reactionary express. Once Trump took office, it was clear the party's base and congressional leaders were solidly in the president's corner while being criticized by conservative intellectuals such as Max Boot, Jennifer Rubin, Michael Gerson, David Brooks, and George Will. If the party did implode, as did the Whigs in the 1850s, where would the illiberal portion of the GOP go? In reality, the illiberal activist base and its business supporters are already the right-wing reactionary party they want to be. Among a large field of GOP contenders in 2016, Donald Trump understood this better than anyone else; he won the nomination because he embodies and reflects the new Republican Party. Scholars have shown that it is not just the elites of the Republican Party who have shifted right; rather, the elites are following the lead of the activist base in kissing American ideals as well as conservatism goodbye.[15]

The political dilemma we face is that there is no way to bridge the stark philosophical and policy differences that exist between liberals and reactionaries. The gap is too wide, the distrust too deep, and liberals believe that concessions on their part will be interpreted as weakness, not compromise as in the days of old. In a two-party system, and that is what American politics is, such an ideological divide is untenable. In the multiparty systems that populate Europe, the solution would be easy. Republicans would split into two separate parties—classic conservatives in one and reactionaries in the other. Yet, because of our winner-take-all elections, the multiparty option does not exist in the United States. We are stuck with two major parties and if one party abandons the broad liberal-conservative center and marches to the far left or far right, the system breaks down.

It is likely that we will muddle along in our bitter interregnum. However, to exit this cul-de-sac, Americans have three options: Conservatives can push the reactionaries aside and reassert control over the Republican Party; Democrats can decisively defeat the reactionaries in national elections and elect a charismatic Franklin Roosevelt/Ronald Reagan founder-type president who realigns politics by capturing a strong chunk of the middle of the electorate; or the reactionary Republican Party scores a landslide triumph in national elections and installs its own dominant president.

Option One would be most welcome but appears unlikely; the reactionary cast of the contemporary GOP is baked in. Option Two is possible yet daunting. To win in 2020 and beyond, Democrats must not only mobilize their base, but expand the electorate. They must convince infrequent voters and the apathetic that we are in the midst of a constitutional crisis and the republic needs them to participate in choosing who governs. Option Three is the nightmare we must prevent. If President Trump or a future reactionary president understood the nuances of power in a way similar to Lyndon Johnson, he or she might well succeed as an authoritarian leader who crushes liberals, amends the Constitution, and violates civil rights at will. Such a president could usher in a political era that mirrors the one-party dictatorships of the Old South, radically shrinking the public sector and giving capitalists freedom from "burdensome" taxes and regulation. Only the first two options preserve the liberal-conservative America established by the founders and Lincoln and shaped into a modern form by Franklin Roosevelt, Lyndon Johnson, Ronald Reagan, and Barack Obama. In the coming months and years, conservatives and liberals must fight for the country in which they believe.

LIBERALS ANSWER BACK

The genius of American politics is fragile. With our Madisonian system, we depend on energetic transformational presidents to respond vigorously to internal crises and foreign threats, and get the country moving in a new direction when the old ideology wears thin. But the success of these superstar presidents depends on both major political parties agreeing on fundamental political values so that both compromise and loss are acceptable. Today, the consensus about who we are and what we value has broken down. The Republican Party holds values outside the mainstream and the result is the interregnum we're now experiencing. Madisonian politics is a wonderful system of government when the players abide by the norms of compromise and Lockean liberalism. But it also can become a system of politics in which a determined minority sows chaos and creates ongoing dysfunction if it so chooses. Republican Party leaders believe they have every right to resort to "politics by other means" if the elections continually give the other party the presidency and majority status.[16] At the beginning of the Obama administration, then Senate Minority Leader Mitch McConnell and his lieutenants made the determination that the best strategy against the president was to stonewall—to reject any and all policy proposals made by the president and Democrats.[17] At the end of Obama's presidency, Senator McConnell, by then the majority leader, again played the obstructionist card announcing only hours after Justice Antonin Scalia's death that "this vacancy should not be filled until we have a new president." The rest of the Republican Party agreed. The reactionary right's insistence that the Senate could flatly ignore President Obama's choice for the Court after Justice Scalia died and not hold a confirmation hearing for Judge Merrick Garland—behavior that clearly contradicts the Constitution—was a dramatic, concrete example of illiberals ignoring the Constitution because it stood in the way of their political goals.

Another occurred in December 2019, when McConnell announced, "Everything I do during this [impeachment trial], I'm coordinating with White House Counsel. There will be no difference between the President's position and our position as to how to handle this. There's no chance the President's going to be removed from office. My hope is there won't be a single Republican who votes for these articles of impeachment." Speaking on MSNBC, Pulitzer Prize–winning historian and author Jon Meacham said McConnell is "arguably going to be one of the two or three most important Senate leaders in American history, most influential. No other senator that I can think of actually stopped a president from having a Supreme Court appointment, thereby shifting American jurisprudence for arguably forty years or so going forward. And what he's done, again, is sort of put his caucus and the Republican base on notice that, in fact, the Trump agenda will continue no matter what the facts are" in the impeachment trial.[18]

The aim of the illiberal right is not only to delegitimize any Democratic president but also to roll back and repeal as much of the 20th century as possible.[19] All entitlement programs and domestic discretionary spending including the safety nets on which millions of Americans depend, as well as government investments in scientific research and infrastructure, are targeted for drastic reductions in GOP budget plans; in some cases, the radical right wishes to eliminate them. Cut programs, reduce staffing to marginal levels, put incompetents in charge of critical government programs, pass laws with no enforcement budget, contract with private companies to provide services—these are just some of the ways antigovernment ideologues seek to damage the public sector.[20] Destroying people's faith in government and the modern liberal state has long been the goal of zealots on the right. In their pursuit of a society based almost entirely on the market, the right has every interest in government failing.[21]

Culture is at the heart of the war between liberals and illiberals.[22] A prime reason our Madisonian institutions work is due to the Lockean liberal and civic republican values that we pour into them. As Tocqueville rightly stressed it is not geography, it is not laws, it is not constitutions that enable democratic nations to survive and flourish; instead, it is mores—the norms of our political culture—that protect and nourish democracy in America.[23] In many nations, constitutions are pieces of paper readily discarded in a fashion similar to Jonathan Swift's description of the various humiliating fates of unsold books, with the pages being used as toilet paper, in bakers' ovens, and as a cheap alternative to glass in lanterns and windows.[24] Madison, as a Virginian and as a slave owner, understood that slavery itself would, at some point, seriously challenge the American experiment in self-government. But for more than two centuries, with the great exception of the Civil War, America had thrived under the umbrella of its Lockean norms.

The quarrels between the progressive wing of the Democratic Party and the more centrist Obama-Clinton-Biden wing pale in comparison to the civil war between conservatives and illiberals for the soul of the Republican Party. The clash between Democrats is nowhere as deep and irreconcilable. We should remember that Bill Clinton was a successful Democratic president during the time when Reagan's influence still dominated the nation and this fact profoundly shaped Clinton's outlook and opportunities. Had Hillary Clinton won the electoral college in 2016, in all likelihood she would have enacted policies far more liberal than her husband and governed more in the tradition of the New Deal. "If we would preserve a free democracy, we must keep rescuing capitalism from the capitalists . . . The plutocracy thinks in terms of class and not nation," wrote Arthur M. Schlesinger Jr.[25] Most Democrats, including "progressive realists" such as Minnesota senator Amy Klobuchar, understand this. Senator Elizabeth Warren, for example, is an updated 2.0 version of a progressive New Dealer focused on making capitalism work "for the rest of us." Some on the left use the term neoliberal to denigrate liberals who are seen as not sufficiently progressive. The label should be reserved for the attempt by libertarian reactionaries associated with the Chicago school of economics to force stringent pro-market reforms on countries such as Chile.[26]

Liberals (and their conservative allies) are the heroes of the American saga. Sometimes greatness and goodness coincide. In sharp contrast to illiberals, our best political leaders and thinkers—among them Alexander Hamilton, Thomas Jefferson, Thomas Paine, James Madison, Abraham Lincoln, Harriet Tubman, Thaddeus Stevens, Theodore Roosevelt, Ida Tarbell, John Dewey, W. E. B. Du Bois, Franklin Roosevelt, Frances Perkins, Arthur M. Schlesinger Jr., Dwight Eisenhower, Earl Warren, Martin Luther King Jr., Lyndon Johnson, Robert F. Kennedy, Dolores Huerta, John Rawls, Gloria Steinem, and Barack Obama—voice the liberal refrain that America is an exceptional society *not* defined by the age-old restrictions of hierarchy, privilege, inequality, and exclusion. When we define liberalism this way, it reminds us of why we left the Old World, what we left behind, and what we were escaping *to* in the New World of Paine, Jefferson, Madison, and Hamilton.

American conservatives know they cannot champion Old World exclusionary values; they operate in a liberal universe. Illiberals do not. That
is the cultural divide that has fractured both the Republican Party and
American politics as a whole. What illiberals do not understand—or rather,
fail to accept—is that America is about more than unlimited individual
liberty for a wealthy few. If this were the case, the United States would
resemble a number of other nations that bow to an oligarchy. Instead,
America is a special political culture that gives liberty and equality and
democracy equal value.[27]

One way to articulate the idea of a genuine democratic culture is to reflect
on the aesthetics of greatness. In sports and the arts, an audience knows when
it is witness to greatness—whether it be watching Aaron Rodgers play quar-
terback or Kobe Bryant score from the three-point range, reading William
Faulkner, or listening to Yo-Yo Ma play Bach. The aesthetics of greatness
is a thing of beauty in which others take pleasure. Performance at this level
of perfection is not a selfish act; it is not an act of complete egoism, which
would cause some people—less narcissistic than others—to refrain from the
attempt and pull back. It is not a will to power and domination over others
or a humiliation and demeaning of them to build oneself up. No, when one
achieves at such a high level, the act is a giving of oneself, a striving to show
what is possible. As such, the effort and the achievement are part of an open
democratic culture that encourages and allows everyone to develop their
unique talents and flourish, and in so doing provide an inspiring example
for others to attempt to do the same. The aesthetics of greatness is a key
component of American liberalism. It can be seen in the infinite possibilities
for the diverse life plans that Rawls speaks of in *A Theory of Justice*; it is alive
in the emphasis on the possibilities of individual growth, development, and
self-control that is central to John Locke's liberal vision; it pulsates in John
Dewey's belief in every individual developing their distinctive personality
and thereby contributing to the community; and it is defended when John
Stuart Mill values the unconventional and the bold against the sometimes
stifling confines of social pressure in *On Liberty*.

In America, success and the pursuit of greatness are not limited to the
very few, as in Rand's vision. No, the American idea is far more liberating
and radical. Pioneered by Locke, Paine, and Jefferson, the radical liberalism
of the founders gambled that average people—unshackled by the traditions

of privilege, hierarchy, class, and irrevocable inequality—could create a
new civilization. Our goal has been to unleash human potential. Following
Locke and Jefferson, our aim has been to create a robust, dynamic middle-
class society that avoids the extreme wealth and permanent underclass
of the Old World and is committed to political equality and democracy.
Given the social limits of growth, there are a finite number of goods (such
as a beachfront home in Southern California or the Hamptons) with
which people can distinguish themselves from the crowd.[28] One path is
to follow the Old World temptations of an oligarchic culture that fosters
a fetish for exclusive private schools and Ivy League institutions designed
to cultivate, protect, perpetuate, and replicate an elite. The other is the
liberal democratic culture fostered by governors Pat and Jerry Brown in
California—based on the idea of making a middle-class life available to all,
built on a high-powered innovative business culture, an inclusiveness that
accepts and values people of all backgrounds, an environmental consciousness, and a system of top-flight higher education affordable and open to
all. If we want to dampen and then extinguish the reactionary impulse, we
must work to build an economy that values workers instead of discarding
them and understand that economic loss and dislocation breed anger and
despair. We must build a political culture that values equality and diversity,
and deals with issues directly instead of scapegoating the weak and the less
numerous. White, black, and brown—these are artificial concepts. The
reality is that every human being is mixed race. Identity politics divides us;
it is not a coincidence that the most successful nation in economic history
is also the most cosmopolitan.

ACKNOWLEDGMENTS

B ooks take time and authors are lucky to have family and friends to encourage them along the way. I am incredibly grateful to my wife, Lita Robinow, who has been exceptionally patient and supportive of this project, and to my two wonderful and talented daughters now pursuing their own careers and lives, Allie and Becca O'Leary. My sister Kerry O'Leary and her husband Keith DiGiorgio have been pillars of support as has my mother, Charlene O'Leary, my in-laws, Larry and RickaLee Robinow, my brother-in-law Steve Robinow and his wife, Rena Duhl, and Lita's cousin Laurie Nussbaum and her husband Paul. On the East Coast, special thanks to Lita's cousin, Jessica Herzstein and her husband, Elliot Gerson, who have been enthusiastic about the book from the beginning. My late father was always a source of encouragement. His example helped inspire this project.

Two special friends who have been supportive both in reading and commenting on the manuscript are Steve Thomas and Heidi Lyons. Heidi copyedited more drafts of the manuscript than we can count. Ann Haley, a veteran journalist, provided important feedback on the final draft. Early in the process, both the late Charles Lindblom and Bob Kuttner told me I was on to something and to forge ahead. Bob set me to work writing an article for *The American Prospect* about Donald Trump and the South on the eve of the 2016 Republican National Convention, a portion of which is incorporated into Chapter 9. In the literary world, Joni Praded and Peter Matson were supportive of the project in its early stages. In the academic world, Tony Smith of the University of California, Irvine, hosted a talk as did David Menefee-Libey at Pomona College. I gained valuable feed-back from the participants of both events. At Chapman University, John Compton provided wise advice on several chapters as did Gordon Babst. Former Political Science Chair Nubar Hovsepian provided important support as did Jeanne Gunner, Tom Zoellner, Carmichael Peters, Nina LeNoir, and Chapman University president Daniele Struppa. I tried out my argument in several of my Chapman classes and I want to thank my students for their thoughtful reactions. At UC Irvine, the Jack W. Peltason Center for the Study of Democracy has been my academic home since 2002, and I owe a special debt of gratitude to founding director Russ Dalton and immediate past director Louis DeSipio, as well as to Center administrator Shani Brasier and Patty Jones of the Department of Logic and Philosophy of Science. My adviser at Yale University, Rogers M. Smith, now at the University of Pennsylvania and the immediate past president of the American Political Science Association, first introduced me to Locke, whom I came to appreciate many years later. Rogers's pathbreaking book, *Civic Ideals: Conflicting Visions of Citizenship in U.S. History* helped shape my conception of American politics being divided into liberals, conserva-tives, and illiberal reactionaries.

I want to thank the five prominent public intellectuals who read an early draft of the book and wrote blurbs praising my effort. I am grateful for the support of Erwin Chemerinsky, dean of the UC Berkeley School of Law, Robert Kuttner, co-editor of *The American Prospect*, Norman Ornstein of the American Enterprise Institute, Alan Wolfe of Boston University, and Kevin Mattson of Ohio University. In addition, my thanks go to two accomplished authors, Sven Beckert of Harvard University and Patrick Phillips, who saw the merit of the project and offered important assistance. When I was covering the West Coast for *Time*, Howard Chua Eoan was a wonderful editor and sent me on an assignment to cover a Tea Party rally in Scottsdale, Arizona, that started me thinking about the right.

Numerous friends have been supportive in a variety of ways. These include Oliver Avens and Nicky Shilliam, Steve Colome and Kathy Lottes, Jim Bernstein and Andrea Neff Bodenstein and the late Deborah Graham, Suzanne and Barry Ross, Paul Vandeventer and Mary Malecha, Michael and Katy Kaufman, Jack Mervis and Donna Miller, Julie Tapp and Peter Jipsen, Meredith and Jason Feldman, Antonio Morawski and Francoise

Schmutz, Robert Bachelor, Peter Blasini and Nancy Yedlin, Meredith Michaels, Sam Gardner and Marci Sternheim, Simon Ho, Rita Rich, Warren Nelson and Lillian Swords, Anita Mishook, Teri Sorey, Dan and Jeanne Stokols, Marcy Tieger, Becky Cioffi, Mary Thomas, Cathy Unger, Julian Willis, Katie Porter, Ian Masters, Larry Wilson, Rabbi Arnold Rachlis, Dan Chmielewski, Sara Ruckle Harms, Cindy Hadden, Deborah Newquist, Melahat Rafiei, Geoff Cowan, Dana Wing, and Julie Brickman.

In a way, this book was inspired by the ethos of the Coro Foundation program in public affairs. After graduating from UCLA, I was fortunate to be a Coro Fellow in Los Angeles where I received an intensive immersion in public policy and business in a major metropolitan region. Coro follows the approach of asking liberals and conservatives to find common ground and to realize the irrationality of believing that one side can win and govern without building bridges. Our year together helped us understand the importance of not seeing political opponents as villains. For this to happen, however, society needs a common set of values.

This book got to the finish line because Don Fehr of Trident Media provided wise guidance throughout the journey and Claiborne Hancock and Jessica Case gave an enthusiastic "yes" to the project. At Pegasus Books, Claiborne and Jessica warmly embraced and supported the book, editor Dan O'Connor offered sage advice while shaping the final text, and Maria Fernandez did great research on photos in addition to demonstrating her design skills. Victoria Wenzel assisted with the edits and Drew Wheeler was the proofreader. It's been a pleasure to work with the entire team. A special shout out to Catherine Green, Don's assistant, and Jamie Goto, who took my author photo.

ENDNOTES

PREFACE

1   Zara Anishanslin, "What we get wrong about Ben Franklin's 'a republic, if you can keep it': Erasing the women from the founding era makes it harder to see women as leaders today," *Washington Post*, October 29, 2019, https://www.washingtonpost.com/outlook/2019/10/29/what-we-get-wrong-about-ben-franklins-republic-if-you-can-keep-it/.

INTRODUCTION: THE BIRTH OF REACTIONARY AMERICA

1   *Congressional Record—Senate*, June 18, 1964, 14318.

2   Elizabeth Stordeur Pryor, "The Etymology of Nigger: Resistance, Language, and the Politics of Freedom in the Antebellum North," *Journal of the Early Republic* 36, 2, Summer 2016: 203–245, https://muse.jhu.edu/article/620987.

3   Dan T. Carter, *The Politics of Rage: George Wallace, The Origins of the New Conservatism, and the Transformation of American Politics*, Second Edition (New York: Simon & Schuster, 1995 and Baton Rouge: Louisiana State University Press, 2000). Narrative based on pp. 218–222. Emphasis in original.

4   Goldwater's nomination was fiercely contested; in the pivotal California primary, the Arizona senator defeated New York governor Nelson Rockefeller by a single point.

5   Alan I. Abramowitz, *The Great Alignment: Race, Party Transformation, and the Rise of Donald Trump* (New Haven: Yale University Press, 2018), pp. 101–106.

6   "Trump won the nomination in large part because he thrived in the right-wing political ecosystem the party establishment had constructed over the previous two decades," Paul Pierson, "American Hybrid: Donald Trump and the strange merger of populism and plutocracy," *British Journal of Sociology* 68 (2017), p. 4, https://onlinelibrary.wiley.com/doi/full/10.1111/1468-4446.12323.

7   https://www.washingtonpost.com/news/post-nation/wp/2018/06/16/america-is-better-than-this-what-a-doctor-saw-in-a-texas-shelter-for-migrant-children/.

8   https://www.nytimes.com/2019/06/16/us/baby-constantine-romania-migrants.
        html; https://www.buzzfeednews.com/article/adolfoflores/separated-immigrant
        -children-trump-detention-report; https://www.washingtonpost.com/politics
        /pence-tours-detention-facilities-at-the-border-defends-administrations
        -treatment-of-migrants/2019/07/12/993f54e0-a4bc-11e9-b8c8-75dae2607e60
        _story.html?utm_term=.dbfda259127d; https://www.theatlantic.com/family
        /archive/2019/07/congress-releases-new-report-child-separations/593905/.

9   https://www.vox.com/2018/7/16/17576956/transcript-putin-trump-russia
        -helsinki-press-conference. The following day, President Trump claimed he
        meant to say "why it wouldn't be Russia." But Associated Press reporter Jonathan
        Lemire, who asked questions in Helsinki, said on MSNBC to believe that
        Trump misspoke "defies all believability because to take that as fact means you
        had to ignore the rest of the press conference."

10   When I write as a news reporter, I strive to be fair and have been praised for my
        accuracy and objectivity. For example, after I reported for *Time* from Scottsdale,
        Arizona, about a Tea Party protest on the afternoon of President Obama's 2010
        State of the Union Address, the Tea Party leader sent me an email commending
        the accuracy and fairness of my story. Here, I wear a different hat. In this
        book, I write as a critic of the right and defender of liberalism, the mainstream
        American political tradition.

11   See Charles Krauthammer, "Donald Trump: Defender of the Faith," op-ed,
        Washington Post, March 3, 2016, https://www.washingtonpost.com/opinions
        /donald-trump-defender-of-the-faith/2016/03/03/33fae7a4-e172-11e5-8d98
        -4b3d9215ade1_story.html. For the fascinating story of how the America's
        Protestant churches shifted from liberal to conservative to illiberal see John
        Compton, *The End of Empathy: Why White Protestants Stopped Loving Their
        Neighbors* (New York: Oxford University Press, forthcoming).

12   "A Letter to a Young Gentleman, Lately Entered into Holy Orders," *Jonathan
        Swift: A Modest Proposal and Other Writings*, Edited with an Introduction by
        Carole Fabricant (New York: Penguin Classics, 2009), p. 110.

13   Obviously, the reforms of the Progressive Era and the New Deal changed the
        nature of what the federal government does, and together with superpower
        status, placed the president into more of a leadership role in terms of public
        policy than was the case in the 19th century, but the basic structure and
        dynamics of Madisonian democracy have continued.

14   See Russell J. Dalton, *Political Realignment: Economics, Culture, and Electoral
        Change* (New York: Oxford University Press, 2018), Chapter 9 The American
        Experience. In each election survey since 1972, the American National Election
        Studies (ANES) Guide to Public Opinion and Electoral Behavior has asked
        citizens to locate the parties on the Liberal-Conservative (Left-Right) scale.
        These are the parties' political images as perceived by the public. Dalton writes:
        "Americans saw Jimmy Carter in 1976 as the most centrist of the Democratic
        candidates across this time series . . . Obama in 2012 and Clinton in 2016 are
        seen as almost as liberal as McGovern. A linear trend line shows a half-point
        leftward shift by Democrats over the full time span. Conversely, in the eyes

of the public (but probably not the pundits or the experts), the Republican candidates have followed a fairly constant position over time. The Reagan candidacy registers as a slight shift to the right, which moderates by his reelection in 1984. The Bush candidacy in 2004 and Romney in 2012, show a similar rightward shift. But most surprising, in 2016, the American public sees Donald Trump as the most moderate Republican candidate since Richard Nixon . . . With the exception of Reagan's two victories in 1980 and 1984, the median voter is closer to the Republican candidate in all the other elections since 1972 . . . The combination of Trump's unorthodox populist rhetoric on economic and cultural matters may have convinced voters that he was not straying from Republican Party orthodoxy in significant ways . . . The public's perception of Democrats' cultural liberalism became more pronounced with Obama's election and the identity campaign of Hillary Clinton in 2016, just as perceptions of the Republicans on cultural issues became more conservative," pp. 185–187, 192.

15   https://www.nytimes.com/2019/05/27/us/auto-worker-jobs-lost.html.

16   The phrase "creative destruction of capitalism" was coined by Joseph Schumpeter, *Capitalism, Socialism and Democracy* [1942] (New York: Harper Perennial, 1962).

17   Seymour Martin Lipset, "The Revolt Against Modernity," in Per Torsvik, ed., *Mobilization, Center-Periphery Structures and Nation-Building* (Bergen: Universitetsforlaget, 1981), pp. 255–56. Quoted by Dalton, *Political Realignment*, pp. 4–5.

18   Dalton, *Political Realignment*, p. viii.

19   See Geoffrey Kabaservice, *Rule and Ruin: The Downfall and the Destruction of the Republican Party, From Eisenhower to the Tea Party* (New York: Oxford University Press, 2012).

20   Edmund Burke, *Reflections on the Revolution in France* [1790], Edited with an introduction and notes by Conor Cruise O'Brien (New York: Penguin, 2004), pp. 90–91. Burke compared liberty to a "wild *gas*" and wrote he "would suspend my congratulations on the new liberty of France, until I am informed how it had been combined with government; with public force; with the discipline and obedience of armies; with the collection of an effective and well-distributed revenue; with morality and religion; with the solidity of property; with peace and order: with civil and social manners. All these things (in their way) are good things too; and, without them, liberty is not a benefit. . . ."

21   Chris Mooney and John Muyskins, "2°C: Beyond the Limit: Dangerous New Hot Zones are Spreading Around the World," *Washington Post*, September 11, 2019, https://www.washingtonpost.com/graphics/2019/national/climate-environment/climate-change-world/; David Wallace-Wells, *The Uninhabitable Earth: Life After Warming* (New York: Tim Duggan, 2019); David Wallace-Wells, "The Uninhabitable Earth: Famine, economic collapse, a sun that cooks us: What climate change could wreak——sooner than you think," *New York*, June 10, 2017, http://nymag.com/intelligencer/2017/07/climate-change-earth -too-hot-for-humans-annotated.html.

22   https://www.nytimes.com/2019/08/23/opinion/sunday/david-koch-climate
      -change.html.

23   Burke, *Reflections on the Revolution in France*, pp. 194–95.

24   John Gottman, *Why Marriages Succeed or Fail: And How You Can Make Yours
      Last* (New York: Simon & Schuster, 1995) and Juan Linz, *The Breakdown of
      Democratic Regimes: Crisis, Breakdown and Reequilibration. An Introduction.*
      (Baltimore: Johns Hopkins University Press, 1978).

25   Paul Woodruff, *First Democracy: The Challenge of an Ancient Idea* (New York:
      Oxford University Press, 2005), Chapter 4.

26   https://www.nytimes.com/2019/08/21/us/facebook-disinformation-floyd
      -brown.html.

27   Thomas E. Mann and Norman J. Ornstein, *It's Even Worse Than It Looks: How
      the American Constitutional System Collided with the New Politics of Extremism*
      (New York: Basic, 2013). In this book, two distinguished political scientists
      present evidence that the extremism exhibited by the Republican Party goes far
      beyond that of the Democratic Party.

28   https://www.nytimes.com/2019/07/14/us/politics/trump-twitter-squad
      -congress.html.

29   https://www.nytimes.com/2019/07/16/us/politics/trump-election-squad.html.

30   https://www.wsj.com/articles/
      trump-rests-his-2020-hopes-on-some-old-tactics-11563376363.

31   Donald Trump likes to tweet that he'll leave the White House "in six years, or
      maybe 10 or 14 (just kidding)." Roger Cohen, "Trump's Ominous Attempt to
      Redefine Human Rights, *New York Times*, July 12, 2019, https://www.nytimes
      .com/2019/07/12/opinion/trump-pompeo-human-rights.html.

32   Jamelle Bouie, "The Joy of Hatred: Trump and 'his people' reach deep into the
      violent history of public spectacle in America," *New York Times*, Sunday, July 21,
      2019, https://www.nytimes.com/2019/07/19/opinion/trump-rally.html. Philip
      Freeman, "Meet the Trump of Ancient Rome, a Populist Demagogue Who
      Helped Bring Down the Republic," https://www.huffpost.com/entry
      /trump-rome-populist_b_9659660.

33   John Higham's classic *Strangers in the Land: Patterns of American Nativism;
      1860–1925* [1955] (New York: Atheneum, 1988) and Rogers M. Smith, *Civic
      Ideals: Conflicting Visions of Citizenship in U.S. History* (1997) are two seminal
      studies of nativism.

ONE: JOHN LOCKE INVENTS AMERICA

1   This is the argument of John Micklethwait and Adrian Wooldridge, *The Right
      Nation: Conservative Power in America* (New York: Penguin, 2005).

2   See Carl Becker, *The Declaration of Independence: A Study in the History of Political
      Ideas* (New York: Harcourt, Brace & Company, 1922).

3   James T. Kloppenberg, *Toward Democracy: The Struggle for Self-Rule in European
      and American Thought* (New York: Oxford University Press, 2016), p. 158.

4   Thomas Paine, *Rights of Man* [1791–92], with an introduction by Eric Foner
      (New York: Penguin, 1984), p. 33.

5   For example, Eisenhower, Ford, and Dole, by and large, endorsed the inclusive reforms of the New Deal and civil rights eras to bring workers, minorities, and women into the polity and economy as full-fledged members even as they were more cautious about government spending than the Democrats.

6   Mary Wollstonecraft, *A Vindication of the Rights of Men* [1790] and *A Vindication of the Rights of Woman* [1792], edited by Sylvana Tomaselli (New York: Cambridge University Press, 1999) and Paine, *Rights of Man*.

7   Arthur M. Schlesinger Jr., *The Vital Center: The Politics of Freedom*, with a new introduction by the author (New Brunswick, N.J.: Transaction Publishers, 2009), p. xvii.

8   For another author who sees this see Kloppenberg, *Toward Democracy*, p. 159.

9   Locke was hugely influential due to his accessible style (especially in the great *An Essay Concerning Human Understanding* [1689]) and because his philosophy corresponded to how most people experienced and perceived the world. To understand Locke, one must read more than the second *Treatise*. The founders as well as generations of Americans also read his *Essay*, the first *Treatise* (in which the author attacks the argument for absolute monarchy), and *A Letter Concerning Toleration*. John Locke, *Two Treatises of Government* [1690], with an introduction by Peter Laslett (New York: Cambridge University Press, 1960), John Locke, *An Essay Concerning Human Understanding*, edited with an introduction by Peter H. Nidditch (New York: Oxford University Press, 1975); John Locke, *A Letter Concerning Toleration*, with an introduction by James Tully (Indianapolis: Hackett Publishing Co., 1983).

10   The centrality of equality to the founding generation is highlighted in Danielle Allen, *Our Declaration: A Reading of the Declaration of Independence in Defense of Equality* (New York: Liveright/W.W. Norton, 2014).

11   Rogers M. Smith, "The 'American Creed' and American Identity: The Limits of Liberal Citizenship in the United States," *Western Political Quarterly*, Vol. 41, No. 2 (June 1988), p. 230.

12   At the forefront of the Enlightenment, Locke, along with Descartes, Spinoza, and Voltaire, launched a frontal assault on tradition and authority.

13   Lee Ward, *John Locke and Modern Life* (New York: Cambridge University Press, 2010), p. 4.

14   Ward, p. 5.

15   Locke, *Essay*, p. 52.

16   Ibid., p. 105.

17   Ibid., Book III, Chapter V "On the Names of mixed Modes and Relations," pp. 428–38.

18   Ward, *John Locke and Modern Life*, pp. 33–35, 46.

19   In the *Essay*, Locke defines liberty as the "Power in any Agent to do or forebear any particular Action, according to the determination or thought of the mind" (p. 237). Beginning with the contrast between pleasure and pain, Locke argues that these two psychological states are the motivating factors in human life. People search for happiness, but it is the dread of "unease" and the desire to escape it that drives much of human behavior. Locke writes that "a great many

uneasinesses" are always on our minds, demanding our attention, ready to determine our *will*, and asking that we act. Yet, human beings are specially blessed with "a power to *suspend* the execution" and immediate satisfaction of these desires; this suspension of action, this ability to resist our momentary impulses, is the source of human liberty.

20   Locke, *Essay*, p. 263. Emphasis added.

21   Ibid., pp. 263–264. Emphasis in original.

22   Martin E. P. Seligman and John Tierney, "We Aren't Built to Live in the Moment: Scientists are beginning to recognize that foresight is what distinguishes human beings from other animals," Sunday Review, *New York Times*, May 21, 2017, https://www.nytimes.com/2017/05/19/opinion/sunday /why-the-future-is-always-on-your-mind.html?_r=0.

23   The "exercise of all the *liberty* Men have, are capable of, or can be useful to them," depends on their ability to "*suspend* their desires, and stop them from determining their *wills* to any action, till they have duly and fairly *examin'd* the good and evil of it." Locke, *Essay*, p. 267. Emphasis in original.

24   See Rogers M. Smith, *Liberalism and American Constitutional Law* (Cambridge, Mass.: Harvard University Press, 1985), esp. Chapters 1, 8, and 9.

25   Smith, *Liberalism and American Constitutional Law*, p. 200.

26   Scholars such as Laslett in the introduction to his edition of Locke, *Two Treatises of Government*, John Dunn, *The Political Thought of John Locke: An Historical Account of the Argument of Two Treatises of Government* (Cambridge, UK: Cambridge University Press, 1969), and James Tully, *A Discourse on Property: John Locke and His Adversaries* (New York: Cambridge University Press, 1980) retrieved the historical Locke and view his Calvinist faith as the centerpiece of his thinking. See more recently Steven Forde, *Locke, Science, and Politics* (New York: Cambridge University Press, 2014). For contrasting views on how Locke's religious convictions affect how we read him in a more secular age see Dunn, *The Political Thought of John Locke*, pp. 262–67, and Jeremy Waldron, *God, Locke, and Equality: Christian Foundations in Locke's Political Thought* (New York: Cambridge University Press, 2002), pp. 240–43.

27   In this sense, there is not a lot of distance between Locke and John Dewey's articulation and understanding of pragmatism—America's major contribution to philosophy.

28   Locke, *Two Treatises*, p. 311. Emphasis in original.

29   "And being furnished with like Faculties, sharing all in one Community of Nature, there cannot be supposed any such *Subordination* among us, that may Authorize us to destroy one another, as if we were made for one anothers uses, as the inferior ranks of Creatures are for ours." Locke, *Second Treatise*, p. 311, emphasis in original. This paragraph draws on Kloppenberg, *Toward Democracy*, pp. 166–67, 158.

30   Ward, p. 5.

31   Ibid., p. 18.

32   Locke, *Essay*, p. 444: "Therefore we in vain pretend to range Things into sorts, and dispose them into certain Classes, under Names, by their *real Essences*, that are so far from our discovery or comprehension." Emphasis in original.

33 Ibid., p. 46.

34 James Madison was in agreement with Locke and Dewey as to the contingent, limited quality of our knowledge. As James Kloppenberg observes, "James Madison recommended combining a historicist commitment to the particularity of all vital political discourses, a pragmatist commitment to testing the workability of political ideas in practice, and a democratic commitment to deliberation as the method of resolving political disputes." See James T. Kloppenberg, *The Virtues of Liberalism* (New York: Oxford University Press, 1998), Chapter 1 "Introduction: Rethinking America's Liberal Tradition," p. 9.

35 Locke, *Essay*, p. 70.

36 Ward, *John Locke and Modern Life*, p. 4.

37 While Locke accepted monarchy, his epistemology undercut the very idea of divine right and his theory of revolution allowed the people to revolt against a bad or wicked king. Paine took Locke's ideas the next logical step and rejected hereditary monarchy altogether.

38 Obviously, I exaggerate here. The norms persisted and thus illiberalism.

39 The classic exposition of this position is C. B. MacPherson, *The Political Theory of Possessive Individualism: Hobbes to Locke* (New York: Oxford University Press, 1962). Both the neo-Marxist left and the illiberal right are invested in viewing Locke as having an atomistic philosophy and being primarily about property rights. The most influential misreadings are those of MacPherson, *The Political Theory of Possessive Individualism* and Leo Strauss, *Natural Right and History* (Chicago: University of Chicago Press, 1953).

40 See Richard Ashcraft's argument about Locke's purposes in publishing the *Two Treatises*. Richard Ashcraft, *Revolutionary Politics & Locke's Two Treatises of Government* (Princeton, N.J.: Princeton University Press, 1986).

41 Robert Filmer, *Patriarch* (1680).

42 Kloppenberg, *Toward Democracy*, p. 153 agrees with this assessment. See Laslett's introduction in *Two Treatises of Government*. In the decade that stretched from 1679 to 1688, the English political world stood on knife's edge. The English Civil War, which raged from 1640 to 1660 and cost King Charles I his head in 1649, had been over for twenty years. Yet there existed widespread fear that England could again descend into bloodshed and chaos, especially if the wrong man assumed the throne. Specifically, Lord Shaftesbury, Locke, and the Whig party feared that when Charles II died his younger brother, James, would assume the throne. James was a Catholic and to many Englishmen, including Locke, a Catholic king translated into monarchical despotism and the forced conversion of Protestant England to the Church of Rome. The Whigs sought to block or exclude James from the throne by an act of Parliament in what came to be known as the Exclusionary Crisis. In a test of wills, Charles II, an Anglican Protestant, sided with his Catholic brother. Shaftesbury, who had previously been jailed in the Tower of London, was again arrested in 1681 and when a grand jury acquitted him, he fled to Holland in 1682. Locke followed in 1683 and proceeded to work on the *Essay*, the *Letter Concerning Toleration*, and the *Two Treatises of Government*—all of which he had been drafting and redrafting for

a number of years. When James became king upon Charles's death in 1685, the new monarch's policies were indeed markedly Catholic. In the ensuing political struggle, James was forced to give up the throne to his nephew and daughter, William of Orange and his wife Mary, and thus the much celebrated Glorious Revolution of 1688 saved England from a king whose loyalty was to Rome.

43   Locke, *Two Treatises*, p. 175. In the actual text, the last clause reads, "that 'tis hardly to be conceived, that an *Englishman*, much less a *Gentleman* should plead for't." I have modernized 'tis and for't for today's readers.

44   Dunn, *Locke*, p. 34.

45   Locke, *Two Treatises*, p. 175. I modernized the original text that reads: "System lies in a little compass, 'tis no more than this."

46   Ibid., pp. 175, 182.

47   Ibid., p. 271.

48   Ibid., p. 274.

49   Ibid., p. 286. Emphasis in original. I have modernized this portion of the sentence: "'tis not to argue from the Authority of Scripture."

50   Dunn, *Locke*, p. 33.

51   Locke's proposition about rational liberty in the *Essay* both predates the second *Treatise* and is more foundational because it underlies the main argument of the second *Treatise*, specifically in that it is the right and duty of each individual to make a judgment with one's rational mind as to whether trust in the ruler is justified. See John Dunn, *Locke* (New York: Oxford University Press, 1984), esp. Chapter 2 "The Politics of Trust."

52   Unlike the Americans in the next century, Locke did not call for an end of monarchy. As a result of the English Civil War (1640–1660), Parliament gained power it would never forfeit. Locke developed a theory of revolution so that the Parliament and the people could act against a bad king, but he accepted monarchy as a fact of English life.

53   Prominent statements on liberalism include Alan Wolfe, *The Future of Liberalism*, with a new introduction (New York: Vintage, 2010); Michael Walzer, *Politics and Passion: Toward a More Egalitarian Liberalism* (New Haven: Yale University Press, 2004); Patrick J. Deneen, *Why Liberalism Failed* (New Haven, Conn.: Yale University Press, 2018); Smith, *Liberalism and American Constitutional Law*; J. G. Merquior, *Liberalism Old & New* (Boston: Twayne Publishers, 1991); William A. Galston, *Liberal Purposes: Goods, Virtues, and Diversity in the Liberal State* (Cambridge, UK: Cambridge University Press, 1991); William A. Galston, *Liberal Pluralism* (Cambridge, UK: Cambridge University Press, 2002); Kloppenberg, *The Virtues of Liberalism*; Steven B. Smith, *Hegel's Critique of Liberalism: Rights in Context* (Chicago: University of Chicago Press, 1991); and Ian Shapiro, *The Evolution of Rights in Liberal Theory* (Cambridge, UK: Cambridge University Press, 1986).

54   David Armitage, "John Locke, Carolina, and the 'Two Treatises of Government,'" *Political Theory* 32 (2004): pp. 602–27. See also Dunn, *The Political Thought of John Locke* and Jeremy Waldron, *God, Locke, and Equality: Christian Foundations of John Locke's Political Thought* (Cambridge, UK: Cambridge University Press, 2002).

55   Jill Lepore, *These Truths: A History of the United States* (New York: W.W. Norton, 2018), p. 55.

56   This section draws from groundbreaking research by University of Maryland history professor Holly Brewer. Holly Brewer, "Slavery, Sovereignty, and 'Inheritable Blood': Reconsidering John Locke and the Origins of American Slavery," *American Historical Review* (October 2017). Holly Brewer, "Slavery-Entangled Philosophy: John Locke took part in administering the slave-owning colonies. Does that make him, and liberalism itself, hypocritical?" https://aeon .co/essays/does-lockes-entanglement-with-slavery-undermine-his-philosophy.

57   Holly Brewer, "Slavery-Entangled Philosophy."

58   David Brion Davis, *The Problem of Slavery in Western Culture* (Ithaca, N.Y.: Cornell University Press, 1966) and David Brion Davis, *The Problem of Slavery in the Age of Revolution 1770–1823* (Ithaca, N.Y.: Cornell University Press, 1975).

59   Brewer, "Slavery-Entangled Philosophy."

60   Ibid.

61   Brewer, "Slavery, Sovereignty, and 'Inheritable Blood,'" p. 1043.

62   "Slavery is so vile and miserable an Estate of Man, and so directly opposite to the generous Temper and Courage of our Nation; that 'tis hardly to be conceived, that an *Englishman,* much less a *Gentleman,* should plead for't," Locke, *Two Treatises,* p. 175. Emphasis in original.

63   Brewer, "Slavery, Sovereignty, and 'Inheritable Blood,'" p. 1078.

64   Ibid., p. 1072. Emphasis in original.

65   Ibid., pp. 1074–1075. Emphasis in original.

TWO: OUR IMPERFECT FOUNDERS

1   The powerful civic republican tradition, which both sparked and fueled the American Revolution, views political freedom as central to human freedom, and fears that without active civic engagement on the part of vigilant and virtuous citizens, the wealthy and powerful will slowly corrupt the organs of government and doom the republic to a gradual but sure decline. This part of our political identity waxes and wanes. When active, civic republican norms of strong public participation ignite populist protests of both liberal and reactionary persuasions. Recent examples include participatory democracy in the 1960s and the Tea Party during Obama's presidency. Leading authors in the civic republican revival include Hannah Arendt, *On Revolution* (New York: Penguin, 1984); Bernard Bailyn, *The Ideological Origins of the American Revolution* (Cambridge, Mass.: Belknap Press/Harvard University Press, 1992); Gordon S. Wood, *The Creation of the American Republic, 1776–1787* (Chapel Hill: University of North Carolina Press, 1998); and J. G. A. Pocock, *The Machiavellian Moment: Florentine Political Thought and the Atlantic Republican Tradition* (Princeton, N.J.: Princeton University Press, 2003).

2   On the one hand, Jefferson was a slavemaster whose first draft of the Declaration included a paragraph condemning slavery and who later drafted a law for general emancipation. Yet he never introduced this piece of legislation believing that, as Hofstadter wrote, "the public mind would not bear the proposition." On the other

hand, Jefferson, in his *Notes on the State of Virginia*, offered scientific "proofs" of Negro inferiority. These arguments anticipated later claims justifying racism based on supposed scientific fact. See Richard Hofstadter, *The American Political Tradition*, with a foreword by Christopher Lasch (New York: Vintage, 1974), p. 26 and Smith, *Civic Ideals*, p. 203.

3   "During much of his mature life Thomas Jefferson owned about 10,000 acres and from one to two hundred Negroes. The leisure that made possible his great writings on human liberty was supported by the labors of three generations of slaves." Hofstadter, *The American Political Tradition*, p. 23.

4   V. O. Key Jr., *Southern Politics in State and Nation* [1949] (Knoxville: University of Tennessee Press, 1984), p. 549; and C. Vann Woodward, *Tom Watson: Agrarian Rebel* (New York: Macmillan, 1938), p. 221.

5   America's strong tradition of illiberal reaction always has resisted the Lockean ideals of freedom and equality. From the beginning of the American experiment, a number of groups were relegated to the sidelines. But the American and French revolutions ushered in new expectations of what people who were not part of the upper class or the white race or the male gender were entitled to and could expect in their lives. The abolitionist movement in Great Britain in the early 19th century succeeded at a time when slave plantations in the British West Indies represented the cornerstone of English capitalism (similar to the importance of the Silicon Valley for the contemporary United States). The abolitionist campaign in Great Britain and the Civil War in the United States demonstrated that efforts to bring about liberty and equality would not be limited simply to white males of the Third Estate—the non-aristocrats and non-clergy who led the French Revolution. See Adam Hochschild, *Bury the Chains: Prophets and Rebels in the Fight to Free an Empire's Slaves* (New York: Houghton Mifflin, 2005).

6   https://www.huffpost.com/entry/turns-out-white-millennials-are-just-as -conservative-as-their-parents_n_5ce856fee4b0512156f16939.

7   Louis Hartz, *The Liberal Tradition in America: An Interpretation of American Political Thought Since the Revolution* (New York: Harcourt, Brace, 1955) is the classic statement of this view.

8   Patrick Henry, "Give me liberty, or give me death!" in William Safire, *Lend Me Your Ears: Great Speeches in History* (New York: W.W. Norton, 1992), pp. 87–89, https://www.history.com/news/patrick-henrys-liberty-or-death-speech-240 -years-ago.

9   This is the argument of Wood, *The Creation of the American Republic* and Andreas Kalyvas and Ira Katznelson, *Liberal Beginnings: Making a Republic for the Moderns* (New York: Cambridge University Press, 2008).

10   Kevin O'Leary, *Saving Democracy: A Plan for Real Representation in America* (Stanford, Calif.: Stanford University Press, 2006), pp. 69–71; Lance Banning, "Jefferson's Ideology Revisited: Liberal and Classical Ideas in the New American Republic," *William and Mary Quarterly* 43 (1986): pp. 3–19; Drew R. McCoy, *Elusive Republic: Political Economy in Jeffersonian America* (New York: W.W. Norton, 1982); and Joyce Appleby, *Capitalism and a New Social*

Order: The Republican Vision of the 1790s (New York: New York University Press, 1984).

11   Eric MacGilvray, *The Invention of Market Freedom* (New York: Cambridge University Press, 2011), p. 19.

12   Arendt, *On Revolution*, p. 119.

13   Kalyvas and Katznelson, *Liberal Beginnings*, especially Chapter 1, "Beginnings," pp. 1–17 and Chapter 3, "After the King: Thomas Paine's and James Madison's Institutional Liberalism," pp. 88–117. For what was lost when democracy became representative democracy see Bernard Manin, *The Principles of Representative Government* (New York: Cambridge University Press, 1997).

14   Garry Wills, *Inventing America: Jefferson's Declaration of Independence* [1978] (New York: Vintage, 2018) Second Edition, brings our attention to the influence of the Scottish Enlightenment on Jefferson. Ronald Hamowy, "Jefferson and the Scottish Enlightenment: A Critique of Garry Wills's *Inventing America: Jefferson's Declaration of Independence*," *William and Mary Quarterly*, Vol. 36, No. 4 (Oct. 1979), pp. 503–523 is an important corrective to Wills's thesis. Hamowy agrees that Francis Hutcheson may have influenced Jefferson but argues that Hutcheson was "heavily influenced" by Locke, p. 521.

15   *The Declaration of Independence & The Constitution of the United States*, with an introduction by Pauline Maier (New York: Bantam Classic, 2008), pp. 53–54.

16   In these critical paragraphs—the announcement of the American creed—Jefferson drew from his memory, his earlier essay, "A Summary View of the Rights of British America" (1774), and James Mason's draft of Virginia's *Declaration of Rights*.

17   Allen, *Our Declaration*, p. 145.

18   Pauline Maier, *American Scripture: Making the Declaration of Independence* (New York: Vintage, 1998), p. 125.

19   In the Second Treatise, Locke writes ". . . to unite for the mutual *Preservation* of their Lives, Liberties and Estates, which I call by the general Name, *Property*." Locke, *Two Treatises of Government*, Second Treatise, sec. 123.

20   Maier, *American Scripture*, Appendix C: The Declaration of Independence: The Jefferson Draft with the Congress's Editorial Changes, p. 239.

21   Thomas Jefferson, *The Life and Selected Writings of Thomas Jefferson*, edited by Adrienne Koch and William Peden (New York: Modern Library, 1944), p. 293.

22   Joseph J. Ellis, *American Dialogue: The Founders and Us* (New York: Alfred A. Knopf, 2018), p. 22.

23   Maier, *American Scripture*, Appendix C: The Declaration of Independence: The Jefferson Draft with the Congress's Editorial Changes, p. 240. Joseph J. Ellis, *Revolutionary Summer: The Birth of American Independence* (New York: Alfred A. Knopf, 2013) mentions this passage in his discussion of the major editorial changes made by the Congress to Jefferson's draft, pp. 62–63.

24   Thomas Paine, *Common Sense*, ed. Isaac Kramnick (New York: Penguin, 1986), pp. 99–100. Jefferson's emotional final charge against the king is central to the argument of Wills's *Inventing America* in which Wills sees a strong connection between Hutcheson and Jefferson and points to the parallel in *Common Sense*, pp. 313–15.

25   See Maier, *American Scripture*, pp. 126–27.

26   Maier, *American Scripture*, p. 134.

27   Ibid., pp. 134–35. Hamowy agrees, writing, "When Jefferson spoke of an inalienable right to the pursuit of happiness, he meant that men may act as they choose in their search for ease, comfort, felicity, and grace, either by owning property or not, by accumulating wealth or distributing it, by opting for material success or asceticism, in a word by determining the path to their own earthly and heavenly salvation as they alone see fit," Hamowy, "Jefferson and the Scottish Enlightenment," p. 519.

28   After writing, "the mutual *Preservation* of their Lives, Liberties and Estates, which I call by the general Name, *Property*" in Sec 123 of the Second *Treatise*, Locke immediately followed in Sec 124 to write, "The great and chief end, therefore, of Mens uniting into Commonwealths, and putting themselves under Government, *is the Preservation of their Property.*" Locke, *Two Treatises of Government*, second *Treatise*, secs. 123 and 124. Emphasis in original.

29   Ellis, *American Dialogue*, pp. 21–22. Above this quote Ellis writes, "The claim that 'all men are created equal' has assumed many mystical meanings, but all of them are incompatible with slavery, and there is no reason to believe that Jefferson was oblivious to that fact."

30   Franco's Spain was a good example of an authoritarian regime that, in its later years, left most of the population alone.

31   Arendt, *On Revolution*, p. 127. The quote from Jefferson is in his letter on the "republics of the wards" to Joseph Cabell, February 2, 1816, in Thomas Jefferson, *The Life and Selected Writings*, p. 661.

32   "To remind him (the king) that our ancestors, before their emigration to America, were the free inhabitants of the British dominions in Europe, and possessed a right, which nature has given to all men, of departing from the country in which chance, not choice, has placed them, of going in quest of new habitations and of there establishing new societies, under such laws and regulations as, to them, shall seem most likely to promote *public happiness.*" Jefferson, *The Life and Selected Writings of Thomas Jefferson*, pp. 293–94. Emphasis added.

33   Julian P. Boyd, ed., *The Papers of Thomas Jefferson*, I (Princeton, N.J.: Princeton University Press, 1950), p. 423, cited in Hamowy, "Jefferson and the Scottish Enlightenment," p. 523.

34   Joseph J. Ellis, *The Quartet: Orchestrating the Second American Revolution 1783–1789* (New York: Vintage, 2016), pp. 139, 151.

35   Ellis, *American Dialogue*, p. 123.

36   Ellis, *The Quartet*, p. xvi.

37   On Madison's constitutional vision see O'Leary, *Saving Democracy*, Chapter 2 "Building on the Founders," pp. 57–63 and Samuel H. Beer, *To Make A Nation: The Rediscovery of American Federalism* (Cambridge, Mass.: Belknap Press/ Harvard University Press, 1993).

38   On Congress as a deliberative body see Joseph M. Bessette, *The Mild Voice of Reason: Deliberative Democracy and American National Government* (Chicago: University of Chicago Press, 1997).

39   O'Leary, *Saving Democracy*, p. 60 and Beer, *To Make a Nation*, Chapter 9
      "Auxiliary Precautions."

40   https://en.wikipedia.org/wiki/Areopagitica citing George H. Sabine,
      Introduction to *Areopagitica* and *On Education* (Appleton-Century-Crofts, 1951),
      p. ix.

41   "Unless a people can command resources independent of the state, no basis
      exists for individual freedom and political opposition." Schlesinger Jr., *The Vital
      Center*, p. xvi.

42   Only representation by population, not by state, would bestow full democratic
      legitimacy on a Constitution which self-consciously desired the election of
      the "best men" to serve in the national legislature. Madison was committed
      to the principle of every voting citizen having an equal voice in the government
      because he wanted the new federal government to literally speak for the
      American people as a collective whole. Ellis, *The Quartet*, p. 124.

43   For a convincing, cogent argument on why majority rule is the fairest decision
      rule see Robert A. Dahl, *Democracy and Its Critics* (New Haven, Conn.: Yale
      University Press, 1989), Chapter 10 Majority Rule and the Democratic Process.

44   Robert A. Dahl, *How Democratic Is the American Constitution?*, Second Edition,
      (New Haven, Conn.: Yale University Press, 2003), pp. 52–53. Emphasis in
      original. On the racism of the New Deal, see Ira Katznelson, *When Affirmative
      Action was White: An Untold History of Racial Inequality in Twentieth-Century
      America* (New York: W.W. Norton, 2005).

45   The population numbers in the paragraph and the subsequent paragraphs are
      drawn from U.S. States Ranked by Population—2019 http://worldpopulation
      review.com/states/.

46   My analysis here is informed by Thomas Geoghegan, "The Infernal Senate,"
      New Republic (November 20, 1994). https://newrepublic.com/article/62471
      /the-infernal-senate.

47   Ibid.

48   William W. Freehling, *The Reintegration of American History: Slavery and the
      Civil War* (New York: Oxford University Press, 1994), p. 29.

49   Paul Finkelman, "Making a Covenant with Death: Slavery and the
      Constitutional Convention," in *Beyond Confederation: Origins of the Constitution
      and American National Identity*, eds. Richard Beeman, Stephen Botein, and
      Edward C. Carter II (Chapel Hill: North Carolina Press, 1987), p. 3.

50   Finkelman, "Making a Covenant with Death" and *The Declaration of Independence
      & The Constitution of the United States*, with an introduction by Pauline Maier
      (New York: Bantam Classics, 2008), pp. 59–76. The euphemism "peculiar
      institution" came into use when John C. Calhoun defended the "peculiar labor" of
      the South in 1828 and the "peculiar domestick institution" in 1830, https://www
      .encyclopedia.com/history/dictionaries-thesauruses-pictures-and-press-releases
      /peculiar-institution.

51   Finkelman, "Making a Covenant with Death," pp. 7–8 and *The Declaration of
      Independence & The Constitution of the United States*, with an introduction by Pauline
      Maier, pp. 59–76. The five provisions and supporting articles are listed here:

- Article I, Section 2, Paragraph 3—The infamous three-fifths clause provided for counting three-fifths of all slaves for purposes of representation in Congress. "Representatives and direct taxes shall be apportioned among the several states which may be included within this Union, according to their respective Numbers, which shall be determined by adding to the whole Number of free Persons, including those bound to Service for a Term of Years, and excluding Indians not taxed, three fifths of all other Persons." (Deleted by the 14th Amendment)
- Article I, Section 9, Paragraph 1—Known as the "slave trade clause," this provision prohibited Congress from banning the "Migration or Importation of such Persons as any of the States now existing shall think proper to admit" before 1808.
- Article I, Section 9, Paragraph 4—This clause stated that any "capitation" or other "direct tax" had to take into account the three-fifths clause. "No Capitation, or other direct, Tax shall be laid, unless in Proportion to the Census or Enumeration herein before directed to be taken."
- Article IV, Section 2, Paragraph 3—The infamous "fugitive slave clause" prohibited the Northern states from emancipating fugitive slaves and required that runaways be returned to their owners "on demand." "No Person held to Service or Labour in one State, under the Laws thereof, escaping into another, shall, in Consequence of any Law or Regulation therein, be discharged from such Service or Labour, but shall be delivered up on Claim of the Party to whom such Service or Labour may be due." (Changed by the 13th Amendment)
- Article V—This article prohibited any amendment of the slave importation or capitation clauses before 1808. "Provided that no Amendment which may be made prior to the Year One thousand eight hundred and eight shall in any Manner affect the first and fourth Clauses in the Ninth Section of the first Article; and that no State, without its Consent, shall be deprived of its equal Suffrage in the Senate."

In addition, slavery received important indirect support in Article I, Section 8, Paragraph 15, which empowered Congress to call "forth the Militia" to "suppress Insurrections" including slave rebellions; Article II, Section 1, Paragraph 2, which provides for the indirect election of the president through an electoral college based on congressional representation, involving the three-fifths counting of slaves and thus whites in slave states having a disproportionate influence on the election of the president; and Article V, which by requiring a three-fourths majority of the states to ratify any amendment to the Constitution, ensured that the slaveowning states would hold a veto over any constitutional changes against their interests.

52   Joseph J. Ellis, *Founding Brothers: The Revolutionary Generation* (New York: Knopf, 2001), pp. 81–83, 100–101. The quote from William Loughton Smith on p. 100 Ellis cites as coming from *First Congress*, vol. 12, pp. 750–61.

53   Freehling, *The Reintegration of American History*, p. 25.

54   On the importance of intensity in politics see Robert A. Dahl, *A Preface to Democratic Theory* (Chicago: University of Chicago Press, 1956).

55   Sean Wilentz, *No Property in Man: Slavery and Antislavery at the Nation's Founding* (Cambridge, Mass.: Harvard University Press, 2018).

56   Abraham Lincoln, Cooper Union Address, February 27, 1860, https://www. nytimes.com/2004/05/02/nyregion/full-text-abraham-lincolns-cooper-union-address.html?mtrref=undefined&gwh=F4510D69F58979B1D1D4B7D499F3A B23&gwt=pay.

57   Michael J. Klarman, *The Framers' Coup: The Making of the United States Constitution* (New York: Oxford University Press, 2016), pp. 296–97.

58   Klarman, *The Framers' Coup*, p. 291.

59   Freehling, *The Reintegration of American History*, p. 28.

60   Wilentz, *No Property in Man*, pp. 97–99, quoting Madison from Max Farrand, ed., *The Records of the Federal Convention of 1787* [1911], rev. ed. (New Haven, Conn.: Yale University Press, 1966), Vol. II: p. 417.

61   Wilentz, *No Property in Man*, p. 147 quoting Patrick Henry in "Virginia Convention," June 17, 1788, in Merrill Jensen, et al., eds., *The Documentary History of the Ratification of the Constitution* (Madison: Wisconsin Historical Society Press, 1976), Vol. X: p. 1341.

62   Wilentz, *No Property in Man*, p. 146.

63   Klarman, *The Framers' Coup*, p. 303.

64   In a May 1787 letter to Jefferson, George Washington wrote that the federal government was "at an end, and unless a remedy is soon applied, anarchy and confusion will inevitably ensue." Washington to Jefferson, May 30, 1787, *The Papers of George Washington* (Confederation Series) W. W. Abbot, ed., Charlottesville: University of Virginia Press, 1995), 5: p. 208, quoted by Klarman, *The Framers' Coup*, p. 126.

65   For example, his idea of a federal veto over state legislatures went down to defeat as did his plan for proportional representation in the Senate.

66   They also invented a federal system with two legislatures—congressional and state—with different powers and responsibilities while having jurisdiction over the same territory. For example, the Americans states have primary responsibility for criminal law and public education while the federal government is responsible for immigration and customs. Gordon S. Wood, *The Idea of America: Reflections on the Birth of the United States* (New York: Penguin Press, 2011), Chapter 5 "The Origins of American Constitutionalism," p. 184.

67   More than any other delegate Wilson championed popular participation in the election of senators and the president. Klarman, *The Framers' Coup*, p. 146.

68   Ellis, *The Quartet*, p. 127.

69   Klarman, *The Framers' Coup*, p. 131–32, quoting from James Madison, "Vices of the Political System of the United States," William T. Hutchinson et al. eds., *The Papers of James Madison* (Congressional Series) Robert R. Rutland and William M. E. Rachal, eds., (Chicago: University of Chicago Press, 1977), 9: pp. 355, 357, a research memo Madison penned in the early months of 1787.

70   Wood, *The Idea of America*, Chapter 6 "The Making of American Democracy," pp. 190–91. O'Leary, *Saving Democracy*, p. 109 and Manin, *The Principles of Representative Government*, p. 41.

71   Klarman, *The Framers' Coup*, p. 245, quoting Farrand, *The Records of the Federal Convention of 1787*, Butler, July 6, 1: pp. 541–2.

72   Ibid., pp. 244, 172–73. The original Congress had sixty-five members representing districts of 30,000 constituents.

73   Drew R. McCoy, review of Gordon S. Wood, *The Radicalism of the American Revolution, Journal of American History*, Vol. 79, No. 4 (March 1993): p. 1563.

74   Wood, *The Idea of America*, Chapter 6 "The Making of American Democracy," pp. 194–195.

75   Gordon S. Wood, *The Radicalism of the American Revolution* (New York: Vintage, 1993), pp. ix, 8.

76   Ibid., Chapters 1–2, with Washington quote on p. 27 coming from Richard Bridgman, "Jefferson's Farmer Before Jefferson," *American Quarterly*, XIV (1962), p. 576.

77   Ibid., p. 38.

78   Wood, *The Creation of the American Republic*, p. 415.

79   Sean Wilentz, *The Rise of American Democracy: Jefferson to Jackson* (New York: W.W. Norton, 2005), p. xix.

80   O'Leary, *Saving Democracy*, pp. 9, 55 and Wood, *The Creation of the American Republic*, pp. 232, 366.

81   Wood, *The Idea of America*, Chapter 6 "The Making of American Democracy," pp. 196–98.

82   In America, people were freer from aristocratic patronage and control and the divide between people with wealth and property and the lower class was not as extreme nor as rigid as in Europe. Wood, *The Radicalism of the American Revolution*, p. 171.

83   Wood, *The Idea of America*, Chapter 6 "The Meaning of American Democracy," p. 199.

84   Ibid., p. 206.

85   Ibid., pp. 206–209.

86   Wilentz, *The Rise of American Democracy*, p. 138, quoting Abraham Bishop, *An Oration on the Extent and Power of Political Delusion*, (Whitefish, Mont.: Kessenger, 2010), pp. 45–46.

87   Joyce Appleby, "Thomas Jefferson and the Psychology of Democracy," in eds. James Horn, Jan Ellen Lewis, and Peter S. Onuf, *The Revolution of 1800: Democracy, Race and the New Republic* (Charlottesville: University of Virginia Press, 2002), p. 155.

88   Appleby, p. 157.

89   Wood, *The Idea of America*, Chapter 2 "The Meaning of American Democracy," pp. 192, 206.

90   A rephrasing of Wood's passage: "the most liberal, the most democratic, the most commercially minded, and the most modern people in the world," Wood, *The Radicalism of the American Revolution*, p. 7.

91   Paine, *Rights of Man*, p. 180.

92   Paine, *Common Sense*, p. 65.

93   Ibid., p. 76. Emphasis in original.

94   Wood, *The Idea of America*, "The Radicalism of Jefferson and Paine Considered,"
      pp. 214–17.
95   Ibid., pp. 224–26.
96   Paine, *Rights of Man*, pp. 41–42, 45.
97   Ibid., p. 71. Emphasis in original.
98   Ibid., pp. 210, 59, 241, 240, 251.
99   Alexis de Tocqueville, *Democracy in America*, translation George Lawrence,
      edited by J. P. Mayer (Garden City, N.Y.: Anchor, 1969), p. 19.
100   Tocqueville, *Democracy in America*, pp. 305, 68–70, 9.
101   While Tocqueville feared citizens of democracies would become inward-looking
      and too focused on themselves and their own careers and families to keep a
      watchful eye on government and public affairs, he believed that in the United
      States, with its decentralized system of governance and participation, these "local
      liberties, then, induce a great many citizens to value the affection of their kindred
      and neighbors, bring men into contact, despite the instincts that separate them,
      and force them to help one another." Tocqueville, *Democracy in America*, p. 511.
102   Ibid., pp. 525–27.
103   Ibid., p. 512.
104   Ibid., p. 346.

THREE: ILLIBERAL CHALLENGE FROM THE PLANTATION ELITE

1   Kevin M. Kruse, *White Flight: Atlanta and the Making of Modern Conservatism*
      (Princeton, N.J.: Princeton University Press, 2005), p. 163.
2   Smith, *Civic Ideals*. In his history of public law from the founding to the 1920s,
      what Smith terms "ascription" occurs when social class or stratum placement
      is primarily hereditary. People are placed in positions in a stratification system
      because of qualities beyond their control. Race, sex, age, class at birth, religion,
      ethnicity, and residence all are good examples of these qualities.
3   More than sixty years ago, Harvard political scientist Louis Hartz celebrated
      the moderation, sanity, and even boredom of the American political world.
      The Liberal Tradition in America is an ode to the powerful, pervasive, and
      largely *unconscious* influence of Locke's ideas on American society and builds
      from Tocqueville's famous insight that Americans were "born free": "The
      Americans have this great advantage [in] that they attained democracy without
      the sufferings of a democratic revolution and that they were born free instead
      of becoming so." Though Americans may disagree about politics, Hartz saw
      our battles over tariffs in one generation and social welfare spending in another
      as family feuds within the liberal faith. According to Hartz, "a society which
      begins with Locke . . . stays with Locke . . . It has within it, as it were, a kind of
      self-completing mechanism, which insures the universality of the liberal idea."
      Hartz, *The Liberal Tradition in America*, p. 6.
4   Smith, *Civic Ideals*, p. 200.
5   Ibid., pp. 1–39, 165–212; Rogers M. Smith, "Beyond Tocqueville, Myrdal and
      Hartz: The Multiple Traditions in America," *American Political Science Review*,
      Vol. 87, No. 3, (September 1993), pp. 549–566.

6   Smith, "Beyond Tocqueville, Myrdal and Hartz," p. 563, note 4.

7   George M. Fredrickson, *Racism: A Short History* (Princeton, N.J.: Princeton University Press, 2002), pp. 93, 95.

8   Smith, *Civic Ideals*, p. 28.

9   Gunnar Myrdal, *An American Dilemma: The Negro Problem and American Democracy* [1944] 20th Anniversary edition (New York: Harper & Row, 1962).

10   See Michael Tesler and David O. Sears, *Obama's Race: The 2008 Election and the Dream of a Post-Racial America* (Chicago: University of Chicago Press, 2010).

11   Michelle Alexander, *The New Jim Crow: Mass Incarceration in the Age of Colorblindness* (New York: New Press, 2010), p. 23–25.

12   Edmund S. Morgan, *American Slavery, American Freedom: The Ordeal of Colonial Virginia* (New York: W.W. Norton, 1975), pp. 129, 158–59. This section is based on Morgan's pathbreaking book.

13   Ibid., pp. 220, 238, 239–270.

14   Ibid., pp. 269–70.

15   In an important footnote, Morgan wrote that "in times and places where land was abundant and rents consequently low"—as was the case in America and Russia in the late 16th and 17th centuries—the dominant class often developed "some form of serfdom or slavery." Morgan, *American Slavery, American Freedom*, p. 218, citing Evsey D. Domar, "The Causes of Slavery or Serfdom: A Hypothesis," *Journal of Economic History*, XX (1970), pp. 18–32.

16   Ibid., p. 296.

17   Ibid., pp. 180–182, 297–298.

18   Ibid., p. 313.

19   Ibid., p. 314, citing the British Public Record Office, Colonial Office, 1/45, folio 138.

20   Ibid., p. 320, quoting Edgar S. Furniss, *The Position of the Laborer in a System of Nationalism: A Study in the Labor Theories of the Later English Mercantilists* [1920] (London: August M. Kelly, 1957), pp. 128–130.

21   Ibid., p. 331, emphasis added, citing William Waller Hening, *The Statutes at Large: Being a Collection of All the Laws of Virginia* (Richmond, Va.:, 1809–23), Vol. II, p. 280.

22   Wilentz, *No Property in Man*, p. 27.

23   Ta-Nehisi Coates, *Between the World and Me* (New York: Spiegel & Grau, 2015), p. 7.

24   Ira Berlin, *Many Thousands Gone: The First Two Centuries of Slavery in North America* (Cambridge, Mass.: Harvard University Press, 1998), pp. 8–10. Berlin says the transformation of the Chesapeake from a society with slaves to a slave society came when "in 1676 planters smashed Nathaniel Bacon's motley army of small holders and indentured servants, black and white. Following their victory, planters slowly replaced indentured servants with slaves as their main source of plantation labor." Ira Berlin, *Generations of Captivity: A History of African-American Slaves* (Cambridge, Mass.: Harvard University Press, 2003), p. 55.

25   Berlin, *Many Thousands Gone*, pp. 96–97. The second quote, cited by Berlin, comes from Morgan Godwyn, *The Negro's and Indians Advocate* (London, 1680), p. 36.

26   Berlin, *Many Thousands Gone*, p. 99.

27   Ibid., p. 106; Edward E. Baptist, *The Half Has Never Been Told: Slavery and the Making of American Capitalism* (New York: Basic, 2014), p. 10.

28   See Hochschild, *Bury the Chains*.

29   Sven Beckert, *Empire of Cotton: A Global History* (New York: Vintage, 2015), p. 102.

30   Bruce Levine, *The Fall of the House of Dixie: The Civil War and the Social Revolution That Transformed the South* (New York: Random House, 2013), p. 9.

31   Berlin, *Generations of Captivity*, p. 161–62; Baptist, *The Half Has Never Been Told*, pp. 1–2.

32   While acknowledging the brutality of slavery, Eugene Genovese highlights the paternalistic aspect of slavery that minimized coercion and allowed slave owners hegemony—when domination is not seriously questioned—while acting as the benevolent, stern father figure. There was a complex psychological relationship between the slave, the often brutal overseer, and master. Eugene D. Genovese, *Roll, Jordan, Roll: The World the Slaves Made* (New York: Vintage, 1974), pp. 3–26.

33   Berlin, *Many Thousands Gone*, p. 98.

34   Barrington Moore Jr., *Social Origins of Dictatorship and Democracy: Lord and Peasant in the Making of the Modern World* (Boston: Beacon Press, 1966), pp. 121–122.

35   Moore, *Social Origins of Dictatorship and Democracy*, p. 123.

36   Berlin, *Many Thousands Gone*, pp. 97–99, Baptist, *The Half Has Never Been Told*, p. 97.

37   Thomas Jefferson, *Notes on the State of Virginia*, cited by Levine, *Half Free and Half Slave*, p. 6.

38   Levine, *The Fall of the House of Dixie*, p. 20.

39   Ibid., p. 18 citing *Selections from the Letters and the Speeches of the Hon. James H. Hammond of South Carolina* (New York, 1866), p. 318.

40   Ibid., p. 21.

41   Ibid., pp. 4–6.

42   Moore, *Social Origins*, pp. 116–117.

43   Levine, *The Fall of the House of Dixie*, p. 26.

44   This is a central argument of Beckert, *Empire of Cotton* and Baptist, *The Half Has Never Been Told*, esp. pp. 113–142. The argument that the plantation South was a rapidly growing, economically dynamic region, and that slave plantations were highly profitable, efficient, and fully capable of out-competing free farms was pioneered by Robert W. Fogel and Stanley L. Engerman, *Time on the Cross: The Economics of American Negro Slavery* (Boston: Little, Brown, 1974).

45   Beckert highlights "the crucial distinction between merchant and industrial capitalism" that many historians gloss over. It is a myth that the Old South resisted the money-grubbing values of the market. By calling merchant capital, "war capitalism," Beckert emphasizes how "southern slave society stood out by the extremity and ruthlessness of its exploitation," James Oakes, "Capitalism and Slavery and the Civil War," *International Labor and Working-Class History* (89) Spring 2016, pp. 212–16.

46   Beckert, *Empire of Cotton*, pp. xv–xvi, 108.

47   Levine, *The Fall of the House of Dixie*, pp. 3–4 and Beckert, *Empire of Cotton*, p. 108.

48   Beckert, *Empire of Cotton*, pp. 221–223.

49   Baptist, *The Half Has Never Been Told*, p. 18.

50   Beckert, *Empire of Cotton*, pp. 79, 81.

51   Baptist, *The Half Has Never Been Told*, p. xxi.

52   Beckert, *Empire of Cotton*, p. 110.

53   "It was the gang system that forced men to work at the pace of an assembly line (called the gang) that made slave laborers more efficient than free laborers," Robert W. Fogel and Stanley L. Engerman, *Without Consent or Contract: The Rise and Fall of American Slavery* (New York: W.W. Norton, 1989), p. 79.

54   Eric Foner, "A Brutal Process," Review of Edward Baptist, *The Half Has Never Been Told*, https://www.nytimes.com/2014/10/05/books/review/the-half-has-never-been-told-by-edward-e-baptist.html.

55   Berlin, *Many Thousands Gone*, p. 98.

56   Baptist, *The Half Has Never Been Told*," p. 128. Baptist writes, "The total gain in the productivity per picker from 1800 and 1860 was almost 400 percent. And from 1819 to 1860, the increase in efficiency of workers who tended spinning machines in Manchester cotton mills was about 400 percent," p. 128.

57   Ibid., p. 113. Baptist's numbers and his characterization of slavery as "torture" are criticized by Oakes, "Capitalism and Slavery and the Civil War," pp. 203–209. See also Alan L Olmstead and Paul W. Rhode, *Creating Abundance: Agricultural Innovation and American Agricultural Development* (New York: Cambridge University Press, 2008) and Alan L. Olmstead and Paul W. Rhode, "'Wait a Cotton Pickin' Minute!' A New View of Slave Productivity," April 2005, working paper, who report that in the fifty years preceding the Civil War the amount of cotton picked per slave in a day increased by two and one-half times, and Franklee Gilbert Whartenby, *Land and Labor Productivity in United States Cotton Production, 1800–1840* (New York: Arno Press, 1977), pp. 54, 104–105, who reports that between 1800 and 1840, annual Southern cotton production surged from 40 to 871 million pounds.

58   John C. Calhoun, "The Positive Good of Slavery," Speech in the U.S. Senate, February 6, 1837.

59   Among Marx's writings see Karl Marx, "On the Jewish Question," *The Marx-Engels Reader*, Second Edition, ed. Robert C. Tucker (New York: W.W. Norton, 1978), pp. 26–46.

60   John C. Calhoun, "The Positive Good of Slavery," Speech in the U.S. Senate, February 6, 1837. See Drew Gilpin Faust, ed., *The Ideology of Slavery: Proslavery Thought in the Antebellum South, 1830–1860* (Baton Rouge: Louisiana State University Press, 1981) and Clyde N. Wilson, ed., *The Papers of John C. Calhoun* (Columbia: University of South Carolina Press, 1959).

61   George M. Fredrickson, Chapter 1 "Masters and Mudsills: The Role of Race in the Planter Ideology of South Carolina," in *The Arrogance of Race: Historical Perspectives on Slavery, Racism and Social Inequality* (Middletown, Conn.: Wesleyan University Press, 1988), p. 22.

62   Fredrickson, *The Arrogance of Race*, p. 3. Emphasis added.

63   Beckert, *Empire of Cotton*, p. 283.

64   Moore, *Social Origins*, p. 145.

65   Ibid., p. 144, emphasis in original, citing Thaddeus Stevens, speech of September 6, 1865, in Lancaster, Pennsylvania, as given in Richard Nelson Current, *Old Thad Stevens: A Story of Ambition* (Madison: University of Wisconsin Press, 1943), pp. 2, 15.

66   Eric Foner, "Thaddeus Stevens and the Imperfect Republic," *Pennsylvania History*, Vol. 60, No. 2 (April 1993), p. 147.

67   Staughton Lynd, "Rethinking Slavery and Reconstruction," *Journal of Negro History*, Vol. 50, No. 3 (July 1965), p. 207.

68   W. E. B. Du Bois, *Black Reconstruction in America 1860–1880*, introduction by David Levering Lewis (New York: Atheneum, 1992), p. 624.

69   Foner, "Thaddeus Stevens and the Imperfect Republic," p. 149.

70   Ibid., p. 148.

71   Moore, *Social Origins*, p. 145, citing Thaddeus Stevens, speech of September 6, 1865.

72   Eric Foner, *Reconstruction: America's Unfinished Revolution 1863–1877* (New York: Harper & Row, 1988), p. 236.

73   Kenneth M. Stamp, *The Era of Reconstruction 1865–1877* (New York: Vintage, 1967) and Foner, *Reconstruction*.

74   Ron Chernow, *Grant* (New York: Penguin, 2018), pp. 550, 562–563.

75   Ibid., pp. 565, 581, 583–592.

76   Beckert, *Empire of Cotton*, pp. 284–286.

77   Lynd, "Rethinking Slavery and Reconstruction," p. 209.

78   Oakes, "Capitalism and Slavery and the Civil War," p. 214.

79   Key, *Southern Politics in State and Nation*. Key's discussion of the power of the Black Belt whites remains fascinating and is discussed in Chapter 7.

80   Kevin O'Leary, "Alabama Senate Special Election Hinges on African American Turnout," *American Prospect* (Dec. 4, 2017). http://prospect.org/article/alabama-senate-special-election-hinges-african-american-turnout.

FOUR: SOCIAL DARWINISM WITH A VENGEANCE

1   Key, *Southern Politics in State and Nation*, p. 666.

2   Jack Beatty, *The Age of Betrayal: The Triumph of Money in America 1865–1900* (New York: Vintage, 2008).

3   Charles Perrow, *Organizing America: Wealth, Power, and the Origins of Corporate Capitalism* (Princeton, N.J.: Princeton University Press, 2002), p. 54.

4   H. W. Brands, *American Colossus: The Triumph of Capitalism: 1865–1900* (New York: Doubleday, 2010), p. 5.

5   McCoy, *The Elusive Republic: Political Economy in Jeffersonian America*.

6   Tocqueville, *Democracy in America*, p. 558.

7   In the 1820s, Speaker of the House Henry Clay famously argued for a program of economic nationalism, that would stand on three legs: tariffs to protect America's emerging industrial sector; infrastructure such as bridges, canals, and roads; and a financial system based on a national bank and strong currency. At Clay's insistence, Congress placed tariffs averaging 40 percent on imported

manufactured goods and often spiked tariffs on some agricultural products to 60 percent. The tariffs not only protected American businesses, they also funded the government; before 1860, tariffs produced 85 percent of the federal government's revenue. The national bank played villain to President Andrew Jackson in the 1830s and met a sorry end. But state governments filled the void by funding the infrastructure necessary for commerce and industrial growth. From 1790 to 1860, national outlays for transportation infrastructure totaled $54 million, while the states spent more than $450 million. Michael Lind, *Land of Promise: An Economic History of the United States* (New York: HarperCollins, 2012), pp. 107, 117.

8   Desmond King and Marc Stears, "Capitalism, Democracy, and the Missing State in Louis Hartz's America," in Mark Hulling, ed., *The American Liberal Tradition Reconsidered: The Contested Legacy of Louis Hartz* (Lawrence: University Press of Kansas, 2010), p. 130. King and Stears go on to note that in *Economic Policy and Democratic Thought* (1948), Hartz saw state governments as being crucial to early American capitalism in four ways: creating a transportation and communication infrastructure, providing venture capital, adopting a regulatory environment that fostered fair competition (and, on occasion, direct economic involvement such as "chartering" to force mergers between firms), and creating sanctioned monopolies when state officials believed industries would benefit by being protected from competition or economies of scale, p. 131.

9   Perrow, *Organizing America*.

10   Ibid., p. 219.

11   Nineteenth century economic growth was promoted through the legal system, and this choice had significant consequences for the distribution of capital and power in American society. Morton Horowitz, *The Transformation of American Law, 1780–1860* (New York: Oxford University Press, 1992), p. xv.

12   Perrow, *Organizing America*, p. 41.

13   Ibid., p. 42.

14   Ibid., pp. 41–42.

15   In the case at hand, the state of New York had granted exclusive navigation rights to a steamship operator and the company's competitors argued that the federal government's commerce power superseded state laws.

16   Brands, *American Colossus*, pp. 19–20 citing Kermit L. Hall, ed., *The Oxford Companion to the Supreme Court of the United States* (New York: Oxford University Press, 1992), pp. 337–38.

17   Perrow, *Organizing America*, p. 42.

18   Ibid., p. 94.

19   Karen Orren, *Belated Feudalism: Labor, the Law, and Liberal Development in the United States* (Cambridge, UK: Cambridge University Press, 1991), p. 164.

20   Perrow, *Organizing America*, pp. 103, 224.

21   Ibid., pp. 108–111.

22   Ibid., p. 109.

23   Dobbin, *Forging Industrial Policy*, p. 160, quoted by Perrow, *Organizing America*, p. 109, emphasis added.

24   Stephen Skowronek, *Building A New American State: The Expansion of National
      Administrative Capacities 1877–1920* (New York: Cambridge University Press,
      1982).

25   Perrow, *Organizing America*, p. 115, and Albert Fishlow, *American
      Railroads and the Transformation of the Ante-bellum Economy* (Cambridge,
      Mass.: Harvard University Press, 1965) and https://eh.net/book_reviews/
      american-railroads-and-the-transformation-of-the-ante-bellum-economy/.

26   Alfred D. Chandler, *The Visible Hand: The Managerial Revolution in American
      Business* (Cambridge, Mass.: Harvard University Press, 1977) and Perrow,
      Organizing America, pp. 158–159, 115, 111.

27   Brand, *American Colossus*, p. 23.

28   "Bureaucracy has proved to be the best unobtrusive control device that elites
      have ever achieved." Perrow, *Organizing America*, p. 225.

29   Oakes, "Capitalism and Slavery and the Civil War," pp. 206–207, and Charles
      Post, *The American Road to Capitalism: Studies in the Class-Structure, Economic
      Development and Political Conflict, 1620–1877* (Chicago: Haymarket, 2012).

30   Orren, *Belated Feudalism*, pp. 73, 15.

31   Lind, *Land of Promise*, p. 173.

32   The seminal work on the master-servant concept in American labor relations is
      Orren, *Belated Feudalism*.

33   Ibid., pp. 25, 13, 24, 8, 11, 74.

34   Ibid., pp. 163, 196, 174–178, 184–185.

35   *Autobiography of Andrew Carnegie* (Boston, 1920), p. 327, quoted by Richard
      Hofstadter, *Social Darwinism in American Thought, 1860–1915* (1944), with a
      new introduction by Eric Foner (Boston: Beacon Press, 1992), Chapter 2 "The
      Vogue of Spencer," p. 45.

36   Hofstadter, *Social Darwinism in American Thought, 1860–1915*, p. 40.

37   "We are undergoing the process of adaptation," Spencer wrote. "We have to lose
      the characteristics which fitted us to our original state, and to gain those which
      will fit us for our present state." Herbert Spencer, *Social Statics or The Conditions
      Essential to Human Happiness Specified and the First of Them Developed* [1851]
      (New York: Augustus Kelley, 1969), p. 281.

38   Contemporary anarchist and libertarian Murray Rothbard declared *Social
      Statics* "the greatest single work of libertarian philosophy ever written." Murray
      Rothbard, "Recommended Reading," *The Libertarian Forum*, (1971), Vol. II,
      p. 5, http://mises.org/daily/6688/Herbert-Spencer-Freedom-and-Empire.

39   In his autobiography, Spencer wrote that his belief in the Lamarckian theory
      "never afterwards wavered," quoted by John Offer, *Herbert Spencer: Political
      Writings* (New York: Cambridge University Press, 1994). "Introduction," p. xi,
      quoting Herbert Spencer, *Autobiography*, Vol. I, pp. 176–7.

40   Spencer, *Social Statics*, p. 281.

41   Ibid., Chapter XXV Poor Laws, pp. 322–23. Emphasis added.

42   "The time was when the history of a people was but the history of its government.
      It is otherwise now. The once universal despotism was but a manifestation of
      the extreme necessity of restraint. Feudalism, serfdom, slavery—all kinds of

tyrannical institutions, are merely the most vigorous kinds of rule, springing out of, necessary to, a bad state of man. The progress from these is in all cases the same—less government. Constitutional forms mean this. Political freedom means this. Democracy means this. In societies, associations, joint-stock companies, we have new agencies occupying fields filled in less advanced times and countries by the State . . . Thus, as civilization advances, does government decay. To the bad it is essential; to the good, not." Spencer, *Social Statics*, pp. 13–14. Spencer makes the case for minimal government, but he does not stop there. In a chapter titled "The Right to Ignore the State," he develops an anarchist position, insisting that every citizen has the right to withdraw, "that he is free to drop connection with the state—to relinquish its protection, and to refuse to pay its support." Spencer argues that government is "essentially immoral," that violence is necessary to maintain it, and "all violence involves criminality." Spencer, *Social Statics*, pp. 206–07.

43　He explained his motivation for writing *The Man Versus The State*: "For some time past I have been getting more and more exasperated at the way in which things are drifting toward Communism with increasing velocity and though I fear little is to be done I am prompted to make a vehement protest." Offer, *Herbert Spencer: Political Writings*, "Introduction," p. xxii, quoting a letter by Spencer to Youmans on November 13, 1883.

44　Offer, *Herbert Spencer: Political Writings*, "Introduction," p. xx, quoting John Stuart Mill's letter to Alexander Bain in 1863, *Collected Works of John Stuart Mill*, Vol. 15, p. 901.

45　Hofstadter, *Social Darwinism in American Thought, 1860–1915*, pp. 31, 32–33.

46　Investigative journalist Ida Tarbell, for one, certainly thought that the Standard Oil Co. had infringed on the equal freedom of other entrepreneurs to enter and engage in business in the petroleum industry. See Tarbell, *The History of the Standard Oil Company*. Alternatively, in *The Public and Its Problems* [1927], John Dewey writes about how third parties—the public—standing outside of commercial agreement or dispute can feel its impact, and thus their freedom to act or to be left alone can seriously be affected.

47　Spencer, *Social Statics*, p. 114.

48　Ibid., "Our first principle requires, not that all shall have like shares of the things which minister to the gratification of the faculties, but that all shall have like freedom to pursue those things."

49　In his mind, this is not necessary. According to his biological theory, those with "greater strength, greater ingenuity, or greater application" are the rightful winners in the grand race of life. Spencer, *Social Statics*, p. 131.

50　Spencer, The Man Versus the State, "The New Toryism," p. 71 in Offer, *Herbert Spencer: Political Writings*.

51　Why call this the "coming slavery?" Spencer asks rhetorically. "The reply is simple. All socialism involves slavery." This is hyperbole. Some forms of socialism, specifically Lenin's version of Marxism that jump-started Soviet totalitarianism, lead to slavery. Others, such as the democratic socialism found in Sweden and Denmark, successfully combine constitutional democracy, a robust private market economy and an expansive state. Spencer, *The Man Versus The State*, "The Coming Socialism," pp. 92, 95.

52   Grover Norquist presents a dichotomy between the "leave us alone coalition" and the "takings coalition" in Grover G. Norquist, *Leave Us Alone: Getting Government's Hands Off of Our Money, Our Guns, Our Lives* (New York: HarperCollins/William Morrow, 2008).

53   Spencer, *The Man Versus The State*, "The New Toryism," p. 71.

54   Hofstadter, *Social Darwinism in American Thought, 1860–1915* (1944), pp. 47–48.

55   Ibid., p. 50.

56   Robert S. and Helen M. Lynd, *Middletown in Transition* (New York, 1937), p. 500, quoted by Hofstadter, *Social Darwinism in American Thought, 1860–1915*, p. 50.

57   Arlie Russell Hochschild, *Strangers in Their Own Land: Anger and Mourning on the American Right* (New York: New Press, 2016), pp. 217–18.

58   In the eighteenth and nineteenth centuries, "Great Britain, was hardly a liberal, lean state with dependable but impartial institutions as it is often portrayed. Instead it was an imperial nation characterized by enormous military expenditures, a near constant state of war, a powerful and interventionist bureaucracy, high taxes, skyrocketing government debt, and protectionist tariffs." Beckert, *Empire of Cotton*, p. xv.

59   Beckert, *Empire of Cotton*, p. 155.

60   Charles E. Lindblom, *Politics and Markets: The World's Political Economic Systems* (New York: Basic, 1977).

61   Beckert, *Empire of Cotton*, pp. 389–90.

FIVE: WHY LIBERALS LOVE GOVERNMENT: THE PROGRESSIVE ERA

1   Robert A. Dahl, "On Removing Certain Impediments to Democracy," in *Toward democracy–a journey: reflections, 1940–1997* (Berkeley: Institute of Governmental Studies Press, University of California, 1997), p. 731.

2   Karl Marx and Friedrich Engels, *The Communist Manifesto*, introduction by Eric Hobsbawm (New York: Verso, 2012), p. 38.

3   Perrow, *Organizing America*, p. 103.

4   Lawrence Goodwyn, *The Populist Moment: A Short History of the Agrarian Revolt in America* (New York: Oxford University Press, 1978), p. viii.

5   Goodwyn, p. 295.

6   http://en.wikipedia.org/wiki/United_States_presidential_election,_1896. On the controversy surrounding 1896 as a realignment election, see Walter Dean Burnham, *Critical Elections and the Mainsprings of American Politics* (New York: W.W. Norton, 1970), and David R. Mayhew, *Electoral Realignments: A Critique of An American Genre* (New Haven, Conn.: Yale University Press, 2002).

7   Goodwyn, p. 297.

8   Robert L. Heilbroner, *The Worldly Philosophers*, (New York: Time Inc. Book Division, 1962), Chapter 2 "The Wonderful World of Adam Smith," p. 52.

9   Perrow, *Organizing America*, Chapter 1.

10   Ida M. Tarbell, *The History of the Standard Oil Company*, briefer version, edited by David M. Chalmers (Mineola, N.Y.: Dover Publications, 1966).

11   Steve Weinberg, *Taking on the Trust: How Ida Tarbell Brought Down John D. Rockefeller and Standard Oil* (New York: W.W Norton, 2008), p. 141, quoting Ron Chernow, *Titan: The Life of John D. Rockefeller Sr.* (New York: Random House, 1998).

12   Tarbell, *The History of the Standard Oil Company*, p. 196.

13   Ibid., p. 21.

14   Locke famously speaks about individuals creating property by combining their labor with the fruits of the earth. Locke, *Second Treatise*, Chapter 5.

15   Tarbell, Sinclair, and Steffens were three of the famous "muckrakers" of the Progressive Era who told the truth about early 20th century America. Sinclair penned best-selling novel *The Jungle* about the meatpacking industry and Steffens, who worked with Tarbell at *McClure's* magazine, wrote *The Shame of the Cities* about the corruption of municipal government.

16   Richard Hofstadter, *The Age of Reform: From Bryan to F.D.R.* (New York: Vintage, 1955), p. 5.

17   Brands, *American Colossus*, p. 610.

18   Ibid., pp. 611, 465.

19   Weinberg, *Taking on the Trust*.

20   Louis Brandeis, "The Regulation of Competition Versus the Regulation of Monopoly," address to the Economic Club of New York, November 1, 1912, http://www.law.louisville.edu/library/collections/brandeis/node/260.

21   Brandeis, "The Regulation of Competition Versus the Regulation of Monopoly."

22   Brands, *American Colossus*, p. 618.

23   David Von Drehle, *Triangle: The Fire That Changed America* (New York: Grove Press, 2003), p. 3. Emphasis in original.

24   Ibid., p. 159.

25   Ibid., pp. 195, 199.

26   Ibid., pp. 206, 211.

27   Ibid., pp. 210–212.

28   Ibid., pp. 213, 201.

29   On this point, the avowed "democratic socialist," Vermont senator Bernie Sanders, is in agreement with other American liberals.

30   Michael Walzer, *Spheres of Justice* (New York: Basic, 1983) and John Rawls, *A Theory of Justice* (Cambridge, Mass.: Harvard University Press, 1971).

31   I borrow from Theodore Roosevelt who wrote that central to the human condition is "the conflict between men who possess more than they earn and men who have earned more than they possess."

32   Locke, *Two Treatises of Government*, "*Labour* being the unquestionable Property of the Labourer, no Man but he can have a right to what that is once joined to, at least where there is enough, and as good left in common for others," p. 329. Emphasis in original.

33   For Locke, political power consists in the right to make and enforce laws regulating property for the sake of the public good. As Kloppenberg writes, "Although Locke devoted considerable attention to origin and justification of property rights, he never doubted that property rights are not only secured but

also may legitimately regulated by government," Kloppenberg, *Toward Democracy*, pp. 157, 163. At the start of the second *Treatise*, Locke writes: "*Political Power* then I take to be *a Right* of making Laws with Penalties of Death, and consequently all less Penalties, for the Regulating and Preservation of Property, and the employing the force of the Community, in the Execution of such Laws, and in the defense of the Commonwealth from Foreign Injury, and all this only for the Publick Good," Locke, *Two Treatises*, p. 308. Emphasis in original.

34 Schlesinger, *The Vital Center*, pp. xvi–xvii.

35 http://www.mortgagerates.info/30-year-mortgage-rates/.

36 On the success of the HOLC and FHA and the New Deal's relevance to the Great Recession's housing crisis see Price Fishback, *Well Worth Saving: How the New Deal Safeguarded Home Ownership* (Chicago: University of Chicago Press, 2013).

37 David Hackett Fischer, Editor's Note, Glenn C. Altschuler and Stuart M. Blumin, *The GI Bill: A New Deal for Veterans* (New York: Oxford University Press, 2009), pp. ix–x.

38 Altschuler and Blumin, *The GI Bill*, pp. 3–4.

39 Eric Laursen, *The People's Pension: The Struggle to Defend Social Security Since Reagan* (Chico, Calif.: AK Press, 2012), p. 5.

40 https://www.fool.com/retirement/2018/10/28/americans-average-social-security -in-2019-how-do-y.aspx and https://www.ssa.gov/policy/docs/chartbooks/fast _facts/2019/fast_facts19.pdf, p. 16.

41 On the unraveling of America's private and public safety net see Jacob S. Hacker, *The Great Risk Shift: The New Economic Insecurity and the Decline of the American Dream*, revised edition (New York: Oxford University Press, 2008).

42 Max J. Skidmore, *Social Security and Its Enemies: The Case for America's Most Efficient Insurance Program* (Boulder, Colo.: Westview Press, 1999), p. 10.

43 Laursen, *The People's Pension*, p. 12.

44 Skidmore, *Social Security and Its Enemies*, p. 9 citing the *1998 Annual Report of the Board of Trustees of the Federal Old-Age and Survivors Insurance and Disability Trust Funds*, pp. 2, 7.

45 Nancy Altman and Eric Kingson, *Social Security Works!: Why Social Security Isn't Going Broke and How Expanding It Will Help Us All* (New York: New Press, 2015).

46 Skidmore, *Social Security and Its Enemies*, Chapter 1 "Myth Versus Reality in Social Security, esp. pp. 10–17.

47 Laursen, *The People's Pension*, pp. 9–10.

48 Laursen, *The People's Pension*, p. 19.

49 https://www.jec.senate.gov/public/_cache/files/5f4be5d9-b297-467a-948a- e7525d04f924/medicare-final.pdf.

50 Paul Starr, *The Social Transformation of American Medicine: The Rise of a Sovereign Profession and the Making of a Vast Industry*, second edition (New York: Basic, 2017), pp. 368–70.

51 Stephanie O'Neill, "As Medicare turns 50, the Lee family recalls its key role," 89.3 KPCC, Southern California Public Radio, July 30, 2015. http://www.scpr .org/news/2015/07/30/53461/as-medicare-turns-50-the-lee-family-recalls-its-ke/.

52   Tom Lewis, *Divided Highways: Building the Interstate Highways, Transforming American Life* (New York: Viking, 1997), p. ix.

53   http://en.wikipedia.org/wiki/Interstate_Highway_System.

54   http://www.eisenhower.archives.gov/research/online_documents/1919_convoy .html.

55   Kevin Starr, *Golden Dreams: California in an Age of Abundance 1950–1963* (New York: Oxford University Press, 2009), p. 248.

56   Peter Edelman, *So Rich, So Poor: Why It's So Hard to End Poverty in America* (New York: New Press, 2012), p. 2.

57   Kevin O'Leary, "Last Refuge for the Homeless: Living in the Car" (*TIME*.com, Feb. 12, 2010), http://www.time.com/time/nation/article/0,8599,1963454,00.html.

SIX: THE NEW DEAL AND REACTION: THE LIBERTARIAN FALLACY

1   John Maynard Keynes, "The End of Laissez-Faire," in *The Collected Writings of John Maynard Keynes*, Vol IX *Essays in Persuasion* (London: Macmillan St. Martin's Press, 1972), pp. 272–286.

2   President Hoover was not totally laissez-faire, but his governmental actions to deal with the Great Depression were clumsy and woefully inadequate.

3   Cass R. Sunstein, *The Second Bill of Rights: FDR's Unfinished Revolution and Why We Need It More Than Ever* (New York: Basic, 2004), pp. 36–40.

4   Nick Taylor, *American-Made: The Enduring Legacy of the WPA: When FDR Put the Nation to Work* (New York: Bantam, 2008), pp. 117–122, 133–136, 129.

5   https://en.wikipedia.org/wiki/Harry_Hopkins.

6   David M. Kennedy, *Freedom From Fear: The American People in Depression and War, 1929–1945* (New York: Oxford University Press, 1999), p. 378.

7   Kennedy, *Freedom From Fear*, pp. 324, 118.

8   Raymond Moley, *After Seven Years* (New York: Harper and Brothers, 1939), p. 14, and *The Public Papers and Addresses of Franklin D. Roosevelt* (New York: Random House and Harper and Brothers) 1928–32, pp. 75–76, 15, cited by Kennedy, *Freedom From Fear*, p. 116.

9   Sunstein, *The Second Bill of Rights*, p. 41, and Kennedy, *Freedom From Fear*, p. 248.

10   Kennedy, *Freedom From Fear*, p. 365.

11   Ibid., pp. 366–368.

12   Ibid., pp. 365–370.

13   Bruce Schulman, *From the Cotton Belt to the Sunbelt: Federal Policy, Economic Development, and the Transformation of the South, 1938–1980* (New York: Oxford University Press, 1991), p. 53, quote cited by Kennedy, *Freedom From Fear*, p. 348.

14   James T. Patterson, *Conservative Conservatism and the New Deal: The Growth of the Conservative Coalition in Congress, 1933–1939* (Lexington: University of Kentucky Press, 1967), pp. 160–162, cited by Kennedy, *Freedom From Fear*, pp. 338–339.

15   For the argument that the modern right took shape in the 1920s and 1930s because of "widespread concern that pluralistic, cosmopolitan forces threatened America's national identity" as a white Protestant nation see Allan J. Lichtman, *White Protestant Nation: The Rise of the Conservative Movement* (New York: Atlantic Monthly Press, 2008), p. 2.

16   Jennifer Burns, *Goddess of the Market: Ayn Rand and the American Right* (New York: Oxford University Press, 2009), p. 2. Corey Robin, *The Reactionary Mind: Conservatism From Edmund Burke to Sarah Palin* (New York: Oxford University Press, 2011), p. 76.

17   In Rand's idealized projection of herself, her major female characters—Kira in *We the Living*, Dominique in *The Fountainhead*, and Dagny Taggart in *Atlas Shrugged*—are romantically and sexually involved with two or three men—including the Neitzschean hero. Similar to Katharine Hepburn in their fierce independence and spirited personalities, Kira, Dominique, and especially Dagny stand tall as strong women—beautiful, highly intelligent, and capable.

18   http://www.cnn.com/2017/01/20/politics/trump-inaugural-address/.

19   Walter Kaufmann, *Nietzsche: Philosopher, Psychologist, Antichrist*, fourth edition (Princeton, N.J.: Princeton University Press, 1974), p. 85.

20   Ibid., p. vii.

21   Michael Tanner, *Nietzsche: A Very Short Introduction* (New York: Oxford University Press, 2000), p. 26.

22   Tanner, *Nietzsche*, p. 4.

23   Burns, *Goddess of the Market*, p. 304, note 4, and https://en.wikipedia.org/wiki/The_Philosophy_of_Friedrich_Nietzsche.

24   Friedrich Nietzsche, *On the Genealogy of Morals*, trans. Walter Kaufman (New York: Vintage, 1967), III, p. 14, and https://plato.stanford.edu/entries/nietzsche/.

25   See Jacob Golomb and Robert S. Wistrich, eds., *Nietzsche, Godfather of Fascism? On the Uses and Abuses of a Philosophy* (Princeton, N.J.: Princeton University Press, 2002).

26   Tanner, *Nietzsche*, p. 30.

27   Kaufmann, *Nietzsche*, pp. 363–364 quoting Nietzsche, *Beyond Good and Evil*, aphorism no. 39.

28   Friedrich Nietzsche, *Beyond Good and Evil*, translated by Marion Faber (New York: Oxford University Press, 2008), aphorism no. 39. Emphasis in original.

29   Tanner, *Nietzsche*, p. 30.

30   Kaufmann, *Nietzsche*, pp. 365–367.

31   As examples of sophisticated studies of Nietzsche see Kaufmann, *Nietzsche*, Erich Heller, *The Importance of Nietzsche* (Chicago: University of Chicago Press, 1988), Henry Staten, *Nietzsche's Voice* (Ithaca, N.Y.: Cornell University Press, 1990), and Tracy B. Strong, *Friedrich Nietzsche and the Politics of Transfiguration* (Berkeley: University of California Press, 1988).

32   Robert C. Holub, "Introduction," Nietzsche, *Beyond Good and Evil*, p. xxiii.

33   Nietzsche, *Beyond Good and Evil*, p. 152. Section 258. Emphasis in original.

34   Burns, *Goddess of the Market*, pp. 40–41, 43.

35   Nietzsche, *Beyond Good and Evil*, p. 151, Section 257. Quotes in original. Emphasis added.

36   Ayn Rand, *Atlas Shrugged* [1957] (New York: New American Library, 1985), p. 90.

37   Rand, *Atlas Shrugged*, p. 974.

38   Burns, *Goddess of the Market*, p. 373.

39   Rand introduces John Galt as having a "clear, calm, implacable voice," and portrays him as being an "implacable enemy." *Atlas Shrugged*, p. 936.

40   Robin, *The Reactionary Mind*, p. 79.

41   Burns, *Goddess of the Market*, p. 9.

42   Ibid., p. 25.

43   Ibid., p. 16.

44   Ibid.

45   Pete A. Gunter, "Nietzsche Laughter," *Sewanee Review*, Vol. 76, No. 3 (Summer 1968), p. 500.

46   In *Thus Spoke Zarathustra*, we learn about the contemptible Last Man who is perfectly happy to be, well, the same as everyone else. Bernd Magnus, *Nietzsche's Existential Imperative* (Bloomington: Indiana University Press, 1978), p. 33, quoted by John Lippitt, "Nietzsche, Zarathustra and the Status of Laughter," *British Journal of Aesthetics*, Vol. 32, No. 1 (January 1992), p. 39.

47   Burns, *Goddess of the Market*, p. 42.

48   On Nietzsche and laughter, see Mark Weeks, "Beyond a Joke: Nietzsche and the Birth of 'Super-Laughter,'" *Journal of Modern Nietzsche Studies*, Issue 27 (Spring 2004), esp. p. 13.

49   In notes about Roark's personality, Rand told herself, "See Nietzsche on laughter." Burns, *Goddess of the Market*, p. 42.

50   Friedrich Nietzsche, *The Gay Science*, translated with commentary by Walter Kaufmann (New York: Vintage, 1974), p. 207, Section 200. Emphasis added.

51   http://en.wikipedia.org/wiki/Schadenfroh.

52   Rand, *The Fountainhead*, p. 107.

53   Burns, *Goddess of the Market*, p. 42 and Rand, *The Fountainhead*, p. 207.

54   Rand, *The Fountainhead*, p. 220.

55   Burns writes that before Rand was smitten with Wendell Willkie and his pro-capitalist message in the 1940 presidential campaign, she "had been suspicious of American democracy. Instead of government of, for, and by the people; she thought the state should be 'a means for the convenience of the higher type of man.'" In the 1940 campaign, however, Rand was "impressed by the questions her working-class audience asked and their responsiveness to her capitalist message." Burns, *Goddess of the Market*, p. 56.

56   F. A. Hayek, *The Road to Serfdom* [1944], with a new introduction by Milton Friedman (Chicago: University of Chicago Press, 1994). An Austrian economist who fled to London, Hayek fashioned a new argument for laissez-faire based on the idea that socialist ideas were responsible for both Nazi and Soviet totalitarianism. In Hayek's worldview, the Nazis and the Marxist Leninists are rival branches of the socialist faith, brothers under the skin.

57   Hayek accepts some minimal government intervention in the economy, but his overall message is clear.

58   Kim Phillips-Fein, *Invisible Hands: The Businessmen's Crusade Against the New Deal* (New York: W.W. Norton, 2009).

59   See William F. Buckley Jr., *Up From Liberalism*, with a foreword by John Dos Passos [1959] (Honor Book, 1965); Milton Friedman, *Capitalism and Freedom*

[1962] (Chicago: University of Chicago Press, 2002); Barry Goldwater, *The Conscience of a Conservative* [1960], with an introduction by Patrick J. Buchanan (New York: MJF, 1990).

60   Here Friedman puts forth a purer illiberal antistatist argument than Hayek. For Friedman, like Spencer, state action should be limited to the police, national defense, and the courts. See Friedman, *Capitalism and Freedom*. Unlike Friedman, Hayek concedes that health and safety regulations and a social welfare safety net are "fully compatible with the preservation of competition." Thus, Hayek is open to some state intervention in the economy. But Hayek's caveat that the advantages gained must be greater than the social cost imposed by such state action means that this apparent concession can be vigorously contested by market diehards. See Hayek, *The Road to Serfdom*, pp. 86–87. "To prohibit the use of certain poisonous substances or to require special precautions in their use, to limit working hours or to require certain sanitary arrangements, is fully compatible with the preservation of competition. The only question here is whether in the particular instance the advantages gained are greater than the social costs which they impose. Nor is the preservation of competition incompatible with an extensive system of social services—so long as the organization of these services is not designed in such a way as to make competition ineffective over wide fields."

61   In the second sentence of the Preface Hayek writes, "This is a political book." *The Road to Serfdom*, p. 37.

62   Isaiah Berlin gives the classic exposition of negative liberty, in his "Two Concepts of Liberty," [1958] in *Four Essays on Liberty* (New York: Oxford University Press, 1969). For critiques of Berlin see MacGilvray, *The Invention of Market Freedom*, pp. 9–15, and Kloppenberg, *The Virtues of Liberalism*, p. 14.

63   Lindblom makes this point in his modern classic *Politics and Markets*.

64   Hayek, *The Road to Serfdom*, pp. 83, 95, 96, 134, 136.

65   Schlesinger, *The Vital Center*.

66   In addition, and as Hayek concedes, it was the socialists, more than any other group, who fought and contested the Nazi's rise to power. See William Sheridan Allen, *The Nazi Seizure of Power: The Experience of a Single German Town, 1930–1935* (New York: Quadrangle, 1965).

67   http://fcit.coedu.usf.edu/holocaust/timeline/nazirise.htm.

68   This is the argument of John Maynard Keynes, *The Economic Consequences of the Peace* [1919].

69   Moore, *Social Origins of Dictatorship and Democracy*, highlights the sharp differences between the landed gentry in England and Germany, p. 38.

70   See Alexander Gerschenkron, *Bread and Democracy in Germany* [1943] (Ithaca, New York: Cornell University Press, 1989), preface.

71   John Gray, "The Road to Serfdom: Forty Years On," *Hayek's Serfdom Revisited: Essays by Economists, Philosophers and Political scientists on The Road to Serfdom after 40 years*. Contributors Norman Barry, John Burton, Hannes H. Gissurarson, John Gray, Jeremy Shearmur, and Karen I. Vaughn (Westminster, UK: Centre for Independent Studies, 1985), pp. 21–22. Ludwig von Mises,

Hayek's teacher, promoted the term interventionist. See John Burton, "The Instability of the 'Middle Way,'" in *Hayek's Serfdom Revisited*, p. 70.

72   Gray, "The Road to Serfdom: Forty Years On," p. 28.

73   For example, see Gray's conclusion, "The Road to Serfdom: Forty Years On," pp. 30–31.

74   For Hayek, "the fundamental principle in the ordering of our affairs is that we should make as much use as possible of the *spontaneous forces* of society, and resort as little as possible to coercion," which he defines as arbitrary personal power or the power of government. Hayek, *The Road to Serfdom*, p. 71. Emphasis added.

75   Ibid., p. 73.

76   Hayek's fear is "Who plans whom, who directs and dominates whom, who assigns to other people their station in life, and who is to have his due allotted by others? . . . It is the extent of the activities of the government which decides whether everything that any person gets any time depends on the government." Here Hayek speaks not just about planning, but extends his argument to "the extent of the activities of the government." Hayek, *The Road to Serfdom*, p. 139.

77   MacGilvray, *The Invention of Market Freedom*, p. 170.

78   William Graham Sumner, *What Social Classes Owe to Each Other* [1883] (Caldwell, Idaho: Caxton Press, 1983), p. 15.

79   MacGilvray, *The Invention of Market Freedom*, pp. 145–46.

80   Ibid., p. 165.

81   Hayek, *The Road to Serfdom*. Hayek followed Joseph Schumpeter's elitist definition of democracy in arguing that it is "essentially a means, a utilitarian device for safeguarding internal peace and individual freedom," p. 110. See Joseph Schumpeter, *Capitalism, Socialism and Democracy* (New York: Harper & Row, 1942), Chapters 20–22.

82   Hayek, *The Road to Serfdom*, p. 109, 102.

83   Dahl, *Democracy and Its Critics*, Chapter 10 "Majority Rule and the Democratic Process," p. 138. Emphasis added.

84   Hayek, *The Road to Serfdom*, p. 71. Emphasis added.

85   Hayek writes, "as decentralization has become necessary because nobody can consciously balance all the considerations bearing on the decisions of so many individuals, the coordination can clearly be effected not by 'conscious control' but only by arrangements which convey to each agent the information he must possess in order effectively to adjust his decisions of others . . . all the details of the changes constantly affecting the conditions of demand and supply of the different commodities can never be fully known." Hayek, *The Road to Serfdom*, p. 55.

86   Others see the utopian aspect of Hayek as well. In the conclusion to his book on Hayek, Norman Barry writes, "What Hayek is offering is a kind of algebraic utopia which is characterized by a set of general rules which allow a plurality of ends and purposes to be pursued. It is also a pessimistic utopia in that Hayek doubts that there will ever be agreement about fundamental ends and does not trust politicians to do anything but impose their conception of the good life on others. It is here that Hayek's study of economics has a

strong impact on his political philosophy, for the economist's conception of the market is a kind of utopia in that theoretically it allows all tastes to be satisfied, it is impersonal and end-independent. It is politics that is disequilibriating: it replaces exchange by coercion and put 'social ends' over individual purposes." Norman P. Barry, *Hayek's Social and Economic Philosophy* (London: Macmillan Press, 1979), p. 195.

87   Albert O. Hirschman, *Exit, Voice and Loyalty* (Cambridge: Harvard University Press, 1970).

88   On the connection between Plato and Hayek, I am indebted to my daughter Rebecca O'Leary and her 2013 paper "Platonism Central to Mises, Hayek, and Polanyi," written for Professor Adam Sitze of Amherst College and his Law, Jurisprudence and Social Thought class, LJST 54, "The Crisis of Neoliberal Legal Theory."

89   Karl Polanyi, *The Great Transformation* [1944], with an introduction by R. M. MacIver (Boston: Beacon Press, 1968), p. 72. Emphasis in original.

90   Polanyi writes that "the commodity fiction, therefore, supplies a vital organizing principle *in regard to the whole of society* affecting almost all its institutions . . . namely, the principle according to which no arrangement or behavior should be allowed to exist in that it might prevent the actual functioning of the market mechanism on the lines of commodity fiction." Polanyi, *The Great Transformation*, p. 73. Emphasis added.

91   Hayek, *The Road to Serfdom*, p. 174. Emphasis added.

92   Paine, *Rights of Man*, pp. 41–42.

93   Hayek, *The Road to Serfdom*, pp. 222–23. Emphasis added.

94   Hayek allows government more of a role than Friedman. See *The Road to Serfdom*, pp. 86–87.

95   Mary Wollstonecraft, "A Vindication of the Rights of Men, in a Letter to the Right Honourable Edmund Burke; Occasioned by his Reflections on the Revolution in France," Mary Wollstonecraft, *A Vindication of the Rights of Men* and *A Vindication of the Rights of Woman*, pp. 7, 13.

96   Paine, *Rights of Man*, p. 71. "In doing this, we shall easily discover that governments must have arisen, either *out* of the people, or *over* the people." Emphasis in original.

97   Charles E. Lindblom, *The Market System: What It Is, How It Works, and What to Make of It* (New Haven: Yale University Press, 2002).

98   For wise endorsement of both see Lindblom, *Politics and Markets*, and Robert B. Reich, *Saving Capitalism: For the Many, not the Few* (New York: Penguin/ Random House, 2015).

SEVEN: RAGE AGAINST GOVERNMENT: GEORGE WALLACE

1   Barrington Moore writes that slave societies (and former slave societies) do not have the same social norms and political forms "as those based on free labor." Moore, *Social Origins of Dictatorship and Democracy*, p. 114. The plantation elite ruled an oppressive class structure that did great harm not only to African Americans, but poor whites as well. The GOP's push to reduce the voting rolls

is nothing new; the white elite in the Old South systemically disenfranchised African Americans *and* poor whites, especially after 1900.

2   Keith O'Brien, "Ole Miss Turns Scary Racial Incident Into Teachable Moment," National Public Radio, July 2, 2013, http://www.npr.org/blogs/codeswitch /2013/07/02/195292757/Ole-Miss-Turns-Scary-Incident-Into-Teachable -Moment.

3   On the controversy surrounding "Sweet Home Alabama" see https://www.npr .org/2018/12/17/676863591/sweet-home-alabama-lynyrd-skynyrd-southern -discomfort-american-anthem. Skynyrd maintains that the words "boo boo boo" following Wallace is a subtle repudiation of Governor Wallace, but other lyrics "and the Governor is true" support the racial interpretation: https://www.theguardian .com/music/2007/nov/16/3; http://thrasherswheat.org/jammin/lynyrd.htm.

4   Richard K. Scher, *Politics in the New South: Republicanism, Race and Leadership in the Twentieth Century*, second edition (Armonk, N.Y.: M.E. Sharpe, 1997), p. 23.

5   Kruse, *White Flight*.

6   David Leonhardt, "Geography Seen as Barrier To Climbing Class Ladder: Study Finds Areas, Including Southeast and Midwest, Resist Upward Mobility," *New York Times*, July 22, 2013.

7   Bill Moyers, "What a Real President Was Like: To Lyndon Johnson the Great Society Meant Hope and Dignity," *Washington Post*, November 13, 1988. Quoted in Nancy Isenberg, *White Trash: The 400-Year Untold History of Class in America* (New York: Penguin, 2016), p. 264.

8   John Gaventa, *Power and Powerlessness: Quiescence and Rebellion in an Appalachian Valley* (Urbana: University of Illinois Press, 1980). Emphasis in original.

9   Hochschild, *Strangers in Their Own Land*, pp. 217–218, 208, 221. Hochschild draws on W. J. Cash, *The Mind of the South* [1941] (New York: Vintage, 1991).

10   Isenberg, *White Trash*, p. 319.

11   Tom Watson, "The Negro Question in the South," cited in Stokely Carmichael and Charles V. Hamilton, *Black Power: The Politics of Liberation in America* (New York: Random House, 1967). Quoted in Alexander, *The New Jim Crow*, p. 33.

12   Michael Perman, *Struggle for Mastery: Disfranchisement in the South 1888–1908* (Chapel Hill: University North Carolina Press, 2001), p. 6.

13   Key and Woodward argued that the disenfranchising campaigns amounted to a "Bourbon coup d'etat," and contemporary research by Michael Perman supports their claim. Key, *Southern Politics in State and Nation*, Chapter 25, "Southern Suffrage Restrictions: Bourbon Coup D'Etat?" and Perman, *Struggle for Mastery*.

14   Perman, *Struggle for Mastery*, p. 5, and J. Morgan Kousser, *The Shaping of Southern Politics: Suffrage Restrictions and the Establishment of the One-Party South 1880–1910* (New Haven, Conn.: Yale University Press, 1974), pp. 250–257.

15   Carter, *The Politics of Rage*, p. 247. Emphasis in original. In Georgia, an 1877 poll tax left only one of every ten blacks on the voting rolls by 1900. Next, a whites-only primary became established for the Democratic Party and a constitutional amendment in 1908 established a grandfather clause, literacy test, and property qualifications. These hurdles effectively erased the presence of African Americans in Georgia politics for the first half of the 20th century. Kruse, *White Flight*, p. 21.

16   Douglas A. Blackmon, *Slavery By Another Name: The Re-Enslavement of Black Americans from the Civil War to World War II* (New York: Random House, 2008), p. 99.

17   C. Vann Woodward, *Origins of the New South 1877–1913* [1951], revised edition (Baton Rouge: Louisiana State University Press, 1971), p. 327.

18   Key, *Southern Politics in State and Nation*, p. 5. Key compared it to the situation faced by the British colonialists in Africa and India.

19   Ibid., p. xxi.

20   Ibid., p. 44.

21   Ibid., pp. 540, 551. If a majority of whites, both in black-belt and hill counties, supported Negro disenfranchisement, then "white supremacy could be assured in local governments of the black counties" where the planter elite lived.

22   W. E. B. Du Bois, *Black Reconstruction in America*, pp. 700–701.

23   Fredrickson, *Racism*, p. 6.

24   Scher, *Politics in the New South*, p. 55.

25   Fredrickson, *Racism: A Short History*, p. 93.

26   Ibid., p. 87.

27   Ibid., p. 90.

28   Ibid., p. 9.

29   Born to a black-belt Alabama planter family in 1879, Collins was a lawyer and public servant dedicated to preserving segregation. Educated at the University of Alabama, the University of Chicago, and Harvard, he wrote about economics, constitutional law, states' rights, and race relations. Charles Wallace Collins, *Whither Solid South?: A Study in Politics and Race Relations* (New Orleans: Pelican, 1947).

30   Joseph E. Lowndes, *From the New Deal to the New Right: Race and the Southern Origins of Modern Conservatism* (New Haven, Conn.: Yale University Press, 2009), Ch. 1–2, esp. pp. 4–6, 16, 19, 21–22, 37, and Ch. 7.

31   Jason Morgan Ward, *Defending White Democracy: The Making of the Segregationist Movement and the Remaking of Racial Politics, 1936–1965* (Chapel Hill: University of North Carolina Press, 2011), p. 107.

32   In trying to stop an anti-poll tax bill, Stennis explained the emerging national strategy of the Dixiecrats: "If we present our case to the rest of the nation in a calm, dispassionate manner, stressing the threat to the freedom of the whole nation that is implied in these unconstitutional attempts to abridge the freedom of the people of one section (the South), we will make valuable friends among people who have been so misinformed as to regard the 'Civil Rights' fight as a moral issue." Ward, *Defending White Democracy*, pp. 107–108.

33   Ibid., pp. 107, 102, and Lowndes, *From the New Deal to the New Right*, p. 37.

34   Both Nixon and Reagan reassured white Southern audiences that while they were committed to civil rights in principle they would oppose measures such as affirmative action, busing, or housing legislation aimed at assisting African Americans and other minorities.

35   For example, the threat Wallace posed in the 1972 presidential race forced Nixon to shift to the right and abandon Daniel Patrick Moynihan's Disraeli

strategy of the president playing the liberal moderate to the left-wing politics of the McGovernite Democrats. Instead of pushing ahead with the Family Assistance Program, with its guaranteed income floor, the nation's second Reconstruction was abandoned as Nixon scurried to find favor in the South to head off the Wallace challenge. President Nixon insisted that he was following an "American strategy," not a Southern strategy, and his protest points to the larger truth.

36   John Egerton, *The Americanization of Dixie: The Southernization of America* (New York: Harper's Magazine Press, 1974), pp. 17, 22.

37   When Senator Goldwater voted against the Civil Rights Act of 1964, Wallace could have penned his brief speech on the Senate floor. Goldwater said he personally opposed racial discrimination, but national legislation would create a "federal police force of mammoth proportions" and create a situation in which neighbors, workers, and businessmen would spy on each other, leading to a "police state." Carter, *The Politics of Rage*, p. 218.

38   Ibid., p. 41.

39   Ibid., p. 72.

40   Ibid., p. 62.

41   Tom Wicker, "George Wallace: A Gross and Simple Heart," *Harper's*, April 1967, p. 47.

42   Carter, *The Politics of Rage*, p. 85.

43   Ibid., p. 96. In the footnote on page 96, Carter acknowledges that Wallace's official biographer denies that Wallace ever made the racist remark. But Carter draws on numerous other sources who say that Wallace did.

44   George C. Wallace, "'The Inaugural Address of Governor George C. Wallace,' January 14, 1963, Montgomery, Alabama, For Release Monday, P.M. January 14, 1963," p. 2.

45   Lowndes, *From the New Deal to the New Right*, p. 143.

46   Wallace, 1963, Inaugural Address, pp. 4–5.

47   Ibid., p. 7.

48   Carter, *The Politics of Rage*, p. 293. Emphasis in original.

49   Wallace, 1963, Inaugural Address, pp. 11–12. Emphasis added.

50   Master orator King said Wallace gave only four speeches, "but he works on them and hones them, so that they are little minor classics." Carter, *The Politics of Rage*, p. 156.

51   Carter, *The Politics of Rage*, p. 253.

52   Wicker, "George Wallace: A Gross and Simple Heart," p. 46.

53   Carter, *The Politics of Rage*, p. 109.

54   Ibid., p. 10.

55   Wayne Greenhaw, *Watch Out for George Wallace* (Englewood Cliffs, N.J.:, Prentice-Hall, 1976), p. 122.

56   Carter, *The Politics of Rage*, pp. 207–08.

57   Greenhaw, *Watch Out for George Wallace*, pp. 155–56.

58   Carter, *The Politics of Rage*, p. 217.

59   Ibid., p. 424.
60   Carter, *The Politics of Rage*, pp. 425, 467.

EIGHT: ZEALOTS IN CHARGE

1   Kabaservice, *Rule and Ruin.*
2   Ibid., p. 50.
3   In *Rule and Ruin,* Kabaservice tells the story of the downfall of moderation
      and the destruction of the Republican Party from the time of Eisenhower
      to the Tea Party. He writes: "The appearance of a Republican Party almost
      entirely composed of ideological conservatives [read: illiberal reactionaries] is
      a new and historically unprecedented development . . . While there are many
      possible reasons to explain the present American political dysfunction, the
      leading suspect is the transformation of the Republican Party over the past
      half-century into a monolithically conservative organization," an ideological
      battering ram instead of a coalition of interests as has been the American
      tradition with the Federalists and Whigs, and Democrats and Republicans
      for most of our history. Kabaservice, *Rule and Ruin*, pp. 24–25, 112, xvi.
4   See for example, See Binyamin Appelbaum, "Blame Economists for the Mess
      We're In," *New York Times,* August 25, 2019, https://www.nytimes
      .com/2019/08/24/opinion/sunday/economics-milton-friedman.html, and
      Binyamin Appelbaum, *The Economists' Hour: False Prophets, Free Markets, and
      the Fracture of Society* (New York: Little, Brown, 2019) and Kevin Phillips,
      *The Politics of Rich and Power: Wealth and the American Electorate in the Reagan
      Aftermath* (New York: Random House, 1990).
5   Kevin Mattson, *Rebels All! A Short History of the Conservative Mind in Postwar
      America* (New Brunswick, N.J.: Rutgers University Press, 2008), pp. 9, 34–37,
      44, 32.
6   In a 1958 *National Review* article, Frank Meyer summarized why liberalism was
      not to be trusted: liberalism was in agreement with communism on the necessity
      and desirability of socialism, had abandoned "all inherited values" theological,
      philosophical, and political as being "without intrinsic virtue or authority," and
      differed from communism only in method and means. George H. Nash, *The
      Conservative Intellectual Movement in America Since 1945* [1976] (Wilmington,
      Del.: Intercollegiate Studies Institute, 2006), p. 227.
7   Nash, *The Conservative Intellectual Movement in America Since 1945*, p. 236.
8   Kabaservice, *Rule and Ruin*, pp. 14–15.
9   "Why the South Must Prevail," *National Review* (August 24, 1957), p. 149
      quoted in Nash, *The Conservative Intellectual Movement in America Since 1945,*
      p. 308. Emphasis in original.
10   Damon Linker, "William F. Buckley and the Odyssey of Conservatism," book
      review of *A Man and His Presidents: The Political Odyssey of William F. Buckley Jr.*
      by Alvin S. Felzenberg, *New York Times*, May 8, 2017.
11   Mattson, *Rebels All!* pp. 12, 9–10, 140.
12   See Chris Matthews, *Tip and the Gipper: When Politics Worked* (New York:
      Simon & Schuster, 2014).

13   George Packer, *The Unwinding: An Inner History of the New America* (New York: Farrar, Straus and Giroux, 2013), p. 23.

14   Matt Grossmann and David A. Hopkins, *Asymmetric Politics: Ideological Republicans and Group Interest Democrats* (New York: Oxford University Press, 2016), pp. 285–292.

15   In the Obama era, Majority Leader McConnell and Speaker Ryan sometimes reached across the aisle, but Ryan was dedicated to making radical cuts to the federal budget and McConnell plotted and executed a strategy of rigid obstruction against any and all of President Obama's initiatives. In President Obama's first year in office, McConnell and his GOP Senate caucus launched more filibusters than had occurred during the entire decade of the 1950s, thereby transforming "an extraordinary expression into a routine obstructive tactic." Theda Skocpol, *Obama and America's Political Future*, with commentary by Larry M. Bartels, Mickey Edwards, and Suzanne Mettler (Cambridge, Mass.: Harvard University Press, 2012). "Under Barack Obama, Republican obstructionists decided to invoke the supermajority rule on almost every issue small and large . . . Remarkably, the filibuster was invoked more often during 2009 than during the entire decade of the 1950s," pp. 26–27. Skocpol cites Ezra Klein, "The Rise of the Filibuster: An Interview with Barbara Sinclair," *Washington Post*, September 26, 2009, and Ben Frumin and Jason Reif, "The Rise of Cloture: How GOP Filibuster Threats Have Changed the Senate," Talking Points Memo blogpost, January 27, 2010.

16   Daniel K. Williams, *God's Own Party: The Making of the Christian Right* (New York: Oxford University Press, 2010), pp. 12–13.

17   In the 1920s as "a gulf had opened between Americans still devoted to a national identity defined by late-19th-century Victorian values and those tied to the increasingly pluralistic cultural forces of the 20th century." Lichtman, *White Protestant Nation*, p. 9.

18   Williams, *God's Own Party*, pp. 14–17 and Kevin M. Kruse, *One Nation Under God: How Corporate America Invented Christian America* (New York: Basic, 2016).

19   Kruse, *One Nation Under God*.

20   Jerry Falwell, "Segregation or Integration—Which?" Sermon preached at Thomas Road Baptist Church, and reprinted in Word of Life, October 1958. Cited in Williams, *God's Own Party*, p. 33.

21   Jonathan Merritt, "Segregation Is Still Alive at These Christian Schools: Diversity is sorely lacking at many private Christian schools, some of which were originally founded to keep blacks out," *Daily Beast*, July 18, 2016, https://www .thedailybeast.com/segregation-is-still-alive-at-these-christian-schools?ref =scroll.

22   https://www.theatlantic.com/national/archive/2012/12/ in-southern-towns-segregation-academies-are-still-going-strong/266207/.

23   Williams, *God's Own Party*, pp. 1, 159.

24   Martin Durham, *The Christian Right, the far right and the boundaries of American conservatism* (Manchester and New York: Manchester University Press, 2000), pp. 24–25, Thomas B. Edsall and Mary D. Edsall, *Chain Reaction: The Impact*

of Race, Rights, and Taxes on American Politics (New York: W.W. Norton, 1992), and Dan T. Carter, *From George Wallace to Newt Gingrich: Race in the Counterrevolution, 1963–1994* (Baton Rouge: Louisiana State University Press, 1996).

25   Daniel Schlozman and Sam Rosenfeld, "The Long Right and the World It Made," paper prepared for the American Political Science Association meetings, Boston, August 31, 2018 (January 2019 version). Schlozman and Rosenfeld quote the longtime publisher of *National Review*. William Rusher saying, "Conservatism is the wine, the GOP is the bottle." p. 2. Emphasis in original.

26   Ibid., pp. 4, 6, footnote No. 20.

27   Richard A. Viguerie, *The New Right: We're Ready to Lead* (Falls Church, Va.: Viguerie Company, 1981), p. 37.

28   Schlozman and Rosenfeld, "The Long Right and the World it Made," pp. 60–62. Gingrich quote, cited by Schlozman and Rosen, is from Newt Gingrich, "The GOP Revolution Holds Powerful Lesson for Changing Washington," in *The Republican Revolution Ten Years Later: Smaller Government or Business as Usual?*, eds. Chris Edwards and John Samples (Washington: Cato Institute, 2005), p. 2.

29   In the decades since Ronald Reagan left the White House, the illiberals who purged and primaried all those who refused to join the "movement" have shifted the GOP far to the right; this was apparent before the emergence of the Tea Party. As detailed by Jacob Hacker and Paul Pierson in *Off Center* (2005), President George W. Bush and the congressional Republicans led by House Majority Leader Tom "the Hammer" DeLay leveraged tiny majorities in the House and Senate to push a hard right agenda. Jacob S. Hacker and Paul Pierson, *Off Center: The Republican Revolution and the Erosion of American Democracy* (New Haven, Conn.: Yale University Press, 2005).

30   According to University of California, Berkeley Law School Dean Erwin Chemerinsky, twenty-one of twenty-four justices nominated to the Supreme Court during the last year of a president's term have been confirmed by the U.S. Senate.

31   Kabaservice, *Rule and Ruin*, pp. 14–17, 25; Charles R. Kesler, *I Am the Change: Barack Obama and the Crisis of Liberalism* (New York: Broadside, 2012), pp. ix–xxi.

32   In his review of Will's *The Conservative Sensibility* (2019), Andrew Sullivan writes, "I found it just as interesting that Will now puts the 'Reagan Revolution' in quotation marks. Unlike so many others, he never fell for the idea that deficits don't matter, and correctly concludes that Reagan did not demand hard choices from self-governing citizens but instead promised them all the benefits of larger and larger government, without any of the fiscal costs. Those costs were to be sloughed off on future generations—a violation of any kind of responsible conservatism. But Will doesn't acknowledge that this was central to the revival of 'conservatism'—fiscal fecklessness that has now morphed into staggering levels of public debt—or ask himself if conservatism as properly understood could honestly sell restraint and austerity to a modern citizenry. Thatcher believed so; but Reagan sure didn't." Andrew Sullivan, "George Will's Eternal Truths," review of George Will, *The Conservative Sensibility*, *New York Times Book Review*, June 16, 2019, pp. 8–9.

33   Kesler, *I Am the Change*, pp. 57–63. Kesler speaks of modern liberalism as
      a Hegelian experiment in "endless State-building." George F. Will, *The
      Conservative Sensibility* (New York: Hachette, 2019).

34   Will, *The Conservative Sensibility*, p. xxviii.

35   For a critique of Presidents Woodrow Wilson, Franklin Roosevelt, Lyndon
      Johnson, and Barack Obama, see Kesler, *I Am the Change*, and Will, *The
      Conservative Sensibility*.

36   Sam Tanenhaus, *The Death of Conservatism* (New York: Random House, 2009).

37   Andrew Sullivan, "George Will's Eternal Truths," *New York Times*, June 16, 2019.

38   Max Boot, *The Corrosion of Conservatism: Why I Left the Right* (New York:
      Liveright, 2018), and Michael Lind, *Up From Conservatism: Why the Right is
      Wrong for America* (New York: Free Press, 1997).

39   Mann and Ornstein, *It's Even Worse Than It Looks*, p. 9. Emphasis added.

40   David Von Drehle, J. Newton-Small, S. Jewler, K. O'Leary, S. Yan, and W.
      Mallory, "Tea Party America," *Time*, Vol. 175, No. 8, pp. 26–31, March 1, 2010.
      Retrieved from EBSCOhost Academic Search Complete. My initial *Time* story
      appeared January 31, 2010, (Kevin O'Leary, "On Scene: With the Tea Party
      Patriots of Scottsdale"), http://www.time.com/time/politics
      /article/0,8599,1957726,00.html.

41   See Michael Tomasky, "Something New on the Mall," *New York Review of Books*
      (October 22, 2009). Tomasky points out that AFP appeared to be a key group
      involved in organizing protests and the disruption of congressional town halls
      discussing the Affordable Care Act in summer 2009, http://www.nybooks.com
      /articles/23150.

42   Quotes and interviews from Tea Party protest rally in front of Representative
      Harry Mitchell's office January 27, 2010 protest rally.

43   Elizabeth Price Foley, *The Tea Party: Three Principles* (Cambridge, UK:
      Cambridge University Press, 2012). However, I would place constitutional
      originalism in the illiberal, not conservative, camp.

44   Christopher S. Parker and Matt A. Barreto, *Change They Can't Believe In: The Tea
      Party and Reactionary Politics in America* (Princeton, N.J.: Princeton University
      Press, 2013), p. 35. They go on to write, "In the American context, racism, sexism,
      and the Protestant work ethic are all ideologies that serve to enhance hierarchy,
      legitimating discrimination as a means of maintaining a social order in which a
      group of dominants presides over subordinates." pp. 24 and 89–90.

45   Christopher Parker, "Race and the Tea Party: Who's Right?" *Salon*, May 3,
      2010, p. 2. http://www.salon.com/2010/05/03/race_and_the_tea_party/.
      Emphasis added. The link between support for small government and the desire
      by some whites not to have their taxes used in ways that might benefit blacks
      and other minorities was recognized in research about California's Proposition
      13 and other tax revolts around the nation in the late 1970s. David O. Sears and
      Jack Citrin, *Tax Revolt: Something for Nothing in California* (Cambridge, Mass.:
      Harvard University Press, 1982).

46   Alan Abramowitz, "Partisan Polarization and the Rise of the Tea Party
      Movement," APSA 2011 Annual Meeting Paper, September 2011, pp. 2, 5.

Emphasis added. Table showing five political activities: registering to vote, contacting a public official, giving money to a campaign, attending a rally /meeting, and displaying a sign/bumper sticker, on p. 24, http://papers.ssrn. com/sol3/Papers.cfm?abstract_id=1903153. Also see Abromowitz, *The Great Alignment.*

47   Like Parker, Abramowitz found Tea Party supporters scoring substantially higher on racial resentment survey questions than other Republicans. Abramowitz, "Partisan Polarization and the Rise of the Tea Party Movement," p. 12.

48   A modern Madison might argue that government should be designed to inhibit a relatively apathetic majority from forcing public policy down the throats of a relatively intense minority. Dahl, *A Preface to Democratic Theory*, p. 90.

49   http://www.ushistory.org/us/33b.asp.

50   For example, it is true that Donald Trump swept the field to become the 2016 presidential nominee of the Republican Party. But only a fraction of the public at large votes in presidential primaries, and Trump won many of the early contests against multiple opponents with 30 to 35 percent of the vote. Only in the later primaries did he break 40 and 50 percent. And this 40 to 50 percent of the Republican primary vote represents approximately a quarter of the adult voting population. Another example: According to the Yale Project on Climate Change Communication, the hard-core global warming deniers are approximately 15 percent of the nation's population. Neela Banerjee, "What do Americans think about global warming? Tony Leiserowitz can tell you. It's not what you might expect." *Yale Alumni Magazine* (January/February 2015), pp. 46–52. This loud, intense group, however, dominates the Republican Party and intimidates the so-called moderate conservatives, such as Jeb Bush, who ran for president in 2016. As the campaign began, the former Florida governor made sure that Republican voters knew that he was as skeptical about climate change as any of the illiberals to his right. Suzanne Goldenberg, "Jeb Bush may be 'the smart brother'—but he's as much of a climate denier as any conservative," *Guardian* (December 16, 2014), http://www.theguardian.com/commentisfree/2014/dec/16/jeb-bush -climate-denier-republican-presidential-candidate-2016#img-1.

51   E. J. Dionne Jr., "Mike Castle's Defeat—and the End of Moderate Republicanism," *Washington Post* op-ed, September 15, 2010. http://www.washingtonpost.com /wp-dyn/content/article/2010/09/15/AR2010091502969.html.

52   Tim Alberta, *American Carnage: On the Front Lines of the Republican Civil War and the Rise of President Trump* (New York: HarperCollins, 2019), pp. 64–67.

53   Dan Balz, "The real story in Texas primary is the ascendancy of Republican right wing," *Washington Post*, March 5, 2014. Emphasis added; http://www .washingtonpost.com/politics/the-real-story-in-texas-primary-is-the-ascendancy -of-gop-right-wing/2014/03/05/1010fb34-a48f-11e3-84d4-e59b1709222c _story.html.

54   Jon Herskovitz and Marice Richter, "Cruz steering Texas Republicans further right in primary fights," *Reuters*, March 3, 2014, http://www.reuters.com /article/2014/03/03/us-usa-politics-texas-idUSBREA221MW20140303.

55   The libertarian doctrine of Manchester liberalism, laissez-faire, and the monarchy
      of the market arrived in the United States after the publication of *The Communist
      Manifesto* in 1848 and Lenin unleashed the Russian Revolution in 1917.

56   McCoy, *The Elusive Republic.*

57   David Rogers, "*Politico* analysis: At \$2.3 trillion cost, Trump tax cuts leave big
      gap" *Politico*, February 28, 2018, https://www.politico.com/story/2018/02/28
      /tax-cuts-trump-gop-analysis-430781.

58   The public blamed the Republicans, and others in the GOP's congressional
      delegation were livid. "What he did was stood up for Ted and threw the
      Republican Party under the bus," said South Carolina Senator Lindsey Graham.
      Adele M. Stan, "The GOP's Primary Lesson: Be Careful What You Wish For,"
      American Prospect, April 6, 2016, quoting an interview on Fox News Radio's
      Kilmeade & Friends, http://prospect.org/article/gop's-primary-lesson-be
      -careful-what-you-wish.

59   Hayek is not as absolute as Spencer, Rand, or his apprentice, Milton Friedman,
      because he does allow for regulations for health and safety concerns to curb
      market operations. See *The Road to Serfdom*, pp. 86, 118.

60   This, in turn, perpetuates and strengthens norms of privilege and class
      advantage among the economic elite while at the same time undermining
      democratic values and stirring discontent among those excluded from enjoying
      the economic rewards of growth. Thomas Piketty, *Capital in the Twenty-First
      Century*, translated by Arthur Goldhammer (Cambridge, Mass.: Belknap Press
      /Harvard University Press, 2014).

61   Jonathan Chait, "Paul Ryan: No, I Want to Help the Poor! Really!" *New York*,
      October 24, 2012, http://nymag.com/daily/intelligencer/2012/10/paul-ryan-no
      -i-want-to-help-the-poor-really.html.

62   Meaning, the Constitution is "limited to the precise terms of the document,
      and nothing more." Jeffrey Toobin, "The Absolutist: Ted Cruz is an unyielding
      debater—and the far right's most formidable advocate" *New Yorker*, June 30,
      2014, http://www.newyorker.com/magazine/2014/06/30/the-absolutist-2.

63   Toobin, "The Absolutist," *New Yorker*, June 30, 2014. The quote from Dellinger
      goes on to say, "It's still around now. I think it's wrong, but Ted does a very
      sophisticated version of that view."

64   Matt Flegenheimer, "Ted Cruz's Conservatism: The Pendulum Swings
      Consistently Right," *New York Times*, April 17, 2016.

65   As a teenager, Ted Cruz earned money giving speeches on the free-market
      principles of Hayek and Mises to Rotary and Kiwanis clubs. See Ryan Lizza,
      "The Party Next Time: As immigration turns red states blue, how can
      Republicans transform their platform?" *New Yorker*, November 19, 2012,
      http://www.newyorker.com/magazine/2012/11/19/the-party-next-time.

      As the candidate of the Tea Party in the GOP primary for U.S. Senate in
      2012, Cruz sang the praises of the Milton Friedman. In his victory speech, Cruz
      told his supporters that he was "walking in Uncle Milton's footsteps," to honor the
      100th birthday of the Chicago School economist and Hayek disciple famous for
      his best seller, "Free to Choose." See Flegenheimer, "Ted Cruz's Conservatism."

66   Friedman, *Capitalism and Freedom.*

67   Jonathan Chait, "7 Ways Paul Ryan Revealed His Love for Ayn Rand," *New York*, July 10, 2014, http://nymag.com/daily/intelligencer/2014/07/7-ways-paul -ryan-revealed-his-love-for-ayn-rand.html.

68   "Paul Ryan and Ayn Rand's Ideas: In the hot seat again," a speech to The Atlas Society, April 30, 2012 (a full audio of Ryan's 2005 address), http://atlassociety .org/commentary/commentary-blog/4971-paul-ryan-and-ayn-rands-ideas -in-the-hot-seat-again.

69   Robert Greenstein, "Statement of Robert Greenstein, President, on Chairman Ryan's Budget Plan," Center on Budget and Policy Priorities, March 12, 2012, http://www.cbpp.org/press/statements/statement-of-robert-greenstein-president -on-chairman-ryans-budget-plan-0.

70   Robert Draper, *When the Tea Party Came to Town* (New York: Simon & Schuster, 2012), pp. 144, 140.

71   Greenstein, "Statement of Robert Greenstein, President, on Chairman Ryan's Budget Plan," Center on Budget and Policy Priorities, March 12, 2012. Emphasis added.

72   Ibid.

73   Ibid.

74   "A Budget That Promises Little But Pain," editorial, *New York Times* (May 23, 2017), https://www.nytimes.com/2017/05/23/opinion/trump-federal-budget .html?_r=0.

75   This is the argument of Heather Cox Richardson, *To Make Men Free: A History of the Republican Party* (New York: Basic, 2014), quote from p. xiii.

76   Fear of big government, as opposed to fear of big business or big labor, has escalated dramatically since the 1990s. In the 1970s and 1980s, from 30 to 51 percent of the public said they were most fearful of big government. It spiked to 65 percent of the public fearing big government as the "biggest threat to the country," with the Republican attacks on the Clinton administration. It shot up to 70-plus percent during President Obama's second term, with the emergence of the Tea Party and a mature right-wing noise machine shaping a substantial segment of public opinion. Graph of respondents answering "big government," "big labor," and "big business" as the "biggest threat facing the country." Data drawn from Gallup polls available at: http://www.gallup.com/file/poll/166568 /Greatest_Threat_131218.pdf. Cited in Grossmann and Hopkins, *Asymmetric Politics*, p. 60.

77   Jefferson Cowie, *The Great Exception: The New Deal & The Limits of American Politics* (Princeton, N.J.: Princeton University Press, 2016), p. 29.

78   Only during the New Deal did modern liberals accept Hamiltonian big government as the vital center of American politics. It was not that Franklin Roosevelt and his advisers worshiped statism and saw a powerful federal state as their goal. Rather, they grew to understand—as Herbert Croly had counseled Teddy Roosevelt in *The Promise of American Life* (1909)—that if large corporations were inevitable in a modern economy and breaking them up was economically unwise, then regulating them was the second-best option.

Only the federal government had the potential power and resources to play a
countervailing role to the corporations that dwarfed individual states.

79   See Galbraith, *The Predator State.*

80   Katznelson, *When Affirmative Action Was White.*

81   Liberals and conservatives understand that rights are secured by government.
Private property, for example, would not exist without a government to sanction
the idea and enforce its protection. While we might believe in pure rights as
an abstraction, in real life, people have rights, and are able to enjoy them, only
because of laws and government. Cass Sunstein writes that those "who object to
'government intervention' depend on it every day." Sunstein, *The Second Bill of
Rights*, pp. 11, 2, 24, 4.

82   Gary Gerstle, *Liberty and Coercion: The Paradox of American Government from the
Founding to the Present* (Princeton, N.J.: Princeton University Press, 2015).

83   Gerstle, *Liberty and Coercion*, pp. 23, 3, 287–295, 86.

84   Erwin Chemerinsky, *The Case Against the Supreme Court* (New York: Penguin,
2014), See Chapter 4, What About the Warren Court?, pp. 120–138. While the
Warren Court is widely viewed as liberal, many of its most important decisions
are today regarded as correct by legal scholars on the left and the right. In *Brown
v. Board of Education* (1954) the Court held that separate schools are inherently
unequal using the Equal Protection clause in the Fourteenth Amendment; *Brown*
began a train of cases in which the Supreme Court invalidated racial apartheid
in the South. *Baker v. Carr* (1962) proclaimed the doctrine of "one person, one
vote" to ensure that state legislatures redrew election districts so that the ballots
of every citizen would carry the same weight. Asserting the power of the central
government over the states, *Baker v. Carr* paved the way for the Voting Rights Act
of 1965. In *Loving v. Virginia* (1967), the Court ruled "Under our Constitution,
the freedom to marry, or not marry, a person of another race resides with the
individual and cannot be infringed by States." In criminal law, the Warren Court
ruled that the provisions of the Bill of Rights protecting criminal suspects and
defendants applied to state and local governments. In *Gideon v. Wainwright*
(1963), the Court held that all criminal defendants facing possible imprisonment
are entitled to a lawyer. In a criminal justice system in which an overwhelming
majority of cases result in guilty pleas—97 percent in federal courts and 94
percent in state courts—the presence of a defense attorney makes a great deal of
difference in the length of the sentence and the nature of the plea deal. In *Mapp
v. Ohio* (1961), the High Court held that the exclusionary rule—the principle that
evidence gained via an illegal search must be excluded from use against a criminal
defendant—applies to the states. In a series of other cases, the court ruled for the
Fifth Amendment's prohibition against double jeopardy and its protections against
self-incrimination; the Sixth Amendment's provisions for a trial by an impartial
jury, the right to confront adverse witnesses, and the right to subpoena witnesses
to testify; and the Eighth Amendment's prohibition against cruel and unusual
punishment be applied to the states. Famously, in *Miranda v. Arizona* (1966), the
court limited the coercive environment of arrest by insisting that the police remind
people of their rights to remain silent and be represented by an attorney.

NINE: DONALD J. TRUMP: REVIVAL OF THE SOUTHERN DEMAGOGUE

1   https://www.washingtonpost.com/opinions/global-opinions/mick-mulvaney
     -just-told-house-investigators-everything-they-need-to-know-about-trump-and
     -ukraine/2019/10/17/e756cb4c-f104-11e9-8693-f487e46784aa_story.html.

2   https://podcasts.apple.com/us/podcast/trumps-re-election-rally
     /id1200361736?i=1000442028359. Emphasis added.

3   A narcissist of massive proportions, Trump loves to dominate every news cycle.

4   See Neil Postman's savage indictment of how television and now 24/7 online
     news have driven sanity and reasoned discussion out of the serious business of
     politics. Neil Postman, *Amusing Ourselves to Death: Public Discourse in the Age
     of Show Business*, revised edition (New York: Penguin, 2004). Also see Nicholas
     Carr, *The Shallows: What the Internet is Doing to Our Brains* (New York: W.W.
     Norton, 2011).

5   "Trump Supporters Think Obama is A Muslim Born in Another Country,"
     Public Policy Polling, September 1, 2015, http://www.publicpolicypolling.com
     /main/2015/08/trump-supporters-think-obama-is-a-muslim-born-in-another
     -country.html.

6   "Trump, Clinton Continue to Lead in SC," Public Policy Polling, February 16,
     2016. http://www.publicpolicypolling.com/pdf/2015/PPP_Release_SC_21616.pdf.

7   https://www.nytimes.com/2019/07/14/us/politics/trump-twitter-squad
     -congress.html.

8   https://www.latimes.com/politics/la-na-pol-trump-reelection-kickoff-rally
     -arena-immigration-orlando-20190618-story.html; https://www.nytimes.com
     /2019/06/18/us/politics/donald-trump-rally-orlando.html. Emphasis added.

9   https://www.nytimes.com/2019/06/18/us/politics/donald-trump-rally-orlando.html.

10   https://www.washingtonpost.com/politics/2019/06/19/fact-checking-president
     -trumps-reelection-campaign-kickoff/?utm_term=.27f077592f97; https://www
     .cnn.com/2019/06/19/politics/fact-check-trump-orlando-rally/index.html.

11   https://podcasts.apple.com/us/podcast/trumps-re-election-rally/id1200361736?i
     =1000442028359.

12   https://www.nytimes.com/2019/07/23/us/politics/trump-working-class.html.

13   Paul Pierson, "American Hybrid: Donald Trump and the strange merger of
     populism and plutocracy," *British Journal of Sociology* 68 (2017): 105–119,
     https://onlinelibrary.wiley.com/doi/full/10.1111/1468-4446.12323.

14   https://www.nytimes.com/2019/06/17/opinion/trump-populist.html.

15   https://www.marketwatch.com/story/manufacturing-employment-in-the-us-is
     -at-the-same-level-of-69-years-ago-2019-01-04. Source of data: BLS/Haver
     Analytics.

16   https://www.nytimes.com/2019/06/24/us/politics/trump-manufacturing-jobs
     -2020.html.

17   https://www.factcheck.org/2018/01/manufacturing-jobs-roaring-back/.

18   Mark Twain, *The Adventures of Huckleberry Finn*, Third Norton Critical Edition,
     Edited by Thomas Cooley (New York: W.W. Norton, 1999), Chapter XXII–XXIII,
     pp. 165–67.

19   https://www.nytimes.com/2019/06/18/us/politics/michael-savage-trump.html.

20   Reported by Garry Wills in "The Politics of Grievance," *New York Review of Books*, July 19, 1990. Cited by Schlozman and Rosenfeld, "The Long New Right and the World It Made," p. 7.

21   Alan I. Abramowitz and Steven Webster, "The rise of negative partisanship and the nationalization of U.S. elections in the 21st century," *Electoral Studies* 41 (2016), p. 14.

22   Mark Z. Barabak, "Trump may pay price for his suburban blight: Defection of female Republicans over his presidency puts states like Arizona in play," *Los Angeles Times*, November 29, 2019, https://www.latimes.com/politics/story /2019-11-29/2020-battleground-suburban-women-voters.

23   Abramowitz and Webster, "The rise of negative partisanship and the nationalization of U.S. elections in the 21st century," p. 15.

24   Interview with Hodding Carter III, May 13, 2016.

25   http://time.com/3923128/donald-trump-announcement-speech/.

26   On disenfranchisement see Perman, *The Struggle for Mastery*.

27   Hodding Carter interview.

28   I am indebted to Robert Kuttner for these observations on Wallace's 1968 campaign.

29   Interview with Ferrel Guillory, May 9, 2016.

30   Eugene Robinson speaking on *Hardball with Chris Matthews* on MSNBC, May 12, 2016. In a March column, he wrote, "Trump doesn't tweet dog whistles, he blasts foghorns." Eugene Robinson, "Trump's dangerous dance with bigotry," *Washington Post*, March 3, 2016. https://www.washingtonpost.com /opinions/trumps-dance-with-bigotry/2016/03/03/d78f735a-e17f-11e5-8d98 -4b3d9215ade1_story.html.

31   James K. Vardaman, Wikipedia profile, http://en.wikipedia.org/wiki/James _K._Vardaman.

32   Bruce Bartlett, *Wrong on Race: The Democratic Party's Buried Past* (New York: Palgrave Macmillan, 2009), p. 71. Original diction.

33   James K. Vardaman, Wikipedia profile, http://en.wikipedia.org/wiki/James _K._Vardaman.

34   Scher, *Politics in the New South*, pp. 58, 53.

35   Ibid., p. 58.

36   See Hochschild, *Strangers in Their Own Land*.

37   Scher, *Politics in the New South*, p. 59.

38   Ibid., p. 59.

39   Interview with Representative David Price, May 5, 2016.

40   Interview with Reverend Dr. William J. Barber II, May 6, 2016.

41   The strategy of the reactionary program to secure the white working-class vote is familiar: Weaken the unions, as Governor Scott Walker did in Wisconsin; take aggressive steps to eliminate Democrats from the voting rolls; and vilify liberals, minorities, women, and immigrants to turn out a solid base.

42   In *The Two Reconstructions* (2004), Swarthmore political scientist Richard Valelly argued that it was strong support across both the courts and parties (specifically the Democratic Party) that allowed the second Reconstruction to

become institutionalized and durable. Whereas the original Reconstruction was destroyed in 1876 by a cynical alliance between a resurgent Southern planter class and Northern Democrats, it seemed as if the modern civil rights movement had moved the nation into a new era. The culmination of America's new maturity on race was the election of Barack Obama. Richard M. Valelly, *The Two Reconstructions: The Struggle for Black Enfranchisement* (Chicago: University of Chicago Press, 2004).

43   Representative David Price interview.

44   Charles S. Bullock III and Ronald Keith Gaddie, *The Triumph of Voting Rights in the South* (Norman: University of Oklahoma Press, 2009), pp. 77, 162. The exception to the rule is Virginia, whose Northern suburbs are distinctly non-Southern, and where former Governor Mark Warner claimed an open Virginia Senate seat in 2008 winning with 64 percent that included an impressive 56 percent of the white vote.

45   Valelly, *The Two Reconstructions*, p. 3.

46   The Brennan Center for Justice at New York University has estimated that the changes put in place in just 2011 and 2012 have made it "significantly harder for 5 million citizens to vote." Michael Waldman, *The Fight to Vote* (New York: Simon & Schuster, 2016), p. 205.

47   William Barber II, "The Retreat From Voting Rights," *New York Times*, op-ed, April 28, 2016, http://www.nytimes.com/2016/04/28/opinion/the-retreat-from -voting-rights.html?_r=0.

48   Others have tried to explain the GOP's continuing shift to the right over the past four decades. For example, E. J. Dionne argues that having been repeatedly frustrated by the empty promises of conservative elected officials saying they will go to Washington and cut government down to size, the GOP base responds to false promises by moving to the right and hoping for a messiah who will match deeds to words. Certainly, this action-reaction paradigm is at work, but the deeper dynamic is the one described in this book. E. J. Dionne Jr., *Why the Right Went Wrong: Conservatives from Goldwater to the Tea Party and Beyond* (New York: Simon & Schuster, 2016).

49   In academic circles this is called "path dependency." See Paul Pierson, "Increasing Returns, Path Dependence, and the Study of Politics," *American Political Science Review* 94 (June 2000): pp. 251–267. https://doi. org/10.2307/2586011, and Paul Pierson, *Politics in Time: History, Institutions, and Social Analysis* (Princeton, N.J.: Princeton University Press, 2004), and Jeffrey Haydu, "Reversal of Fortune: path dependency, problem solving, and temporal cases," *Theory and Society*, (2010) 39: p. 25, https://doi.org/10.1007 /s11186-009-9098-0.

50   Galbraith, *The Predatory State*.

51   Since the Reagan revolution, reactionaries successfully tilted the "balance of benefits and protections away from ordinary Americans" and toward the affluent and financial elite who constitute the core of the GOP base. Hacker and Pierson, *Off Center*, pp. 14–15.

52   https://www.newyorker.com/news/george-packer/irving-kristols-long-strange-trip.

53   Hailing from Texas, a state with a weak, emasculated public sector similar to most Southern states, Bush was the first Southern Republican president. See Michael Lind, *Made in Texas: George W. Bush and the Southern Takeover of American Politics* (New York: Basic, 2002). His rise to power coincided with the elevation of Southern reactionaries in Congress such as Gingrich, House Majority Leader Tom DeLay (Texas), and Senate Republican leader Mitch McConnell (Kentucky).

54   Hacker and Pierson, *Off Center*, pp. 9–10.

55   Christine Todd Whitman, *It's My Party Too: The Battle for the Heart of the GOP and the Future of America* (New York: Penguin, 2005). Quoted by Hacker and Pierson, *Off Center*, p. 4.

56   Alberta, *American Carnage*, p. 164.

57   Durham, *The Christian Right, the far right and the boundaries of American conservatism*, Chapter 8 Pat Buchanan and the Post-Reagan Right, p. 161.

58   https://buchanan.org/blog/1992-republican-national-convention-speech-148.

59   Schlozman and Rosenfeld, "The Long Right and the World It Made," p. 65.

60   Patrick J. Buchanan, *Right From the Beginning* (New York: Little, Brown, 1988), p. 306.

61   https://www.newsweek.com/why-buchanan-so-angry-197834.

62   Michael Brendan Dougherty, *The Castaway*, America's Future Foundation, January 14, 2007, https://americasfuture.org/the-castaway/.

63   Durham, *The Christian Right, the far right and the boundaries of American conservatism*, Chapter 8 Pat Buchanan and the Post-Reagan Right, pp. 154–155. Durham quotes David Brooks, "Buchananism: An Intellectual Cause," *Weekly Standard*, 11, March 17–21, (1996).

64   D. C. Denison, "Patrick Buchanan: The Interview," *Boston Globe Magazine*, June 12, 1988, quoted by Schlozman and Rosenfeld, "The Long Right and the World It Made," p. 65.

65   Samuel Francis, *Beautiful Losers: Essays on the Failure of American Conservatism* (Columbia: University of Missouri Press, 1993), p. 142.

66   Ibid.

67   Timothy Shenk, "The dark history of Donald Trump's rightwing revolt: The Republican intellectual establishment is united against Trump—but this message of cultural and racial resentment has deep roots in the American right," *Guardian*, August 16, 2016, https://www.theguardian.com/news/2016/aug/16/secret-history-trumpism-donald-trump.

68   Schlozman and Rosenfeld, "The Long Right and the World It Made," p. 76.

69   https://www.washingtonpost.com/archive/local/2005/02/26/conservative-writer-samuel-t-francis/8f0d59be-94fe-43ec-93ce-0d24676cb608/.

70   Francis, *Beautiful Losers*, pp. 2–3, 9, 220, 230.

71   https://www.theguardian.com/news/2016/aug/16/secret-history-trumpism-donald-trump.

72   Francis, *Beautiful Losers*, pp. 31–32.

73   https://www.theguardian.com/news/2016/aug/16/secret-history-trumpism-donald-trump.

74   Ibid.

75   Samuel Francis, "From Household to Nation: The Middle American Populism of Pat Buchanan," *Chronicle Magazine*, February 1, 1996, https://www .chroniclesmagazine.org/1996/March/20/3/magazine/article/10838366/.

76   Ruy Teixeira and Joel Rogers, *America's Forgotten Majority: Why the White Working Class Still Matters* (New York: Basic, 2000) and John Judis and Ruy Teixeira, *The Emerging Democratic Majority* (New York: Scribner, 2002).

77   Michael Brendan Dougherty, *The Castaway*, America's Future Foundation, January 14, 2007, https://americasfuture.org/the-castaway/.

78   Rick Perlstein, *Nixonland: The Rise of a President and the Fracturing of America* (New York: Scribner, 2007).

79   https://www.theguardian.com/news/2016/aug/16/ secret-history-trumpism-donald-trump.

80   Francis, *Beautiful Losers*, "The Secret of the Twentieth Century," p. 206.

81   Ibid., p. 26.

82   Francis, "From Household to Nation."

83   Michael Brendan Dougherty, *The Castaway*, America's Future Foundation, January 14, 2007, https://americasfuture.org/the-castaway/.

84   Francis, *Beautiful Losers*, "Message From MARs: The Social Politics of the New Right," p. 75.

85   David Brooks, "The Coming War on Business," *New York Times*, September 22, 2017, https://www.nytimes.com/2017/09/22/opinion/business-war-trump.html. Dinesh D'Souza, "Racism: It's a White (and Black) Thing," *Washington Post*, September 24, 1995, https://www.washingtonpost.com/archive/opinions/1995 /09/24/racism-its-a-white-and-black-thing/46284ab5-417c-4c0c-83e1 -029d51655d91/.

86   https://www.chroniclesmagazine.org/about/; Michael Brendan Dougherty, *The Castaway*, America's Future Foundation, January 14, 2007, https://americas future.org/the-castaway/; https://www.splcenter.org/fighting-hate/extremist -files/group/occidental-quarterly.

87   Jerry Woodruff, Editor, Middle American News, book blurb for Samuel T. Francis, *Essential Writings on Race*, edited and introduced by Jared Taylor (Oakton, Va.: New Century Foundation, 2007).

88   https://en.wikipedia.org/wiki/Samuel_T._Francis.

89   Grover Norquist, "Remarks to the American Conservative Union," February 11, 2012, https://www.c-span.org/video/?304376-9/grover-norquist-remarks. Emphasis added. To be fair, Norquist argued that this is the job of any president, Republican or Democrat. Still, it is striking that a sophisticated political operative such as Norquist would endorse the "warm body" theory of the presidency for the world's leading democracy.

90   https://www.washingtonpost.com/opinions/trump-has-a-dangerous-disability /2017/05/03/56ca6118-2f6b-11e7-9534-00e4656c22aa_story.html?utm_term =.b914628dc1da.

91   https://www.nytimes.com/2019/07/05/us/politics/trump-airports-revolutionary -war.html. Emphasis added.

92   Thomas Frank, *The Wrecking Crew: How Conservatives Ruined Government, Enriched Themselves, and Beggared the Nation* (New York: Metropolitan, 2008).

93   Jan Jones, "Nihilistic Sentiments," *Lethbridge Undergraduate Research Journal*, Vol. 3, No. 1, 2008, https://lurj.org/issues/volume-1-number-1/nihilist.

94   http://www.pbs.org/newshour/rundown/ justice-souters-old-warning-finds-new-life-election/.

TEN: AMERICA'S REACTIONARY REVOLUTION

1   Crane Brinton, *The Anatomy of Revolution* [1938] revised and expanded edition (New York: Vintage, 1965), p. 24. The French Revolution set the template for subsequent revolutions with its rapid movement from a decaying Old Order to a moderate revolution and regime, to radicals seizing control and the escalation of violence in the Terror, to the overthrow of Robespierre and the Jacobins in the Thermidor counterrevolution, so named because of the Jacobins' downfall on 9 Thermidor year II (July 27, 1794, in the French republican calendar).

2   Some argue that the Southern elite joined the revolution because they feared that abolition would be successful in England and they wanted no part of it.

3   For example, in *Federalist* No. 10 and 49, Madison wrote about the importance of protecting republican government from immediate popular influence fueled by passion instead of reason. In *Federalist* No. 10, Madison said representative government at the federal level would "refine and enlarge the public views, by passing them through the medium of a chosen body of citizens, whose wisdom may best discern the true interest of their country, and whose patriotism and love of justice will be least likely to sacrifice it to temporary or partial considerations." Alexander Hamilton, James Madison, and John Jay, *The Federalist Papers*, introduction by Clinton Rossiter (New York: New American Library, 1961).

4   Drew R. McCoy, *The Last of the Fathers: James Madison and the Republican Legacy* (New York: Cambridge University Press, 1989), pp. 50–60.

5   William W. Freehling, "The Founding Fathers, Conditional Antislavery, and the Nonradicalism of the American Revolution," in Freehling, *The Reintegration of American History*, p. 13.

6   http://www.nytimes.com/2012/04/03/science/civil-war-toll-up-by-20-percent -in-new-estimate.html.

7   A column by E. J. Dionne Jr. highlights one aspect of the counterrevolution's anti-democratic nature. https://www.washingtonpost.com/opinions/what -unites-trumps-apologists-minority-rule/2019/11/24/152c5d06-0d6c-11ea-97ac -a7ccc8dd1ebc_story.html.

8   For examples of racism and violence against blacks in the northern cities see Carol Anderson, *White Rage: The Unspoken Truth of Our Racial Divide* (New York: Bloomsbury, 2016).

9   Wood, *The Radicalism of the American Revolution*.

10   Tanenhaus, *The Death of Conservatism*, p. 15. Tanenhaus credits conservative political scientist Willmoore Kendall, "The Civil Rights Movement and the Coming of the Constitutional Crisis," for making this observation. Willmoore

Kendall, *Willmoore Kendall Contra Mundum*, editor Nellie Kendall (Lanham, Md.: University Press of America, 1994).

11 Boot, *The Corrosion of Conservatism*, p. xxi.

12 Nate Cohn and Alicia Parlapiano, "Trump's Coalition: Broad, Loyal and Conflicted," *New York Times*, August 10, 2018, https://www.nytimes.com /interactive/2018/08/09/upshot/trump-voters-how-theyve-changed.html?em _pos=small&ref=headline&nl_art=1&te=1&nl=upshot&emc=edit_up_20180810.

13 https://www.washingtonpost.com/news/monkey-cage/wp/2017/06/05/its-time -to-bust-the-myth-mo.st-trump-voters-were-not-working-class/.

14 Ta-Nehisi Coates, "The First White President: The Foundation of Donald Trump's presidency is the negation of Barack Obama's legacy," *Atlantic* (October 2017), https://www.theatlantic.com/magazine/archive/2017/10/the-first-white -president-ta-nehisi-coates/537909/.

15. https://www.theatlantic.com/magazine/archive/2017/10/the-first-white -president-ta-nehisi-coates/537909/.

16 https://www.wsj.com/articles/white-house-moves-testing-republican-support -for-trump-11571614388.

17 Serwer, "The Nationalist's Delusion," *Atlantic* (November 2017), https://www .theatlantic.com/politics/archive/2017/11/the-nationalists-delusion/546356/. While millennials as a whole lean Democratic, a majority of young white men identify as Republicans and more than half of white millennials believe that discrimination against whites is as significant as against other groups; https://www .washingtonpost.com/news/politics/wp/2018/03/21/a-bright-spot-for -republicans-among-millennials-young-white-men/?utm_term=.d97f9eb88957.

18 Putting the point bluntly, Coates writes, "Not every Trump voter is a white supremacist. But every Trump voter felt it acceptable to hand the fate of the country over to one." https://www.theatlantic.com/magazine/archive/2017/10 /the-first-white-president-ta-nehisi-coates/537909/.

19 Samuel P. Huntington, *American Politics: The Promise of Disharmony* (Cambridge, Mass.: Belknap Press/Harvard University Press, 1983).

20 Hartz, *The Liberal Tradition in America* counseled that Americans continually think of their political opponents as being extreme when, in fact, they are moderate and restrained compared to the real extremes on display in other nations.

21 https://www.nytimes.com/2016/12/16/business/dealbook/women-majority-of-us -law-students-first-time.html. Vivia Chen, "Female Equity Partner Rate is At All-Time High. (But It's Not That Great.): The National Association of Women Lawyers just released its annual report. And the news flash is this: It's not totally depressing. Women now represent . . ." *Law.com*, September 20, 2017, https://www .law.com/sites/almstaff/2017/09/18/female-equity-partner-rate-is-at-all-time-high -but-its-not-that-great/.

22 Coates, *Between the World and Me*, pp. 20, 26.

23 Du Bois, *Black Reconstruction in America 1860–1880*, p. 700.

24 My analysis draws on Princeton historian Arno Mayer, *Dynamics of Counterrevolution in Europe, 1870–1956: An Analytic Framework* (New York:

Harper Torchbooks, 1971). The goal of the reactionary is to preserve the privilege and power of society's traditional elite.

25 For one reading of reactionary thinking across the centuries see Robin, *The Reactionary Mind*.

26 Woodward, *Origins of the New South 1877–1913*.

27 Brinton, *The Anatomy of Revolution*, Chapters 5–6. Scholars pointing to Brinton's continuing relevance include Bailey Stone, *The Anatomy of Revolution Revisited: A Comparative Analysis of England, France and Russia* (New York: Cambridge University Press, 2014) and Michael Kimmel, *Revolution: A Sociological Interpretation* (Philadelphia: Temple University Press, 1990).

28 Alan Serwer, "The Nationalist's Delusion," *Atlantic* (November 2017), https://www.theatlantic.com/politics/archive/2017/11/the-nationalists-delusion/546356/.

29 James Miller, *"Democracy is in the Streets": From Port Huron to the Siege of Chicago* (New York: Touchstone, 1988).

30 See Moore, *Social Origins of Dictatorship and Democracy*.

31 For influential interpretations see Albert Soboul, *A Short History of the French Revolution 1789–1799* (Berkeley: University of California Press, 1977) and Simon Schama, *Citizens: A Chronicle of the French Revolution* (New York: Knopf, 1989). More recently, see Jonathan Israel, *Revolutionary Ideas: An Intellectual History of the French Revolution from the Rights of Man to Robespierre* (Princeton, N.J.: Princeton University Press, 2014) and the exchange between David Bell and Israel, David Bell, "A Very Different French Revolution," *New York Review of Books*, July 10, 2014 and "The French Revolution: An Exchange," *New York Review of Books*, October 9, 2104.

32 Moore, *Social Origins of Dictatorship and Democracy*, p. 38.

33 The famous marriage of iron and rye, a coalition of the landed elite and industrial interests "around a program of imperialism and reaction," resulted in disaster for German democracy and tragedy for European civilization. Moore, *Social Origins*, p. 38.

34 Moore, *Social Origins*, pp. 111–112.

35 Lynd, "Rethinking Slavery and Reconstruction," p. 201.

36 Moore, *Social Origins*, p. 153. In rough outline, Russia faced this dilemma at the start of the 20th century.

37 John Hope Franklin, *Reconstruction After the Civil War*, second edition (Chicago: University of Chicago Press, 1994), p. 214.

38 https://historycollection.co/10-famous-companies-collaborated-nazi-germany/7/; https://allthatsinteresting.com/major-brands-nazi-collaborators. On Koch Industries, see Jane Mayer, *Dark Money: The Hidden History of the Billionaires Behind the Rise of the Radical Right* (New York: Doubleday, 2016), "Fred Koch's willingness to work with the Soviets and the Nazis was a major factor in creating the Koch family's early fortune" and Fred Koch's company Winkler-Koch built the third largest oil refinery in the Third Reich in 1935. This was significant because it was one of the few refineries in Germany that could produce the high-octane gasoline needed to fuel fighter planes, from Chapter 1 "Radicals: A Koch Family History," pp. 30–31.

39   From the back cover of Noel Ignatiev, *How the Irish Became White* [1995] (New York: Routledge Classics, 2009).

40   https://www.motherjones.com/politics/2012/09/full-transcript-mitt-romney -secret-video/.

41   Lindblom, *Politics and Markets* and Ann Crittenden, The 'Veto Power' of Big Business, *New York Times*, January 29, 1978, https://www.nytimes.com /1978/01/29/archives/the-veto-power-of-big-business-business-under-fire.html.

42   Ruchir Sharma, "Why Wall Street Loves Strongmen," *New York Times*, September 27, 2019. Examining the records for 150 countries between 1950 and 2010, the author found "43 cases in which an economy grew at an annual pace of 7 percent or more for a full decade. An astonishing 35 of those economies— more than 80 percent of them—were run by an autocrat." https://www.nytimes .com/2019/09/27/opinion/why-wall-street-loves-strongmen.html.

43   Phillips-Fein, *Invisible Hands* and Mayer, *Dark Money.*

44   Given a face by Charles and David Koch, the libertarian 1 percent has followed a disciplined, sophisticated political strategy: Funding think tanks, public intellectuals, and grassroots organizations; focusing not just on congressional and presidential races but on expanding a citadel of red states to control redistricting and nurture future political talent. For example, the Cato Institute is devoted to disseminating Charles Koch's strict libertarian vision: the government's only legitimate role is to "serve as a night watchman, to protect individuals and property from outside threat, including fraud. That is the maximum" as Koch told the Wichita Rotary Club before the Reagan revolution. Quote from Mayer, *Dark Money*, p. 88. See also Theda Skocpol and Alexander Hertel-Fernandez, "The Koch Network and Republican Party Extremism," (2016) *Perspectives on Politics* 14 (3): pp. 681–99. https://www.cambridge.org/core/services/aop-cambridge -core/content/view/035F3D872B0CE930AF02D7706DF46EEE /S1537592716001122a.pdf/koch_network_and_republican_party_extremism.pdf.

45   Thomas B. Edsall, *Building Red America: The New Conservative Coalition and the Drive for Permanent Power* (New York: Basic, 2006), pp. 15, 35. Hacker and Pierson, *Off Center* and Tom Hamburger and Paul Wallsten, *One Party Country: The Republican Plan for Dominance in the 21st Century* (New York: John Wiley & Sons, 2006) make similar points about the illiberal drive for power.

46   Karen Stenner, *The Authoritarian Dynamic* (New York: Cambridge University Press, 2005), p. 1. Emphasis added.

47   This psychological predisposition is more than a personal distaste for difference. Instead, it is a worldview about the proper balance of obedience and conformity, freedom and difference, group authority and individual autonomy, and the appropriate uses and limits that should be placed on authority. Norm enforcers who despise nonconformist rule breakers, authoritarians cheerlead those in power. In presenting social science evidence that many people have a hard time with racial diversity, civil liberties, disorder, variety, and moral freedom, Stenner is not making a moral claim. Karen Stenner, "Three Kinds of 'Conservatism,'" *Psychological Inquiry*, 20, 2009, pp. 143, 145, and 150 and Stenner and Haidt, "Authoritarianism is Not a Momentary Madness," p. 183.

48   A survey across 29 democracies just after Trump's election victory in the United
      States and the Brexit vote in Britain and just prior to the French presidential
      election featuring the candidacy of Marine Le Pen found "about a third of white
      responders" to be predisposed to support authoritarian leaders in a time of real
      or perceived threat. Stenner and Haidt, "Authoritarianism is Not a Momentary
      Madness," p. 192.

49   Jonathan Haidt says, it is "as though a button is pushed on their forehead that
      says 'in case of moral threat, lock down the borders, kick out those who are
      different, and punish those who are morally deviant.'" https://righteousmind.
      com/the-key-to-trump-is-stenners-authoritarianism/.

50   Stenner, "Three Kinds of 'Conservatism,'" p. 154.

51   Ibid., p. 150.

52   Ibid., p. 152. Emphasis added.

53   https://psmag.com/news/
      authoritarianism-the-terrifying-trait-that-trump-triggers.

54   Steven Levitsky and Daniel Ziblatt, "Is Our Democracy in Danger?" *New York
      Times*, December 18, 2017.

55   Robert Mickey, Steven Levitsky, and Lucan Ahmad Way, "Is America Still Safe
      for Democracy? Why the United States Is in Danger of Backsliding," *Foreign
      Affairs*, May/June 2017, pp. 24, 27.

56   Juan J. Linz, *Crisis, Breakdown, & Reequilibration*, Vol. 1 *The Breakdown of
      Democratic Regimes*, edited by Juan J. Linz and Alfred Stepan (Baltimore: Johns
      Hopkins University Press, 1978), p. 17. Emphasis added.

57   https://www.washingtonpost.com/politics/office-of-special-counsel-
      recommends-removal-of-kellyanne-conway-from-federal-office-for-violating
      -the-hatch-act/2019/06/13/0786ae2e-8df4-11e9-8f69-a2795fca3343_story
      .html?utm_term=.b120cf7dab90; https://www.washingtonpost.com/politics
      /2019/06/13/what-is-hatch-act-why-did-kellyanne-conway-get-accused
      -violating-it-so-egregiously/?utm_term=.555cfe7eb7cd.

58   Masha Gessen, "Incompetence Won't Save Our Democracy," Sunday Review,
      New York Times, June 4, 2017. https://www.nytimes.com/2017/06/02/opinion
      /sunday/trumps-incompetence-wont-save-our-democracy.html?_r=0.

59   Karl Dietrich Bracher, *The German Dictatorship: The Origins, Structure, and
      Effects of National Socialism*, translated from the German by Jean Steinberg, with
      an introduction by Peter Gay (New York: Praeger Publishers, 1970).

60   This paragraph draws on Carlos de la Torre, "Will Democracy Survive Trump's
      Populism? Latin America May Tell Us," *New York Times*, December 15, 2016,
      and Carlos de la Torre, *Populist Seduction in Latin America*, second edition
      (Athens: Ohio University Press, 2010).

61   Jeremy Peters, "Trump Keeps His Conservative Movement Allies Closest," *New
      York Times*, August 2, 2017. https://www.nytimes.com/2017/08/02/us/politics
      /trump-conservative-republicans.html. See also https://www.politico.com
      /story/2017/04/trump-republican-party-takeover-states-237075.

62   https://news.gallup.com/poll/203198/presidential-approval-ratings-donald
      -trump.aspx.

63   For example, only four House Republicans voted with Democrats to condemn President Trump's racist tweet against four minority congresswomen. https://www.nytimes.com/2019/07/16/us/politics/republicans-who-voted-for-resolution.html.

64   Yascha Mounk, "Trump is Destroying Our Democracy," *New York Times*, August 1, 2017.

65   Christopher H. Achen and Larry M. Bartels, *Democracy for Realists: Why Elections Do Not Produce Responsive Government* (Princeton, N.J.: Princeton University Press, 2016), and Suzanne Mettler, "Democracy on the Brink: Protecting the Republic in Trump's America," *Foreign Affairs*, May/June 2017, pp. 122–123.

66   Embracing liberal goals while navigating the fears of working-class whites that they are losing the country they knew is a delicate political task, but it can and must be done by Democrats. See suggestive essay, Franklin Foer's "What's Wrong With the Democrats?" *Atlantic*, July/August 2017.

67   Michael Ignatieff, *Blood and Belonging: Journeys into the New Nationalism* (New York: Farrar, Straus and Giroux, 1995).

68   Hochschild, *Strangers in Their Own Land*, "Trump is an 'emotions candidate.' More than any other candidate in decades, Trump focuses on eliciting and praising emotional responses from his fans rather than detailed policy prescriptions. His speeches—evoking dominance, bravado, clarity, national pride, and personal uplift—inspire an emotional transformation," p. 225.

69   Edmund Burke, *Reflections on the Revolution in France*, p. 183. "[B]ecause prejudice, with its reason, has a motive to give action to that reason, and an affection which will give it permanence."

CONCLUSION: LIBERALS ANSWER BACK

1   J. G. A. Pocock, "Political thought in the English-speaking Atlantic, 1760–1790, Part 2: Empire, revolution and the end of early modernity," in *The Varieties of British Political Thought, 1500–1800*, edited by J. G. A. Pocock with the assistance of Gordon J. Schochet and Lois G. Schwoerer (New York: Cambridge University Press, 1993), note on p. 283.

2   As one example, see Robert Kuttner, *Obama's Challenge: America's Economic Crisis and the Power of a Transformative Presidency* (White River Junction, Vt.: Chelsea Green Publishing, 2008).

3   See Taylor, *American Made: The Enduring Legacy of the WPA*.

4   Jonathan Alter, *The Promise: President Obama, Year One* (New York: Simon & Schuster, 2010), p. 86.

5   See Skocpol, *Obama and America's Political Future*.

6   https://theweek.com/speedreads/852099/trump-just-joked-about-being-president-life--6th-time; https://www.nytimes.com/2019/07/12/opinion/trump-pompeo-human-rights.html.

7   Richard E. Neustadt, *Presidential Power and the Modern Presidents: The Politics of Leadership from Roosevelt to Reagan*, revised ed. (New York: Free Press, 1991).

8   My view of presidential dynasties builds from Stephen Skowronek, *The Politics Presidents Make: Leadership from John Adams to Bill Clinton*, revised ed.

(Cambridge, Mass.: Belknap Press/Harvard University Press, 1997) *Presidential Leadership in Political Time: Reprise and Reappraisal?* second edition, revised and expanded (Lawrence: University Press of Kansas, 2011).

9　Making their position more secure, elite reactionaries realize that many Americans resist criticizing the upper crust because, even as the middle-class dream deteriorates for many, the Horatio Alger myth of striking it rich has an allure for Americans of both illiberal and liberal persuasions.

10　Arthur Schlesinger Jr. argued that the business class is a bad bet for political leadership because it lacks a fundamental commitment to the national interest. His argument is particularly relevant today. To date, a majority of America's business elite and managerial class have stayed loyal to the GOP because of the right's promise of lower taxes and less regulation. Schlesinger, *The Vital Center,* pp. 24–25: "power gravitates to business as the strongest economic group in society; but it has never been able to use that power long for national purposes."

11　O'Leary, *Saving Democracy.*

12　See Michael Lind, "How the South Skews America: We'd be less violent, more mobile and in general more normal if not for Dixie," *Politico Magazine,* July 3, 2015, http://www.politico.com/magazine/story/2015/07/how-the-south-skews -america-119725.html.

13　http://en.wikipedia.org/wiki/List_of_automotive_assembly_plants_in_the _United_States.

14　Bernie Sanders's 2016 presidential campaign, Michael Moore's film *Where to Invade Next,* and Thomas Geoghegan's *Were You Born on the Wrong Continent?: How the European Model Can Help You Get a Life* (New York: New Press, 2011), speak to this point.

15　Abromowitz, *The Great Alignment.*

16　See Benjamin Ginsberg and Martin Shefter, *Politics by Other Means: The Declining Importance of Elections in America* (New York: Basic, 1991).

17　Using the extraordinary powers of the Senate minority in an extraordinary way was one path the illiberal right followed to derail the Obama presidency. The orgy of filibusters continued well into Obama's second term until the Democratic chief, Senate Majority Leader Harry Reid, finally had had enough and took the extraordinary action to modify the filibuster rule. Beginning in 2011, the Tea Party wing in the House, sometimes with then Speaker John Boehner's approval and sometimes with a rejection of his proposals, followed the same approach even more rigidly than the Senate, in which the number of filibusters, threatened filibusters, and cloture votes in the early Obama years spiked exponentially compared to past Congresses.

18　Jon Meacham speaking on *The 11th Hour with Brian Williams,* December 13, 2019, http://www.msnbc.com/transcripts/11th-hour-with-brian-williams/2019-12-13.

19　For a prescient early report on this goal see William Greider, "Rolling Back the Twentieth Century: The right-wing ideologues are dead serious about dismantling government," *Nation,* May 12, 2003, http://www.thenation.com /article/rolling-back-20th-century.

20   Famously, FEMA director Michael Brown was praised by President George W.
        Bush—"Brownie, you're doing a heck of a job"—during the disastrous federal
        response to Hurricane Katrina in 2004.

21   Frank, *The Wrecking Crew.*

22   The culture wars are one way of speaking about the liberal versus illiberal
        divide. However, this concept is limited because it applies to social issues as
        opposed to economics. We need a broader frame of reference. James Davison
        Hunter, a University of Virginia sociologist, introduced the phrase "culture
        wars" and it quickly became media shorthand for the differing values that divide
        Americans. Some analysts, such as Thomas Frank, argue that an irrational
        fixation on social issues causes some people to vote against their (economic)
        self-interest. See James Davison Hunter, *Culture Wars: The Struggle to Define
        America* (New York: Basic, 1992) and Thomas Frank, *What's the Matter with
        Kansas?: How Conservatives Won the Heart of America* (New York: Metropolitan,
        2004). More recently, see Daniel T. Rodgers, *Age of Fracture* (Cambridge, Mass.:
        Belknap Press/Harvard University Press, 2011).

23   Tocqueville, *Democracy in America*, Vol. 1, Part II, Chapter 9 "The Main Causes
        Tending to Maintain A Democratic Republic in the United States."

24   Jonathan Swift, "A Tale of a Tub" in *The Essential Writings of Jonathan Swift,*
        Norton Critical Edition, edited by Claude Rawson and Ian Higgins (New York:
        W.W. Norton, 2010), p. 17. "Books, like Men their Authors, have no more than
        one Way of coming into the World, but there are ten Thousand to go out of it,
        and return no more."

25   Schlesinger, *The Vital Center*, pp. xvii, 13.

26   David Harvey, *A Brief History of Neoliberalism* (New York: Oxford University
        Press, 2005).

27   John Dewey's democracy theory, never articulated in one place but spread across
        his work, is based on the realization of five values—individuality, equality,
        community, intelligence, and the public good. He puts forth a civic republican-
        liberal understanding of democracy that conceives of democracy not as a political
        process but as a "way of life," a distinctive political culture. In this, Dewey
        was similar to Tocqueville and Whitman, his two 19th-century predecessors.
        See Kevin O'Leary, "Herbert Croly, John Dewey and Progressive Democratic
        Theory," unpublished dissertation, Yale University, Department of Political
        Science, 1989, and Richard Rorty, *Achieving Our Country* (Cambridge, Mass.:
        Harvard University Press, 1999).

28   Fred Hirsch, *The Social Limits to Growth* (New York: Routledge & Kegan Paul,
        1978) and Michael J. Sandel, *What Money Can't Buy: The Moral Limits of Markets*
        (New York: Farrar, Straus and Giroux, 2012).

INDEX